Sticks and Balls

A Sexologist Pokes Fun at Sports

Lita-Luise Chappell

Published by
Templar Media
24881 Alicia Parkway #E-144
Laguna Hills, California 92653
www.templar-media.com

Preview Edition

Cover model Nena Cunningham
Photographed by Vere Chappell

Printed in the United States of America

Visit the author at www.LitaChappell.com

Dedication

This book is dedicated to the sex educators, counselors, and therapists who preserve the history of human sexuality, promote its importance, and help people to live happier and more fulfilling sex lives.

Acknowledgements

I am grateful to the following people who impressed upon me the importance of preserving our sexual heritage, and who inspired me to write this book.

A very special thank you goes to the late Dr. Robert "Ted" McIlvenna, who gave up pursuing an athletic scholarship in order to dedicate his life to the above goals. It was his belief that research and effective training in human sexuality were necessary in our society, and with that mission he created the Institute for the Advanced Study of Human Sexuality.

I am very thankful for my husband Vere Chappell, who brought to my attention the existence of the Institute and proposed the idea that we should get our doctorates in human sexuality. Together, through his research and my clinical work, we have strived to make meaningful contributions to the field. He also did the final editing, layout, and cover photography.

I would like to thank my friend and agent, Kat Sanborn, who saw greater possibilities for this book, and encouraged me to take it to a larger public arena.

I would also like to thank my dear friend and amazing promoter, Sharon Sheinker, who helped to edit this book and created my website.

And I will always be grateful to my readers who have followed my works.

Lita-Luise Chappell

Sticks and Balls

A Sexologist Pokes Fun at Sports

Table of Contents

Introduction

Can you guess what is going on in the following description?

A man appeared in a fitted pinstriped suit ready to get a good piece of it for the evening and deliver. He was waiting for a hot box, because when you have it, you get it. He knew it was just a matter of time before he would get a nibble and be ready for that sweet spot. There was no need to pimp himself, just show that he was ready to play. He wanted it high and tight, and up and in with a cock-shot. There was no reason to force his play. He had good wood and was ready to go deep.

You might have thought you just read the desires of a well-dressed man entering a bar and looking for a good time, but you would be wrong. It is the description of a baseball player ready to play, and every expression is a baseball term. Most ball players wear either white pants or a white shirt, or both, with a pinstripe. Getting a good piece of it is when a ball player swings his bat hoping to get a solid hit. To deliver is to pitch a ball. A hot box is the area between two fielders during a rundown. The "I have it" or "you get it" is the call between two players in the field to indicate who will catch a fly ball. A nibble is when a pitcher focuses on pitching to the edge of the plate. The sweet spot is where a batter hits the ball with the strongest spot on the bat. When a player hits a home run and knows he did well, he might swagger or flaunt it to get cheered by his fans. A play is an action during a game. High and tight and up and in, mean the same thing; that is, when a pitch is thrown above the strike zone and close to the batter. A cock-shot is a belt-high fastball thrown down the middle of the plate. To force a play is when a runner must advance to another base because the batter has a runner behind him or when a fly ball is caught and a runner is forced out. Good wood is to hit a ball hard, and to go deep is to hit a home run.

This book is about words in sports that also have a sexual meaning. It exposes the unconscious human need for humans to insert their sexuality into another arena in which they participate, and sports is the perfect recipient. The list of terms for just about every sporting game out there abounds with sexual innuendo and slang. All the sports terms presented in this book have a second meaning.

This book was written for several reasons. They all have to do with what sex and sports share. First, sexuality and sports are two of the most popular activities that humans enjoy. Second, they share the same hormonal responses. Yes, there is real chemistry behind it. And third, as shown in the opening above, a significant number of sports terms also have sexual meaning. In fact, nearly one quarter of the terms in the lexicon of the games listed in this book can be interpreted as sexual. Science and language brings them close together. You could call the two interests natural bedfellows.

There are other reasons to enjoy this book. If you are a sports enthusiast, you most likely strive to be well-acquainted with a sport's rules, you stay on top of the nomenclature, and you possess excellent historical acumen. An aficionado wants to discuss a sport with perception and insight. Becoming knowledgeable in how to speak about a sport shows a keen observation, proficiency, and expertise on the subject. You don't need to be a seasoned coach or sports commentator to possess the skill. You only need to learn the lingo. When you add the awareness of a sport's special sexual language to your commentary, you will not only sound savvy and display a sense of humor, but your friends will enjoy the sport even more.

This book was also written for those who are curious about and fascinated by the oddities of the English language. Within these pages you will be able to feel the *frisson* of sexual words in sports. You do not need to be a sports fan. All you need is curiosity about words. If you want to express your knowledge with more of a zing, the dual terminology is clear. Or you may want a private moment to simply enjoy a chuckle over some sexual words. It is fascinating to see how our culture has introduced sexual terms into sports, and vice-versa.

How does a sports word become a sexual term? What in the world has sex got to do with sports, anyway? Why do sports terms take on a sexual meaning? Since when has this exchange been taking place? And why do fans get so excited about sports? This book will answer all of these questions.

What led me to focus on sports and sexuality? Why would I want to write a book about this connection between sex and sports? I'm a sexologist, a doctor of human sexuality. A sexologist studies sexuality in all its forms, which includes anatomy and physiology, along with sexual development, sexual experience, gender, sexual identification, orientation, disorders, and dysfunctions. Sexologists study the sexual behaviors, feelings, and interactions of people who must learn to deal with their sexuality in a personal manner, within their family, religious beliefs, and cultural environment.

A good part of the work of a sexologist is to educate, and we may do so for an individual, a couple, or a group. Aside from educating, we assist clients to better understand their sexual function or dysfunction. We may help them to monitor or moderate their sexual feelings or behavior. We also counsel clients so that they may feel more confident and gain a better understanding of who they are and what they like and don't like, sexually.

There are various aspects to the field of sexology. Some sexologists are medical doctors who evaluate and treat physical maladies and diseases with surgery or medications. Others are trained counselors and therapists who work with their clients using talk therapy from a psychological perspective. There are other approaches that also contribute to the field's knowledge. These include anthropological, historical, biological, epidemiological, criminological, and sociological perspectives.

I am retired now, but I had a private practice as a sex therapist for many years. I was a member of the American Association of Sexuality Educators, Counselors and Therapists (AASECT), the Society for the Scientific Study of Sexuality (SSSS), and a member of the American College of Sexologists (ACS). My early years in the field were more specifically psychological, as my bachelor's and master's degrees were in psychology with emphasis in health education. I was also certified in hypnotherapy and neurolinguistics, and have studied the sexuality of the greater animal kingdom. When I finally decided what my specialty would be, I continued my schooling and became certified in erotology, sex education, and clinical sexology, then received my doctorate in human sexuality.

At the beginning of my career I was completely unaware of any overlap between sexuality and sports. But one day, a client came to me with a certain problem. He was a baseball player who was having a difficult time with his game affecting his erections. If he did well in the game that day, he got a good erection that night, but if he did poorly that day, he was unable to maintain his erection. I knew very little about baseball. I was not much of a sports enthusiast, as my world was focused more on science and psychology. But it gave me the opportunity to learn about what motivates athletes and how to help them focus on improving their skills, as well as helping them sexually. It also allowed me to see the very interesting relationship between sports and sexuality.

People want to succeed but often don't because they either lack the knowhow, falter in their determination to achieve a goal, or experience an underlying feeling of unworthiness so they don't believe they should achieve success. I am not just speaking about sports, but pretty much every human endeavor.

This ball player got me into researching baseball, which helped me understand the connection between sports and sexuality. We both came to discover that his problem began when a guy on his team teased him about not being able to "get it up enough" to take a good swing when it was a perfect pitch. A misplaced comment from someone we care about can affect us deeply. When he realized *that* was where his fear came from, things began to change. With counseling and positive reinforcement, he began to believe in himself again. He was a good player, but all players now and then make poor judgements during a game. Instead of focusing on the fear of not achieving a good erection, he was better served by replacing that fear with his love and focus for the game. Once he did that, both his game and his sex life turned around.

That experience introduced the connection, but not the words that sex and sports share. This happened with another client. A woman came to me, frustrated with her husband because all he wanted to do on the weekend was watch sports on television, when she was hoping for something more intimate. What could she do? He was especially into football and the season was fast approaching. She was not sure how she was going to cope. After that initial meeting, I looked into football like I had with baseball, and although I had not spotted it the first time, I noticed a list of terms for the game that also seemed to have a sexual meaning.

When she came to see me the following week, I suggested that she study the game's terminology. I handed her a sheet of football terms I determined also had strong sexual implications. I suggested she study the terms, and when watching the game with her husband, whenever any of those terms were used by the sportscaster, she was to touch her husband, preferably his thigh, to get his attention, and with a sexual gleam in her eye repeat that term. Then wait to see what might happen. She was surprised by his response. Her actions did not take his attention away from the program during the game, but it definitely made for fun halftime and after-game entertainment!

As a therapist in the field, it became increasingly obvious to me that a vast number of people, not just clients, have a difficult time speaking about sex and using real terms to describe their sexuality and their desires. I'll talk about why. Writing this book seemed a good way to openly address these terms. When a person cannot speak about sex, their thoughts and feelings about it can become camouflaged by other actions and sublimated. I'll express how that can affect an individual. I'll introduce studies by leaders in the fields of psychology, physiology, and sports medicine that describe how hormones work to activate desire and excitability in human sexuality, in sports with athletes, and in sports fans.

How prevalent are sexual terms in sports games? How many sports games with these terms will this book talk about? How did I decide to focus on the sports I chose? There are approximately 8,000 different sports games that have been played around the world. It would be impossible to cover them all in one book. The task of identifying sexual terms used in every game played would be as long as a set of encyclopedias. A limit had to be considered. I decided to focus on those sports with the most direct sexual connotations — those which are played with a stick and a ball — because they are the most unambiguous words for the penis and testes. Although these two pieces of equipment — the stick and the ball — are male-oriented and the choice for the title of this book, sexual slang terms for female anatomy will also be included.

In the first chapter, *Sticks and Balls* begins with a look at the development and history of sports around the world that use a ball and a stick. The second chapter will investigate the hormones that influence both sexuality and sports. The reader will discover how certain hormones like amines, peptides, and steroids are directly related to our love for sex and our love for sports. In the third chapter, I will speak about how difficult it is for people to come to terms with real sexual terms.

In the chapters that follow, thirty-five sports will be discussed. Each will include a brief overview of its history and short descriptions of how the game is played, the playing area, and especially the stick and/or ball used. Then those terms which have a second meaning which are sexual will be listed, and the sexual definition will be given. Each of the sexual meanings for these terms were found to be used in the English-speaking countries of Australia, Britain, Canada, and the United States. The sexual words may be terms utilized by professionals, or as past or present slang jargon used by specific sexual groups. All the terms were drawn from the vernacular lingo within these cultures.

After carefully going through every official list of terminology for these thirty-five sports and determining all of the sexual terms I could find in these past and present cultures, I was taken aback by the number of sports terms that could have a sexual meaning, but have *not* yet entered the public arena. These additional terms seemed so sexually obvious. Even though many sports words and phrases seemed like they would be a natural in the domain of sexual nomenclature, they were not to be found in any sexual, slang, or urban dictionary. I was surprised. In all the sexual references I consulted in both common and urban usage from three continents, they were not found, but the words seemed too sexually connotative to ignore.

Perhaps it was all in the mind of this sexologist, interpreting something sexual from these terms, but perhaps not. If enough time goes by and these cultures shift, these words and phrases may eventually become a part of the urban culture, and then eventually be accepted into sexual usage, like so many have already. Or perhaps they never will be accepted and we will continue to accept them just as they are, as a sports term and nothing else. Regardless, I could not help myself from taking a deeper look at these terms.

Here is where the focus of this book turns from the use of present-day terms to possible future sexual terms that may someday come into use. I call these the words "most likely to succeed." Naming them would not be any different than a baseball player boasting of attaining "a home run" with his girlfriend. The meaning is clear and the euphemism is obvious. This is where I had the most fun. With so many of these sports terms catching my attention that did not have a sexual reference, I began to make a list of them as a curiosity. I admit that I may have widened my perspective in order to conceive of a second understanding, but I didn't need to go too far afield. I hope you enjoy what I came up with. After all, it is my book, so I think I can poke fun at sports from a sexological point of view if I want.

After completing the list of those slang words most likely to succeed, I was still left with a pile of notes on each sport. These were similar to the kind of notes that a therapist might make when speaking with a client, jotting down key words or phrases. After a session, a therapist typically goes over their notes and does their best to analyze the words and thoughts the client had expressed, along with various insights they might have garnered concerning the client's situation. I found myself enumerating potential meanings for the sport's equipment, player names, and language of play. Instead of there being a person I was analyzing, each sport came under analysis for any possible underlying aspects that were sexual. These notes have been added at the end of each chapter and I labelled these "sexual commentary."

The number of sports terms that also have a sexual meaning was calculated for each of these thirty-five sports, and it was surprising. There are 981 terms listed, to be exact. If you are curious about the percentage of terms which are sexual for any of these stick and ball games, you can find out by going to the last chapter on Term Comparisons, for a breakdown of this information. Which stick and ball game has the most sexual terms within its list of terminology? And which sport has the highest amount of sexual terms compared to its sport terms? Finally, there is a bonus at the end of the book: an extensive list of sexual slang, so that you may see the vast range of secondary words that have been used in place of real sexual terms.

There are things this book will not cover. A complete and thorough historical background for each game will not be given, only a few interesting highlights. Also, specific ways in which a game can be played with all its strategies, rules, codes, tactics, violations, techniques, fouls, and regulations, will not be covered, unless one of the sports terms refers to it, as part of its definition.

In this book you can hone in on one sport, or enjoy learning about the sexual language from each of these stick and ball sports. Discover how much sports and sexuality share, hormonally and linguistically. Each game creates a common base for understanding why sports have become so important to our species, and even more interesting, how sports reflect the sexuality in our culture. By the time you finish this book, you will be an expert on the use of sexual terms in the most popular sports using a stick and a ball. Have a stroking good time!

Part One

Chapter 1
The Development of Sports

Sports are ancient and have benefited mankind both as entertainment during peaceful times and as training for war during disruptive times. This book will focus on sports as entertainment. Games of all kinds have existed since the time when the basic needs of the family unit were met and people began to have free time. They give the populace a sense of satisfaction, belonging, and sharing, a sense of reward, and ultimately a sense of pleasure and happiness. Sports allow a person to enjoy watching, or to join with others and participate. Some forms of sports were derived from ancient skills or proficiencies that a person would have originally needed to survive, such as hunting, but then evolved into a hobby in which the skill was turned into a competitive pursuit.

Those ancient skills provided the public with a spectacle and brought the community together. Armed men fought wild and exotic animals in a colosseum, fought other men in gladiatorial struggles or jousted on horses, or participated in displays of combat skills as part of a team. Forms of these ancient contests are still practiced today, such as men challenging animals with an artistic flair in bullfighting. Every sport has been influenced by the culture, politics, and institutions in which it developed, and the popularity of each sporting game has changed over time. Johan Hizinga, a Dutch cultural historian, wrote in his book *Homo Ludens* that games were a primary condition of the generation of human cultures, and were the foundation of different forms of art, language, law, philosophy, and war.[1]

What makes sports especially important in our modern time is that games are extremely diverse in what they have to offer. They can be enjoyed by solitary individuals who want to better themselves, as an archer, a figure skater, or a swimmer who wishes to improve their skill, timing, or precision. Sports can be enjoyed as part of a team, as in football, soccer, baseball, or volleyball, which promote teamwork. Sports can be played indoors as well as outdoors, and some sports can be played in both. Athletic games may be played by anyone with just a passing interest and a little skill, or by professionals who have developed their skills as a career. Sports actively stimulate within the athlete, as well as the fan, an element of stress which produces emotional jousting back and forth between joy and disappointment with the ups and downs of a game. It may be surprising to learn that the stress in sports is what makes it exciting, and *that* is what we call entertainment!

A Historical Look at Ball and Stick Games

How did we get to where we are now? Where did it all begin? Let's briefly look at some historical sports that used a stick and ball, and find out how and where they developed. Historians have concluded that games and sports developed in both spontaneous and organized forms, with organized play being both noncompetitive

---

[1] Johan Huizinga, *Homo Ludens*, *Proeve Ener Bepaling Van Het Spelelement Der Cultuur*, [No direct translation, but the book is basically about the "play element of culture".] trans. unknown. (London: Routledge & Kegan Paul Ltd., 1938).

and competitive with contests. Those specialized competitive games turned into both intellectual contests and physical sports.[2] Since thousands of sports have been created, the following will only include some of the best-known sports from major sites around the world.

In approximately 2600 BCE in ancient Egypt, there were several games of sticks and balls: a type of hockey, handball, archery, javelin throwing, fishing, and tug of hoop, all of which can be seen in tomb paintings, but no names are known for these games.[3]

Another ancient sport was invented in Mesoamerica c. 1600 BCE. Surprisingly enough, the ball was made of rubber, and the game was called *Ōllamaliztli*.[4] Two or four players passed a ball around huge stone courts, which still remain as evidence of the game.[5] Another sport developed by the Mesoamericans was much like field hockey. About a hundred years later, the game of *Pelota purépecha* was played at night. The ball was soaked in resin and lit on fire so it could be seen.[6] At nearly the same time, the Mayan civilization developed a game called *Pok-A-Tok*. (It was also known as *pitz*, though the Aztecs called it *Tlachtli*, and present-day players call it

---

[2] Joseph Anthony Maguire, William N. Thompson, David Charles Rowe, and Allen Guttmann. "Sports." Encyclopedia Britannica, 2018. https://www.britannica.com/sports/sports

[3] Joshua J. Mark, "Games, Sports & Recreation in Ancient Egypt," *Ancient History Encyclopedia.* April 11, 2017. https://www.ancient.eu/article/1036/

[4] V. L. Scarborough and D. R. Wilcox, "The Mesoamerican Ballgame," Health and Fitness History, 2017. https://healthandfitnesshistory.com/ancient-sports/mesoamerican-ball-game/

[5] Ibid.

[6] Ibid.

Ulama.) It is played without using hands or feet, the object being to get a ball through a narrow stone hoop high on a court wall.[7]

The early Greeks held four major sports festivals called the Panhellenic Games. These were the Olympic Games, where the prize was an olive wreath, the Pythian Games with a prize of a bay laurel wreath, the Nemean Games, awarding crowns of wild celery, and the Isthmian Games, giving a garland of pine leaves.[8] The main events held at each of these games were similar, and each were performed nude (except for the chariot races). Besides chariot racing, other events were boxing, foot races, other hand-combat sports, and a pentathlon, which included the first stick sport of javelin-throwing.[9] Even though the earliest Greek games began in 776 BCE, the first stick event with the javelin throw was not introduced until 684 BCE, and it wasn't until 573 BCE that they added archery and spear-throwing.[10] Also in the 5th century BCE, the Ancient Greeks began playing a fairly violent football-like game called *episkyros,* which developed into the game

---

[7] Bryan Hill, "Ulama, The Mesoamerican Ball Game: Deadly Sport of the Ancient Americas," *Ancient Origins,* 2018. https://www.ancient-origins.net/news-history/ulama-mesoamerican-ball-game-deadly-sport-ancient-americas-003156

[8] O. Broneer, "The Isthmain Victory Crown," *American Journal of Archaeology,* Vol. 66 (1962): 259. https://www.jstor.org/stable/501451

[9] Broneer, "The Isthmain Victory Crown," 259.

[10]Olympic Games, "Welcome to the Ancient Olympic Games." https://www.olympic.org/ancient-olympic-games/long-jump-javelin-discus

17

of *harpastum* during the Roman Empire from 100 BCE to 400 CE.[11]

The game of polo is believed to have originated with the nomadic tribes of Iran and Turkey beginning in the sixth century BCE.[12] Interest in the game continued and became a Persian national sport for the nobles, known as the "sport of kings," then eventually spread to Arabia, Tibet, China, Japan, India, and England.[13]

One of the first recorded games in China, appearing much like soccer with a ball getting kicked through an opening into a net, seems to have begun c. 300 BCE, called *Cuju (Tsu Chu),* and soon afterward developed into similar games called *zhuqui* and *baida.*[14]

Two stick and ball games, *Shinty* in Scotland and *Hurling* in Ireland, developed about the same time, at the beginning of the first millennium.[15] The Irish game of *caid,* referred to as Medieval mob football,[16] and the Welsh *cnapan,* also known as Celtic Medieval Football, eventually led to Association Football and Rugby.[17]

---

[11] Wikipedia, "Harpastum."
https://en.wikipedia.org/wiki/Harpastum

[12] Richard C. Latham, "Polo Sport," *Encyclopedia Britannica Online.*
https://www.britannica.com/sports/polo

[13] Darren Heitner, "The Economics of Polo, The Sport of Kings."
https://www.forbes.com/sites/darrenheitner/2015/05/17/the-economics-of-polo-the-sport-of-kings

[14] Charles Benn, China's Golden Age: Everyday Life in the Tang Dynasty (Oxford: Oxford University Press, 2002), 41.

[15] Hugh Dan MacLennan, "Shinty's Place and Space in World," *The Sports Historian,* Vol. 18, No. 1 (1998), 23.

[16] C. Rowley, *The Shared Origins of Football, Rugby, and Soccer,* Rowman & Littlefield Publishers, 2015.

[17] Robert Wood, "About Cnapan Medieval Football."
https://www.topendsports.com/sport/extinct/cnapan.htm

Another type of Medieval football game was the French ball game *la Soule*, developed in 1283.[18]

More sports appeared in the new millennium. Sometime between 4 to 6 CE, the Ethiopians began to play the game of *genna*, which is much like field hockey and is still played to this day.[19] And in Australia in the late 1700s, they played a ball game called *marn grook*, with an orange-sized ball made from possum skin filled with charcoal or grass.[20]

Thousands more sports using a ball and/or a stick have been created throughout history, and new ones get invented all the time. But sports also have another side to them, another reason for coming into existence: war. Combat sports began with wrestling. This type of sport was instituted to determine male strength and endurance for those best-suited to fight. Sports were developed by men in antiquity to demonstrate male domination over other males. In training armies, men learned to fight together to improve their skills, and staging competitions helped stimulate the need to prove one man against another. But there had to be a way in which this dominance did not always lead to severe body trauma and death, an unfortunate side-effect of these early games. Thus, the competitive spirit was born through sports. Since these skills could only be developed when there were men to fight against and more men were

---

[18] Robert Wood, "La Soule Medieval Football."
https://www.topendsports.com/sport/extinct/la-soule.htm

[19] P. Briggs, "Ethiopia."
https://healthandfitnesshistory.com/ancient-sports/ethiopian-genna-field-hockey/

[20] Zachary Gates, "The Story of Marn Grook."
http://www.sydneyswans.com.au/news/2018-05-28/the-story-of-marn-grook.

needed to be trained all the time, it is easy to see how the concept of sports developed into teams to provide a group effort in competition play-fighting. From what we know so far, over 8,000 different kinds of sporting games have been developed around the world.[21]

Once men realized that they could gain advantage over other men by picking up a stick, the battle for male dominance began with a vengeance. The earliest balls batted around a field were animal or human skulls, pig or cow bladders, and stuffed stitched skins. Since kicking and batting a head and other body parts around a field always ended up being a bloody mess, something had to be substituted, so objects were formed from various natural materials such as wood, then vulcanized rubber, and inflatable balls. Consequently, a variety of sticks and bats were developed to have better control over the ball. In addition, games evolved to make a particular goal the object of the game, so nets, baskets, and goal posts were added. Rules were implemented so that competitions took more than raw strength to win, but required strategy and mental skill as well.

Throughout the history of sports, specialized terms have been created to describe different aspects of each game. As time went on, the populace of every country benefited from the entertainment, and likewise, the culture of the people contributed to the development of the games with new rules, terms, and improvements to the equipment. Sports games using sticks and balls have especially experienced this reciprocal exchange.

There is another element that also enters into the arena. It is something that has driven people all over the world to develop those 8,000 sports. It is an exhilirating

[21]Liponski, Wojciech, "World Sports Encyclopedia," Minneapolis: MBI-UNESCO Publishing Company LLC, 2003.

and enlivening experience for the fans who watch these sports. There is a visceral tension that speeds up the heart, makes us sit focused in full concentration, causes us to breathe hard during a tense moment, and then brings us to our feet with exultation. It is the fear of losing and the elation of winning. The body, mind, and spirit of a fan base melds with the team. *That* is what has catapulted the popularity of all sport games. We enthusiastically call it "getting off" on sports.

Why Do Sports Get Us Off?

Why do people watch and participate in sports? There are many reasons. Tim Urban, a well-known TED presenter, wrote an article called *Why Sports Fans are Sports Fans.*[22] In it, he explains more reasons than you might expect. First of all, sports are a form of entertainment that offer drama, and what happens can create a dramatic effect upon both the players and the viewers.[23] Sports are an active energetic force[24] that can be subtle and measured, as in the game of curling, or explosive and dangerous, as in Pelota, one of the fastest games in the world. A viewer can become involved in not only the action, but also the personalities of each participant.[25] The viewer feels the players' stress, their struggles, their challenges, and their achievements. When a fan develops an attachment for a sport, they often develop an empathy for a particular player. If the player achieves something difficult, then he or she becomes a

---

[22] Tim Urban, "Why Sports Fans are Sports Fans."
https://waitbutwhy.com/archive

[23] Ibid.

[24] Ibid.

[25] Ibid.

hero to the viewer.[26] That way, the fan catches a glimpse of what it feels like to be a hero, simply by watching the player, his or her teammates, and even the televised cheering of the crowd.

Sports connect with a primitive aspect within us.[27] We experience many different feelings while watching the drama. If we favor one player or team, we develop positive feelings for them, and if we don't want the other player or team to win we can get aggressively offensive and angry with them. It harkens back to the days of the Roman arena, watching men fight to the death. We consciously don't want to have anyone really get hurt, but subconsciously we just want to see our favorites win at all cost.

Some sports are simply aesthetically pleasing to watch,[28] whether they feature petite women in short skirts delicately gliding across ice, or tall and agile men with long lean bodies jumping high to reach a hoop. Televised sports often show a play in slow motion, not just so one can see the play better, but to look more graceful and aesthetically pleasing to the eye, attracting more viewers.

Sports bring family, friends, and even strangers together,[29] whether sitting around the TV at home with loved ones, a group of men enjoying guy time together in a sports bar, or being part of a crowded stadium with thousands of people. The action is shared, and consequently feelings of support for a team helps to bond

---

[26] Ibid.

[27] Ibid.

[28] Ibid.

[29] Ibid.

people together.[30] It allows people who have never met before to open up, find common ground, and share their feelings about a sport.[31] Sports comments are a basic conversation opener. "So, what did you think of that ball game on Sunday?" Fans can share their knowledge about the game or statistics on a player, give an opinion about what happened, and enjoy conversing on all aspects of the event, even sharing their hopes and dreams for that team in the future.

Life is not all fun, however. In fact, sometimes life seems to have more trials than rewards, so anything that can take one's mind off 'one's problems and shift it to a more enjoyable experience,[32] helps to restore balance. Sports provide an escape from the usual routine of work, eat, and sleep. Sports can serve as a physical and motivating outlet for the body, and an alternative focal point for the mind. This shift allows a person to turn from doing something for someone else (such as a boss or company), to doing something for him or herself.

Sports also allows one to see perfection in another.[33] Younger people see older accomplished professional athletes and idolize them. Believing in Spider Man is one thing, although consciously, even a child knows he is not real. But a well-known star athlete, who seems he or she can do no wrong, becomes a real live hero and someone that a kid can look up to. Sometimes those heroes can seem to be more than just human men or women. Their greatness can take on such a stature of splendor that a fan can also feel their glory.

---

[30] Ibid.

[31] Ibid.

[32] Ibid.

[33] Ibid.

There is more to sports than just watching them. One can also become an athlete oneself. When a young boy or girl grows up, after admiring a star performer after another, he or she also wants to experience that loved status.[34] And with popularity comes access to things one might not otherwise think one can achieve or be able to have, such as national or international fame, money for a fancy car and a big house, the prospect of travel, an opportunity for long-term employment, respect, a better class of partner or lover, and becoming a prominent man or a woman of the world.

In several studies, Buss (2012),[35] Dunbar and Barrett (2009),[36] and Wrangham (1999),[37] determined that men enroll in physical competition to achieve status, access to resources, and reproductive opportunities. In his paper *On the Evolution of Sport,*[38] Michael P. Lombardo summarized his findings about what sexuality has done to sports. It "influenced the evolution of sport, the primary driving force shaping the characteristics of male sports," because participating was an "intrasexual competition." Intrasexual selection is when members of the same sex compete with each other in order to gain opportunities to compete for the opposite sex. In other words, people, especially men, literally get off by pushing

[34] Ibid.

[35]David M. Buss, "Evolutionary Theories of Dominance and Status," In *Evolutionary Psychology: The New Science of the Mind*, 4th Ed., (Austin: University of Texas, 2012), 351-353.

[36] Robin Dunbar and Louise Barrett (Eds.), *Oxford Handbook of Evolutionary Psychology.* (New York: Oxford University Press, 2009).

[37] Richard Wrangham, "Evolution of Coalitionary Killing," *American Journal of Physical Anthropology.* Vol. 110, no. 29 (1999), 1-30.

[38] Michael Lombardo, "On the Evolution of Sport," *Evolutionary Psychology Journal,* Vol. 10, No. 1 (2012), 18.

their bodies to compete with other men for the attention of women.

Ultimately, we watch and participate in sports because we get enjoyment out of viewing them and performing in them. Sports make us feel good. Emotions affect performance, and positive moods contribute to winning. Sports also give us pride when we win or when our favorite team wins. On the other hand, when an athlete or team loses, we may experience a sense of failure and shame.

There are several studies which talk about what makes one a winner and how that affects them. In Ian Robertson's book, *The Winner Effect: The Neuroscience of Success and Failure,* he relates, "All species have hierarchies, and your position in that hierarchy will determine your health, your mental function, your mood."[39]

In Rosabeth Moss Kanter's book, *Confidence,* she tells us that there are ten advantages a person receives as a result of winning.[40] Winning puts one in a good mood, emotions affect performance, and when teammates feel that success, they receive a residual effect.[41] Winning also produces an attractive situation.[42] Children are absent from school less, people are tardy to work less, and when people gather together and share their ideas, they

---

[39] Ian Robertson, "The Winner Effect: The Neuroscience of Success and Failure. (New York: Thomas Dunne Books, 2012), 64.

[40] Rosabeth Moss Kanter, "Confidence: How Winning Streaks and Losing Streaks Begin and End, (New York: Crown Business, 2006), 127-128.

[41] Ibid.

[42] Ibid.

accomplish more and better things.[43] Another advantage is that winners want to learn more about how to be even better, so they look to improve every possible small routine and process.[44] Winners gain freedom to focus better because they don't have to worry about what might have made them lose.[45] Winners create a positive culture of mutual respect and are more generous, while losers tend to blame others for their mistakes.[46] A winning team receives more support, while those who don't win will lose support.[47] Better press goes to the winner, whereas losers only get bad press.[48] No one invites the losing team to special events, but winners get invited to the best places. Someone who wins also experiences more self-determination and accomplishment, and seems to have more control over his or her life.[49] Winning allows a smooth continuity, whereas losing destabilizes and disrupts long-term strategies.[50]

In our modern society, we have been conditioned to believe that it is not a matter of wanting to win, but *needing* to win, and when an athlete or a team loses they experience disappointment, frustration, distress, regret, anguish, guilt, and shame. Much of this problem stems from childhood, where we are taught that *winning is everything*. This is a major problem because there can be only one winner and that means that everyone else is a

---

[43] Ibid.

[44] Ibid.

[45] Ibid.

[46] Ibid.

[47] Ibid.

[48] Ibid.

[49] Ibid.

[50] Ibid.

loser. The odds are stacked against us. Winning is *not* everything. That is a misnomer. The most important thing for a young person to grasp is that sports are for developing the body physically and learning to always work toward improving oneself.[51] Both produce a psychological advantage, and understanding how to work with others in teamwork eventually prepares them for the workplace.

Sean Cumming succinctly put it this way: "The primary goal... should be to develop desirable psychological and social characteristics as well as physical skills and fitness... Winning should be viewed as a consequence of the athlete's physical and psychological development and not the primary focus of athletic involvement".[52]

One has to learn from one's mistakes or one will never improve. Failure is often what is needed to experience humility, a valuable lesson in our culture.[53] The best athletes learn this early and use their newfound knowledge of that failure to overcome their adversity to become a better athlete and competitor. Poetry and proverb writer William Arthur Ward wrote, "Adversity causes some men to break; others to break records."[54] More still, defeat tests an athlete in other ways. Jerry Lynch, a nationally acclaimed sports psychologist, writes that the best way to play is with passion. Athletes

---

[51] Sean P. Cumming, Frank L. Smoll, Ronald E. Smith, and Joel R. Grossbard, "Is Winning Everything? The Relative Contributions of Motivational Climate and Won-Lost Percentages in Youth Sports," *Journal of Applied Sport Psychology, Vol. 19*, No. 3 (2007), 322-336.

[52] Ibid.

[53] Ibid.

[54] William Arthur Ward, *Fountains of Faith: The Words of William Arthur Ward* (Anderson, S. Carolina: Droke House, 1970).

understand what it means to play with heart, but very few have been shown how patience, perseverance, and compassion are the most important ingredients of national champions.[55]

---

[55] Jerry Lynch, "The Way of the Champion," *Podium Sports Journal,* Vol. 1, No. 1 (2007), 5.

Chapter 2
Hormones at Work

So, what is it that makes sports so exciting? The answer is hormones. Hormones have an immense influence upon the human organism's entire life. They are present and functioning no matter what we involve ourselves in. They help to send messages, control functions, and coordinate activities throughout the body, whether we are awake and active, or at rest and asleep.

Hormones have a wide range of responsibilities that affect the body. First, we will take a look at what those responsibilities are and how they work within the body. Most importantly, a comparison will show that the hormones which are produced in sports are the same hormones produced during sexual arousal and excitation. This surprising connection is what makes sports so popular the world over. Randi Epstein, in his book *Aroused: The History of Hormones and How They Control Just About Everything,* confirms their importance. Hormones "are substances secreted by a gland that target a distant site; they travel via the blood; they are crucial for the maintenance of the body; they are crucial to survival."[56]

---

[56] Randi Hutter Epstein, *Aroused: The History of Hormones and How They Control Just About Everything.* (New York: W. W. Norton & Company, 2018), 7.

The production and regulation of hormones is the work of the endocrine system. Hormones control metabolism, regulate the body's energy, attend to reproductive processes, grow tissue, regulate water levels, create protein for building muscles, help burn fat, and affect a person's mood. Hormones can be divided into three classes: amines, which are the simplest of molecules that contain nitrogen and influence our sympathetic nervous system; peptides, which are amino acid proteins that work within the cell membrane; and steroids, which are from cholesterol and interact with receptors in the nucleus of a cell. Each of these types of hormones affect a person at all times, and when stimulated they go to work, whether it is for that hard-won home run or that long-awaited-for kiss.

A short breakdown of what each hormone does will make it abundantly clear how the body of the lover, the athlete, and the fan share common hormonal reactions. So here is a brief look at amines, peptides, and steroids, and the roles they play. This next section may get a little complicated for some, as it goes into the bio-chemical workings of these hormones. However, it is these precise aspects that show the direct links in how we react to sex and sports in the same way.

Amines

In order to understand what amines are and how they work, it is necessary to first talk about proteins. All the proteins that we eat form an elite group of amino acids which, when broken down in the body, form amines. There are twenty-two proteinogenic amino acids, but nine cannot be produced within the body and must be introduced through eating food. The best foods for essential amino acids are animal proteins like eggs, fish, meats, and poultry. When the amino acids are broken down into amines, they further help many processes within the body.

Amino acids give structure to our cells, muscles, and tissues. They help build the body, give it strength and energy, help tired muscles recover, aid with fat loss, help synthesize hormones and neurotransmitters, and regulate the immune system.[57] The nine essential amino acids are: histidine, isoleucine, leucine, lysine, methionine, phenylalanine, threonine, tryptophan, and valine. Arginine is considered a "conditional" amino acid. Small amounts are produced in the body, but more could be needed to supplement the body under certain circumstances.

Histidine produces histamine, which is a neurotransmitter that is vital to immune response, digestion, sexual function, sleeping and waking cycles. It also protects and maintains the myelin sheath, a fatty protective tissue surrounding all nerve cells.[58] Isoleucine is in the muscle tissue and aids with muscle metabolism, as well as regulating the body's energy, hemoglobin production, and the immune system.[59] Leucine synthesizes protein, repairs muscle tissue, helps to regulate blood sugar levels, produces growth hormones, and stimulates the healing of wounds.[60] Lysine is critical for synthesizing proteins and absorbing calcium, and is needed for enzyme and hormone production, skin cell

---

[57] Jillian Kubala, "Essential Amino Acids: Definition, Benefits and Food Sources," Healthline Newsletter.
https://www.healthline.com/nutrition/essential-amino-acids.

[58] National Center for Biotechnology Information, "Histidine," PubChem Compound database; CID=6274,
https://pubhem.ncbi.nim.nih.gov/compound/6274

[59] PubChem DB, "Isoleucine," CID=6306.

[60] PubChem DB, "Leucine," CID=6106.

production, immune function, and energy.[61] Methionine is needed for tissue growth, selenium and zinc absorption, detoxification, and most importantly, balancing the metabolism.[62] Phenylalanine is important to the function and structure of enzymes, proteins and other amino acids, and is a precursor for the neurotransmitters dopamine, epinephrine, norepinephrine, and tyrosine.[63] Threonine is responsible for the structural proteins in collagen and elastin in skin and the connective tissue, and aids in fat metabolism and immune function.[64] Tryptophan is needed to balance the body's nitrogen levels. The neurotransmitter serotonin regulates appetite, mood, and sleep.[65] And valine helps regenerate and stimulate muscle growth, and aids energy production.[66]

Only a very basic explanation of amino functions will be offered, so that the reader does not get overwhelmed by their chemical structures. Suffice to say, there is a long list of amines that are created by the number of carbon atoms attached to the nitrogen atom, being either polyamines, biogenic amines, or pressor amines. The *Encyclopedia of Food Sciences and Nutrition* offers a chapter on amines with an excellent descriptive summary of their physiological importance:

> Amines participate in important metabolic and physiological functions in living organisms.

---

[61] PubChem DB, "Lysine," CID=5962.

[62] PubChem DB, "Methionine," CID=6137.

[63] PubChem DB, "Phenylalanine," CID=6140.

[64] PubChem DB, "Threonine," CID=6288.

[65] PubChem DB, "Tryptophan," CID=6305.

[66] PubChem DB, "Valine," CID=6287.

Polyamines are essential for cell proliferation, growth, renewal, and metabolism. They are involved in nearly every step of DNA, RNA, and protein synthesis, and regulate the permeability and stability of cellular membranes. Polyamines are needed to replace cells and mediate the action of hormones and growth factors, are essential for the maintenance of the high metabolic activity of the normally functioning and healthy gut, and will repair the damage caused by deleterious components in food or by bacteria. Biogenic amines are generally either psychoactive or vasoactive. Psycho-active amines, such as histamine and serotonin, act on the neural transmitters in the central nervous system. Vaso-active amines act directly or indirectly on the vascular system. Pressor amines — tyramine, tryptamine, and phenyl-ethylamine — cause a rise in blood pressure by constricting the vascular system and increasing the heart rate and contraction force. Serotonin as vaso- and bronchoconstrictor, reduces the volume and acidity of the gastric juice, has an antidiuretic effect, stimulates smooth muscle, and affects carbohydrate metabolism. Histamine can exert many responses within the body. It can directly stimulate the heart, cause contraction or relaxation of extravascular smooth muscle, stimulate both motor and sensorial neurons, and control gastric secretion. It also mediates primary and immediate symptoms in allergic responses.[67]

---

[67] M.B.A. Glória, Encyclopedia of Food Sciences and Nutrition, 2nd Edition. (Amsterdam: Elsevier Science Ltd., 2003), 173.

Peptides

Peptides are precursors of proteins whose functions are determined by size and sequence. They might group together in a chain, from two peptides to perform a simple task, or up to fifty-four for a more complex operation. Peptides are released into the bloodstream where they perform several functions by carrying signals between the glands and cells. There are many different peptides with different functions. Some peptides are naturally antibiotic, stopping the growth of microorganisms in the body. Others work as anti-oxidants, scavenging free radicals. There are peptide chains that form structural support for the body, and some peptides are a component of alkaloids, such as those found in coffee that stimulate the body. Some peptides are used in anti-aging creams for skin cell rejuvenation.

There are many peptide hormones, but one of the most notable is oxytocin, which is produced by the hypothalamus and released by the posterior pituitary gland. It is needed for brain development, cardiovascular activity, digestion, endocrine function, energy balance, excretion of sodium in the urine, feeding, giving birth, immune regulation, lactation, learning and memory, perceiving pain, reproduction, respiration, sex, temperature regulation, tolerance, and dependence.

Oxytocin is found outside the brain in many places in both men and women, but perhaps one of the most interesting places is in the retina of the eye.[68] Upon seeing

---

[68] G. Gauquelin, G. Geelen, F. Louis, A.M. Allevard, C. Meunier, G. Cuisinaud, S. Benjanet, N.G. Seidah, M. Chretien, and J. J. Legros, "Presence of vasopressin, oxytocin and neurophysin in the retina of mammals, effect of light and darkness, comparison with the

an image, cells in the back of the eyeball will trigger nerve impulses to the optic nerve and brain interpreting what is being seen. This could also be a corollary to the fact that oxytocin has been found to modulate fear and anxiety. Seeing a sports team do well may help the viewer feel less anxiety as to a game's outcome. Estrogen increases the secretion of oxytocin and affects social bonding, sexual reproduction in both sexes, and childbirth.[69] Oxytocin has been found to affect a person's generosity, increase trust, enhance a romantic attachment, and many other social behaviors.

This peptide hormone also plays an important role in sexual stimulation and arousal. Increased levels of oxytocin have been noted with masturbation.[70] The hormone serum levels also rise with the anticipation of sexual stimulation alone. And another study reported that genital tract stimulation resulted in increased oxytocin immediately after orgasm.[71]

Steroids

Steroids are organic compounds that are produced in the adrenal cortex, testes, and ovaries, and all are derived

neuropeptide content of the neurohypophysis and pineal gland," Peptides. Vol. 4, No. 4 (1983), 509–515.

[69] H-P. Yang, L. Wang, L. Han, and SC Wang, "Nonsocial Functions of Hypothalamic Oxytocin," International Scholarly Research Notices, Vol. 2013 (2013).

[70] M. S. Carmichael, M.S., R. Humbert, J. Dixen, G. Palmisano, W. Greenleaf, and J. M. Davidson, "Plasma Oxytocin Increases in the Human Sexual Response," The Journal of Clinical Endocrinology and Metabolism. Vol. 64 (1987), 27–31.

[71] W. Blaicher, D. Gruber, C. Bieglmayer, A. M. Blaicher, W. Knogler, and J.C. Huber, "The Role of Oxytocin in Relation to Female Sexual Arousal," Gynecologic and Obstetric Investigation. Vol. 47, No. 2 (1999), 125–126.

from cholesterol. Steroid hormones have two major biological functions. The first one has to do with the communication of cells, called signal transduction.[72] When a cell's internal and external environment is threatened, a biochemical stimulus transmits a message to a molecule receptor which gets amplified, and then a biochemical response generates what the cell needs. The reaction might be in response to a cell's change of location, an increase in cell growth, a needed metabolic change, or a proliferation of that type of cell. The second function has to do with the cell's membrane.[73] Each cell is made up of two layers of lipid molecules that surround and protect its nucleus. This layering is what keeps the ions and proteins where they need to be. The cell's viscosity is important, as it can affect the rotation and diffusion of proteins within the cell.

Steroids can also change their composition. They normally have a core of seventeen bonded carbon atoms in four fused rings and one five-member ring which has five carbon atoms bonded with two hydrogen atoms. This may not mean anything to one who does not have a biochemical background, but if this changes, different steroids can be produced. For example, secosteroid forms vitamin D3, dexamethasone is an anti-inflammatory hormone, and estradiol and testosterone are sex hormones. The way a steroid cell appears will shift with

---

[72] C. M. Klinge, "Steroid Hormone Receptors and Signal Transduction Processes," In Principles of Endocrinology and Hormone Action. A. Belfiore and D. LeRoith (ed.). (Cham, Switzerland: Springer International Publishing, 2008).

[73] Eden, "What is the Phospholipid Bilayer and What Determines Its Fluidity?" Cambridge Coaching. http://blog.cambridgecoaching.com/what-is-the-phospholipid-bilayer-and-what-determines-its-fluidity

its combination of carbon, oxygen, and hydrogen. In fact, one particular structure of these spheres of atoms and their connecting branches is called the ball-and-stick representation!

In the larger picture, there are fungal steroids, animal steroids, plant steroids, and a subset of animal steroids called prokaryotes found in mycobacterium. This chapter will only focus on animal steroids found in the human body, primarily corticosteroids and sex steroids. There are two corticosteroids—glucocorticoids and mineralocorticoids. Glucocorticoids help stimulate glucose production and the breakdown of fat, and are anti-inflammatory and immune-suppressive. Mineralocorticoids increase blood volume by reabsorbing sodium and secreting potassium in the kidneys. The steroid known as cortisol is a glucocorticoid that functions as an immune-suppressor. The steroid known as aldosterone helps regulate blood pressure through electrolytes and water in the cell.

The three main sex steroids are progestogen, androgen, and estrogen. Progesterone is a progestogen. Progestogen supports all aspects in the female body. It regulates the endometrium of the uterus in its cyclical changes, maintains conditions during pregnancy, increases cell growth, reduces spasms by relaxing smooth muscles, reduces inflammation, regulates the immune response, reduces gall-bladder activity, normalizes blood clotting and vascular tone, regulates zinc, copper and oxygen levels, assists in thyroid function, aids bone growth, and regulates collagen, nerve function, and healing.[74] And although progesterone levels rise highest

---

[74] Zulma Tatiana Ruiz-Cortes, Gonadal Sex Steroids: Production, Action and Interactions in Mammals, Chapter 1, (London: IntechOpen. 2012), 3-39.

midway in the luteal phase after ovulation, they do not increase sexual desire.

Testosterone, an androgen, aids in the development and maintenance of male secondary sex characteristics. It contributes to gonad development, deepens the voice, produces hair growth and distribution, adds muscle mass and strength, increases bone density, and supports the needed reproductive hormone levels in the male body. Testosterone is critical for sexual desire, function, and arousal in men.[75] Testosterone therapy also increases sexual desire and arousal in transgender men.[76]

Estradiol, an estrogen, contributes to the development and maintenance of the female secondary sex characteristics. It aids uterine growth, helps maintain blood vessels and skin, allows minerals from bone to be transferred to the blood, increases hepatic production and circulation, improves platelet adhesiveness, helps balance salt and water retention, stimulates growth hormones, and promotes lung function. Estradiol is also the most important hormone for sexual desire in women, and rises to the highest levels during ovulation, just after the follicular phase and right before the luteal phase.[77] For men who undergo surgical or medical castration, estradiol supplementation maintains sexual desire.[78]

---

[75] G. Rastrelli, G. Corona, and M. Maggi, "Testosterone and Sexual Function in Men," Maturitas: The European Menopause Journal. Vol. 112: (2018), 46–52.

[76] M. S. Irwig, "Testosterone Therapy for Transgender Men," The Lancet: Diabetes & Endocrinology, Vol. 5, No. 4 (2017), 301–311.

[77] Cappelletti M, and K. Wallen, "Increasing Women's Sexual Desire: The Comparative Effectiveness of Estrogens and Androgens," Hormone Behavior. Vol. 78 (2016), 178–93.

[78] E. Wibowo, and RJ Wassersug, "The Effect of Estrogen on the Sexual Interest of Castrated Males: Implications to Prostate Cancer

Hormones Shared by Sports and Sexual Activity

All of the hormones mentioned so far operate within the body, regardless of the person and what they do. Now let's examine which hormones specifically affect the body during sports and see how they are also present in sexual activity. There are ten hormones that do this: brain-derived neurotrophic factor, cortisol, dopamine, epinephrine, human growth hormone, insulin, insulin-like growth factor, glucagon, norepinephrine, and testosterone.[79] We have already introduced the hormones of cortisol and testosterone, but more about them is to come.

Cortisol is the first hormone to respond to exercise, low blood sugar, and stress. Cortisol is what keeps one going during long periods of a workout and sexual engagement by supporting metabolic energy. It plays a role in breaking down body tissue, natural fats and oils, and proteins, in order to fuel the body with glucose. If the body becomes too stressed, cortisol levels rise in order to break down muscle protein for fuel, instead of using it for tissue repair.

Testosterone is the primary hormone in the human male, whereas in the female this hormone is one-tenth the concentration. In Ian Robertson's book, *The Winner Effect: The Neuroscience of Success and Failure*, he relates that when a person gets excited from winning a game, their testosterone, and consequently, levels of dopamine, are

Patients on Androgen-deprivation Therapy," Critical Reviews in Oncology/ Hematology, Vol. 87, No. 3 (2013), 224–38.

[79] Pete McCall, "Exercise and Hormones: Eight Hormones Involved in Exercise," American Council on Exercise. https://www.acefitness.org/education-and-resources/professional/expert-articles/5593/exercise-and-hormones-8-hormones-involved-in-exercise

increased. When relayed to the brain, this produces a rewarding feeling of happiness.[80]

In an online article written for the Daily Mail,[81] Jill Reilly describes how a group of researchers took saliva samples from forty-four men and then had them enjoy a strip club. After having the men either just watch the women or they engaged in sexual activity, a second sample was taken. Regardless of what they did or didn't do, the results found that testosterone levels had increased in all of them by a minimum of 36%. Three different studies, by Arce and De Souza,[82] Elias and Wilson,[83] and Hackney,[84] determined that no matter the type of exercise one works at or the kind of sport one participates in, there are always significant increases in testosterone levels. What else can affect testosterone? Alcohol will significantly decrease testosterone levels. This is why coaches tell their players to not drink alcohol the night before a game. Drinking too much alcohol before engaging in sexual activity may lower inhibitions, but it will also lower the degree of sexual arousal.

---

[80] Ian Robertson, *The Winner Effect: The Neuroscience of Success and Failure*. (New York: Thomas Dunne Books, 2012).

[81] Jill Reilly, "It's a Hard Job but Someone's Got To Do It: Scientists Visit Sex Club for Research Into Testosterone Levels," DailyMail. https://www.dailymail.co.uk/news/article-2239621/Researchers-test-mens-testosterone-levels-rise-arousal--visiting-sex-club.html

[82] JC Arce, and M. J. De Souza, "Exercise and Male Infertility," Sports Medicine, Vol. 15 (1993), 146–169.

[83] A. N. Elias, and A. F. Wilson, "Exercise and Gonadal Function," Human Reproduction, Vol. 8 (1993), 1747–1761.

[84] A.C. Hackney, "The Male Reproductive System and Endurance Exercise," Medicine and Science in Sports and Exercise, Vol. 28. (1996), 180–189.

Now on to other hormones: brain-derived neurotrophic factor, dopamine, epinephrine, human growth hormone, insulin, insulin-like growth factor, glucagon, and norepinephrine.

Brain-derived neurotrophic factor (BDNF) directly affects sports activity.[85] It is a neurotransmitter that stimulates brain cell production. With high levels of exercise, BDNF increases cognitive function, so a player can think quickly what their next move will be. Cognitive function is also needed for those engaged in sexual activities, as they will need to be able to think about their actions, assess their partners responsiveness, and interpret their experiences through all of their senses.

Dopamine, epinephrine, and norepinephrine are amine hormones that work with the sympathetic nervous system to regulate body function during cardio-respiratory use to produce energy.[86] They are also neurotransmitters, which cause a person to become more alert and focused, and increase one's motivation to act. Dopamine works to strengthen the pumping of the heart and improve blood flow to the kidneys. It will kick in when the body has trauma or in other serious situations. If an athlete gets hurt, dopamine levels will rise within the body. Dopamine will also release endorphins and serotonins, which make people happy, and are present when an aroused state is reached by a couple during a sexual experience.

Epinephrine increases cardiac efficiency and blood sugar, breaks down glycogen for energy, and supports fat metabolism.[87] Norepinephrine supports the production of

---

[85] McCall, "Exercise and Hormones."

[86] Ibid.

[87] Ibid.

epinephrine which will constrict blood vessels in the body not involved in exercise. Any athlete knows that a good working heart will enable them to achieve more, for a longer time, and this is true for anyone involved in the physical aspects of a sexual workout.

There has been extensive research into how human growth hormone (HGH) is effective in enhancing physical performance in sports.[88] It is a naturally-produced steroid in the body, which is also produced when a couple is physically involved during intercourse. When additional amounts are taken, it augments muscular development and strength. HGH is a naturally-occurring peptide secreted by the pituitary gland, but its production diminishes with age. It can be highly effective for short-term use, but continued and long-term use of this steroid can cause a number of problems: swelling of hands and feet, fluid retention, excessive sweating, blood clotting, tendon damage, hypertension, atherosclerosis, carcinoma, hepatic neoplasms, jaundice, mental irregularities, psychiatric and behavioral disorders, and irreversible organ damage.

Insulin is a peptide hormone that regulates carbohydrate and fat metabolism and is produced by the pancreas.[89] It promotes the absorption of glycogen and glucose into the bloodstream and out of the blood into fat and muscle tissue. The sympathetic nervous system suppresses the release of insulin when exercise starts, whether that exertion is athletic or sexual. That is why avoiding sweet foods before a game is better for the athlete or it will raise insulin levels, and that needed glycogen will be stored instead of being used.

---

[88] Ibid.

[89] Ibid.

Insulin-like growth factor is stimulated much in the same way as human growth hormone and helps to support its function.[90] It is a peptide hormone, and it is produced in the liver. Insulin-like growth factor is important, as it not only repairs protein tissue, it promotes muscle growth. All athletes are cognizant of the need to keep their muscles in good condition. Even the sports fan will need to keep in shape for climbing all those stadium stairs, as will the lover who needs to stay in shape for enjoying their partner during sexual activity.

Glucagon, produced by the pancreas, responds to low blood sugar levels. It stimulates the release of free fatty acids and increases glucose for fueling the body.[91] When glycogen levels fall, glucagon releases more glycogen, which are carbohydrates stored in the liver. Lovers and athletes depend upon the energy of carbohydrates to keep their bodies actively moving.

Norepinephrine (also called noradrenalin), like dopamine and epinephrine, is an organic neuro-transmitting hormone used by the sympathetic nervous system. It mobilizes the brain and body for action, as this is the hormone which, when stress or danger looms, produces the fight-or-flight response. It increases arousal, alertness, vigilance, memory retention and retrieval, blood pressure, blood flow to skeletal muscles, heart rate, and releases glucose for energy to move. It also reduces blood flow to the gastrointestinal tract, and inhibits bowel and urinary activity.[92]

Whether one is involved in sports with a local junior organization, on a national team, or at an international

---

[90] Ibid.

[91] Ibid.

[92] Ibid.

level, sooner or later, apprehension, anxiety, and fear will become a given factor in a competition. This also happens to the young man who is apprehensive about approaching a young woman, a grown man who has anxiety about dating, or a woman who has fear about getting involved with a partner for a life-long relationship. These hormones go to work to support the body in its challenges.

Athletes experience these hormonal surges most directly, but the sport fan watching the action may be going through a similar level of stress, with nail-biting, muscles tensing, and blood pressure rising. Many of the same hormones are going through their bodies in the same way, perhaps not at the same levels, but they are still significantly present.

Dr. Michael Grabowski, professor of communications at Manhattan College, writes about how a sport fan can experience anxiety before and during a game, just by watching. He says it is both a cognitive and somatic anxiety that is experienced, just as if the person were on the field and under that same stress.[93] A viewer may even sweat heavily with that anxiety.

In an article by Scott Muska, he quotes Dr. Richard Shuster, a clinical psychologist at Murray State University, who discusses which hormones are released in the sports fan when following a game.[94] When a fan is watching a team doing well and winning, the brain releases the neurotransmitter dopamine, and when the

[93] Michael Grabowski, (Ed.), *Neuroscience and Media: New Understandings and Representations*, (New York: Routledge, 2011).

[94] Scott Muska, "What Happens To Your Body and Your Brain When You Watch Football," Better Wellness. https://www.nbcnews.com/better/health/what-happens-your-body-brain-when-you-watch-football-ncna814401

fan watches a team losing, the body becomes stressed and releases the hormone cortisol. When enough cortisol is released, it may rob the brain of needed serotonin, which can lead to anger and depression. It is most likely that this is what is occurring when fans grow angry over an umpire's miscall, or the loss of a game.

Paul Bernhardt, professor of educational psychology at the University of Utah, along with his associates, Dabbs, Fielden, and Lutter, produced two studies on testosterone changes during vicarious experiences of winning and losing among fans of sporting events. [95] Saliva samples were taken to assay testosterone levels before and after watching rival college basketball teams and a televised World Cup soccer match. In both studies, mean testosterone levels increased in the fans of winning teams and decreased in the fans of losing teams.

The positive psychological aspects of belonging, sharing, and receiving are rewards in themselves, but hormones will deliver what is needed to the body. Whether one is on the field or off, a fan watching a game winning or losing, observing sex or participating in it, these hormones bring together the captivating combination of mind and body that stimulate and excite. Not only are sports and sex two of the most popular entertainments of human beings, but it is abundantly clear that hormones play a huge part in that popularity.

---

[95] Paul Bernhardt, J. M. Dabbs, J. A. Fieldern, and C. D. Lutter, "Testosterone Changes During Vicarious Experiences of Winning and Losing Among Fans At Sporting Events," Physical Behavior, Vol. 65, No. 1 (1998), 59-62.

Chapter 3
Coming to Terms with the Terms

The third reason I wrote this book has to do with the terms that sports and sexuality share. As a doctor of human sexuality and a therapist, I have had hundreds of conversations with clients about their sex lives. Perhaps the most difficult task is to get people to open up enough to be able to put a voice to their sexual concerns, not just with me, but with their sexual partners, and to have them recognize and use the correct terms when speaking about their bodies. I found that I was often a teacher rather than a counselor, teaching new words and methods of communication to students. It was not their fault. They were raised with parents who did not teach them about sex, let alone use the correct terms. Each emerging sexual person who did not get early instruction had to learn what they needed to know on their own.

There is a persistent avoidance in our culture of the ancient world's belief systems about sex. It stems, without any doubt, from fundamentalist religious convictions that sex is sinful outside of the strictest codes of living. How sinful is it, indeed, to negate the most personal and divine experience a person can have in his or her lifetime? Especially when it can be life-producing and life-enhancing, and truly the most important function two people can embody upon this earth.

When a person is not able to accept his or her own sexuality, the consequences can be dire. At the very least, they experience embarrassment at hearing or seeing something sexual. When parents provide no explanation for what their children may have seen or heard, but tell them not to ask questions and be tempted by the devil, is it no wonder that these children will grow up, have children of their own, and still not be able to discuss any aspect of sexuality with *their* children? This failure to address sexual function and its correct terms has greatly hindered the education of generations of people. Historical embarrassment to address the subject has created shame. If parents do not want to instruct their children, who is going to do it? A tremendous gap exists between what parents will not say and what the U.S. educational system will not teach about this critical information.

In a 2004 NPR survey, 1001 parent-couples were polled, and it was revealed that 80% of them preferred that sex education be taught in school and not by them.[96] Perhaps this isn't the wisest of options. Sex education within the U.S. is inconsistent and limited. All of the following information comes from the National Conference of State Legislatures, the Guttmacher Institute, and Sex, Inc., from 2015. Very little has changed since then.

The following seventeen states and the District of Columbia *do not* require any sex education in their schools: Alaska, Arkansas, Arizona, Florida, Idaho, Kansas, Louisiana, Massachusetts, Michigan, Missouri,

---

[96] National Public Radio, "Sex Education in America," The Kaiser/Kennedy School Poll.
https://www.npr.org/templates/story/story.php?storyId=1622610

Nebraska, New Hampshire, Oklahoma, Pennsylvania, South Dakota, Texas, and Wyoming.[97]

The thirteen states *that do* require sex education in their schools, albeit with still limited instruction, are: Connecticut, Georgia, Indiana, Iowa, Kentucky, Minnesota, Mississippi, Montana, Nevada, North Dakota, Ohio, Tennessee, and Utah.[98]

Only seven states require contraception instruction *when sex education is taught*: Alabama, California, Colorado, Illinois, Virginia, Washington, and Wisconsin.[99] The states that require *both* sex education and contraception instruction are only thirteen: Delaware, Hawaii, Maine, Maryland, New Jersey, New Mexico, New York, North Carolina, Oregon, Rhode Island, South Carolina, Vermont, and West Virginia.[100]

Only twenty-one out of fifty states include information on HIV. Of those states that do include contraception instruction, all are required to stress abstinence *as the only* successful deterrent to pregnancy. They must do so or they will not be granted any federal funding.[101] Is it any surprise that the states that don't

---

[97] Hannah Smothers, "Where are Schools Teaching Kids How to Use a Condom?" August 31, 2015. Splinter News.
https://splinternews.com/where-are-schools-teaching-kids-how-to-use-a-condom-1793850389

[98] Ibid.

[99] Ibid.

[100] Ibid.

[101] Advocates for Youth, "Personal Responsibility & Work Opportunity Reconciliation Act of 1996," Title V, 510(b) (2) (A-H) of the Social Security Act.
http://www.advocatesforyouth.org/publications/publications-a-z/597-abstinence-only-until-marriage-programs-ineffective-unethical-and-poor-public-health

require sex education also have the highest unwanted birth rate for teens?

When sex education falters, either at home or in the schools, parents and school boards fail to realize that simply because sex is not discussed under their tutelage, their child's interest in sex will not go away. But children see things on television and the Internet, and ask their friends who know just as little. Marlene Richie, an international educator, summarizes what happens when parents and schools don't instruct. "Some children get most of their information about sex from their peers, the Internet, or pornography, but these children frequently learn or assume misleading interpretations and use vulgar terms."[102] Consequently, there is a long history of slang terminology that has developed over the centuries. The terms take on different forms such as collocation, euphemism, double entendre, idiom, metaphor, simile, or slang, and reflect the culture in which they are used.

I have spent years wondering and lamenting over our society and its lack of attention to address this lapse of honesty and practicality. Why is it that something so fundamental and so important to our species is not taught in all our schools, or at least introduced with love and acceptance by our parents? It is no wonder that children pick up slang and misinformation from dubious places? With the advent of the Internet, knowledge has become more available. However, there can also be information online that is misleading and judgmental,

---

[102] Marlene Ritchie. "How Are Our Children Learning about Sex? The Responsibility of Parents and Schools to Teach Kids about Human Development and How to Form Caring Relationships." Child Research Net.
http://www.childresearch.net/papers/rights/2016_02.html

produced by religious fundamentalists that claim sex is a sin or punishable by God.

When something so basic as sex and the language it embodies cannot be discussed or shared by our loved ones, those feelings, beliefs, and ideas about basic biological impulses, such as sexual fantasy and desire, can become sublimated. Sublimation is the mechanism whereby those impulses or desires are ignored in order to become more socially acceptable in a person's family, social circle, church, or community. That is, a person finds a way to defend against thinking those thoughts, having those feelings, and acting upon those desires. Sublimation can be something as simple as using an alternative phrase or word for an implied sexual act. Sexual energy can be transformed into something creative, like an artistic endeavor or a consuming hobby. Or it may be directed into a physical fitness program or sports. So many parents, well aware of their children's sexual desires, attempt to funnel those feelings and natural sexual impulses into sports activity. Sublimation may also be directed toward spiritual and mystical pursuits.

A negative shift may produce something as simple as avoidance of the topic and keeping one's thoughts secretive. Sublimation can occur with peer pressure, parental threat, or social jeopardy. Sexual drives and desires may be driven deeply inward. When this happens, the result can cause psychological and emotional harm. It may bring on withdrawal and seclusion in order to avoid any sexual stimulation, which can cause anxiety and depression. In extreme cases, a complete negation and denial of those sexual thoughts and feelings can occur, to the point of a person becoming a sexual predator or a religious celibate. The desire for God may simply take the place of the desire for sex, deemed the safest path for that person. Ever wonder why the virgin is so popular? She is the quintessence of purity, which a person wants to embody. However, repressed and sublimated sexual desires generally do not go away. At the very best, they can only be managed. They are simply buried until some trigger brings them out. This is what happens when a priest comes face to face with a young person who triggers that buried desire. Priests of the Catholic faith have become infamous for their suppressed desires which suddenly burst forth, and the church has continually failed to address and manage.

The use of sexual slang reflects each culture and how its population has dealt with handling proper sexual terms. This goes both ways. Some words are created because the culture in which people find themselves is not able to openly express those words, so substitute words are needed. Then those slang words might get accepted, adopted, and appear in common everyday usage, such as in sports. This back-and-forth sharing of terms has been created and repeated through time, reflecting both maturity and immaturity, where acceptance of sexuality has not been open enough to address the real words for our sexuality in a given culture.

Here are some examples. In the late 1700s, "to tip the velvet" was a kiss, intercourse was "basket-making," and "to strum" and "to bagpipe" were euphamisms for fellatio. "Gingambobs" and "twiddle-diddles" were the gonads, a "godemiche" was a dildo, "a man trap" was a vagina, and a "pego" was a penis. Obviously, these older slang words were eventually dropped, but they serve as examples of sexual slang used during their time.

In the 1920s, birth control was condemned by the church and society at large, homosexuality was thought of as deviant, sex education was limited even for a groom and bride on their wedding night, sex outside of marriage was a sin, and intercourse was thought of as a distasteful means of procreation. Words used during this time reflect the cultural norms of the twenties. An "actress," a "night flower," a "toffer," and a "three-penny-upright" was a prostitute. A woman's genitalia was a "cock alley," a "fruitful vine," a "felt hat," and a "quim". A man's genitalia were referred to as "ballocks," a "lobcock," "plugtail," and "whore pipe". To engage in intercourse was to go "prigging" or "to dock," and an orgasm was referred to as "the melting moment".

Even in the twenty-first century we have developed our own words for very basic parts of the body and sexual activity, which are reflected in the very title of this book. "Balls" are for testes, or refer to the scrotum as a whole, "sticks" are for penises, "pussies" are for vaginas, "eat out" is for cunnilingus, "blowjob" for fellatio, and "hooking up" for intercourse. As each culture matures, it finds its own safe ground in which its members are able to become comfortable talking about the human body and the sexual activities they enjoy.

In our present culture at the end of the second decade of this millennium, people are finally paying more attention to how we use words to speak about gender identity. A person may now identify as transgender, genderqueer, or non-binary. There are now greeting cards from wife to wife and husband to husband. As progressive as that may seem, further progress will have been achieved when cards are to "our favorite Queen," and give "congratulations on your sex change." As I write, women are at risk of losing their right to choose abortion in over twenty states. Our society may claim that it has come a long way, but in many ways, our culture has stagnated with antiquated ways of thinking, and in some cases, is actually reversing its progress toward choice to do what we will with our own bodies. We still have a long way to go.

One very important aspect of this book is the combination of sexual terms found in professional documentation and the use of slang terms found in historical, urban, and slang lexicons. If you are morally opposed to this kind of language, you may feel the need to put this book down and not continue. That would be unfortunate, because you could be the very person who could most benefit from learning the professionally-used real terms.

Throughout this book, you will see many sexual terms appear again and again under the guise of sports terms. These words and phrases may seem odd and unusual. Some may be unpleasant and gross, or even derogatory and hurtful. But they may also be witty, sexy, educational, and humorous. You will most likely see slang words that you have heard and may even have used during your lifetime. Words too raunchy or definitions excessively repulsive will not be listed. There are enough terms that fall this side of that line to fill this book, but there will certainly be some edgy explanations. I promise not to be too clinical, but at the same time, I won't mince my words to describe what is correctly meant.

The expressions I've found are not complete by any means. I will say right now that by listing these terms, it only means that they reflect how male and female genitalia and other sexual terms have been referred to in our culture, and do not intend any racial slur, derogative emphasis, harmful insinuation, or negative implication. They are simply a part of our cultural heritage. *Real terms,* like penis, scrotum, vagina, clitoris, vulva, breast, cunnilingus, fellatio, intercourse, and masturbation will be used. Get used to them now, and be prepared to see them often. The slang and urbanized words will illustrate how sexual names for the body and its functions have been replaced, due to either lack of education and instruction, or simply due to shame and embarrassment by parents.

At the end of this book, the reader will find a long list of slang words used in English-speaking cultures that have taken the place of correct sexual terminology, even though they have not been borrowed for use in sports terminology. Were they simply synonyms, words with a second meaning? Were they just coincidences? Or were their inventers simply casualties of society, forced to sublimate their sexual desires?

Many of these secondary meanings are surprising, and all were created because someone could not bring himself or herself to say or write the correct term. The reader is cautioned to take off their morality hat, put it under your seat, and exchange it for a cultural cap, in order to appreciate how the meaning of words can change through time. Eyebrows are sure to rise. Indignant breaths will be taken. Eyes will roll. But one thing is for sure, you will get an education on how society has learned to deal with its sexuality, and at the same time, you will be entertained.

Part Two
Sticking with a Stick

There are two ways to deliver power, psychologically and physically. Since we cannot *think* a ball across a field, man decided to use his own body or invent a physical extension of himself in order to drive that object across an expanse. Specialized sticks were designed according to the need to attain that goal. Sometimes the smallest of pointed sticks just needs a thrust from a wrist. Other times, such as when playing on ice, the stick just needs to guide an object along. Then there is the arrow which moves by tension, or the rod that extends a line with the flick of a wrist. A long pole is needed to guard, maintain a distance, or to move the entire body through the air.

Mechanical physics play a large role here, involving a mass and force with velocity, speed, and acceleration. Thus the arm, bow, rod, pole, staff, and stick make the object move in a particular and specialized way, keeping in mind all of these mechanical aspects.

For our first look at sports with a stick and the sexual words that belong to them, we will examine the following sports: archery with its arrow, curling with its broom, darts with its point, fishing with its rod, vaulting with its pole, ice hockey with its footed stick, shuffleboard with its pronged cue, and the staff in quarterstaff.

Chapter 4
Archery

The bow and arrow may be one of the oldest weapons for combat and hunting, besides the club and spear, dating to 10,000 BCE.[103] Many primitive civilizations utilized this weapon, most notably the Egyptians, Germanic tribes, British Celts, Native Americans, East Indians, the Chinese, Koreans, Turks, and Yoruban tribes. Several deities were also believed to have used a bow: Apollo, Diana, Cupid, and Heracles, to name a few. There was even a Greek group of worshiped nymphs that attended Artemis, known for their skill of archery in distance, trajectory, and aim.

Competitive archery players use a bow and arrow to shoot across a distance to a target board with colored markings in concentric circles for points. Archery tournaments compete with shooting at set distances of 60, 80, and 100 yards (54.864 m, 73.152 m, and 91.44 m). The round target board used measures from 31.50 to 48.00 inches (80 cm to 122 cm) across, is 51.18 inches (130 cm) above the ground, and it is tilted back about ten degrees off vertical.[104] The target is composed of nine evenly-

---

[103] Wikipedia, "Target Archery."
https://en.wikipedia.org/wiki/Target_archery
[104] Ibid.

spaced concentric rings, two rings for each color, around a central circle.

Scoring is done according to where the arrow lands. The outermost circle on the target board is white for one and two points. Going inward, the next rings are black with three and four points. Next are blue with five and six points. Then red with seven and eight points, and finally gold for nine points with the very center as the bull's eye for ten points. When scores are called or listed at a competition, they are always stated from the highest to the lowest. For indoor competitions an archer shoots three arrows, and when outdoors the player shoots six arrows. The game can be played one individual against another, or in national competitions, several will represent a team. An Olympic player begins the first round by shooting 72 arrows. A perfect score would be 720. The top scores go into a second round for another elimination match, then it is player against player until final playoffs for the gold, silver and bronze medals.

Archery is a highly competitive game. As of 2018, 142 nations participated in competitions, which are governed by the World Archery Federation, with smaller federations in each nation.[105] The largest federations are found in France, Italy, Germany, Japan, Great Britain, and the U.S. There are two distinct archery divisions: Juniors are players under eighteen and Seniors are players over eighteen. Archery entered the Olympics in the early 1900s, but because firm rules for the game had not been established, it wasn't until 1972 that the game was reintroduced for individuals, and finally as a team event in 1988.

---

[105] Ibid.

Now for the equipment. The sport consists of a bendable bow with a strong bowstring attached at both ends, which provides tautness but also flexibility. An arrow is attached to the string by a nock or groove at the back that holds the string in place, and the front of the arrow rests on a small shelf on the bow. The bowstring and base of the arrow are grasped by the hand or by a mechanism, pulled back, and at the height of its tension, both are released toward the target. Bows are made of yew wood, sapwood, and heartwood. Although archery can be played with a longbow, barebow, and a compound bow, the only bow allowed in the Olympics is the recurve bow.

An arrow shaft is made of bamboo, fiberglass, aluminum, carbon fiber, or a composite of materials. The tip, or arrow head, can be made from the sharpened wooden shaft, but more often is made from metal, stone, or some other hard material. Arrows also have fletching, which are bird feathers cut on an angle or curved, but fletching can also have solid plastic vanes or a combination of the two. Three fletches placed around the back of the shaft are most common, helping to make an arrow fly straight. A bowstring is made usually of Dacron, but can also be of linen. A bracer or arm-guard, a finger tab or glove, and sometimes a plastron or chest guard are worn to protect the archer.

Archery Terms and Slang

Belly

Archery: The surface of the bow when drawn toward the bowstring.

Sexual: The front torso, primarily the stomach, used for "belly bumping" as a synonym for intercourse.

Butts
Archery: Practice mounds of earth used as a target.
Sexual: The back end of a person, the buttocks.

Cock feather
Archery: A fletch of feather held at a right angle to the string or perpendicular to the arrow plate, so that when the arrow is released it leaves the bowstring cleanly.
Sexual: A feather used to tickle the penis in sex play.

Cross Dominance
Archery: An adverse way of shooting a bow, that is, the left eye guides a right-sided archer or vice versa.
Sexual: When a cross-dresser spends more time in cross-dress than dressed in the clothes of their gender.

Head
Archery: The front end of an arrow or the arrowhead.
Sexual: The end of the penis, and "getting head" in fellatio.

Kisser
Archery: A plastic button or a tied-on knot of thread designed to be felt by the archer's lips at full draw, which helps to keep the arrowhead straight, and is used to indicate vertical distance.
Sexual: One who kisses something or someone.

Loose
Archery: To shoot or release an arrow from a bow.
Sexual: A person with open sexual practices.

Long rod
Archery: A rod attached to the bow to dampen vibrations.
Sexual: A euphemism for an elongated penis.

Plunger

Archery: A device used to correct an arrow's flex at the point of release.

Sexual: One who thrusts deeply into their partner.

Quill and Quiver

Archery: A quill is a feather shaft, and a quiver is the container for an archer's arrows.

Sexual: The shaft is a synonym for a penis and the container is a synonym for the vagina.

Reed

Archery: The grain of a wooden arrow that the spine is measured against, as opposed to the rift side of the wood.

Sexual: Another synonym for the penis.

Release

Archery: The act of releasing the bowstring at full draw, propelling the arrow away from the bow and the archer.

Sexual: An orgasm, and also an ejaculation.

Shaft

Archery: The main structure or dowel part of the arrow.

Sexual: A term for the length of a penis.

Sin

Archery: Means, "missing the mark," the bull's eye.

Sexual: Acts considered immoral by religious standards.

Upshot

Archery: The last shot in an archery contest.

Sexual: The release of seminal fluid.

Other Archery Terms with Sexual Possibilities

An *arrow* used in archery seems a natural metaphor for the penis, the word *arrowhead* for the head of a penis, an *arrow shaft* would be the shaft of the penis, and an *arrowsmith* seems obvious for the man who uses his penis with distinctive craft. There is also the term *bodkin* in archery, which is a conical arrow point having three or four sides. A bodkin outside of archery is a type of blunted needle with a threading eye for piercing cloth or leather. That certainly sounds like a possible metaphor for a penis with a round blunt end and a large eye. There is also the term, *compressed shaft,* which is when an arrow shaft has been compressed for strength and straightness. Although a penis does not gain strength or straightness when it retracts, in fact, just the opposite occurs, it does still get compressed. The term *target panic,* is what happens when an arrow is shot before a full draw is achieved. A target panic could also be when a man either has sexual fears or in his rush to override them, has a premature ejaculation.

Sexual Commentary

Here is how a game of archery looks to a sexologist. A bowman, having a long slim shaft with a determined head, seeks to embed his rod between a rounded red area and enter into a golden position. The control of the string's tautness with the bending of the bow speaks of a special power. Perhaps the power a male bowman seeks control over his penis, another male's penis, or a woman's clitoral phallus? Don't let this gentlemen's game fool the observer. This is a historic weapon for downing animals for food and killing people in warfare. It is an aggressive play for attention between those believing they are stronger, faster, and better. They will do their best to find their mark with deep intent, and do it from a remote position. Could this be a way for the once hunted to gain control and become the hunter? That is, finding the quickest, quietest, harshest response, in order to make their mark upon the world? Highly competitive players who love the game are called toxophilites, lovers of the bow. The word bow, itself, is a term from Jamaica with a sexual connotation meaning to perform oral sex.

Chapter 5
Curling

In the sport of curling, the stick is a broom. In place of a ball there is a heavy rounded stone, which is called a rock in the U.S. (These two terms will be used interchangeably in this chapter). The stone is thrown by a player called a curler, and it glides down a long narrow rectangular corridor of ice called a sheet, toward the other end to a circular target in the ice called the house. The game is played with two teams called rinks, four players on each rink, and is made up of the lead, the second, the third, and the skip. Each team alternates, playing from opposite ends of the sheet, with each player on a sheet taking turns throwing two stones for a total of eight stones for each team, until all sixteen stones have been played.[106] This is a game of precision and accuracy.

The lead throws the first two rocks and sweeps for the next six throws. The second sweeps for the first two throws, throws the third and fourth rocks, and sweeps again for the last four. The third, (also called the vice, vice-skip, or mate), throws the fifth and sixth rocks, sweeping at other times, sets up the shots that will be thrown by the skip, and posts the score. The skip is the captain, who throws the last two rocks and decides on the strategy of the game.

---

[106] Wikipedia, "Curling." https://en.wikipedia.org/wiki/Curling

After each curler throws the stone and it slides down the sheet, two rink players, called sweepers, race ahead and use their brooms to quickly rub the ice ahead of the stone. This creates friction on the ice, so that the path of the stone is made smoother and enables the stone to curve, curl, go quicker, or go slower. This is done all along the way toward the concentric circles of the house, until the skip tells the sweepers to stop so the stone can come to rest within the house.

When all players on both rinks have thrown their stones, this is called an "end" and the score for each team is marked. This continues back and forth until ten "ends" have been completed. Each rink team is given seventy-three minutes to make its throws. When each rink has thrown all their stones, points are totaled for the most stones that come to rest closest to the very center of the house, called the "button". A rock is counted if it lands within the 12-foot (3.70 m) ring. Scoring may run from one to eight points per end.

Curling has roots in Scotland where it was played on frozen lochs and ponds during the 16th century, and only centuries later began being played in Canada, North America, Switzerland, and Sweden. Now it is played throughout Europe, East Asia, Australasia, and Brazil. The World Curling Federation is the highest governing body. As of 2018, there are an estimated 1,500,000 registered players. There are men's teams, women's teams, and mixed gender teams. The game was presented at the Winter Olympics as a demonstration tournament in the early 1920s and early 1930s, but was not admitted as a medal-awarding game by the International Olympic Committee until 1998.[107] In 2002, the committee voted to

---

[107] World Curling Federation, "Mixed Doubles Curling Confirmed for PyeongChang 2018 Olympics."

retroactively consider both early competitions as part of the Olympic games.

Now for a description of the curling sheet, the curling stone, the curling broom, shoes, and other equipment.

The curling sheet is a large flat rectangular iced area of 14.5 to 16.5 feet wide (4.42 m to 5.03 m) by 146 to 150 feet long (44.50 m to 45.72 m), with each end called the backboard. Often, several sheets may be side by side, allowing several games to be played at the same time. Twelve feet (3.66 m) in from the backboard is the hackline with a hack. A hack is like a starting block where the foot pushes off for throwing a stone. From this point, all the way down to the other end and its hackline, is a central line. Twelve feet in from the hackline is the backline, and from this line begins the large circle or house, which measures 12 feet (3.66 m) across. Marked across the center of the house is the teeline. The center line and the teeline divide the circle into quarters. Inside the house are three concentric circles of 12 feet, 8 feet, and 4 feet. The usual colors are blue, white and red, with some having blue as the outermost color, and some red, but white is always between them. Different teams may use their particular color for any of the rings. Whichever color is in the center is called the "button" and is the bullseye. From this bullseye, twenty-one more feet toward the center of the sheet to the hogline, is called the free guard zone.

The entire curling sheet is specially created and maintained. The original curling sheets may have been frozen lakes and lochs, but modern curling sheets are constructed with an unusual system of pipes that run underneath the ice and pump out a special brine solution with embedded sensors that keep the surface of the ice at

http://www.worldcurling.org/mixed-doubles-curling-confirmed-for-pyeongchang-2018

a constant 23° F. (-5° C.).[108] A person called the ice maker is in charge of monitoring the air and ice temperatures and humidity levels to make sure the playing area is consistent. The surface is not sleek but mottled with sprayed water to form a particular surface called pebble, similar to the outer peel of an orange. It is this surface which contributes to the unexpected movement of the stone.[109]

The earliest curling stones were simply flat-bottomed stones, but they were inconsistent in shape and weight. Then holes were placed in the stones for the curler's finger and thumb, like a bowling ball, for easier maneuverability. Other early stones were a weaver's heavy warp beam from their looms, which had an attachable handle. Other stones were made from wood and some were ice-filled tins. Early players in central Canada made their stones of iron from melted-down cannon balls. Now the stones are made from common green granite from Scotland or Trefor Blue Hone granite from Wales. Each curling stone must weigh between 38 to 44 pounds (17.2 kg), be 4.5 inches high (11.43 cm), and have a circumference of 36 inches (91.44 cm).[110] The stone sides are rounded and curve down to a base ring, which is hollow underneath. On top of the curling stone is an open-ended handle that is attached with a bolt through the center. The handles are either yellow, red, or blue,

---

[108] John Branch, "Curlers Are Finicky When It Comes to Their Olympic Ice," NYtimes.com, 2009.
https://www.nytimes.com/2009/08/17/sports/17curling.html

[109] Mike Celizic, "Smooth Operators: They Make Olympic Ice Nice," Today.com, 2012. https://www.today.com/news/smooth-operators-they-make-olympic-ice-nice-wbna35537168.

[110] World Curling Federation, "The Rules of Curling (Oct 2018)." http://www.worldcurling.org/rules-and-regulations

and each team chooses their color. There are curling stones that come with an electronic eye which will light up if the curler's hand goes over the hog line, which is not permitted.

The curling broom is used to sweep the surface of the ice ahead of where the stone is headed, as brushing the ice creates friction, which forms a thin layer of water on the surface of the ice, making the stone curl less and travel easier. The earliest curling brooms were made of bundled corn strands, much like a household broom. In 1958, the corn straw was inverted in the center of the broom, called the blackjack broom, but the broken straw from hitting the ice tended to leave a mess.[111] In the mid-1960s a horsehair brush was introduced instead of a broom, and gained popularity. In the 1980s, a design called the rink rat was invented, made of three long fingers of springy plastic, covered by cotton and bound together. The cotton covering created more friction for a layer of water on the ice, but the slapping on the ice was quite noisy. The hair brush actually proved to be a better tool, made of hog hair, horsehair, or synthetic hair, with the head of the brush either fixed or able to pivot. Hair brushes do tend to shed hair, but the synthetic ones do not, are easier to clean, and are cheaper. Broom handles went from being corn shafts to wood, fiberglass, aluminum, graphite, or carbon fiber composite. Since the turn of the new millennium, a synthetic broom is now preferred, and although the curling broom is really no longer a broom, but rather a brush, it is still called a broom.

---

[111] Curling Canada, "History of Curling."
https://www.curling.ca/about-the-sport-of-curling/the-history-of-curling

Perhaps just as important as the stone and broom are the curling shoes. Each athletic shoe has a different sole. One shoe's sole is made of Teflon, called a slider, worn by the thrower on the foot that will slide, and worn on both feet by the sweepers. The other shoe is called the gripper, which is worn by the thrower on the hack foot for better traction. A slip-on rubber sole can be fitted over the gripper shoe to easily slide, and a slip-on gripper sole can be fitted over a slider for better footing. There is also other equipment, such as stretchy curling pants for better mobility, curling gloves and mittens, and a stopwatch.

The various process of play for delivery, sweeping, burning or types of shots and strategy will not be discussed, but some may be revealed in the terms. The following terms come from both the World Curling Federation list of terms, and from Wikipedia.

Curling Terms and Slang

Backboard
Curling: The border at the extreme ends of each sheet.
Sexual: The upwards-facing flat plane of the penile shaft that forms when a penis becomes erect.

Barrier
Curling: A board or object behind the hack, used to stop moving stones, also known as a bumper.
Sexual: The use of a condom for safe sex, which forms protection from sexually transmitted infections and diseases.

Biter
Curling: A stone that barely touches the outside of the house.
Sexual: A person who has a habit of biting their lover during sexual play. Also refers to oral sex, a very sexually aroused woman, or is slang for the vagina.

Blast

Curling: A shot delivered with heavy weight and high velocity, usually delivered to break up clustered stones.

Sexual: Refers to a particularly strong ejaculation.

Bounce

Curling: A failed corner freeze where the shooter rolls open.

Sexual: An African American vernacular euphemism for intercourse.

Brushing

Curling: Broom sweeping.

Sexual: The act of two people rubbing their pubic area against one another, and a euphemism for masturbating.

Bump(ing)

Curling: A short shot in which the delivered stone bumps another stone forward.

Sexual: A metaphor for intercourse.

Bumper

Curling: The barrier.

Sexual: Refers to a person's buttocks.

Button

Curling: The circle in the center of the house.

Sexual: A euphemism for a woman's clitoris.

Clean

Curling: To lightly brush the ice in front of a moving rock to remove any debris and ensure a correct line.

Sexual: Refers to a sexual partner with no STIs or STDs.

Club

Curling: The location of the curling sheets.

Sexual: A metaphor for the penis.

Cover(ing)

Curling: Protection given to a stone, by a stone in front of it.

Sexual: A term used for men who cup their scrotum during masturbation in order to feel the intensity of an orgasm. What a gay man or lesbian does when he or she is hiding the fact with a heterosexual relationship. It also refers to an uncircumcised penis and to a condom.

Curling

Curling: A team sport which involves sliding granite stones on ice and sweeping in front of them with brooms to direct them to a desired placement.

Sexual: Refers to a curling experience, an orgasm so strong it makes one's toes curl.

Dish

Curling: A condition with a sheet of ice where the edges of the sheet get slightly rounded up.

Sexual: Refers to a very attractive woman. A simile that says she is "good enough to eat".

Drag

Curling: The effect of a secondary thrown stone with a previously thrown stone when it closely slides behind it or with it.

Sexual: Refers to a person dressed as the opposite gender for a lifestyle change for fun or sexual pleasure.

Easy

Curling: A command called out by the skip to tell the sweepers to sweep a rock more lightly and slowly.

Sexual: Refers to a woman or man who can easily be bedded.

Finish

Curling: The sideways movement in the last ten feet of a rock's path.

Sexual: The final aspect of a man's orgasm in fellatio, when a partner completes the act, often by swallowing the ejaculate.

Flash

Curling: To completely miss an attempted takeout when the rock passes through the house without touching any rocks at all.

Sexual: When a person quickly opens their clothing in public to reveal a part of their body. An act of exhibitionism.

Freeze

Curling: A precise draw weight shot where a delivered stone comes to a rest against a stationary stone, making it nearly impossible to knock out.

Sexual: The retaliation of a person in a relationship who refuses to respond to anything sexual with their partner.

Frost

Curling: A buildup that can occur on ice surfaces when there is excessive humidity in the air. Stones stop faster and curl less.

Sexual: A synonym for the dried residue of an ejaculation.

Grand slam

Curling: The Grand Slam of Curling (currently known as the Pinty's Grand Slam) is a series of curling bonspiels that are a part of the annual World Curling Tour, where games are played in eight ends, instead of the standard 10 ends seen in other major international tournaments.

Sexual: Refers to sexual activity vaginally, anally, and by fellatio with one woman; or having had intercourse with three different women in one night.

Gripper

Curling: A rough sole attached to a curling shoe to improve traction on the ice.

Sexual: A metaphor for the vagina with the ability to grip and clamp down on a penis with kegel muscles.

Hammer

Curling: The last rock in an end, which is a great advantage, as the team with the last rock is said to "have the hammer".

Sexual: A synonym for the penis, and can refer to how an attractive woman can stun a man, simply by her looks.

Handshake

Curling: A traditional sign of goodwill when members of opposing teams shake hands at the end of a game.

Sexual: A euphemism for male masturbation, or a casual sexual encounter with someone.

Hard! (and hurry)

Curling: A skip's command to sweep harder and faster.

Sexual: Refers to a fully erect penis, a woman's erect nipples, and a manner of intercourse.

Hit
Curling: Any shot where the aim is to move another stone. The opposite of a draw.
Sexual: To make advances toward someone for sexual play.

Hog
Curling: A shot that comes to rest short of or on the far hog line and is removed from play.
Sexual: A synonym for a large fat penis.

Inside
Curling: A stone delivered off the broom too close to the desired target and likely to curl past it. Another term for narrow.
Sexual: Refers to either the desire or placement inside the vaginal or anal cavity of another.

Mate
Curling: This player discusses strategy with the skip behind the house and holds the broom while the skip throws his or her rocks.
Sexual: Refers to a sexual partner.

Off!
Curling: A call given by the skip for the sweepers to stop sweeping the rock and take their brooms off the ice.
Sexual: A euphemism for an orgasm, "to get off".

Open
Curling: A rock that is not obscured by another rock, can be open, partial, or covered, or an open takeout, and an open draw.
Sexual: A person amenable for sexual adventure.

Pancake(s)
Curling: A metaphor for a rock or stone.
Sexual: The display of female breasts pressed up against a transparent glass for viewing on the other side.

Pin

Curling: The spot in the center of the house where the tee line crosses the center line.

Sexual: Refers to a prostitute who gestures to a prospective John with a wink, a rolling of the eyes, or a rotating of the hips. It is also a synonym for a small penis.

Rock(s) (ed)

Curling: The rounded granite stone, thrown by curlers during the game.

Sexual: A man may find himself "rocked" by an unsuccessful seduction. It also refers to the testis, especially when engorged. And a euphemism for reaching orgasm, "getting one's rocks off".

Role

Curling: Any movement of a stone after striking another.

Sexual: A gender role or sex role, which implies a range of sexual behaviors and attitudes.

Rub

Curling: When a moving stone barely touches another stationary stone but with less contact than a chip.

Sexual: A euphemism for masturbation, and heavy petting short of intercourse. This is also an acronym, R. U. B., a Random Uncontrollable Boner, which tend to occur in younger men.

Scraper

Curling: A device used by the ice maker to smooth the ice after a period of extended play, performed in conjunction with pebbling the ice.

Sexual: A person who lives life "on the low" and will trade sex for a place to sleep. It also refers to some rough sex during intercourse between two consensual adults.

Second(s)

Curling: The player who throws the third and fourth rocks for a team and sweeps for the prior two and post two throws.

Sexual: An additional fellatio or intercourse experience. It can also refer to the second man who has sexual intercourse with the same woman, after the first man has finished.

Sheepskin

Curling: A wide sheepskin brush used to clean the ice of any loose debris.

Sexual: A prophylactic for the penis, once made of sheepskin, lamb intestine or bladder, and later made with rubber, latex, or polyurethane.

Shooter

Curling: In a hit, this refers to the rock being thrown.

Sexual: Describes a man and his strong ejaculation.

Skip

Curling: The player who calls the shots for the team and traditionally throws the last two rocks.

Sexual: A euphemism for intercourse. Also, when a couple decide to masturbate together, instead of having intercourse.

Slide

Curling: The forward movement of a player throwing a stone.

Sexual: A smooth and efficient intercourse, and what a person may be called who engages with another for casual sex. Also, when a woman slides her vulva along the body or penis of a man, without penetration.

Spinner

Curling: A stone traveling with a rapid rotation.

Sexual: A euphemism for a petite woman who sits upon a penis and can easily be moved, but to actually spin is not possible.

Stone(s)

Curling: A rock.

Sexual: Refers to one testicle or two.

Thick / Thin

Curling: The degree of contact between two rocks. The thicker the hit, the more contact between the stones, and a hit with a small amount of contact is thin.

Sexual: The range of description for the width of a penis.

Tight

Curling: A stone delivered off the broom too close to the desired target and therefore likely to curl past it. Same as narrow.

Sexual: The narrow physical aspect of the vaginal canal.

Up!

Curling: A command shouted by a skip telling the sweepers to raise their brooms and stop sweeping.

Sexual: The upright engorgement of an erect penis. The insertion of the penis into the vaginal canal, "up and in".

Vice (-skip)

Curling: The player who discusses strategy with the skip behind the house and holds the broom while the skip throws his rocks; usually plays third; also known as a mate.

Sexual: The pleasure of promiscuity and prostitution.

Wick

Curling: A shot where the played stone touches a stationary stone just enough so that the played stone changes direction.

Sexual: A synonym for the penis.

Whoa!

Curling: A call given by the skip for the sweepers to stop sweeping.

Sexual: What a new lover says when they see an extraordinarily large penis, or a man sees a beautiful woman naked for the first time.

Other Curling Terms with Sexual Possibilities

Across the face in curling refers to the shooter hitting the object stone on the opposite side from where the broom was placed. In sexual terms, this means that ejaculate is released across the face of one's partner. There is also *around the horn,* which is a double or triple where the shooter ends coming back up the rings. A horn is slang for the penis, so the action around the horn could be speaking about fellatio with the mouth around the penis or a person sitting over the penis. *Calling the shot* in curling is when the skip holds the broom where he or she wants the person to deliver the stone. In BDSM, it is the dominate person who "calls the shots" on what will happen to the submissive.

A *Christmas tree* in curling is a series of rocks in the house arrayed from front to back in such a way that a corner of each successive rock is visible from the hack, that is, angled out like the edge of such a tree. A sexual connotation for Christmas tree can refer to a penis that is thick at the base and tapers to the head, and a female pubic area that was shaved but is growing out, so that it is prickly like pine needles. *Chroming the rock* is grazing a stationary stone without significantly moving it, but enough to alter the path of the shooting rock. Chroming the rock could also be another euphemism for fellatio.

In-off refers to a shot where the delivered stone hits another stone near the outer edge of the sheet at an angle, making the shooter roll into the house. In-off could also refer to a man getting into their partner with intercourse and then "getting off" with an orgasm. A *soft release* is a release that makes the rock curl more, usually by imparting less rotation to the handle. But sexually, a soft release could describe what a penis experiences after intercourse has concluded and is pushed out. There should also be a sexual interpretation for *swing the stick around.* In curling this means to use the measuring device to determine the "shot rock," but it could also be what happens when a man spins his penis around, as a stick, a euphemism for the penis.

Sexual Commentary

Curling is unique among these sports in that the object moved is not a ball, but a rounded stone, and the stick, which is a broom in this sport, never actually comes in contact with the stone. These rounded stones are also called rocks (in the U.S.), which is also a slang term for the testes, commonly heard as, "to get one's rocks off," meaning to orgasm and ejaculate. It is also amusing that the long rectangular white icy surface on which it is played, is called a sheet, like a rectangular white sheet on a bed.

The scoring area with its three concentric rings of red, white and blue is called the house, and the innermost circle is called the button. A stone must at least touch the outer ring to score. One can relate sexually, as a penis must enter through the red circle of the vaginal opening for intercourse, and although it is not physiologically true, with a long penis deeply embedded, feel as though it is coming up behind the navel, or "belly button".

When a curler throws or slides a stone, they lunge to make the delivery. But to lunge has another meaning: to suddenly move forward with force, which is what happens during aggressive play or assault. The broom keeps the ice in front of the moving rock smooth, but it also is used to keep any foreign object off the ice. These foreign objects are called a pick or a pick-up. And as anyone knows, a pick-up is also the act or technique of making the acquaintance of a previously unknown person, especially for amorous purposes.

Chapter 6
Darts

Okay, darts is not in the Olympics, and some would argue that it is not a sport at all. But how it may be considered shifts from a game to a seriously competitive sport when it comes to how the players feel about it and a new level of competition enters the room. It may be deemed a sport because it requires accuracy, patience, talent with a particular skill-set, specific equipment, and meticulous rules. When promotional companies stepped in and big matches between international star players began in the 1990s, this friendly pub game hit the big time. It is still played in pubs in different countries, and has other names, such as Throwers, Arrows, or Tungsten. For our purposes, here and now, it is a sport.

The game of darts has a long history. Darts were first used as weapons in warfare and still remain the weapon of choice for several Amazonian tribes, delivered by blowgun. Fortunately, the modern world has adopted darts as a competative entertainment. Darts became a game in the United Kingdom in the 1860s, when the target became a board instead of a person.[112] At first, blocks of wood were soaked to better allow the points of

[112] James Masters, "The History of Darts and Other Useful Information," The Online Guide to Traditional Games, 1997. http://www.tradgames.org.uk/games/Darts.htm

the darts to stick. These were made from the cross-sectioned butt of a tree. Later they were made from clay, but neither worked well. The darts produced holes in the wood which did not necessarily always come out with soaking, and the clay had to be smoothed out between games and eventually got hard. Finally, someone got the great idea to use the tough sisal fibers of the agave plant. The fibers were bundled, compressed, and bound with a ring of metal to hold them into a round shape. This type of board had the advantage of allowing the darts to easily enter between the fibers, and when removed, the fibers returned to their bound state.

Darts were originally very short arrows made of wood, wrapped with a bit of lead for weight, and turkey feathers to make the flight true. These were called French darts.[113] The metal barrel around the wood was made of brass, but then later plastic took the place of wood. A dart has four parts: the point, barrel, shaft and flight. The point is either 1.26 inches or 1.61 inches long (31.99 mm or 41.00 mm), and the barrels are made from brass, silver-nickel, or tungsten alloy, which gives them each a different weight. They also come in three different shapes. The cylindrical barrels maintain the same diameter for their entire length. Ton barrels bulge in the middle but are thin at both ends. And torpedo barrels are widest at the point and then taper to the end.[114]

As in archery, a flight is added to the end of the dart to give stability and reduce wobble when thrown, but most importantly, to add drag so that the dart does not

[113] Patrick Chaplin, "The History of the Dart." http://www.patrickchaplin.com/Darts.htm

[114] China Tungsten Online (Xiamen) Manufacturers & Sales Corp, "Tungsten Barrell Shape." http://www.chinadart.com/tungsten_dart_barrel_shape.htm

flip over when thrown. Flights can be made of foil, nylon or plastic, and they also come in several different shapes. There is the small kite shape, the teardrop or pear, the slim, the lantern, the number 6, the electro, and the standard. Which one is used depends upon the weight of the dart, and the size of dart depends upon a player's preferred throwing style.

To determine who is first to play and score, each person throws a dart to see whose dart is the nearest to the center. The board is almost 18 inches (45.72 cm) in diameter and is divided by thin metal wires into twenty radial sections. On the outermost ring are numbers printed or made of wire, clockwise from one to twenty. There are three rings, one inside the other. Landing a dart within the outermost ring gives a person double points. A dart that falls within the inner ring gets triple points. In the center is a small green ring giving the player a single count, and the innermost red center or bullseye gives the player a double count of fifty points. Each player begins with a total of 501 points (some games begin with 301). Each player gets three darts per play, and each score is deducted from the player's total. The player to reach zero first wins.

Darts Terms and Slang

Butt

Darts: The old name for the dart board, believed to be first made from a sliced ring of a tree, which was called a "butt".

Sexual: The hind end of a person, the buttocks.

Bag of nuts

Darts: A 45 score, named after the prize given at fairgrounds.

Sexual: A metaphor for the scrotum.

Bed

Darts: A section of a scored number, referring to a double or triple play.

Sexual: A place to sleep and have intercourse.

Bust

Darts: A x01 game, hitting more points than needed to win.

Sexual: Refers to a female's bustline or breasts.

Checkout

Darts: Scoring exactly the score that is left to win the leg.

Sexual: To closely look over a prospective lover.

Conquistador

Darts: Going out with a bull or double bull's eye.

Sexual: A man who has had many sexual conquests.

Cover(ing)

Darts: Aiming for an alternate triple, usually 19, when a previously thrown dart is blocking the triple 20.

Sexual: A term used for men who cup their scrotum during masturbation in order to feel the intensity of an orgasm. What a gay man or lesbian does when he or she is hiding the fact with a heterosexual relationship. It also refers to an uncircumcised penis.

Daddy

Darts: Also known as a "wrong pew," or "right house but wrong bed," meaning that a dart has landed on a double or triple score, but with the wrong number.

Sexual: A name used by a younger woman for an older man who she desires or is having sex with (*not* a family relation). Also, used for a boyfriend or husband while getting into "his bed". And sometimes used by a submissive in roleplay for their dominant partner.

Diddle for the middle
Darts: The throw of a single dart that determines who plays first in a game, by getting closest to the middle of the board.

Sexual: When a person has two of the opposite sex to either side of him or her in bed, for sexual intercourse.

Double trouble
Darts: Not able to hit the double number needed to win.

Sexual: When a man needs to satisfy two women.

Easy in
Darts: A game that requires no special shot to begin scoring.

Sexual: An easy slide into the vaginal or anal cavity of a sexual partner.

He doesn't want it
Darts: A cry from the crowd, recognizing a player who is struggling to successfully complete a leg of scoring.

Sexual: A man who is not game for the taking or does not want sex. Could be a married man or even asexual.

Jugging
Darts: Refers to the person who quits playing when their opponent has reached a score of 200 or more. The punishment for leaving the game is to drink a jug of beer without stopping, following the match.

Sexual: Refers to the action of observing a woman or a man jogging with especially large mammary glands. Also a synonym for "stripping" in Great Britain, because coins are tossed in a mug or "jug" to tip the stripper.

Meatball(s)
Darts: Throwing underhanded and backwards onto the board.

Sexual: A synonym for the scrotum.

Scroat
Darts: A dart that is aimed at hitting the triple 20, but ends up in double 20, instead.
Sexual: One testicle, *scroats* for two.

Shaft
Darts: The part of a dart behind the barrel where the flights are mounted.
Sexual: A synonym for the length of a penis.

Stick
Darts: Refers to the darts themselves.
Sexual: A synonym for the penis.

Straight in (and straight out)
Darts: A game that requires no special shot to begin or end scoring.
Sexual: This implies that a man's penis is going directly into the intended sexual orifice, and straight out means pulling out.

Three in a bed
Darts: When three darts land with the same number, no matter if it is double or triple.
Sexual: A ménage a trios, or three people engaged in sexual activity at the same time.

Wanker's fifty
Darts: A term for scoring 50 points.
Sexual: Masturbating fifty times in a relatively short period of time.

Wanker's off
Darts: When the losing player starts the next leg of the game.
Sexual: Male masturbation to ejaculation.

Woody

Darts: Hitting the dartboard outside the scoring area, and a "wood" is missing the dartboard completely.

Sexual: A hard erect penis.

Other Darts Terms with Sexual Possibilities

Breakfast or *bed 'n' breakfast,* is a score in darts of 26, but if a woman is having breakfast with her date from the night before, it's obvious someone spent the night having intercourse. A *hot toddy* refers to a dart player who throws well despite being intoxicated. Since a woman can be spicy like the hot drink, a hot toddy could also be a woman who is a hottie, or would that be a hottie toddy? The next term is *lipstick,* which usually refers to a triple 20 score, as this portion of the board is commonly red in color and resembles an upper lip, but may refer to any red double or triple pointer. Okay, lipstick is not necessarily a sexual word, but the red color imitates the redness of a vaginal opening, and animal behaviorists tell us that the red coloration on a female baboon monkey's bottom becomes pronounced during ovulation, especially when she is excited. *Spray and pray* in darts means that the darts are thrown aimlessly. But a spray can also be a man's ejaculate, and if there is no protection, the woman could find herself praying she doesn't get pregnant, or contrarily, praying that she does, bringing a new meaning to spray and pray.

Sexual Commentary

Just looking at a dart board produces several thoughts. One, the coloration of the boards are usually black and white, and red and green. Anyone who drives a vehicle knows that red means "stop" and green means "go". This alternation of mixed messages is often what happens in the pursuit of a sexual partner, where there is often an element of hesitation and advancing and retreating. Also, in the very center of the board is a red bullseye. At the beginning of a game, each person throws a dart to determine who will go first. The closest dart to the bullseye goes first. This seems to imitate the process of natural selection in the dating world. A person with strong quick moves, who is sharp-witted, direct, and can arrive "on the dot" is sure to gain the focus of an intended partner. It is a difficult throw to make, but when achieved makes for success.

Now for the dart. One may also make an analogy with the four parts of a dart, with the barrel, the shaft, the point and the flight. The dart is a man's penis, the barrel is his testes, the point is the head or crown of the penis, and the flight is its action of making its way to its intended target. Also, there are three different shapes to the barrel of a dart, cylindrical, ton, and torpedo. Each one may be thought to represent three shapes of a penis. A dart with a cylindrical shape is one with the same diameter along its length, so is long and thin. A ton is a dart with a barrel that is thinner at either end, but bulges in the middle. And the torpedo barrel is thinnest at the base and widest at the point. There is also a difference in lengths of a dart's shaft, which might describe the length of a penis and its process of making its journey into a receiving partner. A shorter shaft makes for more responsiveness and easier headway, and a longer shaft can provide more stability, but requires the member to be harder and have steadier movement.

Chapter 7
Fishing

The broad topic of fishing includes many ways of catching fish and seafood, but for the purposes of this book, the focus will be on fishing that uses a pole for recreation and sport. The stick in this sport, of course, is the fishing rod. Although the ancient practice of fishing 42,000 years ago used only a net or a bone hook on a line,[115] it was revolutionized when done with lines and drift nets deployed by fishing trawlers.

The sport has been written about for centuries, giving instructions on how to fish, what to fish for, and where to fish, but the sport had to wait a couple of hundred years before its equipment was improved upon. During the eighteenth century, fishing rods received a running ring to better control the lines, different kinds of rods were created, and reels were added. Fly-fishing clubs sprung up and consequently, a whole host of tackle items began to be sold in haberdashers. Then larger and stronger reels were created to catch larger fish. The rod, once made of heavy wood, shifted to lighter bamboo or cane, and then to fiberglass. The lines, once made of horsehair, switched

---

[115] Zoë Corbyn, "Archaeologists Land World's Oldest Fish Hook," *Nature: International Weekly Journal of Science.*
https://www.nature.com/news/archaeologists-land-world-s-oldest-fish-hook-1.9461

to silk, and then to synthetic monofilament. The tackle
varies considerably, from rods, reels, lines, bait, hooks,
floats, lures, swivels, and sinkers, to spears, nets, gaffs,
traps, waders, and a tackle box to put it all in. In 1905,
Albert Illingworth patented the fixed spool with line
pickup, revolutionizing the spinning reel.[116]

Fishing for both recreation and sport have their own
set of rules, laws, and licensing. Fishing is a broad term
for catching any kind of seafood, employing cages, nets,
traps, and bow fishing, but the fisherman might also use
extra strong poles, reels and hooks for catching large fish
after throwing chum or fish pieces into the water.
Angling is a more specialized way of catching fish using
only a line, rod and reel, and most specifically a hook
with bait. An angler might not even keep the fish, unless
it is injured or a tasty variety. Once a fish is caught and
logged, the hook is removed and the fish is often
returned, called "catch and release". Fly fishing can be a
relaxing way to escape the office, standing at the edge of
a picturesque lakeshore or streambed; but it can also be a
highly competitive sport for trophy-sized fish. Big-game
fishing enthusiasts stand at the stern of a large boat, using
nothing but brute strength to reel in heavy marlin, shark,
or tuna.

Angling involves a reel that is attached near the
handle of a rod, with a line wound around the reel and
running down the length of the pole through a series of
rings. Bait is attached to the end of the line with a small
hook. Above it is tied a lure, which is often reflective, to
catch the eye of the fish. A float is attached which lies on
the surface of the water so the person fishing can see with

[116] Terence B. Thomas, Frank E. Keating, and Robert Lee Petri,
"Fishing." Encyclopaedia Britannica Online,
https://www.britannica.com/topic/fishing-recreation#ref70275

a bob of the float when a fish nibbles at the bait. Then the line is quickly pulled to hook the fish and reel it in.

The length of a fishing rod can be as short as 4 feet (1.22 m) and as long as 14 feet (4.27 m), but most fall between the range of 6 and 8 feet (1.83 m to 2.44 m). If one has a shorter rod, then the casting distance will be shorter; longer rods allow for a longer casting distance.

Fishing Terms and Slang

Action
Fishing: The flexibility of the rod.
Sexual: A euphemism for intercourse.

Angler (Angling)
Fishing: One who fishes with a pole or rod, line and reel, and a hook and bait. They often follow the rule of catch and release.
Sexual: One who schemes his or her way into the arms of a desired sexual partner, and the process thereof.

Back shot
Fishing: A piece of shot put on the line behind the float to help keep the float steady in windy conditions.
Sexual: The release of ejaculate upon a person's back rather than discharging internally.

Ball
Fishing: The metal, semi-circular arm of an open-face spinning reel that engages the line after a cast.
Sexual: A synonym for testicle.

Bedding
Fishing: Refers to fish laying eggs and hiding in beds of greenery in river beds during the spawning season.
Sexual: Refers to the act of taking another to bed for sex.

Bobber

Fishing: A float attached to the line under which a hook and sometimes a sinker hang.

Sexual: One who has intercourse, a male masturbator, and a person skilled at performing fellatio.

Break off

Fishing: A fish lost when the line breaks, as opposed to losing a fish when the hook breaks.

Sexual: To cause a partner to orgasm during intercourse.

Bumping

Fishing: Refers to the act of making a lure hit an object, such as a log, tree, or rock, in a controlled manner, which can get the attention of a fish and result in a strike.

Sexual: In striptease, a movement that thrusts the pelvis forward.

Butt

Fishing: The end of the handle section of a rod.

Sexual: The hind end of a person, the buttocks.

Cover

Fishing: Natural or manmade objects on the bottom of lakes, rivers, or impoundments that influence fish behavior.

Sexual: A term used for men who cup their scrotum during masturbation in order to feel the intensity of an orgasm. What a gay man or lesbian does when he or she is hiding the fact with a heterosexual relationship. It also refers to an uncircumcised penis.

Cull (ing)

Fishing: A method of removing and releasing lighter-weight fish from a live well so the heaviest or tournament limit is retained.

Sexual: A "cull" is British for a prostitute's customer, and "culling" refers to the process at which she "hooks" him.

Dam

Fishing: A fishing tackle producer. Also, a good place to fish, behind a water-retaining dam.

Sexual: A rubber barrier used in oral sex.

Dap(ping)

Fishing: A method of fly-fishing, in which the fly is allowed to skip or dance on the water while the line and leader are held above the water from a high rod.

Sexual: An acronym for <u>d</u>ouble <u>a</u>nal <u>p</u>enetration, that is, simultaneous penetration of an anus by two men.

Dink

Fishing: A small bass, usually under six to eight inches long.

Sexual: Also a "dinkle". A synonym for penis, which comes from 1888 America, from "dingus," meaning "a thing". Also a "dinkle".

Drag

Fishing: A device on fishing reels that allows the line to play out under pressure, even though the reel is engaged, it ensures against line breakage.

Sexual: Refers to the wearing of clothes of the opposite sex, as "in drag" or doing so for a "drag show".

Edge

Fishing: The borders created by a change in the structure or vegetation in a lake, such as tree and weed lines.

Sexual: A masturbation technique where one intentionally comes to the brink of an orgasm but stops and repeats, to increase the length of time for the pleasure to build. Also, "edge play," which is risky sexual activity.

Fishhook

Fishing: A barbed or barbless hook used for catching fish.

Sexual: A man's maneuver of cupping the hand around the vulva of a woman, often pulling her toward him.

Flat

Fishing: Shallow water where game fish feed or spawn.

Sexual: Refers to a woman's breasts being very small, or no roundness to her buttocks.

Flake

Fishing: A platform built up from poles used for drying fish. It is also the flesh of several species of small shark.

Sexual: One who promises to meet another for a sexual date but doesn't show.

Honey hole

Fishing: Describes an excellent area of water for fishing.

Sexual: Refers to the vaginal canal, considered a "sweet" place for a penis to enter. Also known as a "honey pot".

Hook

Fishing: The strong, curved piece of pointed metal tied to the end of a fishing line that hooks the mouth of the fish.

Sexual: One "hooks up" for a partner in sex. It is also the process that a hooker or prostitute uses to get a John.

Hump

Fishing: An underwater island that generally rises gradually which often is a holding area for groups of fish.

Sexual: A euphemism for intercourse.

Jig (jigging)

Fishing: A fishing lure that attracts fish. It is an up and down movement of the rod while reeling in, which imitates the natural movement of live lure.

Sexual: A euphemism for engaging in sexual activity.

Keeper

Fishing: Any caught fish that is worth taking home to eat.

Sexual: Refers to someone who makes a perfect sexual companion.

Lure

Fishing: Artificial bait designed to attract a fish's attention with movement, vibration, shine, or flashy color.

Sexual: To entice or tempt another with the promise of sexual pleasure or reward. Lures used may be money, power, travel, a home-cooked meal, aftershave or perfume, or good physique.

Nymph

Fishing: An aquatic insect in an immature stage, which hovers under the surface of the water that fish like to eat.

Sexual: Short for nymphomaniac, or a female with uncontrollable sexual desire.

Peg(ging)

Fishing: A predefined fishing area, marked with a peg.

Sexual: The action of a woman who wears a strap-on and penetrates her partner with it.

Pike

Fishing: A long-bodied predatory freshwater fish with a pointed snout and large teeth.

Sexual: A synonym for the penis.

Pick up

Fishing: The act of a fish taking a fishing lure.

Sexual: The act of enticing and luring another person in a public place to go somewhere private for sexual enjoyment.

Pitching

Fishing: A technique in which worms or jigs are dropped into cover at close range with an underhand pendulum motion using a long-bait-casting rod.

Sexual: A term used by gay men to indicate that they are a top or dominate player.

Pole

Fishing: A fishing rod without the eyes and reel seat.

Sexual: A synonym for the penis.

Pro

Fishing: Short for a professional angler, who makes his or her living at fishing and participates in angling tournaments.

Sexual: Short for a professional prostitute, who makes her living from sexual offerings.

Pumping

Fishing: A technique used when fighting a heavy or large fish, by lifting the rod to pull in, and then lowering the rod to wind in the line. This is repeated until the fish surfaces.

Sexual: The action of intercourse.

Quiver tip

Fishing: A special type of rod which has a sensitive tip that curves over when the angler has a bite on his or her line.

Sexual: Refers to the tip of the penis.

Rise

Fishing: Fish breaking the surface of water to eat an insect.

Sexual: When a man gets "a rise" with an engorged penis.

Rod

Fishing: The pole used to cast the bait.

Sexual: A synonym for the penis.

Saddle

Fishing: A thin piece of land that extends out from the shoreline and connects to an island or reef where fish tend to hide.

Sexual: Refers to "in the saddle," that is, intercourse.

Snagging

Fishing: A method of catching fish by jerking an unbaited hook through the water.

Sexual: A successful lure and "picking up" of a person for the intention of a sexual encounter.

Spoon

Fishing: A metallic lure in the shape of a tablespoon.

Sexual: A Victorian term for a couple that lies close together, one behind the other, for sleeping or for intercourse.

Tackle

Fishing: The equipment used by anglers when fishing, which may include, hooks, lines, sinkers, floats, rods, reels, baits, lures, spears, nets, gaffs, traps, waders, and a tackle box.

Sexual: A British word for a man's genitals, his "fishing tackle," also known as a man's "wedding or man tackle," for that special night.

Transition

Fishing: The ground under the water where the structure changes, such as sand to gravel, where fish like to gather.

Sexual: A term that describes a transsexual person's journey from the sex they were assigned at birth to the opposite gender.

Troll(ing)

Fishing: To tow a lure or bait behind a moving boat.

Sexual: A person strolling about, looking for a sexual partner.

Other Fishing Terms with Sexual Possibilities

A *butt pad* in fishing is a cup-shaped pad worn on a belt about the midriff to protect the holder from the butt end of the rod while fly-fishing. A butt pad could also easily be the cushion one uses under the hips of a lover to raise them higher for easier penetration. *Catch and release* refers to catching a fish and immediately releasing it, due to just enjoying the art of catching or if for eating, due to it being too small. Catch and release could also easily be applied to someone who goes fishing for a sexual partner at a bar, entices someone in conversation, but then decides they don't want to have sex with them and backs off.

Flutter bait is any type of fishing bait that is cast and then allowed to flutter down, resembling a dying fish, often used in bass fishing. A flutter bait could also mean the bait used to catch a man by the process of a woman fluttering her eyelashes. *Jerk bait* is a type of soft or hard plastic bait resembling a bat fish, typically worked in a series of quick jerks to resemble a darting baitfish. But it would not be far off base to call an explicitly adult magazine or any other sexual visual aid as jerk bait for masturbation.

Lipping is a method of landing fish by placing a thumb into its mouth and bending the lip slightly down to temporarily paralyze the fish to get it into the boat or unhook and release it. Lipping could easily be anything that human lips do, as in kissing or in oral stimulation of another. *Moontimes* are the first-quarter and second-quarter periods of a moon's progression, best for fishing. Moontimes can also mean the time of a woman's menstruation. *Organic baits* are minnows, insects, worms, fish eggs, cut bait, cheese, or other such items. Organic baits, sexually speaking, could be a winning smile, sexy eyes, full lips, perky breasts, a curvy or muscular body, small buttocks, and long legs. *Peacock ladies* are a type of fly used by fly-anglers, but women who dress up colorfully and ostentatiously could also be considered peacock ladies.

Sexual Commentary

There are so many other terms that could be sexual in fishing, it is hard to know where to call the limit, but just because I can, here are more. An *attractant* in fishing is a solid, powder or liquid form of scent applied to fishing lures for increased productivity. Men and women do this all the time, using colognes and perfumes. Fishermen use *bait* to catch fish, which can be artificial, live or just a shiny lure. Men use their physique, good manners, a good job, fancy car, and money to lure and bait a partner. Women use a flashing smile, fluttering eyes, shapely figure, good cooking, and sexy clothes to bait a prospective partner. Bait is bait.

Soft bottom and hard bottom are also fishing terms to describe the soft sandy bottom of a river or lake, or a lake or river that has a more solid clay, gravel, or rock bottom. However, both of these terms could be used to describe the buttocks of someone. A *pocket* in fishing is a small indentation in a waterway shoreline, but it could also be another slang word for vagina. A *slot* in fishing is the size limit, where the angler may not keep fish shorter than the minimum length or longer than the upper length limit. But a slot might also be considered the same as the slang word slit, which refers to a vagina. And last, a *tight-action plug* in fishing is a lure with a short, rapid side-to-side movement, used when fish are more active. It could also be a butt-plug, which sits snugly while other actions of a sexual nature are acted upon.

Chapter 8
Ice Hockey

In the fast-paced team sport of ice hockey the stick has a foot, stick hits a puck instead of a ball, and the field is an ice rink. There are six skating players on each team: three forwards, a right and left wing and a center; two defensemen, who are behind them; and a goaltender. The players do their best to pass and shoot the puck into a net on the opponent's half of the rink to score a goal.

First, the name "hockey" can be confusing. In Canada, the U.S. and a few other countries, it is known as "ice hockey". In England and most other European countries, when they hear the name "hockey" they understand it to be what we would call "field hockey." To confuse matters even more, there is the game of Bandy, which is similar to ice hockey as it is played on ice and also uses a curved stick, but it directs a small red ball instead of a puck. Bandy has more similarities to association football, which is not U.S. football, but the game that Americans call soccer. Now that the reader has hopefully understood the difference, let's get back to ice hockey.

The sport began in the mid-1500s to early 1600s, when the Netherlands was fighting the Eighty Years War for independence from Spain. The earliest written evidence for the game's name comes from a statute in Galway, Ireland, banning the game of "hokie" in 1573. At this time it was played by launching a small ball with a stick. The word "puck" has Scottish-Gaelic derivation, from *puc,* meaning a blow.[117]

That war-torn era gave birth to a Golden Age. The Dutch painter Jan van Goyen (1596-1656) painted *A Winter Scene* that shows young children playing on ice with curved sticks; and in Hendrick Avercamp's painting, *Winter Landscape with Skaters,* it shows a group of people playing a game similar to hockey called *IJscolf* with a small ball and a curved stick. In the 1700s, a plug of cork or an oak stopper from a barrel was used as the "bung" or puck. Richard Johnson was the first person to write about the game in his 1776 book *Juvenile Sports and Pastimes,* the eleventh chapter of which was titled "New Improvements on the Game of Hockey."[118] And a 1797 engraving shows a player with his bung and stick on the River Thames.

Variations on the game were created as interest in winter games spread to Canada and the U.S. A painting from the early 1800s depicts a basic form of hockey called *shinney* or *shinty* which was played on the St. Lawrence River in Ontario, Montreal, and Quebec City. In 1825, the game was played on Great Bear Lake in Canada. An 1830s painting shows the lieutenant governor of New Brunswick and his family playing the game with soldiers. An 1835 paining by John O'Toole shows the game being played on a frozen stream in West Virginia. In 1839 it was

[117] Patrick Weston Joyce, *English as We Speak it in Ireland.* (Dublin: Longmans, Green, & Co. 1910, "The blow given by a hurler to the ball with his *caman* or hurley is always called a *puck.* Irish *poc,* same sound and meaning," 308.

118 Ian Smith, "This is the earliest surviving Ice Hockey film footage, taken in 1898."
https://www.thevintagenews.com/2016/03/15/earliest-surviving-ice-hockey-film-footage-taken-1898

played on a tributary of the Niagara River called Chippewa Creek. In Thomas Haliburton's 1844 novel, *The Attaché: or Sam Slick in England, 2nd Series,* one of his characters mentions playing Hurly (a similar game) in the early 1800s.[119]

The first organized game of ice hockey was in 1875, held indoors at the Victoria Skating Rink in Montreal. The puck was still a bung, the goal posts were 8 feet across (2.44 m) instead of today's 6 feet across (1.83 m), and there were nine players on a team instead of today's six.[120] Within a few years the Hockey Association had formal rules, and several ice hockey clubs were formed in time to hold world championships for the Carnival Cup at the Winter Carnival in Montreal in 1883. The year 1986 marked the 100th anniversary of the challenge between the Queen's University Gaels and the Royal Military College Paladins, and this rivalry still continues for the Carr-Harris Cup.[121]

By the late 1800s, with almost a hundred teams, Lord Stanley, the Governor General of Canada, decided it was time to have something special to give the winners of championships as a Grand Trophy. He procured a large silver bowl for this purpose which became known as the Stanley Cup. By the end of the century, several things had changed in the game. Goaltenders began to wear cricket padding on their legs for better protection. New moves brought new names like the scoop shot and the

---

[119] Haliburton, Thomas, *The Attaché: or Sam Slick in England, 2nd Series.* (London: Richard Bentley, 1844).

[120] WikiVisually, "Victoria Skating Rink." https://wikivisually.com/wiki/Victoria_Skating_Rink.

[121] Jordan Whitehouse, "The Carr-Harris Cup: Hockey's Oldest Rivalry." https://www.visitkingston.ca/the-carr-harris-cup-hockeys-oldest-rivalry/

wrist shot. The point and cover-point positions were replaced with right and left defense positions, and the goal nets became a standard feature.[122]

The game traveled from Canada to the United States, but Americans were playing ice polo, with a ball instead of a puck. From those beginnings, the U.S. Amateur Hockey League was formed in 1896, based in New York at St. Nicholas rink. In Europe, after Lord Stanley's five sons teamed against a court team of royals, the game's popularity grew quickly. By 1903, a league of five teams had formed, called the *Ligue International de Hockey sur Glace*, which later became the International Ice Hockey Federation.[123]

Many ice hockey rinks have come and gone in Canada, but the oldest rink, built in 1898, is still operating in Ottowa's Aberdeen Pavilion. In 1910, the Matthews Arena was built in Boston and became the home of the Boston Bruins, the oldest U.S. team in the National Hockey League. Teams are formed for major and junior players, college players, and professionals. Ice hockey was introduced into the Olympics in the summer of 1920 with a men's tournament, but it wasn't until 1998 when a woman's tournament was finally admitted.

Now to describe more of the team, rink, puck, hockey stick, and other equipment. The right and left defense, also called wingers, are usually paired against the opposing defensemen, and goaltenders guard each end of the semi-circle, called the crease, against the opposer's puck in their defensive zone. Also, ice hockey is unusual

---

[122] Frank Selke, *Behind The Cheering*, (Toronto, Canada: McClelland and Stewart Ltd., 1962).

[123] Wikipedia, "International Ice Hockey Federation." https://en.wikipedia.org/wiki/International_Ice_Hockey_Federation

in that it is an off-side game, meaning that passes can be made backward and forward.

A North American ice hockey rink is 85 feet wide by 200 feet long (25.91 m by 60.96 m), with rounded corners. And an International rink is 98 feet wide by 197 feet long (30 m by 60 m). A 4-foot-high (1.22 m) wall surrounds the rink, and the inside of the wall is called "the boards". The goal line runs the width of the rink 11 feet (3.35 m) from the furthest walls. In the center of this line is the goal crease with the goal net where the goalie stands. Thirty feet (9.14 m) inward is the blue line, on both sides, and between the goal line and blue line on one side is the attacking zone with two red circles, and on the other side is the defending zone with two red circles.

A right defenseman stands in front of one circle and a left defenseman stands in front of the other. Ten more yards (9.14 m) to the center of the rink is the center red line that goes from side to side. Both sides of the center line are neutral zones in which the right wing, left wing, and center are positioned at the beginning of each game. In the very center is a blue circle and spot for a faceoff. There can also be a neutral zone faceoff spot and an end zone faceoff spot. Outside of the rink on one long side are benches for the players from each team. On the other long side are benches for the scorekeepers, and penalty benches.

Various pieces of equipment are needed to play, most for protection against the puck, other sticks, and slamming bodies. Players wear shin pads, a helmet or visor, a mouth guard, genital guard, a neck protector over heavily padded shorts and jersey, a garter belt if needed to hold up their special hockey socks, and strong skates honed for maneuverability and speed. A goaltender must wear more: larger leg pads and padded jersey, a chest protector, blocking glove and catching glove, a goalie mask, and special goalie skates. Hockey skates are made from thick leather or nylon, and both ends of the blade are rounded for maneuverability. Goalkeepers have skates that are lower to the ice and more square than curved, for stability. The smallest and most important piece of equipment is a 3-inch (7.62 cm) wide, 1-inch (2.54 cm) thick, 6-ounce (170.10 g) rubber puck. It is a disk served cold, frozen that is, which allows it to glide faster and smoother, and eliminates bouncing. But they do thaw, so twelve to twenty are required per game.

The last piece of equipment is the hockey stick, and since Part Two of this book is focused on sticks, we will spend a bit more time here. The oldest sticks were made of hornbeam wood in the mid-1800s. The wood shifted to ash in the 1920s, as it was more durable, but at the same time it added more weight. A notch was made in the shaft and the blade was glued in it. There were also sticks made of willow and birch, and one developed blade was so curved it looked like the curve of a banana.

In the 1940s, lamination with layers of different wood made the stick flexible. Fiberglass was introduced in the 1950s, used to wrap around the wood of the stick, making it lighter, more durable, and cheaper, and the preferred wood became aspen. By the early 1980s aluminum sticks became legal, with a replaceable blade. In the early 1990s, carbon fiber became popular. Now, a composite stick may be made of wood, graphite, Kevlar, or titanium.

An average regular stick measures 2 to 3 inches (5.08 cm to 7.62 cm) thick, and the foot is 12½ inches (31.75 cm) long. The length of the stick is about 5.33 feet (1.63 m), but, the exact length of the stick is determined according to the height of the player. With a stick held upright in front of a person and the stick's toe on the ice, the handle should reach between the chin and nose without skates, or to the chin with skates on. For durability, a goalie's stick is wider at the toe, longer in the foot, and wider half-way up the stick. For handling the stick better, the top of the shaft is wrapped with either black or white cloth tape, and for dealing with the puck better, the blade is often wrapped with a cotton and adhesive friction tape.

A good swing with a stick on a puck can result in speeds of over 100 miles (160.93 km) per hour. An average player goes through six to ten dozen sticks per season. That's 60 to 125 sticks a year, and the average NHL hockey stick costs $185 (€163 as of October 2018). But it is the liveliness or responsiveness of a stick that makes the difference between a cheap and expensive stick.

This chapter must also describe the important properties of a stick, the lie and the flex, along with the pattern on the blade. The angle of the shaft to the blade is called the "lie". A very straight shaft with the blade flat on the ice provides a high lie value, from five to seven for a normal player's stick. A "five lie" means a 135° angle. Goalie sticks have a lie of eleven to fifteen percent. There is also a flex to a hockey stick, which includes the aspects of bend, stiffness and whip. There is a flex range of 40 to 160 psi (275.79 kPa to 1,103.16 kPa), printed on the stick. The pattern on the blade is also important, and includes the curve, the face angle, and the toe. This chapter will not get into all the strategies of the game, but some will be listed in the terms below.

Ice Hockey Terms and Slang

500

Ice hockey: 50% or even. Refers to points earned in relation to the number of points available.

Sexual: 500 is a reference to 500 ml of saline for a breast implant. The number implies large breasts, and the comment is one in recognition of breasts surgically enhanced.

Apple

Ice hockey: A slang term used to describe an assist on a goal.

Sexual: A euphemism for a woman's small breasts, no bigger than an average-sized apple.

Assist

Ice hockey: Attributed to players of the scoring team, who shot, passed, or deflected the puck toward the scoring teammate.

Sexual: When one guy helps his buddy connect with a female friend to be a sexual partner.

Biscuit

Ice hockey: A slang word for the puck.

Sexual: Refers to the buttocks of a person.

Blocker

Ice hockey: The rectangular padded glove that a goaltender wears on the stick-holding hand.

Sexual: Short for "cock-blocker," a person who blocks the way for another to connect sexually with someone.

Butterfly

Ice hockey: A style of goaltending where the goalie drops to the knees to cover the lower half of the net with his or her leg pads.

Sexual: The feeling of butterflies in the stomach alludes to the first aspect of erotic excitement, called limerence. It is also a synonym for the vulva. A butterfly kiss is a blink of an eyelash on someone's cheek; and it is a sexual position where the woman is on her back with legs up, bent, and out.

Bender

Ice hockey: Short for ankle bender, a derogatory term for a player who bends his or her ankles when skating.

Sexual: A euphemism for a gay man.

Cage

Ice hockey: A metal grid that attaches to the front of a helmet to protect the face.

Sexual: In prostitution, it is a room rented for sexual purposes. In BDSM, a cage, usually with bars, is used to hold a submissive for confinement and training, for fantasy play.

Catcher (catching) glove

Ice hockey: The webbed glove that the goaltender wears on the hand opposite the stick.

Sexual: A euphemism for a condom.

Cherry picking

Ice hockey: When a player stays near their opponent's defense, waiting for a pass in order to receive a breakaway.

Sexual: The process of watching and waiting for a sexually inexperienced person in a crowd, usually a bar, in order to seduce them and have sexual relations.

Clipping

Ice hockey: Hitting an opponent below the knees resulting in a penalty.

Sexual: A quick and usually singular sexual encounter.

Crease

Ice hockey: An area of the ice that extends from the goal line in front of the net, often shaped as a semicircle and painted in a different color.

Sexual: The crevice separating the buttocks.

Dangle

Ice hockey: When a player does a series of dekes in a row (a movement where a player handles the puck in such a manner to fool the opponent into moving out of position) in order to get around the opposing players.

Sexual: The "angle of the dangle" refers to the various stages of arousal with the penis. It is from "dangle-dong," a synonym for a limp penis.

Dive, (a)

Ice hockey: When a player exaggerates the contact made against him, in order to entice the referee into calling a penalty against the opposition, but ends up in an unsportsmanlike conduct penalty, being called against the accuser.

Sexual: A euphemism for cunnilingus. And a place of low caliber for picking up loose women.

Duster

Ice hockey: A derogatory term for a player who always sits on the bench, and is there so long they are said to "collect dust".

Sexual: A euphemism for the buttocks.

Flopper

Ice hockey: A goalie prone to going down on the ice to stop pucks. Opposite of a "stand up" goalie.

Sexual: Large saggy breasts that hang low, and refers to a half-erect penis.

Gap

Ice hockey: The space between the opponent and the puck.

Sexual: Slang for the vagina. Also, the upper inner thighs on a female body which are slender enough to show an open space, considered sexually attractive.

Goon(ing)

Ice hockey: A general term for either a pest and agitator, or an enforcer ready for a fight.

Sexual: A sexually aroused state, produced through masturbation with the intent to ride a heightened edge of excitation many times before climaxing.

Grinder

Ice hockey: A player valued more for hard work and checking skills, than scoring ability, and who often sets up goal shots for offensive players.

Sexual: One who grinds their sexual organs against another in copulation, a casual term for the mouth, and what a stripper does when she rotates her hips as if having intercourse.

Hack

Ice hockey: Contacting an opponent's body or stick with one's own, with a swinging motion, which results in a penalty.

Sexual: Refers to a prostitute who is not good at his or her job.

Hat trick

Ice hockey: When one player scores three goals in one game. Fans throw their caps onto the rink in approval.

Sexual: When a man is able to experience fellatio, vaginal, and anal intercourse in one night, or when he has sex with three different partners in one night.

Hooking

Ice hockey: The act of impeding an opponent by placing the blade of a stick into their body, which results in a penalty.

Sexual: Refers to "hooking up" or looking for a sexual partner. It is also the action of a prostitute "hooking" a client.

Icing

Ice hockey: Occurs when a player shoots the puck across both the center red line and the opposing team's goal line without the puck going into the net or being able to be touched by an opposing player in their neutral or defensive zones.

Sexual: The act of playing with an ice cube and surprising a lover with its use for hardening nipples and controlling an erection.

Jock

Ice hockey: From jock-strap, the device used to protect the testicles of a male player.

Sexual: A synonym for the penis, to penetrate with a penis, and a male practitioner of anal intercourse.

Kneeing

Ice hockey: The act of contacting an opposing player when leading an outstretched knee, resulting in a penalty.

Sexual: When a person rubs against another's knee to stimulate their sexual organs.

Light the Lamp

Ice hockey: A light above the net turns on when a goal is scored.

Sexual: A literary metaphor for sexual intercourse.

Line

Ice hockey: A specific line up of a left winger, center, and right winger.

Sexual: Where prostitutes ply their trade, and a line or lineup in a brothel that shows the prostitutes who are available.

Muffin

Ice hockey: A bad shot that wavers in the air when traveling toward the goal that should have been stopped.

Sexual: A euphemism for a woman's outer labia.

One timer

Ice hockey: The act of shooting the puck directly off a pass without playing the puck in any way.

Sexual: A one-time sexual experience with a person.

Overtime

Ice hockey: An extra session of play added on after the full regulation time has concluded in order to resolve a tie.

Sexual: Refers to continuing intercourse after ejaculation has occurred, or a prostitute who allows extra time to his or her client.

Paddle

Ice hockey: The wide portion above the blade of a goalie's stick.

Sexual: Both the implement and the act of paddling with consent, a spanking with sexual dynamics in mind.

Pillows

Ice hockey: The goaltender's leg pads.

Sexual: Can refer to a female's full breasts or round soft buttocks.

Power play

Ice hockey: This occurs when one team has more players on the ice than the other team, when a player is in a penalty box.

Sexual: The intentional demonstration of power to impress and attract another person's attention for their own sexual pleasure.

Puck bunny

Ice hockey: A young female fan more interested in meeting the virile players, than in the game.

Sexual: A woman groupie for field or ice hockey players, who follows the team and has sexual relations with them.

Pull the goalie

Ice hockey: Removing the goalie from the ice in order to temporarily replace him with an extra skater.

Sexual: Ceasing birth control when trying to produce a child.

Rebound

Ice hockey: This occurs when the puck bounces off a goalie, a player, or the net, after a shot to the goal.

Sexual: Going from one relationship to the next to avoid the pain of a breakup.

Save

Ice hockey: Stopping the puck from crossing the goal line and preventing the opposing team from scoring a goal.

Sexual: When a wingman comes through by steering a possible sexual partner toward his buddy.

Shaft

Ice hockey: The long part of the stick that is straight and is held by the player.

Sexual: The shank of the penis, as opposed to the head of the penis.

Shift

Ice hockey: The period of time a player, line, or defensive pairing is on the ice before being replaced by another.

Sexual: An Irish term to kiss deeply, and can also include intercourse.

Sin bin

Ice hockey: The penalty box.

Sexual: Refers to a van with a bed, a "cock-wagon," a "fuck-truck," a house of prostitution, or the drawer next to a bed where sex toys are kept.

Slot

Ice hockey: The area on the hockey rink directly in front of the goaltender between the face-off circles on each side.

Sexual: A synonym for the vagina.

Sniper

Ice hockey: A player with a powerful, accurate shot skilled at finishing plays.

Sexual: One who hides and masturbates while watching two people having intercourse, and who, when ready to orgasm, runs out from their hiding place, ejaculates and then runs away. A male who is above his partner having intercourse and then withdraws, surprising their partner, only to ejaculate on them. And, a woman's erect nipples seen through her top, and a sneaky woman who uses strategies to entrap a lover.

Trap

Ice hockey: A defensive hockey strategy in which a team loads up the neutral zone with players so that the opposing team has a difficult time crossing the blue line.

Sexual: The lure of a transwoman who tests to see how well she passes for a woman by trapping a man in an intimate moment. A woman getting pregnant in order to force marriage is also a trap.

Trapper

Ice hockey: A player who joins his team, loading up the neutral zone with other trappers so that the opposing team has a difficult time crossing the blue line and gaining the zone.

Sexual: A gay man whose sexual preference leans toward overweight men.

Twig

Ice hockey: Another name for a hockey stick.

Sexual: A vibrator with a slender tip, and a synonym for a very small penis.

Wheel(ing)

Ice hockey: When there is time and space to skate with the puck.

Sexual: The charismatic art of seducing a woman with the intention of rolling her into bed. It is also an Elizabethan euphemism for the vulva and the vagina.

Wrap around

Ice hockey: Scoring from behind the net.

Sexual: The position of an arm during anal or vaginal intercourse with rear entry. The arm reaches forward to either manipulate a partner's clitoris or stroke a penis.

Other Ice Hockey Terms with Sexual Possibilities

In this game, body checking is using the hip or shoulder to knock an opponent against the boards or the ice. Body checking is a recommendation before having intercourse with someone new, to make sure no open sores or problems are present. It is also a visual reward for someone who appreciates the human body of a soon to be lover. A face wash in ice hockey is an intentional rubbing of the open palm of a glove in an opponent's face to annoy them. A face wash could also be the spraying of semen on to the face. A goal suck should merit at least one reference to fellatio but in ice hockey, a goal suck is a selfish player who stands near the goal awaiting a pass from teammates so he can score and get the glory. A healthy scratch in ice hockey is an uninjured player on the roster who does not dress for a game, as only twenty players are allowed to dress. A healthy scratch can also be when men need to scratch their scrotum, as one might need to scratch anywhere on their body. Pubic hairs can tickle the groin. Or, it can be a common fungal infection called "jock itch". Holding the stick is the act of grabbing an opponent's ice hockey stick, resulting in a penalty. Holding the stick would obviously be a man holding his penis, most likely for masturbation.

Misconduct is a penalty where the offending player is ruled off the ice for ten minutes but may be substituted back in. Misconduct could also mean any sexual action that crosses the line of bad behavior. The referee's crease is the semi-circular area at the red line, beside the scorer's bench, into which a player may not enter when occupied by a referee. Since a crease is the crevice separating the buttocks, it makes sense that the referee's crease is exposed when he bends over and shows that crack. Riding the pine is when a player is confined to the bench (usually made of pine wood), by a coach due to unsatisfactory performance. Although the word pine does not seem to be listed as a synonym for the penis, if it were, it would be when a man has shaved the hair at the base of his penis and the hair has partially grown out creating stubble. A woman who was to sit on top in intercourse might say that she was riding the pine.

A scoring chance in ice hockey is an attempt or chance for a team or player to score a goal. This can also mean that a person has a chance to be with another in an intimate way. A shot on goal is a shot that will enter the goal if it is not stopped by the goaltender. The term might also mean that an ejaculation has met its mark. Ice hockey has a slapshot, which is a hard shot, usually with a big windup, wherein the player bends his stick on the ice and allows the energy stored in bending it to launch the puck forward. Some consider a slap shot when a man is receiving fellatio, and when ready pulls out, slaps the face of the fellator with his penis and then unloads upon the face. Spearing is another term in ice hockey. It is the act of jabbing an opponent with the blade of his stick, which results in at least a double minor penalty. Sexually, spearing could easily be part of deep-throating in fellatio, or the action of jamming a penis deeply into a partner's other cavity.

Split the D is when an offensive player confuses or outmaneuvers two defensemen in order to get between them. "D" stands for dick, another name for the penis, so split the D, could refer to a penile bisection or splitting, in body modification. Stick checking in ice hockey is using the hockey stick to interfere with an opponent's stick. As in body checking, stick checking would be the process of checking a penis out before having intercourse with someone new, to make sure no open sores or abnormalities are present or could cause any risk, even with a condom. Stick handling is the act of controlling the puck with one's stick, especially while maneuvering through opponents. Since a penis is also known as a stick, this includes all ways of handling a penis.

Sexual Commentary

In amateur and international games, in front of each goal is a goal crease, which is a half-circle surrounded by thin red lines. This is where the goaltender defends the goal and none other can enter this area. Just in front of this is what is now referred to as the Goaltender Trap Zone (or trapezoid). It is prohibited for the goaltender to handle the puck anywhere behind the goal line that is not within the trapezoidal area, or there is a penalty. Think of the red lines of the half circle as the curved entry of a vaginal zone, and the goaltender as a woman's friend who is charged with protecting her from being sexually approached in a public place. However, if he becomes the man who enters that area, he might be the one who gets into trouble.

Chapter 9
Pole Vault

Pole vaulting needs to be included in this overview of sports, not only because it is an international athletics track and field event, and has been included as an Olympic sport since 1896, but because the pole is the longest stick used in any sport. The pole can be as short as ten feet (3.05 m), but as long as 17 feet 5 inches (5.33 m). A vaulter must carry his or her pole while running quickly toward the bar, carefully stab the base of the pole into the box below the bar, and then while firmly holding on to the pole, use the acceleration to hoist him or herself over a high crossbar without dislodging it. The vaulter who can vault the highest over the bar without knocking it down wins the competition.

Originally, pole vaulting was not a competition but a necessity, used to get across a marshy area to solid land without getting wet. This occurred most notably in the Netherlands, in lowlands around the North Sea, and in low-lying areas in England. It is thought that gondoliers in Venice also used their poles to get to land from their boats. At first, pole vaulting was taken into competition strictly for distance, but that changed in England in the 1860s, when the sport shifted to competition for height.[124]

---

[124] Jan Johnson and Ruse Versteeg, *Illustrated History of the Pole Vault*. (Atascadero, CA: Sky Jumpers, 2008), p. 20.

Vault poles were originally made of bamboo and ash, but then changed to aluminum, fiberglass, or carbon fiber, which gave the poles more flexibility and strength, and allowed the vaulter to reach greater heights. A vaulter's weight determines the flex rating of the pole, and the effectiveness of the pole depends upon where the handgrips are placed. A pole vaulter needs a running start with good speed, accuracy to place the butt of the pole into the box at the base of the bar, strength to hold onto the pole as the body ascends, and agility to maneuver the body and swing over the bar. The high crossbar was once a triangular aluminum bar, but now it is a round fiberglass bar with rubber ends.

Each competitor is allowed three attempts to clear a height. If they do, the bar is raised and they get three more attempts to clear that height. If they falter, they are out of the competition. In case of a tie, the loser is the one who had the greatest number of misses. Or if still tied, another jump for each vaulter is conducted. Scoring is much like that in high jumping, and the landing area, once of sawdust or sand, became mats of foam. Vaulters used to land on their feet, but now they land on their back or shoulders. The record for highest vault was set in 2014 by a Frenchman named Renaud Lavillenie, at 20.21 feet (6.16 m).[125]

Pole Vault Terms and Slang

Box

Pole vaulting: The trapezoidal indentation in the ground at the end of the runway, with a metal or

---

[125] BBC Sport, "Sergey Bubka's Pole Valt Record Broken by Renaud Lavillenie," BBC Sports. https://www.bbc.com/sport/athletics/26208821

fiberglass covering, in which the vaulters plant their pole in order to swing over the cross bar.

Sexual: A synonym for the vagina.

Extension

Pole vaulting: Refers to the extension of the hips upward with outstretched legs as the shoulders drive down, causing the vaulter to be positioned upside down.

Sexual: The process by which the penis engorges with blood as excitation begins, extending to full length.

Fly away

Pole vaulting: The phase of the vaulter pushing off the pole and releasing it so it falls away from the bar and mats.

Sexual: A Japanese slang phrase meaning orgasm.

Grip

Pole vaulting: The location of the vaulter's top hand on the pole.

Sexual: The grasp that one has on a lover, either with hands on hips, face, penis, or legs.

Pit

Pole vaulting: The area where mats are located for landing.

Sexual: This can be a slang synonym for an armpit, an anus, or the vagina. It is also British term for a bed or bedroom.

Pole

Pole vaulting: The long fiberglass shaft that propels the vaulter over the bar.

Sexual: Refers to a penis, especially a vertically erect penis.

Swing leg

Pole vaulting: The last foot and leg that leave the ground in a jump, which swings forward and upward to help propel the vaulter up and over the bar.

Sexual: Refers to the penis, with its owner ready to swing either way for a male or female encounter.

Turn

Pole vaulting: The vaulter turns 180° toward the pole while extending the arms down past the head and shoulders.

Sexual: A metaphor for intercourse, "taking or having a turn."

Other Pole Vault Terms with Sexual Possibilities

In pole vault, the *approach* is when the vaulter sprints down the runway with speed and correct position so that he or she can initiate a take-off. One may also consider the term approach to describe what a person does to meet and strike up a conversation with the intention of having a sexual experience. The *bar* refers to the crossbar that is suspended above the ground by the standards. Although the word itself does not have a sexual meaning, a bar or a club with a bar is the number one place people meet up for sex. *Standards* are what hold up the cross bar at a particular height above the ground and can be adjusted to different horizontal heights in competition. Standards are also what a person seeks when looking for a sexual partner, neither setting the standard too high and making the task unattainable, nor lowering the standard too low to admit someone unacceptable. There is also the *swing up,* which is when the vaulter plants the pole in the box and throws his or her legs forward and the pole upward, causing a pendulum motion that propels the body up and over. A sexual swing up can also be when a couple engages in sexual swinging, and ends up swinging with prominent or famous people.

Sexual Commentary

The obvious and very special aspect of this activity is the length of the pole, the longest stick of any sport. Poles are made according to the maximum weight of a person, so that the pole will stand up to the stress of their weight. One side of the pole is more stiff, to stabilize it, while the other end of the pole bends more to help the vaulter over the bar. The pole's stiffness and length, as well as the technical ability of the vaulter, make for the best vault.

A penis is sometimes referred to as a man's pole, which just sounds longer. In fact, men mistakenly equate their penis size with their power and masculinity, and men seem to be more concerned about their body image than women. Dr. Phillippa Diedrichs from the Center of Appearance Research at the University of the West of England conducted a study of 394 men in 2012. It revealed that 80.7% of men were concerned with their weight, lack of hair, or look of themselves, and 12% said they would trade a year of life if they could have their ideal body.[126] In an internet survey 52,031 heterosexual men and women were asked about penile size and satisfaction. Forty-five percent of the men wanted their penis to be larger.[127] Could it be that some men, with an

---

[126] Felicity Spector, "Belly up: Why men don't like their bodies," *4 News*, (Jan. 6, 2012). https://www.channel4.com/news/belly-up-why-men-dont-like-their-bodies

[127] Janet Lever, David A. Frederick, and Letitia Anne Peplau, "Does Size Matter? Men's and Women's Views on Penis Size Across the Lifespan," *Psychology of Men & Masculinity*, Vol. 7, No. 3. (2006), 129-143.

unconscious desire to have a longer penis, consciously turn to a sport with the longest pole imaginable?

Speaking of long poles, an honorable mention needs to be given to the Scottish athletic event of the caber toss. There are few terms for this Scottish Highland game, so it doesn't rate its own chapter, but it certainly ranks as the heaviest stick ever borne in a competitive sport. In the caber toss, men lift huge poles, just under 20 feet long (6 m) and weighing up to 175 pounds (79 kg), carry them across a field, and flip them over. The object is to flip the pole, end-over-end, and have it land at the maximum vertical angle to score the highest. The term *caber*, from Gaelic, means a wooden beam, and the one who performs this feat is called a "tosser" or a "thrower." In British slang, this is one who shows off and brags, and in sexual lingo a tosser is one who masturbates. Suffice to say, this old lumberjack competition seems to be a match to determine which man has the biggest penis that can become erect with the greatest angle. That's one vaulting that definitely impresses.

Chapter 10
Deck Shuffleboard

Deck shuffleboard, also called floor shuffleboard, has its own chapter as it is a sport using a stick and it has some interesting terms with a sexual twist. It can be played indoors or outdoors, with two people or two teams of two. A player will use his or her cue stick to launch four discs down a court to a scoring area. There is also a tabletop version called Table Shuffleboard, which has gained in popularity and can now be found in neighborhood drinking establishments. This chapter will only deal with deck shuffleboard.

The precise origin of shuffleboard is unknown, but it we do know that it developed somewhere in Europe about 500 years ago. There is documentation that England's King Henry VIII gambled over the game of "shovillaborde," and thus it was deemed a royal game and not for commoners. However, the game made its way into the future for all. It used to be played more by the elderly because it does not take much strength or agility, and is still found at retirement homes and on cruise ships, but now the game is enjoyed by all ages, inside and outside, on a floor, deck, or pavement.

The offensive object of the game is to use a cue stick to push weighted discs (also called flapjacks) down a narrow court in order to have each disc end up in a scoring triangle, without falling off the end of the board. The defensive object of the game is to keep the opposing team from knocking the team's disc from a good score or off the board. The point of the triangle, which faces the player, carries the highest score of ten points. The next wider section is eight points, the next is seven points, and at the widest base of the triangle is an area called the 10-off zone. If someone's disc lands there, 10 points are *deducted* from the person's score. Points are only tallied when all discs have been launched and only the weights in front get scored.[128] A game can be played to 50, 75 or 100 points, and the winner is the best two out of three games.

A court can be permanently set and painted with scoring numbers, or a transportable, pre-marked rollout mat can be used. There are different lengths. A non-regulation shuffleboard court, for entertainment, is 6 feet wide by 39 feet long (1.83 m by 11.89 m), with an additional 6-foot area at either end used to shoot from. Two large triangles face each other at either end, 12 feet (3.66 m) apart. A *regulation* outdoor court is six feet wide and fifty-two feet long (1.83 m by 15.85 m), with the two scoring triangles facing each other 18 feet (5.49 m) apart. The triangles have a base of 6 feet (1.83 m) across and two 9-foot (2.74 m) sides, with a line dividing each triangle in half. There is also a court for children that is 3 feet wide by 15 feet long (0.91 m by 4.57 m).

Each team has four corresponding hard plastic colored discs. Yellow and black are traditional, but other colors, such as white, yellow, and red can be used. The team with the color discs always plays first. The discs are 6 inches (15.24 cm) in diameter, 1 inch (2.54 cm) thick, and cannot weigh more than 15 ounces (425.24 g). Each player also uses a stick called a cue or a pole, which

---

[128] McClure Tables, "Shuffleboard Game Rules."
https://www.mccluretables.com/t-Shuffleboard_Game_Rules.aspx

measures 5 to 6 feet and 3 inches long (1.52 to 1.92 m). Attached to the end of the cue are two small outward-facing prongs with hard plastic feet that are 5 inches (12.7 cm) wide. Players use the cue to slide the discs forward along the court. They can come in one piece 6 feet (1.83 m) long, two pieces, or telescoped with one shaft inside the other that pulls out and can be locked into place. The only other addition to the game is wax or shuffleboard powder, which is made of tiny silicone particles that allow the puck to move smoothly.

Shuffleboard is divided into different national tournaments: amateur, junior, and senior classes. The USA National Shuffleboard Association was established in 1931.[129] The U.S. hosts national tournament championships, and the Huntsman World Senior Games. There is also the International Shuffleboard Association, which hosts annual world singles and team championship tournaments. In 2018, the most competitive countries were Brazil, Canada, Germany, Japan, United Kingdom, U.N. teams, and the United States.

Deck Shuffleboard Terms and Slang

Alley

Shuffleboard: The official name of the gutter, the concrete area, two feet wide, between two adjacent courts. Also called "suicide alley".

Sexual: The shortened term for "shaft alley" referring to the area from the vaginal opening to the anus, is originally a nautical term, which is the passage from the engine room to the stern.

---

[129] USA National Shuffleboard Association, "USA – NSA Shuffleboard." http://www.national-shuffleboard-association.us/

Apex

Shuffleboard: The forward point of the scoring triangle.

Sexual: The height, pinnacle, and culmination of sexual foreplay, which ends in a climax.

Bait

Shuffleboard: A disc that is placed on the board, usually in the deep seven without a protective guard, for the purpose of getting the opponent's cue disc into an area where it can be put into the 10-off area.

Sexual: Sex bait is a person in a group that is chosen for both their attractiveness and vulnerability.

Beads

Shuffleboard: Fine glass globules that are sprinkled on a court to lessen the friction of the court surface and the discs.

Sexual: Refers to anal beads, which consist of multiple small spheres attached together, inserted into the anus and slowly removed for a heightened experience when a person orgasms. Also known as a "string of pearls."

Block

Shuffleboard: A disc that is placed so as to interfere with the opponent's next shot, a preventive guard, or a disc that happens to stop in a position that interferes with either player's shot.

Sexual: Short for "cock-block," that is, one who blocks the way for another to connect sexually with a potential partner.

Bunny

Shuffleboard: A disc that represents the winning score.

Sexual: An inexperienced male who thrusts too fast during intercourse, much like a rabbit, due to exuberant inexperience.

Bunt

Shuffleboard: An attempt to move a disc already on the board to a more favorable position by striking it with the cue disc.

Sexual: A Shakespearean term, "a low dirty prostitute, half whore and half beggar."[130]

Double

Shuffleboard: A shot that scores both the cue disc and a liner of the same color. Before the shot, the liner is known as a potential double.

Sexual: Short for double penetration, that is, a woman being penetrated by a man vaginally and another anally. It is also when one man is engaged in sex play with two women.

Frame

Shuffleboard: That portion of a game begun at the head of the court in which each player shoots four discs.

Sexual: A term for the human body, as it is often used to describe a woman having a desirable figure.

Glance

Shuffleboard: A shot in which the disc, after its impact with a target, changes its course to stop in a more favorable position.

Sexual: Refers to someone who gives a quick and discrete look at someone with sexual interest.

---

[130] Gardon Williams, *A Dictionary of Sexual Language and Imagery in Shakespearean and Stuart Literature,* (London: Athlone Press. 1994), 174.

Gutter

Shuffleboard: The alley or concrete area between two adjacent courts.

Sexual: Refers to "gutter sex," that is, the action of one experiencing a humiliating sexual act.

Hammer

Shuffleboard: The last disc to be shot at the end of the court.

Sexual: A synonym for the penis.

Head

Shuffleboard: The end of the court by the scoreboard.

Sexual: The act of giving or receiving oral sex, fellatio or cunnilingus, and also refers to the end of the penis.

Hit and Run

Shuffleboard: A shot that either glances or knocks a disc off of the board.

Sexual: A hurried act of intercourse.

Lag

Shuffleboard: To shoot for the choice of color before a tournament game begins.

Sexual: "Sex-lag" is when a couple has so much sex, their bodies become disoriented with respect to time. A "sexual jetlag" is when a couple are separated and are experiencing separation anxiety. Also, a "fuck-lag," when a couple pauses during intercourse.

Out

Shuffleboard: Black is out, which means, black shoots first.

Sexual: When someone "comes out," as in "out of the closet," they are openly saying they are gay or lesbian.

Pigeon

Shuffleboard: A live disc lying on the line dividing the kitchen (the 10-off area) and the seven-area.

Sexual: This refers to the person who falls victim to receiving expelled ejaculate from someone near or above them. Also, an endearment for a woman, "little pigeon."

Roll

Shuffleboard: The impact of a disc with a target that changes its course. Sometimes used to mean a glance.

Sexual: A euphemism for having sexual intercourse, a "roll in the hay."

Sneak

Shuffleboard: A score safely hidden by exploiting a weakness in the opponent's play.

Sexual: A man that is a cheater, a heel, a rascal, or scoundrel, who cons a woman into sneaking off to surreptitiously have sex.

Snuggle

Shuffleboard: To place a scoring disc close behind one of the opponent's discs for the purpose of protection.

Sexual: To spoon or cuddle the backside of a partner with or without clothes on.

Stick

Shuffleboard: To stop on the board in almost the same place as the disc which was knocked away.

Sexual: A synonym for the penis, and "sex on a stick" refers to a very sexually attractive person.

Other Deck Shuffleboard Terms with Sexual Possibilities

In Shuffleboard, *deep 7, deep 8, deep 10,* and *deep kitchen* all refer to discs that are near the far side of these areas, allowing room for the opponent to score using the discs as backstops. But *deep* can also have a sexual connotation, that is, a deep penetrating thrust of the penis during intercourse. A *friendly game* or a *fun game* in shuffleboard is one in which sociability is more important to the players than excelling. A friendly game or a fun game can be any number of sex games played for fun such as Hearts Are Wild, Around the World, and Bumps and Grinds.

Kitchen bait is a disc that is placed on the board without a protective guard for the purpose of getting the opponent's cue disc into an area where it can be put into the kitchen. Kitchen bait could also be a woman using her skills as a good cook to land a sexual partner. To *lose one's hammer* refers to the hammer player failing to score during the half round of play. Since a hammer is a synonym for the penis, to lose one's hammer could be premature ejaculation. To *rush a game* is to take an unnecessary risk toward the end, for the purpose of getting an extra score on the board to bring the game to a premature close. To rush a game could also refer to the hurried experience of "picking up" a person in a bar near closing time, so that a sexual experience might still be had.

Sexual Commentary

In deck shuffleboard, instead of throwing a ball across a field, discs slide across a smooth-surfaced court, pushed along by a cue, to a triangle that is marked with different levels of points to be gained. The cue stick is called a shaft and the end is called the head, the same as a penis. The pucks are dimpled for easy grip, much like the testes. Triangles are a strong shape, and when the point is facing the person it represents feminine energy, as it mimics the triangle shape of a woman's pubic area, the point at the entrance or clitoris and the wider end internally at the uterus, and externally at either side of the buttocks. With a long stick pushing discs forward and into the triangle, the action rather mimics a penis sliding forward to push semen into the vagina. And if the person is lucky, the ejaculate stays within the scoring boundary of a sexual experience, well-played.

Chapter 11
Quarterstaff

There are approximately thirty-five martial arts that use a stick, staff, cane, pole, walking stick, or a baton, but very few originate in English-speaking countries. Most of these are decisively combative in nature and are Asian. There are several stick sports that are practiced for training with a sword, such as fencing. This chapter will concentrate on one particular stick sport where English terms can be understood, the English quarterstaff.

This original European weapon-turned-sport finds its entire history in England, beginning in the fifteenth century when sticks were used in fighting. Many conclude that it was not a sport but a weapon, but Medieval Chronicles state that it was identified more as being a sport than a non-fatal combat weapon.[131] Quarterstaff's popularity increased through the sixteenth century, and by the early 1700s was used in prizefights and held in an arena with wagering. The sport fell out of popularity as boxing took its place, but it made a comeback in the late 1800s as a Victorian reconstruction of the sport. This was due to a change in materials and a great escalation in the production of sports equipment.

---

[131] Medieval Chronicles, "Medieval Quarterstaff Weapon." http://www.medievalchronicles.com/medieval-weapons/quarterstaff-weapon/

140

The largest interest was due to a resurgence of the Robin Hood legend. The story was originally resurrected from an early 1370s ballad, made popular in the late 1400s, written about again in the early sixteenth century, and then brought to life once more by author Howard Pyle in 1883.[132] In the story, when they first meet, the quarterstaff was used by Little John to best Robin Hood trying to cross a narrow bridge.

The name "quarterstaff" most likely comes from the way it is made. Rather than forming a pole from a single branch of wood, a larger tree's branch was sawn into quarters lengthwise, and then rounded out for strength as well as flexibility. There are short long staffs which measure about 8 feet long (2.44 m), and the long staff measures up to 12 feet long (3.66 m).

As a weapon, the harder the wood the better, so oak and beech were used. Later, when the quarterstaff became more of a sport, the staff was made of softer wood, most commonly bamboo or privet. This gave the staff more flexibility, and a strike upon the body did not make as great an impact. When the object was only to subdue an opponent rather than maim or kill, protective coverings were used for sporting bouts. Head protection with facemasks like those created for fencing and cricket were used, as well as padding for thighs and groin, guards for knees and shins, and gloves for hands and fingers.

The staff is held by two hands, one near the butt end and the other at least a foot or two further forward. Positioning also depends upon the movement that will be

---

[132] John H. Chandler, "Robin Hood: Development of a Popular Hero," The Robin Hood Project, University of Rochester. http://d.lib.rochester.edu/robin-hood/text/chandler-robin-hood-development-of-a-popular-hero

used. There are blows that fall downward or at angles, parries to the legs or arms, thrusts with a step forward, and strikes upon the opponent on any part of the body. A description of the play and terminology of the sport comes to us from the work of Thomas A. McCarthy, an instructor in the art.

"Each one stands facing inwards (i.e., facing each other), about 4 feet apart, with the Staff in the right hand, held between the forefinger and thumb, the elbow slightly bent, the upper part in the hollow of the shoulder, the point on the ground, and in a line with the toe of the right foot." [133] This is called "the ready." After this, the players make a half-turn to the right on their heels, and then raise the staff to the chest horizontally. From there, both engage with attacks and defenses with various moves.

Although this sport is no longer common, it can still be found reenacted at Medieval fairs, and serves as an example of the lengths to which man will go to prove his strength and worthiness.

Quarterstaff Terms and Slang

Attack

Quarterstaff: To strike with the upper end of the staff at the right side of the head.

Sexual: It can mean a sexual attack, or in Japan it simply means to approach someone (without harm) of the opposite gender.

---

[133] Thomas A. McCarthy, "Quarter-Staff: A Practical Manual," Reprinted from the Journal of Manly Arts. (London: W. Swan Sonnenshein & Co., 1883). https://ejmas.com/jmanly/articles/2001/jmanlyart_mccarthy_0901.htm

Change, (the)
Quarterstaff: The particular way in which a staff moves from one hand to the other.
Sexual: The time when a woman reaches menopause.

Engage(d)
Quarterstaff: To actively maneuver and advance upon an opponent.
Sexual: Implies that while preparing for a marriage, sexual intercourse will be practiced before the contract is signed.

Glove(s)
Quarterstaff: They are padded and protect the hands.
Sexual: A synonym for a condom.

Jump
Quarterstaff: The motion of jumping upward so that an attacker's staff, aiming for the legs, passes below the feet.
Sexual: Also known as, "to jump someone's bones," which is to have intercourse.

Pin (ning or pinned)
Quarterstaff: To step forward and strike with the upper end of the staff straight to the front of the head.
Sexual: A synonym for a small penis, long thin legs, or when a partner holds another down, either with force or with ties for sexual play.

Play Loose
Quarterstaff: To be improperly dressed for the sport; that is, without proper protective clothing.
Sexual: To trifle irresponsibly with someone's affections.

Staff
Quarterstaff: The name of the pole used in the sport.
Sexual: A synonym for the penis.

Strike

Quarterstaff: To hit the opponent with a staff.

Sexual: When one decides to refrain from sex with their partner to achieve certain goals.

Other Quarterstaff Terms with Sexual Possibilities

Catching him is when a strike has been made with the staff, and the term could also mean that a woman is in the process of catching the man she wants. There is a stance called *the ready*, which is described above. Although there is no specific sexual equivalent for this term, it might be understood by a lover who has been purposefully warmed up with enough foreplay and is ready for intercourse. They are in the ready for sexual play.

Sexual Commentary

This "stick" is not the longest one in sports, but it is still long, from 8 feet to 9 feet 6 inches (2.44 m to 2.90 m), and four or five inches (10.16 cm or 12.70 cm) in circumference. Perhaps the most interesting aspect of this sport is not so much the length of the staff, but the presentation of each contestant's staff in the opening position, which then moves into the second position called the "prove distance." This is done by a half-turn to the right with both heels, followed by the right hand grasping and raising the staff from the ground. At the same time, the left arm is straightened in front of the body, until the upper end of each staff touches the center of the chest in a horizontal line as high as the shoulder. This movement seems to imitate other animals such as deer, moose and caribou, which show off their large antlers to warn off other males in the mating season. Or like the bonobo ape, which will break off branches and uproot small trees to show their strength. Or, when men, when ready for a fight, inhale deeply to show off a large chest. How quaint and gentlemanly.

Part Three
Who's Got the Balls?

Whether its a large orange rubber ball with a bumpy texture, several hard hand-sized colored wooden balls, small silver or gold metal balls, a very large and heavy ball with three holes, an elongated brown ball with white stitching, a twelve-inch smooth rubber ball with black and white pentagonal divisions, a large rubber ball with hexagonal makings, an egg-shaped plastic ball, a small black rubber ball with a red dot on it, or a smooth and soft rubber ball with alternate running stripes, it is a ball on a mission with a goal to be reached. The one other thing they all have in common is that no other pieces of equipment are used; no bats, cues, poles, rackets, or sticks. Just the body.

Although each one of these balls is used in sports, they can also be a metaphor for the human regenerative organ of the testicles. Testicles produce generations that attempt to take over the world. The one with the most potent ball(s) wins! We will talk about how each of the sporting balls are handled, how they move, what they do, and how they win. These balls will go into hoops, race across courts, knock down pins, fly through goals, bounce off walls, knock into people, get tackled by players, get kicked far, and go over nets. It's a tough life, but someone's balls have got to do it.

In this section on balls, we will bounce from one sport to the next: basketball, bocce, bowling, dodgeball, football, handball, kickball, rugby, soccer, and volleyball.

Once again, I will warn you that the sexual language that follows may be surprising. Instead of being offended, enjoy the double-entendres and the innuendos. Many of the same terms are used in different sports, so you will see some ball terms being repeated. They just inherently share the same intention. There are a lot of balls to be handled, so let's get started.

Chapter 12
Basketball

Basketball is the second-largest sport in the U.S., surpassed only by football. It is widely watched and supported. There are high school teams, college teams, a national association, a professional league, and international leagues for both men and women.

The game has come a long way in its innovations but the number of players has stayed relatively standard. The game is played with five players on each side, although three, two, and even just one on each side can play the game. The object is for a team to get as many basketballs as possible through the opposite court's hoop to score. Additional points can be gained from shooting the ball from behind a three-point line into the hoop, and free throws are granted after a foul is made by the opposite team, worth one point. The ball can be passed from teammate to teammate and bounced while walking or running, but it must stay in motion with the body.

Four timed segments usually make up a game, but the time limits vary. U.S. varsity games give eight minutes per quarter. Ten minutes are given for each session of women's college teams and international teams. Twelve minutes are played for each quarter in American national teams, and men's college games play with two 20-minute halves. Most have a fifteen-minute break in the middle, although in American high schools, ten minutes are given. After halftime, the teams switch sides. Players can be changed out during time-outs and each team has a coach to instruct and guide the team through a game. Players wear shorts, a jersey with a number on the front and back, and high-top sneakers to support ankles when sudden moves are made on the court. Officials referee the teams, keep time, keep score, and enforce the regulations of the game. All teams take on names identified with the city the team is from.

The game includes shooting, dribbling, rebounding, passing, and blocking. There are many rules and regulations, positions, and strategies, but we will discuss only those pertaining to select terms. There are also many types of basketball games: wheelchair basketball, water basketball, beach basketball, dunk hoops, slamball, streetball, and unicycle basketball; along with spin-off games, such as ringball, Korfball, netball, and fantasy basketball.

Basketball was invented by Doctor James Naismith in 1891.[134] The identity of the inventor was not discovered until 2006, when his granddaughter found his handwritten notes in a diary. The game was derived from an old children's game called "duck on a rock". In this game, the ball went into a real basket, a basket for collecting peaches! However, with the bottom of the basket intact, players had to retrieve the ball each time, so the bottom was eventually removed. Originally, the ball was a brown leather soccer ball with laces that were stitched along one side. The laces proved to cause unpredictable bounces, so they were removed. When the laces were eliminated, dribbling the ball became more of a part of the game. The brown ball changed to orange so

[134] Naismith Basketball Foundation, "About Dr. James Naismith." https://naismithbasketballfoundation.com/about-dr-james-naismith/

everyone could see it better, with black lines dividing the ball into eight panels.

A basketball court is rectangular, usually indoors, with basket hoops at both ends. The court is 49 feet wide (15 m) and 92 feet long (28 m). Most courts have polished maple wooden floors with sections divided by lines that designate specific areas of the court.

The ball size has become standardized. For men it is 29.5 inches (75 cm) in circumference and weighs 22 ounces (623.69 g). For women, the ball is 28.5 inches (72 cm) in circumference and weighs 20 ounces (567 g). In 1906, a metal hoop with a backboard replaced the peach basket, and the hoops became a standard 18 inches (46 cm) in diameter, mounted on a board 10 feet (3 m) off the ground.

The first national league of teams for men was formed in 1946, called the Basketball Association of America (BAA). It was composed of teams from the U.S. and Canada, and its first game was held in Toronto, Canada. There was also another league called the American Basketball League (ABL). In 1949, some of the teams on the league joined with the BAA and the name was changed to what it is today, the National Basketball Association (NBA). Over the next five years, the NBA consolidated from eleven to the eight teams, now called franchises. The NBA was also threatened by the formation of the American Basketball Association (ABA) in 1967, when some top players jumped leagues. But the NBA grew, thanks in part to a 1969 iconic symbol that became well-known, a silhouette of legendary player Jerry West dribbling a ball in red, white and blue.[135] By

---

[135] Quora, "How Did Jerry West Become the NBA Logo?" https://www.quora.com/How-did-Jerry-West-become-the-NBA-logo

1970 the league had expanded to eighteen teams, and by 1976 to twenty-two.

Many more changes occurred and several top players made headlines with drug-related issues, which lowered attendance. But big wins with new stars like Michael Jordan took the first basketball team into the Naismith Memorial Basketball Hall of Fame. That raised interest to twenty-seven teams. In 1996 the first women's league as formed as the Women's National Basketball Association (WNBA). As of 2018, there were thirty teams in the NBA, one in Canada and twenty-nine in the U.S. The International Basketball Federation (IBF), was founded in 1932 and began to oversee all international games. By 1936, at the Berlin Games, basketball became a full medal sport for men, and by 1976, it went to women at the Montreal Games. However, it wasn't until the 1992 Barcelona Games that basketball was allowed to be part of the Olympic Games.

Basketball Terms and Slang

2 for 1 play

Basketball: A play that does not consume most of the clock in order to save time.

Sexual: This means two women for one man or two men for one woman for sexual play.

Air ball

Basketball: An unblocked shot that fails to hit the rim or backboard.

Sexual: When a man is receiving oral sex and ejaculates outside of the mouth.

Assist

Basketball: A pass to a teammate who scores a basket immediately or after one dribble.

Sexual: When one guy helps his buddy connect with a woman for a sexual partner.

Ball hog

Basketball: A player who does not pass the ball.

Sexual: When a man is in a threesome with two women, and one of the women takes over the fondling of his scrotum during fellatio and won't let the other woman have a turn.

Backboard

Basketball: The rectangular platform behind the rim that supports it.

Sexual: A woman's flat buttocks, and also a synonym for the flat plane of the penile shaft when erect.

Bank shot

Basketball: A shot that hits the backboard before hitting the rim or going through the net.

Sexual: When a man ejaculates during oral sex into their partner's mouth and it banks down the throat.

Baseline

Basketball: The line that marks the playing boundary at either end of the court.

Sexual: The bare minimum standard of attractiveness that a man or woman might be given when considered for intercourse.

Beef

Basketball: B.E.E.F. is the abbreviation or mnemonic used to teach proper shooting form, which is, "balance, eyes, elbows, and follow through.

Sexual: A synonym for the male genitalia.

Bench

Basketball: Refers to the area where substitutes sit on the sidelines waiting to get into the game.

Sexual: Describes how a woman sits on a man's lap facing him while they kiss. Also, a combination of the words bitch and wench, used to describe a promiscuous woman.

Benchwarmer
Basketball: A player who sits on the bench for most or all of the entire game.

Sexual: The term refers to a woman when a man has had sex with her, but has no plans to do so again unless he is desperate.

Bonus
Basketball: A team is "in the bonus" when it receives extra free throws, due to the opposing team having been called on more than seven fouls during one of the halves of the game.

Sexual: When a man has had the opportunity to insert his penis in a place that he did not expect and was rewarded, usually an anal opportunity.

Dime
Basketball: To make a pass without looking.

Sexual: A woman that is a perfect ten in attractiveness.

Double dribble
Basketball: Dribbling the ball with two hands at the same time.

Sexual: When semen leaks after an ejaculation.

Downtown
Basketball: When a ball lands outside the three-point line.

Sexual: Refers to a man's or a woman's genitals.

Floaters
Basketball: A type of shot that arcs high, in order to prevent a tall defender from blocking the shot.

Sexual: Refers to women's breasts that float in water. Also, to testicles that float, known as testicular buoyancy.

Flop

Basketball: An intentional fall by a player after little or no physical contact from an opponent, with the goal of drawing a personal foul called against the opponent.

Sexual: A woman who drinks a lot and has random sex.

Forward

Basketball: One of the three standard player positions.

Sexual: When a person is very interested in another and approaches them rather quickly.

Key

Basketball: The free-throw lane and circle marking on the court, giving the appearance of a keyhole.

Sexual: Once used frequently in the gay community when a key or keys hung in a certain way from a man's pants, to indicate if he is cruising or not and a top or a bottom. A keyhole is also a synonym for the vagina.

Lay-in

Basketball: A close-range shot using one hand to tip the ball over the rim.

Sexual: Staying in bed to have intercourse.

Layup

Basketball: A close-range shot using one hand to bank the ball off of the backboard.

Sexual: "Hooking up" with a woman who is known to be easy for sex and not specifically for anything else.

Overtime

Basketball: When the score is tied at the end of the regulation play and the play goes into a five-minute overtime period.

Sexual: Refers to the continuing of intercourse, even after ejaculation has occurred.

Palming

Basketball: Refers to the habit of a player holding the ball at the apex of its bounce while dribbling. It's rude in non-organized play, but in professional games it is a dribbling penalty.

Sexual: A euphemism for masturbation.

Pass

Basketball: To throw the ball to a teammate.

Sexual: To "make a pass at" or "come on to" someone.

Pivot

Basketball: When one foot remains stationary and the other moves to avoid a traveling foul.

Sexual: An attractive woman that a man will bring with him out in public, to make him seem like a good partner to have, but she is there just so that he can attract another woman to have sex with.

Rainbow

Basketball: A long high arc shot of a ball into the basket.

Sexual: Refers to a term used by the LGBTQ+ community to acknowledge acceptance among its members. It also refers to the ring of lipstick left on a penis after fellatio, and it is a simile for male ejaculation in an arc, "like a rainbow."

Rebound

Basketball: To obtain the ball after a missed field goal attempt.

Sexual: Getting into a relationship with someone new after a broken relationship, to avoid the pain of the first partner.

Rimshot

Basketball: A shot that hits the rim of the basket hoop.

Sexual: In porn lingo, it refers to a male that ejaculates onto the anus.

Rock

Basketball: A slang word for the ball.

Sexual: A synonym for the testicles when they get hard.

Swish

Basketball: A shot, which goes through the net without touching the rim.

Sexual: An effeminate gay man.

Splash

Basketball: This occurs when a ball hits the net and causes the net to flip up and land over the rim as a result.

Sexual: Slang for female ejaculation.

Trey

Basketball: A three-point field goal.

Sexual: A "trey" guy, short for tremendous, is not only an incredible person but also one with a large attractive penis.

Triangle offense

Basketball: An offensive strategy with the goal of exchanging three positions, creating space among players and allowing each one to pass to four teammates.

Sexual: Aiming a penis during intercourse in three different regions within the vaginal canal forming a triangle of penetration.

Turnover

Basketball: To lose possession of the ball.

Sexual: A term used to describe a gender switch.

Up and down

Basketball: A traveling violation when the ball carrier jumps vertically into the air and does not get rid of the ball before landing.

Sexual: This indicates how a person is checking out another's physical attractiveness.

V-cut

Basketball: A fake move where a player moves toward the player defending him or her and then quickly turns and receives the ball.

Sexual: Refers to the "V" shape made by a person's body at the groin area.

Other Basketball Terms with Sexual Possibilities

A *dish* in basketball is an assist, when a pass goes to a teammate who scores a basket immediately or after one dribble. But most have also heard the term that a man might use when describing an attractive and sexy woman, stating that she is "a dish," that is, good enough to eat. *Heating up* in the sport is when a player continues to make the majority of the shots throughout the game. Foreplay in sexual excitation is specifically necessary for heating up both bodies. It stimulates the production of hormones, races the heart, and increases the blood flow to those stimulated areas, all in preparation for sexual intercourse. A *man-to-man defense* in the game is when each player guards a single opposing player. Also interpreted as two gay men that defend themselves against anti-homosexual comments. A *shot clock* in basketball is a timer designed to increase the pace of the game, by requiring a shot to be released before the timer expires. Sexually speaking, a clock shot (reversing the words) is an ejaculation upon the face, in reference to a person's face representing the face of a clock. In basketball, a *swingman* is a player capable of playing either shooting guard or small forward. In sex-speak, this could also be a wingman who fulfills that same function at a swinger's function.

157

Sexual Commentary

Basketball can claim the title of having the largest ball of all the balls in sports. One can understand a man wanting to have large balls, as it might also imply that he has a large penis. Having the "balls" to do something means to have the gall to accomplish a task. And having large balls means that he is acting brave, as a man should when faced with a difficult situation. It makes him feel daring, gutsy, and fearless. And what does he do with that ball? He does his best to get that large ball past the net (a woman's panties) and into the hoop (the vagina). Probably the most common sexual term in this sport is *penetration*, which is when the ball is dribbled or passed inside the defensive area toward the basket. Sportscasters love this term and use it often. That is because they are making the audience equate the sports play with a euphemistic sexual insertion of a penis, which most men who are watching the sport will readily connect with. Is it no wonder that basketball has over 1 billion followers and is the second most popular sport in the world?

Chapter 13
Bocce

Bocce is an Italian word that means, "to bowl."[136] The game has its roots in the Roman Empire. It became popular with Italian immigrants who came to America, but can also be found in many different countries around the world by different names. Bocce is one of several games that belong to the collective French game of *boules*. Different boules games are played with the balls rolled, thrown underhand or overhand, and either with or without a run before the throw. There are games where the balls are made out of wood, plastic, epoxy resin, steel, bronze, or are stuffed and made out of leather. Some balls are spherical and some have a shape bias that causes them to roll in a curved path. Boules games include bocce, pétanque, bocce volo, boccia, bolas criollas, bowls, jeu provençal, punto, and raffa.

This chapter will focus on the first game listed above, bocce. It is most often played in the U.S., but is very similar to versions played in Australia, South America, and many European and Adriatic countries such as Bosnia, Croatia, Herzegovina, Montenegro, Serbia and Slovenia. There are slightly different rules and names for

---

[136] Collins Dictionary, "Boccia."
https://www.collinsdictionary.com/dictionary/english/boccie

each game, but for our purposes, bocce has a good list of terms in English.

Bocce is played on flat ground or on a flat asphalt court that is 90 feet (27.5 m) long and 8 to 13 feet (2.5 m to 4 m) wide. The balls are made of either plastic or metal, and each team plays with four balls. The game can be played with two, three, or four people, or with teams. The game begins with one person throwing a small ball, called the jack or pallino, from one end of the court ending 2 to 8 feet (.61 m to 2.44 m) from the far end. That team is first to roll a bocce ball toward the jack. Then the opposite team rolls a ball. An opponent can also throw underhand to knock an opponent's ball away. The team which does not have the ball closest to the jack has a chance to bowl, until one side or the other has used their four balls. The team that scores is the one with the closest ball to the jack (pallino) and receives one point for each of their balls that is closer than the closest ball of the other team. A game is played to either seven or thirteen points, as long as it does not exceed four hours.[137]

Bocce Terms and Slang

Bocci or Bocce Balls

Bocce: The word "bocce" is the plural for "bocci," the eight balls used to play in the game.

Sexual: A "ball" is a synonym for one testicle, and in Italian, a *bocchino* is a profane slang word for fellatio.

---

[137] BocceVolo, "Rules – Chapter 2: The Game - Points to be Made and the Duration of the Match."
http://www.boccevolo.com/about/ch2.html

Captain

Bocce: The designated person on a team who coaches and makes all team decisions during the game.

Sexual: A euphemism for an erect penis. It is also the term used for a leader in a gay sex orgy, who takes the central role and often directs what participants should do.

Coin toss

Bocce: The initial flip of a coin at the start of a game to determine which team throws the pallino or jack the first time and chooses the color of the team's bocce balls.

Sexual: Viewing a prospective and attractive lover from the back, without knowing the look of the front of a person.

Dead ball

Bocce: A ball removed from play during a frame for reasons defined in the game rules.

Sexual: After a serious injury to the scrotum has occurred, the spermatic cord that carries blood to one or both of the testicles may have been twisted, called testicular torsion. This can affect the blood flow to the tissues, which will turn the testicle numb. This can also occur in too rapid growth at puberty.

Frame

Bocce: The playing of all the bocce balls in one direction with the total points up to that time.

Sexual: A term for the human body, often referring to a woman having a desirable figure.

Jack

Bocce: The small pallino ball that starts the game.

Sexual: The noun becomes a verb as in "jack off," meaning to masturbate and ejaculate.

Kiss

Bocce: This describes the condition where the bocce ball is just touching the pallino ball.

Sexual: The pressing of the lips of two people, or one's lips to any part of another's body, a pet, or any inanimate object.

Spock

Bocce: A strong underhanded bowling-like throw aimed directly at the balls on the court, meant to purposely hit and move an opponent's ball.

Sexual: This comes from a hand gesture of four fingers divided in half, and refers to sexual activity that involves sticking the index and middle finger into the vagina while simultaneously sticking the ring and pinky fingers into the rectum. This evolved from a greeting used by the Star Trek character named Mr. Spock.

Team

Bocce: When players work together on the same side, either one against one or two against two.

Sexual: Refers to when a guy has a group of women that he may have individual sex with at any given time.

Other Bocce Terms with Sexual Possibilities

In bocce, the term *out team* is the team that does not have the closest bocce ball to the pallino, but an out team with a sexual connotation, might be a small group or team of people who decide to out themselves as being gay or transgender.

Sexual Commentary

Let's examine the balls used in the sport. The pallino ball, also called a jack, is the first small ball thrown down the court, and it becomes the target and object of play, for the players to get their bocce balls as close as possible without touching it. The pallino is an Italian masculine noun meaning "cue ball" but it can also mean "pellet" or "spot," referring to its small size. It is either white or yellow, and the bocce balls are either red or green. White signifies pureness and goodness. Yellow means freshness, honor, intellect, loyalty, and optimism. Red means fiery energy, strength, power, passion and desire. Green is the color of nature, renewal, growth, fertility and harmony. Red and green are contrasting colors, but they also are in harmony with each other, making them perfect opposing colors, and as we know, opposites often attract.

Figuratively, the word pallino means having an inclination or predisposition, but can also mean a mania, or being crazy or obsessive about something. Ask any professional bocce player, and they will tell you that many players do become obsessive about playing the game. Once the pallino is in place and the other players have thrown their bocce balls to get as close as possible to the pallino, a player may utilize a move called *hitting or spock*. This means the ball will be thrown underhand (with an underhanded motive), purposely hard, with the aim of knocking, shooting, or bombing the other balls out of the way. Again, the game's words are often about hurting people, and with this analogy, means that each player is always trying to knock the competition away, in order to get as close as possible to the purist virginal ideal aspect as they can.

Chapter 14
Bowling

There is bowls or lawn bowling, more commonly played in the U.K., and pin bowling, more commonly played in the U.S. and Canada. Target bowling includes games called bocce, boules, bowls, carpet bowls, kegel, pétanque, and skittles. These games are played on carpet, grass, gravel, wood, or another hard surface. Pin bowling consists of players who take turns rolling a heavy ball down a wooden lane, with the intention of knocking down as many standing pins as possible at the far end to make points. There are many games that fall under this heading: five-pin, nine-pin, ten-pin, candlepin and duckspin. When all the pins are knocked down it's called a strike. If some pins are left standing, but are knocked down by the second ball, it is called a spare. The highest score that can be achieved is 300, which is twelve strikes in a row.

Ancient bowling balls have been found in Egypt, dating to 3200 BCE.[138] Some balls were filled with husks of grain and stitched closed in leather. Others were made of porcelain for better rolling. Between c. 300 CE and 400 CE, the Germans may have brought the game back, not as a sport but as a religious rite held in the cloisters of

---

[138] Help with Bowling, "The History and Origins of Bowling." http://helpwithbowling.com/history-origins-of-bowling.php

churches. At the time, men carried a club called a kegel as a weapon. It may have been a way for the parishioners to entertain themselves. They set their kegels up at one end of the courtyard, representing "heathens," and a stone ball was rolled to knock them down, to symbolically cleanse the parishioners of sin.[139]

During the Middle Ages, bowling was played outside on a green. Laws on betting were passed, and the game grew so popular that bowling lanes moved indoors so players could entertain themselves in any weather. In England, in 1299, the first bowling green was made for a public event called Master's Close in Southampton, and is still in use to this day.[140]

Bowling seemed to get banned at one time or another for different reasons. First, because it was in competition with archery. Then the game was banned for the ordinary worker and declared legal only for the upper classes. Later it was banned on Sundays as it conflicted with church-going. Martin Luther King and Sir Francis Drake were said to have enjoyed bowling. By 1670, Dutch immigrants were bowling in New York City, and thirty-three years later in 1733, New York had *its* first official bowling green. Ninepin bowling made its way into American literature in 1819 with Washington Irving's book, *Rip Van Winkle*. And by 1875, the National Bowling Association (NBA) was founded in New York City.

Standards for the alley and the ball follow. The bowling alley or lane is 42 inches (106.68 cm) wide, by 60 feet long (18 m), from the foul line where bowlers stand to the edge of the pin deck where the pins are standing,

---

[139] J. Bruce Pluckhahn, "Bowling Game," Encyclopedia Britannica Online. https://www.britannica.com/sports/bowling

[140] E.J. Linney, *A History of the Game of Bowls*, (Edinburgh: Edinburgh Press. 1933), 22.

with the depth of the pin deck at 2 feet and 10 inches (0.86 m).

The diameter of a bowling ball can be from 8.5 inches to 8.6 inches (21.59 cm to 21.83 cm), with a circumference between 26.7 to 27 inches (67.83 cm to 68.59 cm). The weight should be 16 pounds (7.26 kg). Bowling with ten pins became the standard instead of nine.[141] Twenty years later, the American Bowling Congress (ABC) changed the scoring system from 200 points for twenty thrown balls to 300 points for ten balls. In the late nineteenth century, the balls were made of lignum vitae hardwood, then Ebonite rubber, followed by Mineralite rubber, and then urethane in 1980.

By the early 1900s, bowling alleys were usually in a building with a bar or saloon, but with prohibition they became a place for family entertainment. Four world championships were first held in 1936. In 1948, a bowling alley was added to the White House on the ground floor of the West Wing. Presidents Truman and Nixon played, but the alley was eventually moved out. Finally, during the 1950s, bowling hit the big time with the invention of the automatic pinsetter, and professional bowlers began to make large amounts of money. In 1954, Steve Nagy was the first person to bowl a perfect game of 300.[142] By the mid-1960s it was estimated that there were about 12,000 bowling centers in the U.S. participating in tournaments. The first woman was admitted to the PBA

[141] Steven A. Riess (Ed.), "Rise of Organized Bowling," From *Sports in America from Colonial Times to the Twenty-First Century*, (New York: Routledge, 2015), 187.

[142] J. R. Schmidt, "Steve Nagy's 300 Game on Championship Bowling," Set Them Up Knock Them Down, Bowl-A-Roll Lanes. http://bowl-aroll.blogspot.com/2011/11/perfect-tv-drama-steve-nagy-is.html

168

in 2004, and in 2010, Kelly Kulick was the first woman to win a tournament.

However, bowling has had its ups and downs in popularity. Beginning in the 1970s there was a steady decline, because the cost of operating a large building for the sport became too expensive. Less than half of bowling alleys have survived. From 1997 to 2007, membership declined 36% and old-fashioned alleys were disappearing.[143] In the last ten years, bowling has had a resurgence, mostly with a younger crowd as now there is virtual bowling, but also people are going to newer buildings, due to the fact that anyone can show up to play and not have to be on a team. This open-play bowling is growing in popularity, especially when the alleys are upscale with cocktail seating, fresh food served, and natural light coming in.

Bowling Terms and Slang

ABC

Bowling: An abbreviation for the American Bowling Congress, which was just for men, but now the Congress has become the USBC for men, women, and youth.

Sexual: A cunnilingus technique where the tongue traces the letters of the alphabet for constant and ever-changing stimulation. It is also a slang abbreviation for the area between the scrotum and the anus, known as Ass Ball Connector.

---

[143] White Hutchinson Leisure & Learning Group, "What's Happening to Bowling?"
https://www.whitehutchinson.com/leisure/articles/whats-happening-to-bowling.shtml

Alley

Bowling: A shortened term for a bowling establishment.

Sexual: Short for "shaft alley," referring to an area on the body (between the breasts, vulva, and buttocks), where a penis might enter or rub against.

Backend

Bowling: The last 20 feet (6.10 m) of a bowling lane.

Sexual: Approaching a woman from the backside for either vaginal or anal sex.

Bagger

Bowling: This indicates the number of consecutive strikes preceded by a number (ex: a three bagger = three strikes in a row).

Sexual: A derogatory term for a woman with whom a man might engage in sexual congress, if a bag were put over her head due to an unattractive face.

Blind

Bowling: When a team member doesn't show, they're considered absent and their score is averaged, called a blind score.

Sexual: When someone is so deeply in love that they are unable to see the faults in their partner. Also, an uncircumcised penis with the head hidden is said to be in blind mode.

Bub

Bowling: A player who travels with a group of bowlers and spends more money than he makes. That person is like a groupie, but also does odd jobs around the bowling alley.

Sexual: A generic term of endearment for a good friend, but also a slang term for female breasts, from "boobs."

Cherry (ies)

Bowling: When a bowling ball hits a front pin knocking it straight back past any other standing pins to the right or to the left.

Sexual: Refers to a woman's erect nipples, and a woman's hymen, but is more likely a misunderstanding for the clitoris.

Cranker

Bowling: A bowler who puts revolutions on the ball.

Sexual: An erect penis, a woman who engages many men by having intercourse with them, and since a crank is a slang word for a penis, a cranker is one who masturbates.

Crossover

Bowling: A ball going to the 1-2 pocket side for a right-hander or the 1-3 side for a left-hander.

Sexual: The act of two men involved in manual genital stimulation at the same time. There are also crossover sexual offenses where victims are from multiple age, gender, and relationship categories.

Ditch

Bowling: The gutter or edge of the bowling lane.

Sexual: A vulgar term for a woman's genitals.

Double

Bowling: Two strikes in succession.

Sexual: Performing manual genital stimulation on a penis with two hands; and short for double penetration when a woman is penetrated by a man vaginally and another man anally. It is also when one man is engaged in sex play with two women.

Gutter ball
Bowling: A thrown ball that rolls off the lane into the gutter.

Sexual: The act of pushing one testicle into a woman's vagina, or when a guy rubs his genitalia between two breasts.

Hambone
Bowling: Throwing four strikes in a row.

Sexual: A synonym for the penis.

Helicopter
Bowling: When a ball spins like a top and still rolls straight.

Sexual: When a woman sits on a very lubricated penis and is able to move around with ease, but the idea that she can spin around like a helicopter's blades, is not possible. It is also a movement when a man swings his penis around in a circle, with or without his hands.

Hook
Bowling: A ball that breaks or changes direction sharply toward the pocket.

Sexual: A hot sexy girl. To kiss someone. A short term for "hooking up" or meeting with a lover. A gay term that describes the hooking of a finger in the anus. What a hooker does when she "hooks" a customer, and also refers to a curved penis.

Pap
Bowling: An abbreviation for Positive Axis Point, which is the point on a ball that spins when a bowler releases it.

Sexual: A synonym for breasts that produce milk, a pat or stroke upon a penis, another name for the penis, or to have sexual intercourse. Also, it is short for Pap smear, a test of cervix cells for cervical cancer.

Pin

Bowling: Refers to the manufacture of a bowling ball. It is the stem, which is positioned in the weight block that holds the core in place as the cover stock is poured into the ball mold. A pin in refer to balls with pin to cg distances (before drilling) of less than an inch while pin out refers to pin to cg distances with greater pin to cg distance.

Sexual: This can refer to "pinning" a person down for intercourse, and can refer to a small penis.

Pocket

Bowling: The area between 1-2 pins for a left-hander and 1-3 pins for a right-hander.

Sexual: A synonym for a vaginal or anal cavity, or the act of a man fondling his penis through one of his pants pockets, called "pocket pool."

Sandbagger (Sandbags, Sandbagging)

Bowling: A player who deliberately performs in a competition or league at a lower level than the skill set they have without the competition knowing, in order to lower their average so they can achieve a greater handicap and get extra points.

Sexual: A man's large testicles or a woman's large breasts.

Stroker

Bowling: A bowler who is very smooth with his or her release and approach.

Sexual: One who masturbates, or a girlfriend who will only perform manual genital stimulation instead of intercourse.

Tweener

Bowling: Bowlers who are neither big hook crankers nor smooth arcing strokers.

Sexual: A lesbian or bisexual female that is not considered either butch or fem, having equal male and female qualities. An acquaintance one sleeps with, in between a serious relationship.

Other Bowling Terms with Sexual Possibilities

In bowling, an *angle of entry* is the direction the ball travels when going down the lane to avoid the gutter on the right or the left. In intercourse, the angle of entry into the vagina is important for correct access and comfort. An *approach* in bowling is the way in which a bowler walks to the foul line to release the ball. As to a sexual meaning, there are two main approaches that a man will take when he is interested in a woman; that of the man who loves the excitement of the chase for a lustful encounter, and those who take more time with tenderness because they are seeking a deeper and longer-term connection. There is also a term called *bed posts* in bowling, which is a 7–10 split of the pins. But we all know that bed posts are part of a bed where not only sleep but intercourse takes place, as well as convenient places to tie someone to for sexual play. A *blow* is a miss or an error failing to convert a spare pin other than a split. A blow is also another term for fellatio.

A *double wood* is when any two pins are one behind the other. And since "wood" is another name for a penis, double wood could be interpreted as double penetration, that is, one man's penis is inserted into a woman's vagina and another man's penis is in her anus. *Down and in* refers to a line that is more direct and parallel to the boards in the lane, but it could also be interpreted as "getting down" and inside a lover. *Finger grips* are inserts in the bowling ball where a thumb and two fingers are able to grip the ball. There is also a hold that a man can take by inserting two fingers into a woman's vagina and his thumb into her anus, or vice versa. A *radius of gyration* is what identifies how fast a ball begins to rotate once it leaves the bowler's hand. This could also be interpreted as the width and motion of a penis when it moves within a vaginal or anal canal. A *tap* is an expression used to describe a single pin that is left standing after what seemed to be a shot where the bowler expected to strike. A tap is also a term that could mean to have intercourse.

Sexual Commentary

A bowling ball is by far the heaviest ball of any sport, at 16 pounds (7.25 k). Almost an equal number of the sexes bowl, with female participation averaging at 46%. Apparently, both sexes like to handle these heavy balls. There are smaller, lighter balls without holes used in five-pin, candlepin and duckpin bowling, but in ten-pin bowling, there may be only two finger holes or up to five for each finger and thumb of one hand. The most common hold has been a ball with three holes, one for the middle finger, the ring finger, and the thumb. Since the turn of the century, however, the practice has not been to insert the thumb. This hold is also a technique used to hold or stimulate a woman with digits being placed just inside her anus and vagina.

Aside from the size, weight, and holes in a ball, the other important factor is the hardness of the ball's surface. A hard testicle means it is filled with seminal fluid. The softer the bowling ball surface, the better the ball will "grab" the lane with surface friction. Wooden lanes are often oiled so that the ball rolls more smoothly. Both bowling balls and penises like lubrication.

Now to the pins. The pins in a ten-pin game are taller and heavier compared to the pins in duckpin, which are shorter and squatter. But the pins in candlepin are the tallest and thinnest of the three. The names of the parts of a pin are also interesting. At the base is the core and skirt. Rising up to the widest part is the belly, rising still to the narrowest part at the neck, then widening slightly at the top, which is called a head, and at the very top is the crown. Despite the base being called a skirt, the remaining parts can be likened to a man's body, having a long neck, a head and a crown, and a man's penis, as "pin" is a slang term for a penis. In essence, the pins (no matter how many or what type) may be thought of as a bunch of men standing together. The bowler, who has a big heavy ball, has the opportunity to knock every one of those other "men" out of play. Those pins, which can be considered as a group of penises, lack the balls to stand up and fight back. All they can do is either stand there and hope they are missed, or take it lying down. Men might bowl to psychologically eliminate the competition, and women might bowl to teach those men and their penises a lesson.

Chapter 15
Dodgeball

Dodgeball is a direct contact sport between a ball and a person. Team players spend half their time trying to hit another person with the ball, and the other half trying to avoid getting hit by a person throwing the ball. This aggressive game is played by elementary school children as well as university students, and has made the world stage with two organizations which have tournaments. The objective of the game is to hit the members of the opposing team with a ball below the shoulders or force them to go outside the court boundaries, in order to eliminate them from the game.

What is surprising about this game is that not just one ball is used, but four to ten, depending upon how large the court is and how many are playing. The balls also differ in construction. Some are made from cloth, some with foam, and others are made from rubber. The sport does not have a specific court that it is played on, but it can be played on a basketball or volleyball court, or any large fenced in area, but it must have a centerline.

The game begins with an opening rush of all players to the centerline, where the balls are lined up. In some games the balls are thrown upward. The players must get to the balls as fast as they can, and then roll or throw each ball back to their team players that are behind a "check line". After that, the ball goes "live" and can be thrown at the players of the opposite team. When a person is hit, they are out and go to the bench. If the ball rebounds off a wall, another team player, or another ball, they are also out. Shots thrown to the head are not allowed, and both the thrower and the one hit could be sent out. If a ball is thrown and caught by an opponent with arms or legs, then the thrower is out. There are very few rules to the game, but one movie made the game famous by saying that there were five "D's" in dodgeball: "Dodge, duck, dip, dive, and dodge."[144] All the rest of the rules and aspects of the game won't be discussed here, but if a term comes up that necessitates an explanation, it will be given.

There are many variations of the game in different countries. In Spain the game is called Datchball, in China Da Yi Mao, in India Sekan-tadi, in Israel and Australia Ga-ga, Kings Court in Canada, and Heaven in New Zealand. There are also Greek, German, and Swedish Dodgeball, and more variations called Nationball, Battleball, Trench, Jailball, Jailbreak, Prisonball, Teamball, Killerball, Crossfire, Gauntlet, Warball, Dungeon Dodge, and several more. In the videogame it's called Stikbold. Where the game originated is debatable. Some say that it began in Asia, or Greece, or Mesoamerica in 500 BCE. Other historians believe it is much younger, coming from Africa 200 years ago where it was a test of strength and endurance for a warrior, and rocks were thrown, instead.[145]

---

[144] Patches O'Houlihan, "Dodgeball – A True Underdog Story," Wikipedia.
https://en.wikipedia.org/wiki/DodgeBall:_A_True_Underdog_Story
[145] Rebounderz, "Where Did Dodgeball Start? A Brief History Lesson." https://www.rebounderz.com/lansdale/where-did-dodgeball-start-a-brief-history-lesson

The court's entire length is 60 feet (18 m). It is divided into two halves 30 feet by 30 feet (9 m by 9 m). There is a neutral zone between them 4 feet (1.2 m) wide. Ten feet (3.0 m) from the center line is an attack line running parallel. The U.S. uses a rubber ball, but most other countries use a foam and cloth ball. The size of each of the regulation rubber balls used, called blockers, are 8.5 inches (22 cm) in diameter.

The following terms are from the World Dodgeball Association.

Dodgeball Terms and Slang

Ball(s)
Dodgeball: The primary, junior, or standard size ball used in the game.

Sexual: A synonym for one or both testicles.

Ball control
Dodgeball: This is keeping the majority of the many balls on one side of the court and systematically attacking.

Sexual: The ability to control and prevent ejaculation can be accomplished using an annulus or ring around the neck of the scrotum, which will keep the testes from rising prior to ejaculation.

Buddy up
Dodgeball: In offense, it is the synchronized throwing with one or more teammates. In defense, it is when catchers pair up with snipers (a player who waits in the backline) to block the opposition and protect teammates from counterattacks.

Sexual: Refers to people being overly friendly or familiar, especially in order to gain favor. Also to men doubling up in a dormitory shower, and is a person who acts as a friend to a person suffering from AIDS.

Catcher

Dodgeball: A player who is good at catching the ball.

Sexual: This is "the bottom" in a sexual relationship or a man who receives anal sex from another male. It is also a euphemism for a condom.

Corners

Dodgeball: The pawns of the game. They are primarily a defensive position, but sometimes a sacrificial buffer, and will attack when beneficial. There are two corners to a team who play near the outside edges of the court.

Sexual: The end of a block where street prostitutes work from.

Dead ball

Dodgeball: Refers to a ball that either hits a dead player, hits another dodgeball, or hits any surface of the court.

Sexual: After a serious injury to the scrotum has occurred, the spermatic cord that carries blood to one or both of the testicles may have been twisted, called testicular torsion. This can affect the blood flow to the tissues, which will turn the testicle numb. This can also occur in too rapid growth at puberty.

Equipment

Dodgeball: The tools needed to play the game: at least four balls, a suitable playing surface, and uniforms for the players.

Sexual: A euphemism for male sexual genitals.

Face shot

Dodgeball: When a ball hits a player in the face.

Sexual: An ejaculation discharged over a partner's face.

Head shot

Dodgeball: Either an intentional or accidental shot of the ball that hits a player anywhere above the chest, which results in that player being eliminated from the game.

Sexual: The result of a man pulling his penis out of the mouth of a fellator and the ejaculate landing on the fellator's head, or the result of ejaculate landing on a masturbator's face or head.

Muffins

Dodgeball: This describes bad throws where the ball floats slowly through the air.

Sexual: A synonym for a female's outer labia.

Play

Dodgeball: Any attempt by a player to catch, dodge, or block a directly thrown ball.

Sexual: Refers to sexual play or role play, and the entire sexual response cycle of excitement, plateau, orgasm, and resolution, when orgasm occurs.

Shagger

Dodgeball: A player who stands several feet away from the back wall of the court to ensure that the ball does not roll back to the opponent's half of the court.

Sexual: A British word for a man that seduces and uses women for his own pleasure.

Sniper

Dodgeball: A player with good timing and precision, who waits for someone vulnerable and then throws a surprise ball.

Sexual: One who hides and masturbates while watching two people have intercourse, and when ready to orgasm runs out from his hiding place, ejaculates over the couple and then runs away. Or a male who is above his partner having intercourse and then withdraws, surprising his partner, only to ejaculate on them. It is also a woman's erect nipples seen through her top, and a sneaky woman who uses strategies to entrap a lover.

Trap

Dodgeball: A trap ball is one caught simultaneously with a player's body, another ball, or with something in the environment.

Sexual: The lure of a transwoman who tests to see how well she passes for a woman in trapping a man in an intimate moment. A woman getting pregnant in order to be married is also a trap.

Other Dodgeball Terms with Sexual Possibilities

A *live ball* in this game is any ball that is in motion and getting played. In sex-speak, a live ball can also be interpreted as one or both testicles fully capable of producing sperm, the opposite of a dead ball. Another term is *pumpfaking*. It is when a player tries to fool the opposition into believing that a ball is going to be thrown in their direction. The arms holding the ball may bend and an actual short jerk forward might look like a ball is about to be thrown, but then is not. Sexually speaking, a pumpfaking, or fake pumping, might also be interpreted as a dry hump. It isn't real intercourse, but imitates the movement.

Sexual Commentary

This is an aggressive sport that seemingly teaches young people that the one with the bigger balls wins. It may have begun as a way for men to avoid other men and their weapons, but it may also be a significantly underlying instruction and training signifying the requisite for domination over others.

Chapter 16
Football

Football is America's most favorite sport, but the name is sometimes confusing to those outside the U.S. as it shares a history with rugby and soccer. In the U.S. the game is called American football, in Canada the game is called Canadian football, and both are called gridiron football, due to the lines on the field. There are also Australian rules football, rugby football, and Gaelic football, which are derived from soccer. They all use the foot to move a ball through an opposing team's field in order to score a goal at the far end. In the U.K., soccer is called "association football." In order to discern the difference, Americans took the shortened word "soc" from within association to refer to the British sport as soccer, and called the U.S. sport American Football.[146]

Knowing which ball each sport uses only helps a little. The countries that use a spherical ball call the game association football and Gaelic football. The prolate spheroid ball with rounded ends is used in rugby and Australian football, while American and Canadian football use a prolate spheroid ball with pointed ends.

[146] Brian Phillips, "Why Do We Call It Soccer?"
https://slate.com/news-and-politics/2010/06/most-countries-think-of-the-world-cup-as-a-football-tournament-why-do-we-call-the-game-soccer.html

For the purposes of this chapter, I will limit the discussion to American and Canadian football.

There are several common things that link all of these games: there are two teams with eleven to eighteen players, the game is played in a specific delineated area, and the players must use their bodies to move the ball either by carrying, passing, or kicking it. The goal is to gain as much yardage across a field, while defending the team members with the ball, in order to get the ball into the opponent's end of the field between two goalposts for points.

In American football, there are eleven players on a team. The name for the player positions depends on whether the team is playing defense or offense. For offensive engagements, the quarterback is the leader of the team. He calls the plays, gives the signals at the scrimmage line, and receives the ball from the center where he will hand it off, throw to a receiver, or run with it. The center snaps the ball back to the quarterback on every play. The running back, sometimes called the tailback, halfback or rusher, runs with the ball. Then there is the fullback, who blocks for the running back and blocks to protect the quarterback when passing. Next, there are wide receivers, who do their best to dodge defenders and stay ready to catch the ball. There is also a tight end, who acts as a receiver and a blocker. Left and right guards block and protect the ball carriers, especially the quarterback, and the left and right tackle, are the two outermost players on the offensive line. Canadian football has twelve players on a team and their positions are the same except they call their tight end the slotback.

On the defensive side, two defensive tackles hold their positions to stop any running plays and work to pressure the quarterback to upset the backfield formation. The two outer players are called defensive ends. They must block offensive moves in the backfield and tackle the ball carrier or quarterback. They might even force the ball carrier to go out of bounds or toward other defensive players on their team. There are also three or four linebackers, who station themselves behind the defensive linemen, and might have to defend as well as run. Next are two cornerbacks, who line up at the widest part of the field opposite the offensive receivers. And last are the free safeties and strong safeties, who must defend the deep passes and runs. Canadian football also has a defensive back, but only one safety player. Both countries also have additional special team player positions.

Although there are mentions of football-like games in ancient history, writers describe the game being played in Ireland in the early 1300s, Scotland in the 1400s, Italy in the 1500s, and England in the 1600s. In 1660, Francis Willughby wrote the *Book of Games*, adding some detail about football, including descriptions of fences at each end of the field with gates called "goals." He also described how the teams were selected, along with tactics, scoring, and rules of the game.[147]

By the early 1800s in England, the game took to the streets and was called "mob football." Due to the game's sustained popularity, the sport was promoted in schools to keep children fit and encourage competitiveness. Each school began to devise their own rules, so the first official code of rules was set down in 1815. By then, Europeans were settling in America and they took the game with them. By 1820 the first match was held at Princeton University, soon followed by Harvard, Dartmouth, Rutgers, and Brown. By 1876, Walter Camp, considered

---

[147] Francis Willughby, *Book of Games,* (Nottingham, England: Ashgate Publishing Co., 2003).

the "Father of American Football," introduced new rules for blocking, down-and-distance, line of scrimmage, and the forward pass, which made the game uniquely American.[148]

In the early annals of the ancient game, the ball was an air-filled, round leather bag. Much later, in the 1800s in Australia, the ball was a stuffed possum skin, which gave it an elastic quality but was still firm and strong. Children made balls out of the roots of the bulrush plant, and one tribe made the ball from the scrotum of an old kangaroo. In Mesoamerica the balls were made of rubber. In Europe, the ball was first made out of an inflated pig's bladder but was later covered in leather to better hold its shape. In 1851, two differently-shaped balls were used, one round and the other oval. Four years later, Charles Goodyear patented his spherical ball made from vulcanized rubber, but it was still hard to carry and awkward to throw.

The air-filled rubber ball continued to be a problem because it kept losing air from hard use. Games sometimes had to stop midway so the ball could be re-inflated with a hand pump. In 1886, a syringe-like device allowed the inflation to occur much more quickly. In 1890 the ball became the "prolate spheroid" shape that it is today. A metal stem, like that on a car tire, replaced the rubber valve. The ball had to be unlaced in order to inflate the inner rubber ball, and the stem always left a lump under the laces. But in 1924, the first valve-inflated football eliminated the need for a stem. In 1935, the National Football League standardized the shape and make of the ball. The ball went to half its length, from 21 inches to 11 inches (53.34 cm to 27.94 cm), and the air

---

148 Wikipedia. "Walter Camp."
https://en.wikipedia.org/wiki/Walter_Camp

pressure was set to about 13 psi. The design included hand-sewn ends, a triple lining, and lock-stitched seams. By 1955, the outer skin of the ball was wrapped in "grip-tite" cowhide leather, which made the ball easier to grip. In 1981, it got a pebble-like look and texture, as the ball looks today.

There is also other equipment used by the players. A football helmet with a protective cage gear for the face is required. Special shoes have cleats to better grip the playing field. Gloves, padded jersey tops, pants with under-padding, and girdling at the hips, thighs, and knees complete the uniform. Many teams also wear colored flags for easy distinction on the field.

Competitions are held worldwide by many associations. There are football clubs with leagues in over 130 countries, with competitions for senior men, senior women, young men, and young women. There are also futsal competitions (a variant of football played on a hard court), beach competitions, and competitions between sub-national teams, leagues, and clubs.

There are different rules for the various football games around the world, such as Cambridge rules, Sheffield rules, Australian rules, and NFL rules. The following terms represent predominantly American and Canadian football terms, though some terms transcend international borders.

Football Terms and Slang

Back

Football: Any position not on the scrimmage line, including the positions of running back, tailback, quarterback, halfback, defensive halfback, flankerback, fullback, cornerback, rover, or safety.

Sexual: The buttocks of a woman or a man, sometimes with additional meaning indicating how large or sexy that anatomy is.

Backup

Football: The second-string player who does not start the game but comes in later as a relief to the starter.

Sexual: Refers to a person whose relationship has just ended, and they have another partner with whom they can have intercourse. Can also refer to the state of having unreleased sperm over a long period of time, commonly known as "blue balls."

Ball control

Football: A strategy that is based on low-risk plays in an effort to avoid losing possession of the ball.

Sexual: The ability to control and prevent ejaculation can be accomplished by using an annulus or ring around the neck of the scrotum, which keeps the testicles from rising prior to ejaculation.

Block (ing)

Football: When a player obstructs another player with his body, pushing the opponent back or preventing movement beyond the blocker.

Sexual: Short for "cock-block," one who blocks another from connecting sexually with a prospective partner.

Blowout

Football: A game in which one team dominates another.

Sexual: When the front of a man's pair of pants pops open from a large erect penis, when a man has a strong ejaculation from being fellated, and during intercourse when the male prematurely ejaculates.

Bomb(s)

Football: A long arcing pass of the ball.

Sexual: This can refer to enormous female breasts, or when someone is extremely attractive and sexy. It is also an acronym for Beat Off Memory Bank, meaning that a person who has seen someone that turns them on will remember them later when they masturbate. In the Caribbean, they "make bomb" or have intercourse, and it indicates that the orgasmic experience was exceptional.

Bootleg

Football: An offensive play of misdirection, when the quarterback pretends to hand off the ball, but carries it away.

Sexual: When a person picks up someone they consider easy to get into bed with. Also, a woman who enters a club wearing high boots and a very short skirt, indicating she wants sex. "She's gettin' her bootleg on."

Box, (the)

Football: An area on the defensive side of the ball, directly opposite the offensive linemen and about five yards deep.

Sexual: A slang term that refers to the vagina.

Bust

Football: Refers to a new draftee player who failed to meet the expectations of the drafting team.

Sexual: It can refer to a woman's bosom, an orgasm, an ejaculation by a man or a woman, and an ejaculation that does not go inside of the body but somewhere on the body.

Clipping

Football: An illegal block, in which the victim is blocked from the back, at or below the waist, which is a 15-yard penalty.

Sexual: A euphemism for having a one-night stand.

Cover

Football: The attempt to prevent a receiver from catching a pass. There are five different kinds of cover: cover zero, cover one, cover two, cover three, and cover four.

Sexual: When men cup their scrotum during masturbation in order to feel the intensity of an orgasm, and a term used for a gay man who is hiding the fact with a heterosexual relationship. It is also an uncircumcised penis, and a condom.

Cut

Football: A sharp change of direction by a running player.

Sexual: A circumcised penis, or to have intercourse. Also, a slang description for the vagina.

Dead ball

Football: A ball which is no longer in play.

Sexual: After a serious injury to the scrotum has occurred, the spermatic cord that carries blood to one or both of the testicles may have been twisted, called testicular torsion. This can affect the blood flow to the tissues, which will turn the testicle numb. This can also occur in too rapid growth during puberty.

Dive (diving)

Football: A play in which the ball is handed off to the running back, who attacks the middle of the offensive formation.

Sexual: Oral sex performed on a woman, also known as "muff diving."

Down

Football: A unit of the game that starts with a legal snap or free kick after the ball is ready for play and ends when the ball next becomes dead or out of play. A first down is the first of the plays and occurs after a change of possession of the ball.

Sexual: Refers to "going down," meaning to perform oral sex, fellatio or cunnilingus. Also, to "get down and dirty" means to have intercourse.

Drive

Football: A continuous set of offensive plays gaining yardage and several first downs, and a blocking technique.

Sexual: A powerful penile thrust in intercourse. In the 1950s and 1960s, "going for a drive" meant driving someplace "to neck" or to have intercourse.

False start

Football: A foul in which an offensive player moves before the ball is snapped, drawing defensive players offside.

Sexual: A premature ejaculation.

Field goal

Football: A score of three points made by getting the ball through the opponent's goal other than a kickoff or free kick, following a safety.

Sexual: A man's ejaculation shot out between the knees of their partner.

Field position
Football: A measure of how many yards a team must travel in order to score.
Sexual: Refers to how close a person is to connecting with a possible sexual partner.

Flag
Football: A yellow cloth thrown down by an official indicates that a foul has been made. If an NFL official throws down a red flag they are challenging a call.
Sexual: Colored handkerchiefs worn in a rear pant pocket to indicate specific sexual interests, used by gay, lesbian, and BDSM participants. The rear right pocket indicates a "top" and the left indicates a "bottom." It is also used to describe having had sex with a foreigner, denoting that country's colored flag.

Flanker
Football: A player position on offense.
Sexual: Someone who prematurely ejaculates and then cries about it, or a penis that loses its erection.

Flat
Football: An area on the field between the scrimmage line and the 10-yard line into the defensive backfield, within 15 yards (14 m) of the sideline.
Sexual: A woman with tiny breasts or buttocks.

Forward pass
Football: A pass that touches a person, object, or the ground, closer to the opponent's end line than where it was released from, or is accidentally lost during a forward throwing motion.
Sexual: Refers to a man or woman who is forward in flirting with another in order to engage him or her for sexual relations.

Fullback

Football: An offense player position.

Sexual: A tough, unattractive woman in a group of women whose job it is to make sure that none of the other women get played with. Also, a woman's panties that fully cover her buttocks.

Fumble

Football: When a player loses possession of the ball.

Sexual: Just short of a "rumble," meaning intercourse, where the partners only play with each other's sexual organs.

Gunslinger

Football: A quarterback who plays in an aggressive and decisive manner by throwing deep, risky passes.

Sexual: One who leans against a mirror to masturbate and then quickly turns to see his ejaculation. It is also a woman who rudely rejects a male's attentions.

Hail Mary

Football: A long pass play, thrown toward a group of receivers near or in the end zone in hope of a touchdown.

Sexual: When a person at the end of the night in a bar or club tries to "hook up" with who is left, in order to "get laid."

Hand off

Football: When a player transfers the ball to another player and the receiver takes possession of it.

Sexual: When a person begins to masturbate or perform manual genital stimulation on someone, and then has another person continue. If someone is dating and their interests turn cold, they "hand off" the contact information to a friend. It is also when one hangs out with one woman and then switches to another woman to avoid approach anxiety.

Horse collar
Football: A type of tackle made by grabbing the backside of a runner, going in a different direction.

Sexual: A derogatory name for the shape of the vaginal canal.

Huddle
Football: When a team meets on the field to communicate instructions for the next play.

Sexual: A combination of hugging and cuddling with someone. It is also when a group of women discuss someone's sexual orientation.

Ineligible receiver
Football: A receiver who is not allowed to catch a pass.

Sexual: When a man publicly dates a woman, but she only has eyes for other women.

Kick
Football: A drop kick, a place kick, or a punt.

Sexual: A partner to hang out with, kiss and fondle, but not have intercourse with, a "side kick." Also, a woman's buttocks, *her kick.*

Kneel
Football: After a player receives the ball from a pass, he abruptly stops and kneels down short of the end zone, ending the play until the clock runs out. Same as "take a knee."

Sexual: A dominant lover's demand to their lover to get down on their knees and give them oral sex.

Muff
Football: When a player drops a ball attempting possession.

Sexual: Refers to the outer labia, mistakenly thought of as untrimmed pubic hair. An abbreviation for <u>M</u>andatory <u>U</u>nattractive <u>F</u>emale <u>F</u>riend, or the one "muff" woman in a group of hot women.

Open

Football: When an intended receiver is separated from any defenders who have a very low chance of preventing a reception.

Sexual: Someone who is easy to "hook up" with or at least willing to do anything sexual. Can also mean an open relationship, where each agrees to allow their partner to have another lover.

PAT

Football: An acronym for <u>P</u>oint <u>A</u>fter <u>T</u>ouchdown. It is one point if the ball is kicked through the uprights and two if the ball is rushed or thrown and received in the end zone.

Sexual: An acronym for <u>P</u>itch <u>A</u> <u>T</u>ent, meaning to get an erection. It can also mean a non-gender specific person because the name is used commonly for both sexes. Also, the process of giving a male lover pats or taps on his penis.

Package

Football: Players on the field for a given play.

Sexual: A euphemism for male genitalia, and also refers to the bulge of those organs in a man's pants.

Pancakes

Football: An ideal block taking the opposing defender to the ground. Sometimes just called "cake," for a sweet revenge.

Sexual: Refers to a women's flat breasts or buttocks, or a woman flattening her breasts up against glass in exhibitionism. Also, the areola around nipples, and a euphemism for lying flat and having sex in the missionary position.

Pass

Football: The act of throwing the ball from one player to another, either laterally or forward.

Sexual: "To make a pass" at a woman is to engage her for possible relations. It also refers to the stretch of skin between the vaginal opening and the anus, a combination of "pussy" and "ass."

Pass Interference

Football: When a player illegally hinders an eligible receiver's opportunity to catch a forward pass.

Sexual: A blocked flirt with someone, a "cockblocker."

Play

Football: When the ball is "in play" by getting passed or carried, making it a pass play, or a running play.

Sexual: Refers to any kind of sexual activity alone or with another. In BDSM, it refers to playing out a sexual scene.

Position

Football: A role or place a player has on the field.

Sexual: The body position one takes during intercourse.

Pulling

Football: An offensive lineman, who instead of blocking the player in front of them, steps back or pulls away from the line and runs to block a defender in a trap or sweep play.

Sexual: An alternative term for "hooking up," or masturbating. An Australian slang term, "on the pull," meaning that a man is all dressed up and out looking for a sexual partner.

Pump fake

Football: A faked pass by the quarterback, in order to fool the defensive team.

Sexual: Intercourse from the rear, then pulling out and faking an orgasm by spitting on the back, then turning the partner over to ejaculate on their face. Also, a woman who promises intercourse, but changes her mind.

Punter

Football: A kicker who specializes in punting the ball.

Sexual: British slang for a prostitute's "John."

Quarter

Football: One of four periods of play in a standard American football game.

Sexual: The name for a short guy with a really tall girlfriend, and a woman whose sex appeal is very high. Better than a dime.

Quarterback sneak

Football: A quarterback play used just short of yardage or the goal line, running right behind or beside the center.

Sexual: When intercourse begins but abruptly stops, and then resumes hours later in a surprise aggressive move.

Rover

Football: A hybrid safety player that has dual responsibilities as a defensive back and a linebacker.

Sexual: A person that cruises places for sexual encounters.

Sack

Football: Tackling a ball carrier intending to throw a forward pass.

Sexual: A synonym for the scrotum.

Stick(s)

Football: The pole attached to the end of the 10-yard chain that is used by the chain crew to measure for any down.

Sexual: A synonym for the penis.

Strip(ping)

Football: To remove a football from the player carrying it.

Sexual: To remove clothing from the body quickly or in a teasing and entertaining manner.

Tackle box

Football: The area where the two offensive tackles line up prior to the snap.

Sexual: A box is a slang euphemism for the vagina, and a tackle box is when a woman has genital piercings.

Take a knee

Football: A low risk play in which the player in possession of the ball kneels down after receiving the snap, ending the play while keeping the clock running. Similar to a kneel.

Sexual: When a person rides another's knee, leg, or thigh to stimulate their sexual organs.

Wide Receiver

Football: A player position on offense, split wide from the formation, and plays on the line of scrimmage as a split end or one yard off a flanker.

Sexual: A bottom or submissive gay man.

Other Football Terms with Sexual Possibilities

An *automatic first down* is a first down awarded to an offensive team after a defensive team has made a foul. An automatic first down could also be the first action a lover takes when they drop to their knees to offer either fellatio or cunnilingus to a potential lover. A *ball carrier* is the player currently in possession of the football. A ball carrier could also refer to a jockstrap. *Busted play* is when, due to unforeseen circumstances, a play deteriorates to the point that it no longer conforms to the coach's playbook and leads to confusion or chaos on the field. Busted play could also mean that someone, like a husband or wife, interrupts or busts their lover in the midst of sexual play with someone else.

A *fair catch* is an unhindered catch of an opponent's kicked ball. A fair catch could also refer to a woman who was "picked up" fairly and willingly in a club. A *field of play* is the area between both the goal lines and the sidelines, and in some contexts the space vertically above it, also known as the playing field. A field of play could also refer to the number of sexual options with different people available for sexual play. A *flexbone* is a formation involving three running backs, where a fullback is lined up behind the quarterback and two receivers behind the line of scrimmage at both ends of the offensive line. A flexbon*e* could also be something sexual. To flex is to show off and a bone is a synonym for the penis, so this could mean an exhibitionist who shows off his penis.

A *goal area* is the end zone in Canadian football. A goal area could also be considered the generative organs of both sexes. A *line to gain* is a line parallel to the goal lines, such that having the ball dead beyond it entitles the offense to a new series of downs. A line to gain could also be that line between fumble and rumble, that is, beyond just "petting," to intercourse. A *live ball* is any ball in play, whether in a player's possession or not. If a dead ball in sexual parlance is when a testicle has no feeling due to some accident, then a live ball would be one that is actively producing sperm and viable. *Man-to-man* coverage is a defense in which all players cover a specific

200

player on the offensive team. Man-to-man coverage could also be a description of two gay men engaged in sex play.

Play action is a tactic in which the quarterback fakes either a handoff or a throw, in order to draw the defense away from the intended offensive play. Play action could also mean any sexual activity. A *restraining line* is a team's respective line of scrimmage and on a free kick, the line the ball is to be kicked from. A restraining line could also be considered the point at which a woman decides whether she wants to have intercourse or not. In football, a *tight end* is often a blocker player position on offense, who lines up on the line of scrimmage next to the offensive tackle. A tight end could also be a woman with a narrow vaginal canal or a man with a tight anus. There is also a *vanilla offense*, an offense with very few plays and or formations. A vanilla offense could also be when a couple are involved in sexual play, but at a certain point one person becomes disappointed because they want to go beyond that and get more experimental.

Sexual Commentary

There are many more terms that might also have sexual connotations. Some have already been mentioned, but here are some additional comments. There is an *end zone* at the far end of each field where a *touchdown* is made. An end zone could also be considered the end of the trunk of the human body, with the sexual organs as residing in the end zone. A score is made with a touchdown. When someone sensually touches another going down the body and then touches and plays in that area, they are in the end zone, and upon intercourse will have reached their goal. Also, the entire game is not only about gaining points, it is about gaining territory. The offensive team with man-to-man coverage must stop the team with the ball from getting close to the goal, and will block, grab, tackle, sack, and hold a player down to stop them. There might also be a loose ball or a pass attempt, but if missed, it is an incomplete pass. This rather sounds like a bunch of men striving to show that they possess the biggest ball(s), and will stop any other man from beating them in their pursuit of getting their ball(s) between the legs of a woman (the goal posts).

Chapter 17
Handball

Handball has origins in ancient Rome, where women were said to play the game of *expulsim ludere*. This Latin phrase roughly translates as "expulsed play," or the act of driving something through the air.[149] The game, and variations of it, were also played in medieval France, and then in Greenland, before arriving in the Czech Republic, Denmark, Ukraine, and Germany, where it was finally codified at the end of the 1800s.[150] The first rules were published in 1906, and improved in 1919. The first international games were played in 1925, women had their own teams by 1930, and the game entered the Olympics in 1936 for men and 1976 for women. By 2009, the International Handball Federation oversaw 795,000 teams and 19 million players. Spectator attendance records can reach up to 44,000 people. The game is known as American handball, Basque pelota, European handball, fieldball, international Fronton, Olympic handball, team handball, Valencian fronto, and Welsh

---

[149] Wilhelm Adolf Becker, "The Game of Ball," In *Gallus: or, Roman Scenes of the Time of Augustus,* Rev. Frederick Metcalfe, (trans). (London: Longmann, Green, and Co. 1603), 402.

[150] World Handball, "History: Origins and Development." http://www.hand-ball.org/historia/

handball. In this chapter we will only look at American and European handball.

American handball is different from the rest. It can be played by teams in several ways: by two players called singles, three players called cutthroat, or four players with two on each side called doubles. There are three versions of the game. One is played against one wall, another is played with three walls, and the third is played with four walls. The goal is to pass, bounce, or dribble a ball with hands only, and get it into the opposing team's goal area to score. A game lasts for one hour, having two periods of thirty minutes each with a break in between. A team wins by scoring the most goals. Both are allowed a number of players for substitution. The American game is controlled by the United States Handball Association. European handball is played the same way, but consists of six field players and one goalkeeper, and is regulated by the European Handball Federation.

Handball can be played on an indoor or outdoor court. In American handball, the court is 20 feet wide by 40 feet long (6 m by 12.20 m), and the wall is 20 feet (6.10 m) high. In European handball the court is about 65 feet wide by 131 feet long (20 m by 40 m), and 20 feet high (6.10 m). There is also a half-circle zone which extends forward 6.5 yards (5.94 m) from the back line. Centered at the back line is the goal, which is approximately 3 yards (2.74 m) wide and 2.19 yards (2 m) high with goal posts, a crossbar of aluminum or wood, and a net. Twenty feet (6.10 m) from the back line is a circle where only the goalkeeper is allowed.

Only the goalkeeper is allowed to touch the ball with any part of his or her body, but players can throw with their hands. The ball may be held for no more than three seconds, and players may not take more than three steps when holding the ball before it must be passed to another player or shot through the goal posts. Two referees watch for faults, and consequently, may penalize either team or award a team a free-throw. They will display either a yellow card as a warning, or a red card for a disqualification.

The size of the ball depends upon who is using it. If used by men, it has a circumference of 23 to 24 inches (58.42 cm to 60.96 cm) and weighs 15 to 16.8 ounces (425.24 g to 476.27 g); for women, the ball has a circumference of 21 to 22 inches (53.34 cm to 55.88 cm) and weighs 11.5 to 13.2 ounces (326.02 g to 374.21 g); and for an adolescent, the ball has a circumference of 20 inches (50.8 cm) and weighs 10 to 12 ounces (283.50 g to 340.20 g). The ball is an inflatable sphere made of a synthetic material or leather, and must not have a slippery surface or be shiny. It has hexagonal stitching and comes in either white or any combination of colors, depending upon the team's colors.

Handball Terms and Slang

Ace
Handball: Serving an ace means the receiver does not make any contact with the ball whatsoever.
Sexual: A shortened word for an asexual person.

Assault
Handball: A forceful and deliberate attack against the body of another player.
Sexual: Any unwanted sexual contact or threat on another person's body without consent, through clothes or not.

Ball(s)
Handball: The round object used in the game to bounce and throw into the goal.
Sexual: One or two testicles. "To ball" is also a euphemism for engaging in intercourse.

Block

Handball: The body of a player interfering with the normal shot of the receiver.

Sexual: Short for "cock-block," when one person blocks the way for another to connect sexually with someone.

Crack

Handball: Refers to the short line marking on outdoor courts and is often a simple groove on the ground, which makes it hard for players to receive the return.

Sexual: Refers to the crevice of the labia, and also the cleavage between the buttocks.

Down

Handball: Servers who make a switch because of a mistake on their end (too short or long, out, or not returning the ball).

Sexual: Refers to "going down," meaning to perform oral sex, fellatio or cunnilingus. Also, to "get down and dirty" means to have intercourse.

Dribble

Handball: Maneuvering the ball by bouncing it on the floor.

Sexual: A trickle of semen that is released with sexual excitement or during ejaculation.

Equipment

Handball: The ball, uniform, gloves, and shoes of the players.

Sexual: A euphemism for male genitals.

Flagging

Handball: Flagging occurs when a serve almost hits a player. The serve is retaken and the server does not score if the receiver is unable to return the shot.

Sexual: The act of wearing colored handkerchiefs indicating specific sexual interests, used by gay, lesbian and BDSM participants. A handkerchief worn in the right rear pocket indicates a "top" and worn on the left indicates a "bottom." Also used to describe having had sex with a foreigner, denoting that country's flag.

Foul

Handball: An irregular action in a game, which is usually punished with a free throw.

Sexual: When someone is physically dirty, nasty, raunchy, or foul-mouthed to a point of being very unpleasant.

Free Throw

Handball: What is awarded to the opposing team when a player makes a foul. The ball is thrown from the nine-meter line from the goal.

Sexual: Receiving oral sex, but not returning the favor.

Give and go

Handball: An offensive play that involves passing the ball (giving) followed by running (go) to an open spot to receive the ball back.

Sexual: Having a quick sexual encounter and then leaving.

Glove(s)

Handball: Covering worn by a player to protect the hands.

Sexual: A synonym for a condom.

Goalie

Handball: The person who defends the goal against the opposing team trying to score, and the only person allowed to field in the goal area who can use his body to move the ball away.

Sexual: A person that cannot "score" with a woman and keeps their friend from scoring, too.

208

Handling
Handball: Refers to the skill of dribbling, catching, passing, or throwing the ball.

Sexual: Any sexual interaction between two people that is beyond the intention of friendship.

Interruption
Handball: A referee may temporarily stop the game for a variety of special reasons, especially if a player is injured.

Sexual: This is when a couple uses the withdrawal method of birth control to avoid insemination and pregnancy, called *coitus interruptus*. Proven to be unreliable.

Long ball(s)
Handball: When a ball in play lands outside the long line of the court. Also, a long shot and a down if made during a serve. It is an automatic point to the server if the ball remains in play.

Sexual: A scrotum that hangs low, either because it developed that way, or because the man is older, and it sags due to gravity over time.

Overtime
Handball: When a match ends in a draw, and overtime is called.

Sexual: When a guy works hard and long to convince a woman to engage in sexual relations. Having intercourse over a long period of time, and continuing intercourse after an orgasm.

Passive Play

Handball: This is keeping the ball in a team's possession without making a recognizable attempt to attack and score.

Sexual: Sexual play where the submissive "bottom" or "receiver" is not active him or herself, and is being played with.

Playing time

Handball: There are two halftimes of thirty minutes.

Sexual: The time a couple decides to take to engage in sexual activity.

Rebound

Handball: Refers to the way the ball bounces backward after hitting the bars of the goal post.

Sexual: Going from one relationship to the next to avoid the pain of a breakup.

Save

Handball: When the goalkeeper stops a shot with any part of his or her body.

Sexual: To flirt with a beautiful person in a crowd, trying to "save" them from others trying to pick them up. Also, a "wingman" coming to save his friend from a bad situation.

Score

Handball: The current and end result of a game.

Sexual: To be able to have a kissing session with a person, or to succeed in seducing someone and attaining sexual intercourse.

Short ball

Handball: Refers to instances when the serve lands before or actually on the short line of an indoor court. Making two short serves with the ball results in one down.

Sexual: A short amount of time given for intercourse.

Substitution

Handball: A player who enters the court to replace a teammate, once the first player has left the court.

Sexual: This refers to any sexual toys, tools, or dolls that a person might use to substitute for a real person.

Suspension

Handball: A form of personal punishment, which is usually a two-minute suspension from the game.

Sexual: To suspend a person's body from ropes or chains during bondage sex play.

Three-step

Handball: When a player holding the ball is only allowed to make three steps after dribbling or passing the ball.

Sexual: A technique whereby the stimulator excites a woman in three places at the same time, the vagina, the clitoris, and the breasts. Can also indicate anal stimulation.

Throw

Handball: An overtime free throw with the defensive wall three meters from the shooting player.

Sexual: To engage in sexual intercourse.

Whip(ping)

Handball: A technique where a player swings in a vertical motion to "whip" the ball in a downward motion hitting the wall.

Sexual: In consensual sex play, what a "naughty" sexual partner is punished with. The action of quickly "whipping" the penis out of pants.

Other Handball Terms with Sexual Possibilities

A *forewarning signal* in handball indicates that a time-out will end within ten seconds. Given a sexual meaning, a forewarning signal could be indicators such as rapid breathing or dilated eyes, that an orgasm is imminent. A *goal area* is the D-shaped area 6½ feet (6 m) from the goal that is used only by the goalkeeper. A goal area could also be considered the generative organs of both sexes. *Interception of the ball* means that a player caught the ball before it reached a particular place. In a sexual context, interception of the ball could be what happens in group sex when a person intercepts the play of a couple to have a more involved participation.

Man marking in handball is a defensive strategy where a defender is assigned a specific opposition player to guard rather than covering an area of the court. Man marking could also be the tattooing of a man's name on another person's body, as a sign of possession. Also in the game, *personal punishments* are awarded by the referee after a warning has been given when a foul has been committed, and if severe, could lead to disqualification. A personal punishment in a kink scene could easily be a chastisement or reprimand of a submissive who has not followed directions. *Playing positions* are the seven handball player positions: goalkeeper, left wing, left back, middle back, line player, right back and right wing. In sex play, this could be any position that the participants take with one another.

The game allows a *re-enter*, which is when a player has been punished with a two-minute suspension and then is allowed back on to the court to play again. In a sexual situation, this term would apply when a man re-enters the mouth, vagina or anus after pulling out for any reason. *Shooting on goal* in handball refers to throwing on goal with a shot, which can include the overarm shot, underarm shot, side bend shot, falling jump shot, jump shot and jumping with both feet. Sexually speaking, shooting on goal could also mean when a man ejaculates on top of the sexual organs rather than ejaculating inside the sexual orifice. A *spike* in handball is an overhead smash of the ball leading to a killer shot. A sexual interpretation would be to cause a spike in blood pressure of a submissive, or when a dominant threatens to spike the man with her stiletto heels; then again, it might also bring on a hard spike of a penis with excitement at just hearing that threat. There is one more term which is fun. In handball, there is the *whistle for the throw-off*, which is when the referee gives the signal to start the game. But quite often, when a stripper throws off her clothing, many men will give a wolf-whistle to show their appreciation.

Sexual Commentary

Let's look at the name of the game, handball. The word "ball" is a homonym, as a handball is the ball used in the sport and a "ball" is a testicle in urban usage. Despite the use of the word "ball" for the male anatomy, there is no sport ball that actually is the same weight or dimensions as a testicle. A testicle ends up being somewhere between the size of a golf ball and a racquetball, and is much lighter than any sport ball. Regardless, both pieces of equipment, a handball and a testicle, can be easily held in the hand. But as in anything, it depends on what you do with it. Each does take special handling. A person (or player) may handle the ball with either their left or right hand. In handball, the person can be a left-handed or a right-handed player; and in general, a man will favor masturbating with one hand more than the other for their entire lifetime. A long or short ball in handball is when the ball lands outside the long line or on the short line, but can also refer to the appearance of a testicle. A testicle will elongate when too warm, and will rise and become shorter when it becomes too cold, or simply with age.

Chapter 18
Kickball

Kickball, also called soccer baseball in Canada, is a league game played on a softball diamond, with three bases, a pitcher's mound, and a home plate. The ball is kicked from a home area in a 3-foot circle and must pass beyond a 5-foot line. Runners advance with infield balls. One team tries to score when its players return a ball from home base to the field and then circle the bases, while the opposing team tries to stop them by tagging them out with the ball before they can return to home base. After every player has had a chance to kick the ball, they change sides. The team with the most runs wins.

The game of kickball was first invented in 1917 when it was called "kick baseball," and it had only twelve rules.[151] In 1920, the sport began being played in schools as a physical education tool, and the ball was also used for soccer or volleyball. From ten to thirty players played on a baseball diamond. In 1922, the New York State Department of Education held a conference to teach all teachers the game, so they could in turn teach their students. The adult teams were named Yale and Princeton. Soldiers during the Second World War also played the game in 1942.

---

[151] "Kick Baseball," Chapter in *The Playground: The World at Play*. Vol. XI, No. 1. (New York: Cornell University. 1917), 240.

Although the game was first designed for children and remains a game primarily for children and young adults, adults have grown to enjoy the game, and there are many organized leagues. It is popular in the schools of Canada, China, England, Japan, South Korea, and America.

Originally the ball was 7 to 8 inches long (17.78 cm to 20.32 cm), and made out of an old stocking and rags. In the 1920s, Hutch Sporting Goods produced a ball with running grooves, a mottled texture, and laces. Later, the ball changed to an 8.5 to 16-inch diameter (21.59 cm to 40.64 cm) inflated rubber ball, mostly of a red color, but the ball can also be blue, orange, yellow, green, and purple, though they are still made with a rough texture.

Kickball Terms and Slang

Ball

Kickball: Called when a ball is pitched outside the strike zone and when the ball is higher than one foot in height at the base.

Sexual: A synonym for one testicle, and two are "balls." "To ball" is a euphemism to engage in intercourse.

Bunting

Kickball: This is a short soft kick by the kicker.

Sexual: The act of pulling a penis out of a person's mouth during oral sex and slapping it against the fellator's chin. Also, a "bunt" refers to someone who tries to start something sexual with another person, but doesn't even get a kiss.

Out

Kickball: When a ball touches a running player, when a kicked ball is caught, when there are three strikes, and when a fielder with the ball touches the base before the runner gets there.

Sexual: When someone "comes out" as in "out of the closet," they are openly expressing their homosexuality.

Stealing

Kickball: Running to the next base before a ball is pitched.

Sexual: Refers to "stealing a kiss," or stealing a look at someone else when their partner is not looking.

Tag

Kickball: To touch a runner who is off the base, which puts the player out.

Sexual: It is a price for sexual services. It is also a marking, which could be a man's name marked or tattooed on the lower back of a woman, or a woman's name or picture on a man's body.

Tag up

Kickball: Once a kicked ball is caught in the air, a runner on base may advance.

Sexual: Touching someone and then making the next move – to kiss a breast, a breast to a buttock or genitals, or touching the genitals to penetration. "Tagged up" is leaving a mark on another during sexual excitement, such as leaving a "hicky."

Walk

Kickball: When a kicker is awarded first base after a specific number of balls.

Sexual: What a streetwalker does. She walks the sidewalk waiting for a customer to approach her.

Other Kickball Terms with Sexual Possibilities

A *lead off* in kickball is stepping off a base before the kicker kicks the ball. But it might also be used to describe what happens at the beginning of an orgy when people are hesitant to start, but someone will always lead off with the first move. The term *force out* is used when there is an out at a base, where the base runner need not be tagged, as he or she is out for other reasons. In sexual slang, a force out could easily mean that point after copulation when the woman uses her kegel muscles to push the penis out of her vaginal canal. A *strike* is a ball that is not kicked by the kicker, or when the kicker kicks a foul ball. A strike could also be when a hooker on a corner strikes a pose to lure a motorist to stop for her, and after he stops to strike a bargain for a price with what the customer wants to have happen.

Sexual Commentary

The earliest kickballs had their surface covered in brown leather; more recently, the ball became red. Now they come in five other colors, but the brown and red are significant in that one may suggest that this brown and reddishness aligns with the general coloration of testicles (unless of course one possesses another skin color). Then there is the shape of the field, which is similar to baseball, in that it is a diamond. There are several meanings to this shape, but one of them which is relevant for these notes is that it is the symbol of creation, or a literal image of the birth canal.

Also, when possible, the three field bases are denoted by cones. Cones are an interesting choice, made up of a circle and a triangle. Circles represent wholeness, completeness, movement, unity, protection, integrity, perfection and femininity. Triangles represent action, dynamic tension, aggression, energy, strength, stability, progression, direction, and masculinity because they have a point to them. Also, the movement of the runners going counterclockwise represents the fulfillment of intention. All of these designs and shapes, therefore, have something of a sexual nature. One last thing. There are five innings per game. This number has many, many meanings, but relative to these notes, five is composed of the female number two with the male number three, and therefore denotes marriage. It is said to be the prevailing number in nature and art; it symbolizes fire, sensuality, fecundity, opportunity, vitality, and competitiveness.

Chapter 19
Rugby

The term rugby football can refer to rugby league or rugby union. The Football Association formalized the difference between association football and rugby football in 1863, and the first rugby club was formed in England the following year. The first international match between England and Scotland was held in 1871, when the English formed the Rugby Football Union. Twenty-one years later, the union grew but had a schism. The Northern Rugby Football Union was formed, but one became known as the league and the other the union. At first, they used the same rules, but then became two separate sports. Finally, in 1995, rugby union and rugby league both became professional sports.

Both the union and the league have things in common, but there are some differences. Clarifying these differences will help to understand them, as both deserve to be addressed.[152] They share the same intention of the game, and the ball is almost the same, but there are variations in tackling, scoring, pitch (the field, also called a paddock), players, possession, and demographics. Both aim to win by scoring points through conversions, drop

---

[152] Rules of Sport, "What is the Difference Between Rugby League and Rugby Union?" http://www.rulesofsport.com/faq/what-is-the-difference-between-rugby-league-and-rugby-union.html

goals, penalty goals, and getting the ball over a crossball to score. The ball is ovoid in shape in both games, and can be advanced to the goal by running with it, kicking it, and passing it sideways and backward, but not forward. Game time for both sports is two periods of forty minutes with a ten-minute break in between.

There are also differences in tackling and scoring. In both sports, only the player that carries the ball is allowed to be tackled, but when the play continues, the ball gets transferred in different ways. In league, the player can use their legs to bring an opponent down if they also have both hands on the opponent. And when ready to continue, they can roll the ball back to a teammate. But in union, the game continues with a scramble for possession of the ball. What they share in scoring is when a player touches the ball down beyond the defending goal line and a try is scored, kicking a conversion for two more points can be made. The difference in scoring a try in league is worth four points, but in union it is five points. In league a drop goal is one point, but in union it is three points. And in league, a penalty goal is one point, but in union it is three points.

There are further differences. In league, the pitch can be a maximum size of 74.37 yards wide by 133.42 yards long (68 m by 122 m), and in union their maximum pitch is 76.55 yards wide by 157.48 yards long (70 m by 144 m). In league there are thirteen players to a team, and in union there are fifteen players. Possession is different as well. In league, before handing possession of the ball over, the team is only allowed to be tackled six times. In union, a team can keep the ball for as long as they want until the opposing team takes it from them. The last difference is the biggest. League is generally considered a sport for the working class, and union more a sport for the middle class.

Another thing they share is their ancient history. A fourth century BCE Greek writer named Antiphanes was the first to describe an ancient game resembling rugby football. It was adapted by the Romans and called *harpastum*,[153] and the Roman politician Cicero tells the story of a man killed by a ball gone wild while he was getting a shave.[154] The game continued to be played through history, and finally in 1830 became part of the school exercise program in England. The first match was played in 1857 in Scotland, and in 1892 players were beginning to get paid for playing. Rugby union was admitted into the Olympics in 1900, and participated in the 1908, 1920, and 1924 games as a medal sport, but aside from an exhibition game in 1936, has not been readmitted.

The first rugby balls were made from pigs' bladders of four panels and hand-stitched with leather casings. They were plum-shaped due to the extension of a pig's bladder called a *quanco*. The balls that union rugby and league rugby use are similar but have some differences.

An official rugby union ball is still made up of four panels, but it is oval-shaped. It is 11 to 12 inches long (27.94 cm to 30.48 cm), 23 to 24 inches (58.42 cm to 60.96 cm) in circumference, weighs 14 to 16 ounces (396.89 g to 453.59 g), and when inflated has a pressure of 9.5 to 10 psi (65.50 kPa to 68.95 kPa). The ball is made of a synthetic material or of leather, is water resistant, and has a textured surface for an easier grip. Once made of leather but prone to getting water-logged, since 1980 they are now encased in synthetic water proof materials.

---

[153] Shawn T. Norris, "The Sport of the Roman Army," Rome Across Europe. http://www.romeacrosseurope.com/?p=1118

[154] E. Norman Gardiner, "Athletics in the Ancient World," (New York: Courier Dover Publications. 2002), 229.

League balls are slightly more pointed than union balls. The official rugby league ball is a prolate spheroid shape. Its size is 11 inches (27 cm) long and 24 inches (60 cm) in circumference at its widest, and weighs between 13.5 and 15.5 ounces (383 g and 440 g). Once made of brown leather, they are now synthetic and called a size 5 or international ball. There are also smaller sizes called "mini" and "mod" for junior teams.

For rugby union, World Rugby is the governing body that oversees its 6.6 million players in 119 countries, and every four years holds the Rugby World Cup. For rugby league, the Rugby League International Federation oversees nineteen countries, and members compete for the Rugby League World Cup.

Rugby Terms and Slang

Biff

Rugby: A fight during the game.

Sexual: Slang for a women's genitalia or vagina.

Blindside

Rugby: The narrow side of the pitch in relation to a scrum or play of the ball, the opposite of open side.

Sexual: Refers to approaching a lover sexually when they are not expecting it.

Bomb

Rugby: A high kick in general play, used when close to the try-line, so it comes down in the goal area.

Sexual: This can refer to enormous female breasts or when someone is extremely attractive and sexy. The word is an acronym for Beat Off Memory Bank, meaning that a person they view gets placed into memory to masturbate to later. In the Caribbean, they "make bomb" or have intercourse, used when the orgasmic experience is exceptional.

Break

Rugby: A breach of the line of defenders by the player in possession of the ball on the attacking team.

Sexual: When a couple decides to spend some time separated from their sexual activities. Also a term used in prostitution for collecting money from a customer to break her luck with the first money of the night, and to leave with a client.

Bridging

Rugby: Refers to a team linking or binding players together at the play-the-ball into a scrum-like formation.

Sexual: A prison term for when a non-circumcised inmate takes his penis's foreskin and extends it over the tip of another inmate's circumcised penis.

Bust

Rugby: When a player breaks through an attempted tackle.

Sexual: A woman's breasts, and to ejaculate.

Chicken wing

Rugby: A shoulder lock technique, used to slow down a player. It is punishable.

Sexual: A rear-entry position for intercourse, referred to as "doggy-style" but the male also pulls back one or both arms of the receiving person.

Completion rate

Rugby: The percentage of times in possession that a team holds the ball for a set of sex tackles.

Sexual: Refers to the length of time it takes for men and women to reach orgasm. For a woman the average is about twenty minutes. For a man it takes between three and six minutes.

Dead

Rugby: The ball is deemed to be dead if it goes out of play beyond the dead ball line.

Sexual: After a serious injury to the scrotum has occurred, the spermatic cord that carries blood to one or both of the testicles may have been twisted, called testicular torsion. This can affect the blood flow to the tissues, which will turn the testicle numb, sometimes referred to as "dead." This can also occur with rapid growth during puberty.

Engage(d)

Rugby: An attacking player attracts a defender with the aim of manipulating their defensive position to the advantage of the attacking team.

Sexual: Implies that while preparing for marriage, sexual intercourse will be practiced before the contract is signed. It also refers to when two people are sexually coupled.

Facial

Rugby: A defending player in contact with the ball-carrier during or after the completion of a tackle, who illegally touches the face of the carrier with their hand or forearm, to frustrate, provoke, or establish dominance, only gaining a penalty.

Sexual: When a man ejaculates on his partner's face.

Falcon

Rugby: An unintentional throw of a ball which hits a player's head.

Sexual: The description of a woman who is quick and cunning. When a person places their index finger in a woman's vagina and their middle finger in her anus, in a hooked fashion like a falcon's talon.

225

Fend

Rugby: The action by the ball carrier repelling a tackler using his arm, also known as a "hand off."

Sexual: The need of many women who get approached in a public venue who must "fend-off" a pushy aggressor, thereby protecting themselves and safeguarding their personal boundaries.

Field goal

Rugby: An older term, meaning that there was a goal scored by kicking a ball over the cross bar and between the posts.

Sexual: A man's ejaculation shot out between the knees of his partner.

Flat

Rugby: When an attacking play has a lack of depth along a line of players in close proximity to the defenders. A "flat pass" is when a teammate runs near a ball carrier to receive a pass.

Sexual: A woman with flat breasts or buttocks.

Flop

Rugby: An attempt by a player not involved in a tackle, who delays the player in possession of the ball from getting to their feet quickly, by falling on top of them. A penalty may be awarded to the attacking player.

Sexual: An inebriated woman out to get any guy she can get. A failed pick-up attempt. "Flops" are also flat breasts, and a flaccid penis.

Forward pass

Rugby: This occurs when the ball travels forward relative to the player passing it.

Sexual: Refers to a man who is quite forward in flirting with a woman in order to engage her for sexual relations.

Foul play
Rugby: A non-technical breach of the rules, such as a high tackle.

Sexual: A person who goes beyond the sexual limits of their agreed partnership by playing a dirty trick, a cruel act, or committing violence against their partner.

Fullback
Rugby: A defensive position, but the player may drop out of the defensive line to cover the rear of his team from kicks and runners breaking the line. He may support a runner or run into an attack.

Sexual: Women's panties that fully cover the buttocks. Also, a tough, unattractive woman in a group of women at a club whose job it is to make sure that none of her women friends get approached inappropriately or accosted.

Hand off
Rugby: The action by the ball carrier of repelling a tackler by making sure his arm is straight before contact is made or it is illegal.

Sexual: When one person begins to masturbate or perform manual genital stimulation and then has someone else continue. When someone begins to date a person but their interest turns cold, and they give that person's contact information to a friend. It is also when one hangs out with one girl and then switches to another.

Hand over
Rugby: The surrendering of the ball to the opposition team after a team has been tackled six times, or occurs if a team kicks the ball into the touch line area after the fifth tackle.

Sexual: Much like a hand off, sharing a "hand job."

High ball(s)

Rugby: Describes the ball going up into the air while the attacking players rush underneath it where it is expected to land.

Sexual: Describes testes that fail to descend after birth, which can be caused possibly by genetics, a premature birth, low testosterone, nerve inactivity, or related to the mother having smoked cigarettes, drank alcohol, or was obese or diabetic.

Hit up

Rugby: An Australasian term for crash ball, which is an attacking tactic where a player receives a pass at pace and runs to the opposition's defensive line. By doing so, the runner creates holes in the opposition's defense.

Sexual: Very similar to "hitting on" or making a pass with the intention of having intercourse.

Hooker

Rugby: In defense, he is the player who organizes and defends the middle of the line against the opposition's props and second-rowers. In offense, he is responsible for starting the play by either passing the ball to the right player or running, and will probably make more tackles than any other player.

Sexual: A synonym for a prostitute.

In and out

Rugby: A running arc made by an attacking player, attempting to create indecision in the defender, before turning toward the corner and attempting to reach the goal line to score.

Sexual: A synonym for intercourse.

Interception

Rugby: In an attempt to pass the ball to another team member, someone from the opposing team catches it instead.

Sexual: When someone approaches a person of interest before another can make a move. In group sex, it is someone who intercepts the ejaculate before the intended person does.

Mark

Rugby: A place on the field where the referee awards a penalty kick, free kick, or scrum.

Sexual: An unwise, easy targeted young woman, who is not hip to aggressive men who are just looking to get laid.

Move

Rugby: Often refers to a preplanned passage of play, and a referee calls this in order to allow a tackled player to get back on their feet.

Sexual: The process of hitting on a woman, of "making a move," by a smooth mover.

Offload

Rugby: When a player holding the ball is tackled but passes the ball to a teammate before the tackle is completed.

Sexual: To ejaculate.

Pass

Rugby: To transfer a ball by throwing it to a teammate. There is the flat pass, direct spin pass, short pass, close-quarters pop pass, and the floated pass.

Sexual: "To make a pass" at a person in order to engage them for sexual relations. Also refers to the stretch of skin between the vaginal opening and the anus, a combination of "pussy" and "ass."

Power play

Rugby: The act of running the ball on the fifth tackle instead of kicking it.

Sexual: A person who uses their authority as a dominant in BDSM roleplay to strategically maneuver and control a submissive into doing what they want.

Red zone

Rugby: The area between each goal line and the team's own twenty-meter line.

Sexual: Slang for a woman's vagina when menstruating.

Rook(s)

Rugby: Someone who has great knowledge about the sport.

Sexual: Someone who takes advantage of and tricks a woman into betraying or cheating on their partner by deceiving or hoodwinking a woman into believing they are the better lover.

Scissors move

Rugby: An attempt to cause a disruption and breach in the defense of the opposing team, by passing a ball to a nearby teammate.

Sexual: A sexual position where two females engage in clitoral stimulation by splitting their legs apart and rubbing against each other.

Scramble

Rugby: The state of the defense following a break, with players retreating in order to try to make a cover tackle or to get back on side, if the attacker has already been tackled.

Sexual: When a group of people have a free-for-all or orgy.

Scrum

Rugby: A means of restarting a play after a minor infringement. It involves up to eight players from each team, known as the pack or forward pack, binding together in three rows and interlocking with the free opposing team's forwards.

Sexual: Short for "*scrump*," which means to have intercourse.

Show and go

Rugby: The ball carrier will take a stance and hold the ball in front of him to give the impression that he is passing it to a teammate. With indecision created in the defense, the ball carrier will sprint for a weak point in the defensive line.

Sexual: A teaser, when a woman walks by and purposely shows off skin but keeps on walking. Brief exhibitionism.

Sin bin

Rugby: The penalty box where a player must wait for ten minutes before resuming play, after receiving a yellow card by the referee.

Sexual: An Australian term for a van love nest. It also refers to the top drawer of a nightstand that contains items for sexual use, such as condoms, lubrication, or sexual toys.

Strike

Rugby: Using the foot to attempt to gain possession of the ball in a scrum, and to hit an opponent with a fist, a misconduct.

Sexual: From "sex-strike," in which one or multiple persons refrain from sex with their partners to achieve certain goals.

Support

Rugby: The movement of a player that places him or her in a position, which will assist a teammate.

Sexual: Any sexual activity is a way of showing support to another. It is also a short term for an athletic support or jockstrap.

Tackle

Rugby: When a defending player stops a ball-carrier by bringing them to the ground so they cannot continue the play.

Sexual: A British word for a man's genitals, his "fishing tackle." Also known as a man's "wedding or man tackle," for that special night.

Touch

Rugby: The area outside two touchlines, which define the sides of the playing area.

Sexual: A euphemism to engage in sexual intercourse.

Try

Rugby: The primary method of scoring worth four points in league rugby and five points in union rugby.

Sexual: The testing of another's will and boundaries to determine how much dominance they can apply in order to engage in sexual intercourse. It is also the act of intercourse.

Turnover

Rugby: Same as a handover. The surrendering of the ball to the opposition team, after a team was tackled six times, or occurs if a team kicks the ball into touch on the full after the fifth tackle.

Sexual: Like a hand off when sharing a "hand job," and the strategy of allowing time between lovers after switching relationships.

232

Wing

Rugby: The wings are normally the fastest players on a team, a play on the far left and right fringes of the field, and a player whose primary task is to receive passes and score.

Sexual: A way of defining various types of sexual partners or practices with a color code. Placing a girlfriend under a guy's protection. A short word for "wingman."

Other Rugby Terms with Sexual Possibilities

Ooh, lots of potential slang words here. *Above the horizontal* is one determinant of a dangerous tackle in rugby, where defenders lift an attacking player off the ground to the point when their feet are higher than their head. In sex-speak, horizontal is a euphemism for having intercourse lying down. Whoever is on top is above the horizontal person below them. An *ankle tap* may be used as a last resort by a defender chasing the attacking player carrying the ball, if that player is about to evade them and a conventional tackle is not possible. Tap is a euphemism for intercourse, and with men who have foot and ankle fetishes, they might tap their penis between two beautiful ankles for an ankle tap.

A *club call* is when the highest-ranking team from the regular season that won their match in the first week of the play-offs is able to select their opponents for the next game. A club is a synonym for a penis, and a club could easily refer to a gentlemen's club or strip club. A club call could also be when a man just can't stay away from a lover, responding to a request to go to them. A *cutout pass* in rugby is also sometimes referred to as "cut out ball," which is when the ball is passed by an attacking player across the front of one of their team mates and caught by a team mate positioned further away. A cutout-pass and cut out ball could also be when a person decides to not participate and leaves after a pass has been made for sex.

A *dominant tackle* is a call by the referee which rewards good technique and allows the defender extra time before the attacker must be released to be allowed to play the ball. It could also mean that the dominant partner in a relationship decides to surprise their lover and push for intercourse. *Double movement* in rugby is an illegal movement in the attempt to score a try. This term could also apply to a threesome, where there is sexual movement by two people toward or on a third person. *Downward pressure* is one of several criteria that needs to be met for a try to be awarded by the referee. Downward pressure could also be what is asked for when a lover who is lying below in coitus likes to have the weight of their lover fully on top of them.

A *field of play* is the area bounded by, but not including, the touch lines and goal lines. A field of play could also refer to the type of sexual play that is desired. Will it include erotica, virtual sex, voyeurism, exhibitionism, masturbation, oral, vaginal, anal, toys, role playing, bondage, dominance and submission, or sadism and masochism? The field of possible play is wide with options. The *Great Split* in rugby refers to the different schisms that have occurred in rugby leading to the development of rugby league football. A great split, often seen in dance routines, could also refer to the widest split of a woman's legs during intercourse. A *golden point* is sometimes used to resolve drawn-out rugby league matches by having the two teams play for up to ten more minutes to settle a tie. If there were any golden point in a session of intercourse, it has to be the orgasm, where the moments are blissful, glorious, and resplendent.

An *obstruction* in the sport is when a player tackles an opponent who does not have the ball, which is a penalty.

An obstruction in intercourse could also refer to a tampon within a vagina. A *professional foul* in rugby is a deliberate act of foul play, usually to prevent an opponent from scoring. A professional foul can also be when a prostitute steals money or possessions from a client. When a player in rugby rolls the ball into the scrum and tries to gain possession of it by kicking it backward toward their own side, this is called a *put in*. A put in could also refer to a penis being put into an agreed-upon orifice.

A move involving a decoy runner in rugby is a *second man play*. The term could also apply to a second man who supplies his sexual abilities to a couple. Another term in the game is called *second effort*, which is an attempt by a defending player who tackles another specifically to delay the play. This interferes with the player's attempt to regain their feet, which will be penalized if seen. A second effort could also be the term when a man cannot get an erection and their lover allows them a second effort to do so. *See you later* is a phrase sometimes used in rugby commentary to refer to a hand-off or fend in the game. "See you later" is often the pat line used by a person after having sex with someone who they don't intend to see again. A *sliding defense* requires that gaps are left at either edge of the field at the end of the defensive line, which aims to squeeze more players around the area of play. This could also be the excuse a lover might use when he accidently slides into an anus, when the woman expected him to enter her vagina. His excuse is that they used too much lubricant and he just slid in. Yeah, sure.

Up and under, also known as a "bomb," is a high short punt onto or behind the defending team. It describes the ball going up into the air while the attacking players rush underneath it toward where it is expected to land. Up and under could also describe the process of a person going up to a lover's body and going under their shirt to touch their breasts, or when a couple is up for sexual intercourse and they get under the covers.

Sexual Commentary

The ball that is used in Rugby Union is unique. It is oblong like the ball used in American football but there are no points at the end. Instead, the ends of the ball are rounded, giving the overall look of the ball the appearance of an egg. This shape is the same as that of a man's testicles. Like eggs, the testicles are very fragile, and both represent fertility and regeneration, which can produce new life for the future.

There is only one more comment about this sport, and that is for the term "a try," which garners either four or five points. Why in the world would the rule makers consider something that garners a team that many points *only* a try? "To try" does not mean something was achieved. A try is an attempt that fails, like a guy who tries to get a woman's attention, but fails to get a response. No points should be awarded for only an *attempt* to score. Obviously, something has been misunderstood along the way. Would the rule-makers please change this term to actually stand for what it should mean?

Chapter 20
Soccer

Many people are confused when it comes to distinguishing "soccer" and "football." Are they speaking about association football, U.S soccer, or U.S. football? One must consider the country in which the sport is played. Here are the distinctions: 1. The balls are different. Football played in the U.S. and Canada uses a ball with two pointed ends. In association football and U.S. soccer the ball is round. 2. The games are played differently. Players use their feet to move the ball in U.K. associated football and U.S. soccer, while in U.S. and Canadian football the ball can be carried.

There *are* several similarities. Both have teams of eleven players each. Each team features a player who makes a goal, though they are called by different names. There are offside rules, which require the team on offense to move down the field in unison. And each sport often kicks the ball with the top of their shoe, rather than the bottom.

There are many differences. In U.S. soccer and association football, the players work as a single unit, whereas in U.S. and Canadian football, players have different jobs, that is, as a defensive player or as an offensive player. The fields are different sizes and are marked differently. The U.S. soccer and association football fields are longer and wider. They both have a kickoff circle, midfield line, and two penalty areas, while

U.S. and Canadian football have field markings every ten yards. United States soccer and association football are played in two 45-minute halves, while U.S. and Canadian football is played in four 15-minute quarters. Only goalkeepers can use their hands to touch the ball in U.S. soccer and association football, but any player in U.S. and Canadian football can carry the ball. U.S. soccer and association football allow only three substitutes per game, while substitutions are unlimited in U.S. and Canadian football. U.S. soccer and association football are also stricter when it comes to what constitutes a foul. What they wear is different, too. A U.S. soccer and association football player wears shorts, a jersey, knee socks, shin guards, and cleats on their shoes, while a U.S. and Canadian football player wears a uniform, helmet, and shoulder pads.

Scoring and championships are different, as well. In U.S. soccer and association football, in order to score, the ball must cross the goal line between the goal posts and go under the crossbar for a goal. In U.S. and Canadian football, the ball must go between the goalposts for a six-point touchdown or a two-point conversion, and a kick counts as an extra point, or a three-point field goal. U.S. soccer and association football championships hold a World Cup, while American football has the Super Bowl.

Now that the differences are cleared up, this chapter will concentrate on U.S. soccer and association football. The game's antecedents come from ancient China, Egypt, Greece, and Rome. The game is thought to have been brought into the United States in the mid-1800s, by English, Irish, Italians, German, and Scottish immigrants. The sport is referenced in the Etymology Dictionary in

1863.[155] The first major soccer match where only the feet were used to move the ball was played between Princeton and Rutgers Universities in 1869. Early soccer leagues usually used the name "football," and that confusion existed for many years until 1919, when the sport formed its own league called the American Soccer League. This became the United States Soccer Federation in 1974.

Popularity of the game grew rapidly. By 1967 there were 100,000 players in the U.S. Throughout the 1970s, U.S. soccer became popular in grade schools for boys and girls, and adult teams and leagues were formed. By 1984, when the game entered the Olympics, there were 4,000,000 players. Between 1990 and 2010, it was the fastest growing sport in the U.S. As of 2015, more than 24.4 million people were playing soccer in the U.S. In 2018, 3.572 billion viewers watched the International Federation of Association Football (FIFA) World Cup. That's over half of the earth's total population![156]

Now because this chapter is about balls, here is a description of the ball used by the U.S. soccer and association football teams. As we have learned, the make and style of the ball has changed over time, from very early balls made of animal and human skulls, to pig and cow bladders, to stuffed cloth. The first modern round balls were made from vulcanized rubber inner tubes in 1836 by Charles Goodyear. One from 1855 is on display at the National Soccer Hall of Fame. In 1862, the first

---

[155] Douglas Harper, "Football," Etymology online.
https://www.etymonline.com/word/football

[156] FIFA, "More than half the world watched record-breaking 2018 World Cup." https://www.fifa.com/worldcup/news/more-than-half-the-world-watched-record-breaking-2018-world-cup

inflatable rubber balls were made, which kept their round shape and hardness.

By 1872, the first official size and weight was fixed at 27 to 28 inches (68.58 cm to 71.12 cm) in circumference and 13 to 15 ounces (368.54 g to 425.24 g) in weight. The ball has remained approximately the same, except for the materials it is made of and the design of the panels. The lower quality balls were made from the leather of the cow's shoulder and the best quality from the rump of the cow. Interlocking panels became the norm in the 1900s, comprised of eighteen sections stitched together in six panels of three strips each. However, when the leather got wet, it made the ball heavy. Synthetic paints helped to coat and seal the leather, and the valve of the inner tube was eliminated.

The balls continued to be improved. In 1951, white balls were made so spectators could more easily see the balls on a green field, and then orange balls were introduced to see the ball better when there was snow on the ground. Buckminster Fuller created a series of spherical designs which lent the look of the modern soccer ball. The pattern is a series of twenty hexagons and twelve pentagons. The colors became black and white in 1970, so the players could more easily determine the swerve on a ball. By 2002, the balls became waterproof and faster in flight. They had a soft feel and were safer when they hit the head of a player. After that, the panels changed to a star design in black and white, then to stars with different colors for each team with intricate artistic flourishes, some with player's names on them.

Soccer Terms and Slang

Assist

Soccer: When the ball is passed in play to a teammate who then scores.

Sexual: When one guy helps his buddy connect with a male or female friend for sexual pleasure.

Box

Soccer: The penalty area, sometimes called the 18-yard box.

Sexual: A slang synonym for a woman's vagina.

Dead ball

Soccer: When the play is stopped and the ball is not moving.

Sexual: After a serious injury to the scrotum has occurred, the spermatic cord that carries blood to one or both of the testicles may have been twisted, called testicular torsion. This can affect the blood flow to the tissues, which will turn the testicle numb. This can also occur with rapid growth during puberty.

Hand ball

Soccer: An offense that includes not only the hand touching the ball, but any part of the arm below the armpit.

Sexual: A euphemism for sexual foreplay involving handling a man's scrotum.

Head

Soccer: Also called a "header," where the forehead is used to put the ball in play for a clearance, a pass, or a shot at the goal.

Sexual: The end of the penis, or the act of giving or receiving oral sex, fellatio for men and cunnilingus women.

Mark

Soccer: In man-to-man coverage, the defender is said to mark (rather than guard) the attacker. The closer he plays to him, the tighter the marking, and the further away the looser the marking.

Sexual: An unwise, easily-targeted young woman who is not hip to aggressive men who are just looking to get laid.

Period

Soccer: A standard 45-minute length of play. There can also be a temporary dismissal period any time between.

Sexual: Refers to a woman's time of menstruation.

Pitch

Soccer: The British term for a sports field.

Sexual: The territory, area, or street that a prostitute works along, and the words a person tells another to get them to agree to a sexual liaison.

Scissor kick

Soccer: A side volley, when the player leans sideways, throws his legs upward, and volleys the ball forward with a scissor-like motion as the kicking leg passes forward over the other leg.

Sexual: The movement made when bisexual women or lesbians rub their labia and clitorises together for sexual excitement.

Tackle

Soccer: Using the feet to take the ball from an opponent's feet. A tackle may be accompanied by a legitimate shoulder charge, but there must be no holding, pushing, tripping, elbowing, or hip-checking.

Sexual: A British word for a man's genitals, his "fishing tackle." Also known as a man's "wedding or man tackle" for that special night.

Time

Soccer: The length of a game with two halves of forty-five minutes each.

Sexual: Short for "making time," meaning to engage in sexual activity.

Other Soccer Terms with Sexual Possibilities

To *boot* a ball in soccer is to kick it hard, long and high, without aim. A "booter" is the player who does this. In sex slang, a booter is a man who has unprotected sex. In soccer, the game is played on a soccer *field*, but "field" can also mean "playing the field," meaning that a person dates numerous people but has no serious relationship. An *own goal* is a player who accidently kicks or deflects the ball into his own goal, giving the opponents the score. It could also mean that a person has achieved their own sexual goal, whatever that might be, or masturbated to orgasm. A *wall pass* is when a ball is rebounded off a wall rather than passed to a teammate. A wall pass might also be a pass delivered to a prospective lover, while both are leaning against or next to a wall.

Sexual Commentary

In the rules of soccer, a goal must be placed in the center of each goal line, the vertical posts and horizontal crossbar must be painted white, they cannot exceed the width or depth of five inches (12 cm), and a net may be attached to the goals. This placement, color and depth are of interest. The vertical posts may be likened to a person's legs, with the sexual organs in the center, and may be vertical during intercourse. White is the color of cleanliness, purity, perfection, and virginity, and the average penis when erect is 5 inches long. The goal is to get his "balls" and penis past these "posts" into the scoring zone of the vagina. This is also one of the few sports where matches use a video operation room to review plays. A referee may change his call if the video shows he made a mistake. This sounds rather like a porno being recorded for future enjoyment.

Chapter 21
Volleyball

Volleyball is a ball and net game, in which two teams of six players on each side of the net do their best to score points by grounding a ball on the opposing team's side of the court without a return.

The game was founded in 1895 by a YMCA physical education director, William G. Morgan in Massachusetts. He called it mintonette, taken from badminton, also played over a net (p. 4).[157] He also wrote the first rules. The net was supposed to be 6½ feet (2 m) high, stretched across a court 25 feet (7.62 m) wide and 50 feet (15.24 m) long. Any number of players could be on a team, and the ball could be in contact with members on the same team any number of times before it went over the net. A match had nine innings and each team had three serves in each inning. If the ball hit the net it was a foul. If that was on a serve, a second serve was allowed. Scoring went to twenty-one points and the team to reach that first won the game.

The game spread to other YMCAs and when Alfred Halstead, one of Morgan's professors, saw the volleying

[157] New England Historical Society, "In 1895, William Morgan Invents Mintonette."
http://www.newenglandhistoricalsociety.com/leroy-shear-the-respected-vermont-banker-who-wasnt

of the ball back and forth, he dubbed it "volley ball," with two words.[158] In 1896, the words were combined when the YMCA wrote its official sports handbook.

The game's popularity spread and the rules changed. Canada was the first country, other than the U.S., to play the game, in 1900. Then the Philippines adopted the game in 1916 and coined the terms "set and spike," and the "three hits" rule. The following year, the points per game were reduced from twenty-one to fifteen. Volleyball became a popular outdoor sport for nudists as early as the 1920s, and the court became standard in nudist clubs by the 1960s.[159]

Sixteen thousand volleyballs were given out to American forces in 1919 for entertainment, and thus the game went to wherever forces were sent.[160] The first World Championships were held in 1949 for men and 1952 for women.[161] Soon many countries took up the sport, including Italy, the Netherlands, Brazil, Russia, and countries throughout Asia. Volleyball became part of the Olympics in the summer of 1964. In 1987, beach volleyball began to be played in the sand with only two players per team.

The court dimensions have changed since its beginnings. A volleyball court is now 29.5 by 59.1 feet (9 m by 18 m). For men's competitions, the top of the net is just under 8 feet (2.44 m) high, and for women's

---

[158] Ibid.

[159] M. S. Weinberg, "The Nudist Camp: Way of Life and Social Structure," *Human Organization*. Vol. 26, No. 3. (1967), 91-99.

[160] Volleyball - General Information, "History of Volleyball." http://volleyball.org/history.html

[161] Fédération Internationale de Volleyball, "FIVB History." https://web.archive.org/web/20070919033125/http://www.fivb.ch/EN/FIVB/History.htm

competitions it is a few inches over 7 feet (2.24 m). The court is divided in half where the net is strung, and there is an attack line 9.84 feet (3 m) back on either side of the net. A free zone encircles the court where players enter and play. There are set positions on the court, and after the team gains the serve, the team members rotate clockwise.

The ball is spherical with a circumference of around 26 inches (65-67 cm) and weighs 9½ ounces (269.32 g). It is made of three layers. The innermost layer is made of a rubber bladder covered in cloth. Over the cloth is a covering of real or synthetic leather. The leather is made up of eighteen rectangular panels arranged in six sections of three panels each. Indoor balls have only eight panels and may be all white or a combination of two to three colors. There is a lighter ball for youths, and a beach volleyball is slightly larger, has a rougher texture and a lower pressure, and can be solid white or brightly colored.

Volleyball Terms & Slang

Ace
Volleyball: A serve resulting in a point, usually when the ball hits the floor untouched on the receiving team's side of the court.

Sexual: A shortened word for an asexual person.

Angle
Volleyball: The trajectory of the ball over the net on a serve into the opposite court.

Sexual: An approach that a person uses to "pick up" a partner, usually with sex in mind.

Assist

Volleyball: Passing or setting up the ball to a teammate who attacks the ball for a kill.

Sexual: When a guy helps his buddy connect with a woman or a man for an intimate experience.

Attack

Volleyball: The offensive action of hitting the ball. It is the attempt by one team to terminate the play by hitting the ball to the floor on the opponent's side.

Sexual: It can mean a sexual attack, or in Japan it simply means (without harm) to approach someone of the opposite gender.

Back slide

Volleyball: A quick slide behind the second passer, whose job it is to position a pass to the hitter.

Sexual: To engage in intercourse with an ex-lover.

Baseline

Volleyball: The back boundary of the court.

Sexual: The bare minimum standard of attractiveness that a man or woman might consider for intercourse.

Block

Volleyball: A defensive play by one or more front row players meant to intercept a spiked ball.

Sexual: Short for "cock-block," when a person blocks another from connecting sexually with someone.

Break

Volleyball: An abrupt change of direction in the attacker's approach.

Sexual: When a couple decides to spend some time separated from their sexual activities; and a term used in prostitution for collecting money from a customer to break her luck with the first money of the night, and to leave with a client.

Bump
Volleyball: Slang for forearm passing.
Sexual: A euphemism for intercourse.

Deep
Volleyball: Away from the net toward the baseline.
Sexual: When a penis deeply penetrates the receiver.

Dig
Volleyball: Passing a spiked or rapidly hit ball, having accessed it close to the floor.
Sexual: An abbreviation for Daddy Issue Girl - a young woman who is attracted to an older man. The opposite of a "cougar," which refers to an older woman who prefers young men.

Dink
Volleyball: This is a gentle shot.
Sexual: A synonym for penis which comes from 1888 America, from "dingus," meaning a "thing." Also a dinkle.

Doubles
Volleyball: A game with two players on a side.
Sexual: Performing manual genital stimulation with two different sets of hands. Short for double penetration, when a woman is penetrated by a man vaginally and another man anally. It is also when one man is engaged in sex play with two women.

Dump
Volleyball: Performed by the setter, who delivers the ball into the opponent's court on the second contact.
Sexual: To be rid of a lover.

Floater(s)

Volleyball: A serve with no spin that follows an erratic path.

Sexual: Refers to breasts or a scrotum which floats in water.

Foul

Volleyball: A violation of the rules.

Sexual: When someone is physically dirty, nasty, raunchy, or foul-mouthed to a point of being very unpleasant.

Free ball

Volleyball: Returning the ball to the opponent without the intent of making a kill or a spike.

Sexual: When a guy does not wear any underwear and his scrotum and penis are unhampered in their natural movement.

Hit

Volleyball: To jump and strike the ball with a forceful overhand shot.

Sexual: A euphemism for intercourse.

Inside

Volleyball: Refers to a shot of the ball toward the center of the net.

Sexual: When a person has sexually entered their lover.

Joust

Volleyball: When two opposing players contact the ball simultaneously above the net, causing the ball to momentarily come to rest. If an official calls this, the point is replayed.

Sexual: A euphemism for intercourse.

Key

Volleyball: To discern a team's next play by observation of patterns or habits.

Sexual: Touching someone inappropriately for one's own amusement and then brushing it off as a joke.

Lineup

Volleyball: The serving order of the players, which reflects their starting position on the court.

Sexual: Common in a brothel, where prostitutes are lined up for men to choose from.

Load

Volleyball: To position the blockers so that the most effective blocker confronts the opponent's most effective attacker.

Sexual: The amount of semen from an ejaculation.

Pass

Volleyball: To receive a serve or the first contact of the ball with the intent to send the ball to another player.

Sexual: To make a pass at or "come on to" someone.

Pancake(s)

Volleyball: A one-hand floor defensive technique where the hand is extended and slid along the floor palm down, while the player dives or extension rolls, so that the ball bounces off the back of the hand.

Sexual: Refers to a women's flat breasts or buttocks. A woman flattening her breasts up against glass for public display in exhibitionism. Also, the areola around the nipples, and a euphemism for lying flat to have sex in the missionary position.

252

Penetration

Volleyball: The blocker's ability to reach over the net above the opponent's court.

Sexual: The act of inserting a penis, dildo, or phallic strap-on into an oral or sexual cavity of a real or manufactured body or object.

Play

Volleyball: An attack with a planned fake, usually including two or more hitters.

Sexual: Refers to any kind of sexual activity alone or with another. In BDSM, it refers to sexual role-play.

Power tip

Volleyball: A move that can help a player hit the ball into open gaps, by tipping the ball in a certain way and direction. Also known as dinking.

Sexual: A medium penis with an unusually large head.

Pump

Volleyball: A play in which an attacker fakes spiking a quick set and then hits a medium-high set at the same location.

Sexual: Refers to the in and out action of the penis in intercourse.

Rainbow

Volleyball: A soft shot over the blockers to the back line that has the arc of a rainbow.

Sexual: Refers to a term used by the LGBTQ+ community to acknowledge acceptance among its members. It also refers to the ring of lipstick left on a penis after fellatio, and is a simile for male ejaculation in an arc, "like a rainbow."

Rotation

Volleyball: The clockwise movement of players around the court and through the serving position following a side out.

Sexual: An oral sex musical chairs game.

Set

Volleyball: The tactical skill in which a ball is directed to a point where a player can spike it into the opponent's court.

Sexual: Refers to a woman's pair of breasts or her legs.

Shank

Volleyball: A severely misdirected pass.

Sexual: A prostitute or a woman without virtue.

Shoot

Volleyball: A low fast set to an attacker who is away from the setter.

Sexual: To ejaculate.

Slide

Volleyball: An attack approach that includes a last moment move along the net.

Sexual: A person who is known for his or her open sexual proclivities with no attachments.

Spike

Volleyball: A hit or attack when a ball is contacted with force by a player on the offensive team, who intends to terminate the ball on the opponent's floor or off the opponent's blocker.

Sexual: A euphemism for a hard, penile erection.

Stuff

Volleyball: A ball that is deflected back to the attacking team's floor by the opponent's blockers.

Sexual: Can refer to something sexual, to seduce someone, or a woman or man's genitals. To "get stuffed" means penile penetration.

Swing

Volleyball: To move from one sideline to another, as an approaching move to attack.

Sexual: To have an open sexual relationship with one's partner and with a select group of other partners, called swingers.

Switch

Volleyball: To change court positions after a ball is served.

Sexual: A person who shifts in a sexual relationship between being dominant and submissive.

Tool

Volleyball: When an attacker hits the ball off an opposing blocker's arms, out of bounds.

Sexual: Commonly referred to as the penis, a man's tool.

Touch

Volleyball: A player contacting the ball.

Sexual: An initial manner of body contact, and a euphemism for engaging in sexual intercourse.

Transition

Volleyball: To switch from offense to defense, and vice versa.

Sexual: A term that describes a transsexual person's journey from the sex they were assigned at birth to the opposite gender.

Wing

Volleyball: The defensive players in areas 5 and 1.

Sexual: A system of rating sexual activity with a color code. Placing a girlfriend under a man's protection. Short for "wingman."

Other Volleyball Terms with Sexual Possibilities

A *blocking error* is a violation that consists of touching the net, crossing the center line, blocking a set, or any other violation which pertains to illegal blocking. From sexual slang comes the phrase "cock-blocking" someone. This is when a person blocks another from connecting sexually with someone. A blocking error would be when a person mistakenly interferes for no reason. To *open up* in volleyball is to step away from the ball's path in receiving a serve. To open up can also mean to become more amenable and receptive to new ways of thinking about sexual interests, even if just sharing a sexual fantasy. A *quickslide* is a quick attack that includes a two-footed take-off and a broad jump along the net. Whereas a quickslide could also be when a man enjoys a woman-friend because he knows he can have a quickie.

Also in volleyball, a play that includes both a quick set and shoot set is a *quick shoot*. This could also be a hurried copulation with a quick release. *Ready position* is the flexed, yet comfortable posture a player assumes before moving to the point of contact. It could also be the readiness of a man or woman who is naked and ready for sex. A *three set* is a play set delivered low and fast, midway between the setter and the left sideline, to the spiker. It is designed to beat the middle blocker. A three set could also be a threesome in sexual play.

Sexual Commentary

Volleyball seems to have been a sport played more by women than men. Men may be dominant athletes in the world of sports, but there are several reasons why this game is played more by women. Some say it is because women are more flexible, they can quickly lower themselves closer to the ground when diving for a ball, whereas men tend not to dive, at least forward, due to not wanting their testicles to hit the floor with that kind of force. The other reason is that the average number of scholarships given for the sport in universities are simply not available to men as much as women. There is something about a bunch of women wanting to attack an opposing team by spiking a ball down hard on the opponent's side. Then to call a further attack a "kill" makes one wonder if these woman are simply taking their aggressions out on men in this game.

Part Four
Sticks and Balls

There are over twenty very popular sports played around the world using a stick and a ball. Some are similar to each other, such as hurling and camogie, and pool, carom and snooker. Other sports played outside the U.S. and British Isles include brännboll in Norway, longball in Denmark, and pesäpallo in Finland. Some are usually played only by children, like tee-ball and wiffle ball. All of them provide sports enthusiasts with great exercise and good entertainment. However, for this chapter, only fourteen of the most popular stick-and-ball sports will be explored.

The games I will discuss in this section are bandy, baseball, cricket, croquet, curling, golf, hurling (with camogie), ice hockey, lacrosse, polo, pool (with carom and snooker), quidditch, rounders, and shinty. All of these games are played in Australia, the U.S., or the U.K. This gives the reader the opportunity to learn about these games using terms understandable in English, and also to be surprised by many of the terms have a sexual meaning. Some of these sports may be new to the American reader, like bandy, camogie, and shinty, but I will describe them. One may also be surprised to see the sport of quidditch on the list. The reader may believe this is just a made-up game from the Harry Potter books, but it is more than that. The sport may have originated with the books, but it was so well-described and became so enticing to its readers that the sport took form in the real world.

Various kinds of sticks are used in these games. Some are fat and squat, some long and thin, others rounded and heavy, flat and wide, or have a foot or head on them. The balls are also different. Some are small and hard, others large and soft. They may be striped or a solid color, and made of wood or leather.

Chapter 22
Bandy

Bandy may not be familiar to sports lovers in the U.S, but it is the second-most popular winter sport in the world played on ice after ice hockey. Skaters use a long stick with a curved end to move a small red ball into the opponent's goal to score between goal posts and over a crossbar. There are eleven players per team and they play on an ice rink the size of a football field. The game is played in two halves of forty-five minutes each, with a halftime of fifteen minutes. The team that scores the most goals wins. There are variations of the game called rink bandy, seven-a-side bandy, bandy hockey, ball hockey, ice ball, and bandy ball. The English sport got its name from the British term "to bandy about," and from the French word *bander*, which means, "to strike back and forth." The stick is also called a "bandy."

The origins of the game are debated. Its earliest innovators are found not only in England but also in Holland and Russia. In 1882, the members of the Bury Fen Bandy Club in East Anglia, England, first published the rules of the game. In 1891, the first National Bandy Association began and the first international match was held. In the early 1900s, Sweden established its first national bandy league. A dozen years later, the game was played by eight countries competing for the first European championship. Now, the Federation of International Bandy (FIB) has twenty-seven countries as members.[162] Although the International Olympic Committee recognized bandy as a competitive sport in 2001, it has not been allowed into the Olympics as not enough countries are competing. That may change by 2022, as its popularity is still strong and growing.

There are eighteen official rules to the game that make it specifically the game of bandy. There are no specific player positions except a goalkeeper, but players may act as defenders and midfielders. Players normally use just their sticks to move the ball, but they can also use any part of their skates and legs. Only the goalkeeper can use the head, hands, or arms within their own penalty area. If a player uses his head, there is a penalty. Players can pass the ball to a teammate, take shots, or dribble it closer to the goal. The other team can intercept a pass or even tackle an opponent that has the ball. A game only stops when the ball leaves the field or if a referee calls for a stop; a referee can award a free stroke, a corner stroke, or a penalty shot.

There are certain field and uniform requirements. The field is 148 to 213 feet wide (45.11 m by 64.92 m) and 300 to 360 feet long (91.44 m by 109.73 m). A high border wall on both sides keeps the ball from leaving the field. At each field end is a 16 foot (4.88 m) half-circular penalty area and in the center is a goal cage. There are also two free-stroke areas along the front of this area. Teams must wear different colors to distinguish them from one another. Each player must wear bandy skates, a mouth guard and helmet, and padding to protect their elbows, genitals, knees, and throat. A goalkeeper will also wear a face guard.

---

[162] Federation of International Bandy, "Members." http://www.worldbandy.com/members.html

The stick and ball requirements are also set. The bandy stick is usually made of wood, without any metal or sharp parts. There is a handle at one end and at the other end of the stick is a curved or crooked foot which comes in five different angle variations, one through five, with five having the most angle. Which angle a player uses depends upon his height, hand positions, and the position he takes to play. The stick is about fifty inches long (127 cm) and just under 3 inches wide (7.62 cm). The center of the bandy ball is made of cork and is surrounded by rubber or a rubber-like plastic. The ball is just under 2½-inches wide (6.35 cm). It is painted orange or bright red.

Bandy Terms and Slang

Ball
Bandy: An orange or red tennis-size ball used in the game.

Sexual: A ball is a synonym for one testicle. "To ball" is a euphemism meaning to have intercourse.

Crossbar
Bundy: The bar that goes across the top of the goal and connects to the two goal posts.

Sexual: A furnishing that is used in BDSM play, where a person is attached to a horizontal bar.

Draw
Bundy: When a game ends and both teams are tied.

Sexual: To attract a person or be drawn by a person, usually with a romantic or sexual implication.

Dribbling
Bundy: A maneuver when a player moves a ball in a given direction avoiding interceptions with a bandy stick.

Sexual: The slow trickle of sperm, rather than a quick release. May also be a slight pre-release from excitation.

Duration

Bandy: The length of a game with two 45-minute halves.

Sexual: The length of time for a person to reach orgasm. On average, for a woman it is approximately twenty minutes, and for a man about five minutes or less.

Face off

Bandy: A method to begin or restart a play when two teams line up in opposition to each other and the opposing players attempt to gain control of the ball after it is placed between their sticks by an official.

Sexual: A fraternity game where two guys face each other with a loaf of bread between them. The object is to masturbate while maintaining eye contact and be the first one to ejaculate on to the bread or on the other guy. Or to masturbate while sitting and ejaculate upon one's own face, or masturbate while looking at one's partner on FaceTime or Skype.

FIB

Bandy: Abbreviation for Federation of International Bandy.

Sexual: An abbreviation for Fill in Boyfriend, which describes a situation when one's primary boyfriend is not enough and a secondary man fills in to supply the needs of a person.

Knockout competition

Bandy: When a game goes beyond a draw, and into a play of extra time of two 15-minute periods.

Sexual: A group of women who are all extremely good looking and sexy.

Stick

Bandy: This is the wooden rod that strikes the ball.
Sexual: A synonym for the penis.

Stroke in

Bandy: When one team plays the ball over the touchline, the opposing team is awarded a stroke back into the playing area.

Sexual: The action of intercourse whereby the penis makes its way into a partner.

Stroke off

Bandy: The action that starts each half and after a goal has been scored, which takes place at center ice when all players must remain on their half of the ice away from the ball until it is put back into play.

Sexual: The action of masturbation or intercourse where the last stroke produces an ejaculation, or a person "getting off" with an orgasm.

Winger

Bandy: A non-specific term for a forward, who is neither a center forward, nor a second striker, but a winger. Also, another term for a wing-back.

Sexual: Another word for a "wingman," a buddy who helps his friend get a woman for the night.

Other Bandy Terms with Sexual Possibilities

A *free stroke* is given out against a player who has been called for a foul or has broken the rules outside of the penalty area. A stroke, in sexual terms, refers to the action of placing the index finger and thumb around the penis along the shaft and moving the skin up and down to produce a pleasurable sensation leading to orgasm and ejaculation, known as a "hand job." A *free stroke* could mean that a guy receives a hand job for free. There is also the term *slap shot,* which is when a player places the bandy stick behind him and then swings the stick forward striking the ball, as in golf. A slap shot could also refer to an erect penis when receiving fellatio, involving the penis being slapped across the cheek just before the ejaculate shoots out upon the face.

Sexual Commentary

Okay, bandy doesn't have nearly the amount of sexy terms that kickball or volleyball have, but what it does have is a bent stick that comes in five different angles of crook, and a red ball. Now here is a game that takes into consideration the natural angle of a dangle and the natural color of two stimulated testicles. The sizes are slightly off with the bandy ball being a bit larger than the average testicle. An average testicle is 1.57 inches long, 1.2 inches wide, and .79 inches thick (4 cm by 3 cm by 2 cm). But a bandy ball is somewhat larger at 2.46 to 2.51 inches (62.40 mm to 63.80 mm). Close. A bigger set of "balls" (testes) are thought to indicate a larger penis size, but this is not necessarily true. There is not a hardline ratio of testes to penis size. The size of both varies from man to man. Then to score, by getting that red ball between the goal posts (the thighs) and into the goal net, called a cage (the vagina), ah, now that is a consummation.

Chapter 23
Baseball

Baseball is America's third most popular sport, surpassed only by basketball and football. It is a team sport using a bat and a ball. Two teams of nine players take turns batting and running and then pitching and fielding. Each team gets a chance to do both in an inning, and there are nine innings in a game. The field is a diamond within an open ninety-degree triangle with three infield bases, a pitcher's mound in the middle, a home base that has right and left-handed batter's boxes, and a catcher's box behind the batter's box. Outside of the triangle are foul lines and there is an outfield that can reach as far as 400 feet (121.92 m) beyond, to a fence.

The object of the game is to strike the ball with a bat from the home plate and hit it so far as to allow the player to advance to as many bases as possible without being tagged by the ball. Players advance to each base as a batter puts the ball in play, until they can return to home base and score a home run. The team with the most home runs wins. A neutral empire stands behind the catcher and calls the play.

Historian David Block says the game was based on the British games of rounders, stoolball, and tut-ball.[163]

---

[163] David Block, *Baseball Before We Knew It: A Search for the Roots of the Game,* (Lincoln, NE: Bison Books, 2005), 86-87.

The first mention of the game in writing was from a British book published in 1744, *A Little Pretty Pocket-Book* by John Newbery, which contained a poem describing the game. It included a woodcut depicting the field, although it was more in the shape of a triangle with posts instead of a diamond with bases.[164] Block found that the first recorded game was in 1749 in Surrey, England, then called "Bass-Ball."[165] In 1791, the game made its first appearance in America in Massachusetts, and within five years baseball was a popular sport.

Many early forms of bat and ball games were played throughout America in the early 1800s, some with detailed descriptions, though they were all different. In 1845, a member of the Knickerbocker Club, Alexander Cartwright of New York, was the first to write down the rules for the game, and since then has been known as the "Father of modern baseball."[166] Through the next decade, baseball developed into sixteen national clubs and a governing body called the National Association of Base Ball Players. In 1858, the game was so popular that it was seen as a potential commercial venture and an admission price to watch the game was first charged. A National League began in 1876, and although African Americans were barred from the game, several "black leagues" were formed as well.

Eight years later, although the rules had stipulated that balls should only be thrown underhand, pitching overhand was now allowed, and three years after that, a

---

[164] Ibid, 139-140.

[165] Nate Sulat, "Why Isn't Baseball More Popular in the U.K.?" BBC News Magazine (online), July 26, 2013. https://www.bbc.com/news/magazine-23425907

[166] Wikipedia, "Alexander Cartwright." https://en.wikipedia.org/wiki/Alexander_Cartwright

267

version was developed called soft ball for players of winter games. By 1901, the last of the rules was changed, counting foul balls as strikes. That same year, the American League was established. This created a rivalry with the other league, involving eight teams, and each fought for the best players. A national agreement was reached in 1903 to reconcile their differences, and consequently the first World Series was inaugurated.

That's not to say that everyone was happy, as players often challenged the team owners over contract discrepancies for income and control, and some went on strike, as with the Black Sox Scandal. Sensing an opening for other minority and immigrant groups, many saw their chance to gain acceptance into the American game. The Irish slugger Ed Delahanty, Babe Ruth of German ancestry, and later in 1945, the first African-American Jack Robinson, would each be accepted and each became exceptional ball players.

Through the 1920s new regulations came into effect. The pitched spitball was banned and the ball's composition, shape, and size were set. In 1936, Little League Baseball was founded, and when the Second World War took a lot of men away from the game, women formed their own teams in the All-American Girls Professional Baseball League. Through the 1950s, baseball had a trying time and saw some decline. Whether due to competition with football or national problems with racial integration, attendance went down and no major team had a home in the western states until 1958. Then, the Dodgers moved to Los Angeles and the Giants moved to San Francisco. The Negro National League was closed, and its players were signed to national teams. By 1962, both leagues had ten teams.

Things were changing in the game itself. By 1968 the height of the pitcher's mound was reduced from 15 inches to 10 inches (38.10 cm to 25.40 cm), the strike zone became smaller, and in 1972 the designated hitter rule was adopted, which meant that one man could take the place of the pitcher to be his batter. New teams were added and they were reorganized into two divisions. Unions forced the stopping of the games to protest more player rules, which cancelled the World Series in 1981 and again in 1994.[167]

By 1993, there were three divisions in the major leagues, and the average number of home runs increased, along with game attendance. In 2000, all supervision of players, regulations, and functions were taken over by the Major League Baseball (MLB) organization, overseeing the National and American Leagues, each with divisions in the West, East, and Central U.S. The organization's first major problem developed in 2002 when the use of performance-enhancing drugs was discovered, and many players were involved in a steroid abuse scandal. In the decade that followed, the average number of home runs decreased as the use of steroids was banned, and strikeouts increased as pitchers became more popular. In 1992, baseball was added to the Olympics, but by 2012 it was dropped due to lack of a following over much of the world. It was determined that it was better for the Major Leagues in the U.S. to have their own tournaments for their national teams, culminating in an annual championship called The World Series. A team wins the series by winning the best of

---

[167] Albert Theodore Powers, *The Business of Baseball*. Jefferson, (NC: McFarland Books. 2003), 184–187.

seven playoff games and is awarded the Commissioner's Trophy.[168]

The tools of the game are the bat, ball, and a glove or mitt. There is a standard helmet, cleat shoes, and a uniform which has different colors for each team. The glove has webbing between the fingers and is made of padded leather to protect the hand when catching the ball. The bat is made of solid wood in graduating width from a knobbed handle to 2.5 inches (6.35 cm) in diameter at the hitting end, and the bats are from 34 to 42 inches (86.36 cm to 106.68 cm) long. The ball is made with a cork or rubber center, surrounded by yarn, covered with white cowhide with red stitching, and is 9 inches (22.86 cm) in circumference.

Baseball Terms and Slang

Ace
Baseball: Usually the first and best pitcher on the team.
Sexual: A shortened word for an asexual person.

Airmail
Baseball: When a fielder's throw to the infield goes well over the intended receiver's head.
Sexual: A euphemism for when a man's pants zipper is down, either accidently or on purpose.

Alley
Baseball: Refers to the area where a line drive or ground ball goes into the field along a "power alley" or space to the right or left of the centerfielder.
Sexual: A shortened term for "shaft alley" referring to the area from the vaginal opening to the anus, originally

---

[168] Major League Baseball News, "World Series Trophy Profile." https://www.mlb.com/news/world-series-trophy-profile/c-155729034

a nautical term for the passage from the engine room to the stern.

Assist

Baseball: Something awarded to a defensive player when a ball is in play and touches him before the runner is put out, or another fielder committed an error.

Sexual: When one guy helps his buddy connect with a woman for sexual interest.

Bag

Baseball: Refers to one of the four bases (first, second, third and home) on the diamond, which were originally sandbags called pillows, but are now secured hard rubber shells.

Sexual: When a potential partner is dated with the intent to have intercourse, with success considered to be "in the bag."

Bang

Baseball: This could be the cancellation of a game due to bad weather, to hit a homer, an injured player that keeps playing, when a runner is out within only a second after the ball hit the catcher's glove, and when a pitcher throws the ball inside the plate.

Sexual: A euphemism for intercourse. To "bang" someone or get "banged."

Bases loaded

Baseball: When runners are on first, second, and third base, which means that if the batter hits well, it forces a run to home place, while he makes for first base.

Sexual: Implies that a man is expecting every sexual favor from an intended partner, including fellatio, vaginal (if a woman), and anal intercourse.

Bat (ter) or Bats

Baseball: The wooden stick used to hit the ball, the action of the bat hitting the ball, the person who bats the ball, and "bats" refers to a team with many good batters or hitters.

Sexual: An acronym for <u>B</u>ig <u>A</u>ss <u>T</u>its, meaning large breasts, and an Australian word for one who masturbates.

Batter's box

Baseball: The marked area on the inner field, to either side of the home plate, where a batter stands ready to swing.

Sexual: Refers to being prior to "first base" status, that is, not yet advancing sexually with a potential partner.

Battery

Baseball: The pitcher and catcher working effectively together by strategy and signal.

Sexual: Refers to "sexual battery," a crime in which an unwanted sexual attack has occurred for gratification or abuse.

Batting average

Baseball: The average number of actual hits of the ball per swing of the bat, per player.

Sexual: The average number of times a male has successfully had intercourse per sexual attempts.

Batting practice

Baseball: When a player practices his hitting technique.

Sexual: Refers to a man who uses a woman to practice his sexual approaches upon, to keep his pickup lines working and his ego supported.

Bazooka(s)

Baseball: A very strong throwing arm.

Sexual: Refers to a woman's breasts of great size.

BB

Baseball: Stands for "base on balls," which means it is a walk, or a strong and hard line drive hit, difficult to get to.

Sexual: An abbreviation for "bare back," seen in online forums and escort sites. It means the advertiser is willing to have intercourse without a condom.

Bench

Baseball: Where players sit in the dugout waiting to get to bat or onto the field.

Sexual: Describes how a woman sits on a man's lap facing him while they kiss or have intercourse. It is also a combination of the words bitch and wench in gang slang.

Bender

Baseball: This is a ball thrown in a curve.

Sexual: Synonym for a gay man, with the underlying implication that a man bends over to receive penile penetration.

Blow

Baseball: Can refer to losing a game, a pitch that the hitter cannot hit, to lose a lead, or to "blow-out a game" when a team wins by a large margin of runs.

Sexual: Short for "blow job," that is, fellatio.

Bomb(s)

Baseball: A home run.

Sexual: This can refer to enormous female breasts or when someone is extremely attractive and sexy. Also an acronym for Beat Off Memory Bank, meaning that the person they view gets placed into memory to masturbate to later. In the Caribbean, they "make bomb" or have intercourse, and when the orgasmic experience was exceptional.

Box

Baseball: The area around the pitcher's mound and the area where the batter stands when ready to hit the ball.

Sexual: A slang euphemism for the vagina.

Break

Baseball: A three-day period roughly halfway through the season giving players a break from the 162-game schedule. It also refers to the break down movement of a fastball.

Sexual: When a couple decides to spend some time separated from their sexual activities. Also, a term used by a prostitute, for collecting money from the first customer of the night, and to leave with a client.

Break one off

Baseball: To throw a curveball.

Sexual: A euphemism for male masturbation.

Bump

Baseball: Alternate term for the pitcher's mound.

Sexual: In striptease, a movement that thrusts the pelvis forward.

Bunt

Baseball: To deliberately bat the ball weakly to a particular spot on the infield by holding the bat nearly still and letting the ball bounce from it.

Sexual: A synonym for the buttocks.

Butcher

Baseball: A fielder in bad form.

Sexual: A hostile term for a man who perpetrates rough sexual intercourse. Also, "like a butcher's daughter," which is slang for a woman who is sexually active.

Cannon

Baseball: An arm that throws strongly.

Sexual: A synonym for the penis.

Cellar

Baseball: A team that always seems to be in last place.

Sexual: A metaphor from the 19th century, meaning the vagina.

Cement mixer

Baseball: An intended fast pitched ball that ends up being a slower ball with a sidespin.

Sexual: The rolling and rotating movement of the hips that a stripper makes while dancing, mimicking intercourse.

Chopper

Baseball: A batted ball that either strikes the dirt right in front of home plate or bounces in the infield.

Sexual: A synonym for the penis.

Chuck

Baseball: Another name for a throw by the pitcher.

Sexual: To have intercourse or to ejaculate, with both meanings coming from the 19th century.

Circle

Baseball: The marked circle on the field next to the batter's box where the next batter stands.

Sexual: A synonym for the vagina.

Clubhouse

Baseball: A team's locker room, which may offer facilities more than just lockers.

Sexual: A gay term for a public toilet used for casual sex.

Cockshot

Baseball: A belt-high fastball pitched down the middle of the plate.

Sexual: A rough unit of measurement, approximately equal to an average ejaculation, between ½ to 1 teaspoon (2 to 5 ml). Rate of frequency may affect amount; infrequency may produce more, and a higher frequency may produce less.

Collar

Baseball: To strike out or have a hitless game.

Sexual: A neck leash used in bondage and discipline that a submissive wears, behaving as a pet.

Cookie

Baseball: A pitch that is easy to hit.

Sexual: A synonym for the vagina.

Crank

Baseball: To hit a ball for extra bases, usually for a home run. Also, an older term for a spectator, which comes from the cranking of the turnstile through which they would enter to watch a game.

Sexual: A synonym for the penis, and a euphemism for male masturbation.

Cut

Baseball: A swing of a bat, or to be taken off the team.

Sexual: A circumcised penis, or to have intercourse. Also used as a euphemism for the vagina.

Dance

Baseball: The erratic movement of a thrown knuckleball.

Sexual: A euphemism for intercourse.

Dead ball

Baseball: What happens to the ball after a foul when a fan or player interferes or when an umpire interferes with a catcher, and when no runners may advance.

Sexual: After a serious injury to the scrotum has occurred, the spermatic cord that carries blood to one or both of the testicles may have been twisted, called testicular torsion. This can affect the blood flow to the tissues, which may turn the testicle numb, thought of as "dead." May occur with too rapid growth during puberty.

Double

Baseball: A hit, which takes the batter to second base.

Sexual: Refers to "double penetration," that is, when one man's penis enters vaginally and another man enters anally. It is also when one man is engaged in sex play with two women.

Double header

Baseball: Refers to when the same two teams play two games on the same day.

Sexual: Mutual oral sex at the same time or when the same two people engage in two sessions of intercourse in the same day.

Down

Baseball: Refers to an out in the game.

Sexual: Oral sex, either fellatio or cunnilingus. To "go down" on a person.

DP combo

Baseball: The executors of a double play are the shortstop and second baseman.

Sexual: Refers to "double penetration," that is, when one man penetrates a woman vaginally and another man does so anally.

Draw
Baseball: A batter who has drawn a walk.
Sexual: To attract a member of the opposite sex.

Drive
Baseball: A line drive of a ball down the center.
Sexual: A euphemism for sexual intercourse, or implied when a man asks if the woman wants to go for "a drive."

Drop
Baseball: To lose a game, or to cause another team to lose. Also, the weight of a bat relative to its length.
Sexual: A synonym for the buttocks.

Dump
Baseball: A hitter who uses a bunt instead of swinging.
Sexual: To end an intimate relationship with someone.

Duster
Baseball: A pitch delivered so close to the batter that he drops to the ground.
Sexual: A synonym for the buttocks.

Fisted
Baseball: When a batter swings at a pitch that is inside and the ball hits the bat close to his fists.
Sexual: The act of having a fist inserted into a vagina or anus.

FL
Baseball: An abbreviation for Federal League, which was a major league from 1914 to 1915.
Sexual: An abbreviation for "French Letter," an old term for condom, used by soldiers in the two world wars.

Flamethrower
Baseball: A pitcher who throws a high-velocity fastball, called a fireball, in excess of 95 miles (152.89 km) per hour.
Sexual: A bouncer in a gay bar.

Floater
Baseball: A knuckleball that appears to float or bob on its way to the batter's plate.
Sexual: An occasional short-term gay sexual partner.

Force play
Baseball: When a batter hits a ball and runs to first base, forcing any player on first to go to second base.
Sexual: A forced marriage when the woman becomes pregnant. Used in the BDSM community for play by a dominant who does what they like without asking the submissive's permission.

Free pass
Baseball: When a batter gets thrown four bad pitches, and the umpire calls balls on all of them. Then the batter is allowed to walk to first base without hitting the ball.
Sexual: When a sexual partner is given permission to have a sexual experience outside of the primary relationship without any consequences.

Gap
Baseball: The space between fielders where a ball might go, and if the ball goes there it is called a "gapper."
Sexual: The space between a woman's legs below the pubis, present on a slender woman and considered sexy. It is also a synonym for the vagina.

Glove

Baseball: A large padded leather covering for the hand and worn by most players in the field to catch balls. There are also batting gloves, sliding gloves, and a catcher's "mitt."

Sexual: A synonym for condom.

Go deep

Baseball: To hit a home run.

Sexual: When a penis deeply penetrates.

Grand slam

Baseball: When all the bases are loaded and the batter hits a home run.

Sexual: Refers to intercourse while maintaining penetration in a continuous set of positions. When a man attains sexual reward with oral, vaginal, and anal sex with one woman. Also, having had intercourse with three different women in a short period of time.

Green light

Baseball: What a manager indicates to his batter or runner, with permission to be aggressive.

Sexual: Refers to a non-verbal cue from a person to a potential lover, indicating that they are willing.

Ground ball

Baseball: A batted ball that bounces into the infield. Also known as a "grounder."

Sexual: Refers to an inebriated woman in a bar who appears easy to pick up and have intercourse with.

Ground rule double

Baseball: A condition under which a batter hits a fair ball that no fielder is able to retrieve. The batter is awarded the ability to advance to second base.

Sexual: Refers to when a person touches another person's body in a sexual way with one of their own body parts. A hand on a breast, breasts against a body, hand on a pubis, or a grind against another while dancing.

Gun
Baseball: A strong pitching arm.

Sexual: A synonym for the penis.

Hammer
Baseball: When a batter hits a ball hard. It can also refer to a pitcher's curve ball.

Sexual: A synonym for the penis, and also refers to vigorous intercourse.

Handcuff
Baseball: This can be a ground ball that bounces too close for a fielder to catch, or a pitch thrown so close to the batter's hands that he cannot swing at the ball.

Sexual: When one takes strong actions to shield their object of affection from the advances of others.

Handle
Baseball: Refers to a fielder who cannot keep hold of the ball, that is, the ball lacked a metaphorical handle to grab on to.

Sexual: To take hold of and fondle a penis.

Hat trick
Baseball: This can refer to a player who has hit three home runs in a game, or to someone who has struck out three times.

Sexual: Penetrating a female partner vaginally, anally, and orally within one session.

Headhunter
Baseball: Refers to a pitcher who intentionally throws a ball that threatens to hit the batter, particularly his head.

Sexual: Refers to a person who seeks to perform oral sex with another.

Heavy hitter

Baseball: A powerful batter who hits a lot of home runs and has a high slugging percentage.

Sexual: A person who relentlessly tries to seduce another.

High hard one

Baseball: A ball thrown fast and high above the strike zone.

Sexual: A sexual euphemism for an erect hard penis.

Hit

Baseball: The act of the bat coming into contact with the ball, and the result of it, with the batter making it to a base.

Sexual: To deliver a "pick up" line to a prospective lover. To have intercourse. An acronym for "Hoes in Training" (meaning whores), and for "Homosexual in Training." Also, a young woman dressed up to look older with the intention of getting the attention of an older man for sex.

Hit and run

Baseball: When a base runner starts running to the next base forcing the next batter to swing and hit the ball to right field.

Sexual: When a man seduces a woman only for sex, and then disappears without giving a real name or contact information.

Hole

Baseball: One of the nine places in a batting lineup.

Sexual: A derogatory synonym for an anus or a vagina.

Home

Baseball: When a runner reaches home plate safely.

Sexual: A euphemism for the vagina.

Home Cooking

Baseball: When the official gives a favorable call to the player, or it is a home field advantage where the team plays in its own stadium or town.

Sexual: The sex a person gets from their wife or husband, or live-in partner.

Home plate

Baseball: The fourth base.

Sexual: A euphemism for intercourse.

Home run

Baseball: A strong base hit that allows the batter to run all the bases and come into home for a score.

Sexual: Denotes the process of sexual activity, from kissing and touching, to oral sex, ending in sexual intercourse and orgasm.

Home run derby

Baseball: A competition where batters attempt to hit the most home runs.

Sexual: An orgy, or when many people are having intercourse at the same time.

Hook

Baseball: Refers to the action of the manager who replaces a pitcher. Also, when a pitcher is "on the hook" for leaving the pitcher's mound when his team is behind in scoring, and refers to a curveball.

Sexual: A person who "hooks up" with a partner in sex. It is also short for what a hooker or a prostitute does to get a client.

Hopper

Baseball: A batted ball that bounces in the infield.

Sexual: Refers to a "bed-hopper," that is, a person who goes from one partner's bed to another.

Hose

Baseball: Refers to an outfielder's strong arm for catching a ball, and in turn, throwing it to an infielder to have that batter out, and refers to that player as "being hosed."

Sexual: A synonym for the penis and a slang term used by men, meaning to have intercourse. It is also a gay term, which means that the dominant partner will direct the anal copulation, and a "hose-monster" implies a promiscuous person.

Hot

Baseball: A batter or a team that is on a winning streak.

Sexual: A word used to describe a sexually exciting person.

Hot box

Baseball: The area between two fielders during a rundown.

Sexual: A euphemism for the vagina, or a promiscuous woman.

Jack

Baseball: To hit a homerun.

Sexual: From "jack-off," meaning to masturbate and ejaculate.

Jam

Baseball: A pitched ball that is too close to the batter. A pitcher can be in a jam when good hitters are up next. When the bases are "jammed," they are full with men waiting to run, which is also referred to as a "jam sandwich."

Sexual: To have sexual intercourse, or refers to the ejaculate. A "jam pot" is British slang for the vagina. A "lawful jam" is a wife, and a "jam tart" is a mistress or prostitute. It is also an acronym for Just <u>a</u> <u>M</u>an, meaning a heterosexual male.

Jelly legs

Baseball: What happens to a batter's legs when a curveball hits the bat, traveling on a devastating arc that causes him and his bat to waver before he can move to run.

Sexual: A partner who has had so much intercourse while standing that their legs go weak.

Jerk

Baseball: A hard hit ball that goes over the fence, which results in a home run.

Sexual: A euphemism for masturbation.

Jump

Baseball: Used to express the action of when a fielder quickly catches the ball, or when a base runner leaves a base before the pitch reaches the plate.

Sexual: A figurative metaphor, to "jump her (or his) bones," meaning to engage in sexual intercourse with someone.

Junk

Baseball: A pitch that is difficult to hit due to its movement rather than its speed.

Sexual: A euphemism for the male genital organs.

Knock

Baseball: A hard hit of the ball, and a two-base hit. When a pitcher gets removed from the game he is said to have been "knocked around." Also, an infielder who stops a line drive, a "knock down" of the ball, and a "knock off" is to win the game.

Sexual: A synonym for a playgirl, to have sexual intercourse, and to "knock up" is to cause a female partner to become pregnant.

Lace

Baseball: Another description for a very hard-hit line ball.

Sexual: A gay term that refers to the foreskin of the penis.

Lay down

Baseball: A batter who bunts a ball.

Sexual: A euphemism for intercourse.

Leather

Baseball: Refers to a fielder's glove, and a good defensive player.

Sexual: Refers to male genitalia, a half-hard penis, and used in sadomasochism, as one who wears leather to imply that interest.

Lineup

Baseball: The description that announces the batting order and their defensive position.

Sexual: Common in a brothel where prostitutes are lined up for men to choose from.

Lollipop

Baseball: A soft and straight pitch without an arc.

Sexual: A synonym for the penis, and for a frigid woman.

Masher

Baseball: A player who hits a home run.

Sexual: A man with dishonorable sexual intentions, a womanizer, a persistent flirter, one who either makes unwanted advances or rubs up against a woman in a public place.

Meat

Baseball: A rookie player, an easy out usually with a strikeout, a base runner who is out at a base, and a pitcher or fielder's throwing hand.

Sexual: A euphemism for the penis or the vagina.

Meatball

Baseball: An easy pitch down the middle of the plate.

Sexual: Refers to a prostitute's customer, and can refer to an over-weight woman with large breasts and buttocks.

Mitt

Baseball: A baseball glove worn by the catcher or the first base man.

Sexual: A euphemism for a woman's mons pubis and vagina.

Moon shot

Baseball: A very high-hit ball that makes a home run.

Sexual: A euphemism for anal intercourse, or to drop one's pants and expose their buttocks as a jest or insult.

Mound

Baseball: The raised section in the middle of the baseball diamond where the pitcher stands when throwing the pitch.

Sexual: The mons pubis, or soft cushion of fatty tissue found over the pubic bone on a female.

Muff

Baseball: To make an error on an easy play.

Sexual: A synonym for the vagina. Also, it is an acronym, Mandatory Unattractive Female Friend, meaning the one unattractive woman in a group of women.

Nail (ed)

Baseball: This is a hit to a pitch, the last play of a winning game, and a throw that gets a runner out.

Sexual: A euphemism for intercourse.

Nibble

Baseball: Refers to when a pitcher throws to the right or left edge of home plate.

Sexual: To make tiny bites tenderly and repeatedly, usually on a person's neck, with the intention of exciting them.

Nightcap

Baseball: The second game of a doubleheader.

Sexual: A euphemism often used when asking if a partner would care for some intercourse to top the evening off.

Pearl(s)

Baseball: Another name for a baseball.

Sexual: A synonym for the clitoris. It is also an ejaculation from fellatio that leaves drops in a curved line upon a body, ideally below the woman's neckline, as a pearl necklace.

Peg(s)

Baseball: To throw the ball to one of the base players.

Sexual: A strap-on dildo a woman uses to penetrate another during intercourse. It is also an acronym for Post Ejaculatory Guilt Syndrome, which may occur after a sexual encounter, whereby the person experiences feelings of self-reproach or guilt.

Pill

Baseball: A synonym for the baseball.

Sexual: A short word for the birth control pill.

Pimping

Baseball: Acting ostentatiously or showboating to gain the attention or approval of fans.

Sexual: A person, especially a man, who solicits customers for a prostitute or outside a brothel, usually in return for a share of the earnings. To pander, a procurer of sexual partners.

Pitcher

Baseball: The fielder who is responsible for pitching the ball.

Sexual: The dominate top in a sexual relationship, or a man who anally penetrates another male.

Play

Baseball: Any particular sequence of events during a game.

Sexual: Anything sexual for enjoyment and entertainment.

Poke

Baseball: Refers to an extra base hit or home run.

Sexual: A synonym for intercourse.

Pull

Baseball: To substitute a pitcher or hitter for another, or the ability for a hitter to bat the ball to one side of the field.

Sexual: The ability to draw a potential sexual partner by seduction, touching, or kissing. An Australian slang term, "on the pull," meaning that a man is all dressed up and out looking for a sexual partner.

Rainbow

Baseball: A pitched curveball with a high arc in its path to the plate.

Sexual: Refers to a symbol used by the LGBTQ+ community to acknowledge acceptance among its members. It also refers to the ring of lipstick left on a penis after fellatio, and it is a simile for male ejaculation in an arc, "like a rainbow."

Rake
Baseball: To hit the ball very hard.

Sexual: A late seventeenth century word for a man who had immoral character and conduct, particularly toward women.

Receiver
Baseball: Another term for a catcher.

Sexual: A submissive who is being sexually dominated by a "pitcher," either orally, vaginally, or anally.

Relief pitcher
Baseball: A substitute pitcher brought into the game.

Sexual: Refers to a dildo or vibrator used in place of a penis.

Rookie
Baseball: A player in their first year of play, having fewer than 130 bats for hitters and fewer than 50 innings for pitchers.

Sexual: A semi-hard penile erection.

Rope
Baseball: A hard line drive of a batted ball.

Sexual: A long trail of ejaculate on a partner's body. Also, a binding tie used on a person in bondage to restrict some or all movement.

Roster
Baseball: The official list of players eligible to play a game.

Sexual: A list of potential partners for sex.

Rubber
Baseball: The white rubber strip of the pitching plate.

Sexual: A synonym for a condom.

Sack

Baseball: Synonymous with bag, or 1st, 2nd, or 3rd base. It is also a player who plays a particular base, a "sacker." Most often this is the second sacker (second baseman). Together, the second sacker and the short-stop may be referred to as "sack-mates," because they often share the play at second base.

Sexual: A synonym for the male scrotum.

Salad

Baseball: An easily handled pitch.

Sexual: The expression a male uses about a woman in question, that she may be worth at least experiencing as an appetizer to determine whether to have sexual intercourse with her. Also, a euphemism for "rimming" the anus, and to engage in intercourse (see Tossed, below).

Salami

Baseball: A grand slam home run.

Sexual: A synonym for the penis.

Seed

Baseball: A batted ball hit so hard it flies straight without an arc, or any thrown ball that looks the same way.

Sexual: A synonym for sperm.

Set the table

Baseball: To get runners on base ahead of the power hitters in the lineup.

Sexual: When a man displays his genitals or a woman exposes herself on a dining table.

Shift

Baseball: When all infielders and/or outfielders position themselves clockwise or counterclockwise from their usual position.

Sexual: An Irish term for deep kissing.

Shortstop

Baseball: A fielder positioned in the infield between second and third base, or the position itself.

Sexual: Fellatio that is not completed.

Sinker(s)

Baseball: Usually, a pitched fastball that breaks sharply downward as it crosses the plate.

Sexual: Refers to breasts or testicles that hang low.

Slide

Baseball: When a player drops to the ground when running toward a base to avoid being tagged out.

Sexual: A woman used for intercourse with no obligations.

Slump

Baseball: An extended period when a player or team is not performing well or up to expectations.

Sexual: An extended period of time when a person goes without sex.

Spank

Baseball: To hit a line drive of the ball to the opposite field. Also, to win a game in a decisive manner.

Sexual: The action of consenting adults, whacking a partner on the buttocks, back, and thighs. May also refer to "spank the monkey," meaning male masturbation.

Spitter

Baseball: A spitball pitch in which the ball has been altered by the application of spit, petroleum jelly, or some other substance.

Sexual: One who does not swallow ejaculate after fellatio.

Squeeze play

Baseball: A tactic used to attempt to score a runner from third on a bunt.

Sexual: The action of a woman who uses her kegel muscles to exert a strong squeeze on a penis during intercourse.

Staff

Baseball: The eleven or twelve pitchers on the team's roster.

Sexual: A synonym for the penis.

Stuff

Baseball: An overall evaluation of how effective a pitcher is.

Sexual: A word used to stand in for anything sexual.

Sweet spot

Baseball: The perfect place where the bat hits the ball, which is 6.7 inches (17 cm) from the end of the barrel.

Sexual: A place on the body that pleasurably responds to a touch or caress, referring to either a woman's clitoris or G-spot.

Swing man

Baseball: A pitcher who can function as a starting pitcher or a long reliever.

Sexual: A gay or bisexual wingman who lulls women into thinking he and his buddy are gay and therefore safe, but then he steers a woman to his straight friend.

Switch hitter

Baseball: A player that can bat equally well with either their right or left-hand and arm.

Sexual: A bisexual person, or one who can easily switch from being a top to a bottom and vice-versa.

Tap

Baseball: To hit a slow ground ball toward the pitcher.

Sexual: A euphemism for having intercourse. An abbreviation for <u>T</u>its, <u>A</u>ss, <u>P</u>ussy. Also, to playfully pat a penis into hardness with a hand or an implement.

Tossed

Baseball: When a player or manager is ordered by an umpire to leave a game.

Sexual: This refers to salad (see above), as in a "tossed salad," meaning the action of a lover who "rims" the anus with their tongue.

Triple crown

Baseball: This refers to a batter who leads the league in three categories, home runs, runs batted in, and batting average; and for a pitcher with an earned run average, wins, and strikeouts.

Sexual: When a man has achieved in one night the goal of having oral, vaginal, and anal sex. It also refers to a man having orgasmed thrice in one day with three different women.

Triple play

Baseball: When three outs are made in one play.

Sexual: When in one night a man achieves fellatio, vaginal, and anal penetration with a woman.

Up (and in)

Baseball: When a batter comes "up" to the plate and stands "in" the batter's box, when a team is in the lead by runs, when a batter pops a ball upward, when a pitcher got a pitch up and the ball went sailing in the air, when a player is called up from the minors to the majors, or when an umpire calls for the next batter by saying, "batter up!"

Sexual: When a penis is erect and hard, and describes sexual penetration.

Vulture

Baseball: A reliever who records wins in late innings by being the pitcher of record in the midst of a comeback.

Sexual: A guy who preys on a woman because she is emotionally or physically vulnerable.

Wheels

Baseball: Describes a runner's fast legs.

Sexual: It also describes a man's ability to speak with and seduce women.

Window shopping

Baseball: Caught looking for strike three.

Sexual: Being in a relationship, but still looking, and even flirting with another but without any follow-up.

Wood

Baseball: A baseball bat.

Sexual: A synonym for an erect penis.

Other Baseball Terms with Sexual Possibilities

There is a baseball phrase called *around the horn*, which means that the infielders throw the ball to each other around the bases after recording an out, provided that there are no runners on base. This isn't a sexual slang phrase but it should be. A horn is a synonym for the penis, so it seems obvious that to go around the horn is when either a person wraps their lips around a penis, or when a woman sits upon a man's penis, encircling it. Another term, *ate him up*, goes without question as a sexual phrase that could only mean one thing. But in baseball, it is an expression of the action of a batted ball that is difficult for a fielder to handle. Whereas sexually, this would more than suggest an act of fellatio.

A *bush league* in baseball means a minor league or an unprofessional team located in a small town that is "in the sticks or the bushes." Back in the early 1970s and up to 2000, a "bush," describing a woman's pubic hair, was left natural and unshaved. It only stands to reason that a bush league would be a group of such women. *Charging the mound* refers to a batter assaulting the pitcher after being hit by a pitch. But it could also be interpreted to mean something else. A mound is a reference to the outer fleshy part of a woman's mons pubis, so the entire term of charging the mound could be interpreted as a manner of approaching a woman for intercourse. Also, there are the baseball terms *cut the ball off,* and *find a hole.* Despite the rather drastic meaning of the first, the second seems to obviously refer to a person seeking a sexual orifice. *Flashing the leather* is making an outstanding or difficult defensive play in baseball, but anyone who enters a club wearing leather is letting others know that they are into the leather scene.

Get good wood means to hit a ball hard with the bat, but since wood is a synonym for a penis, it could easily be a good hard penis. *Got a piece of it* is when a batter hits a foul ball or foul tip but still remains at the bat. But getting a piece of it could also mean getting laid, since "getting a piece of ass" is an obvious reference to intercourse, either vaginal or anal. An *intentional pass* is the same as an intentional walk, given by the pitcher throwing four straight balls well outside the strike zone. But the term could equally mean someone who makes a pass at another person with the intention of being with that person sexually. *In the hole* is another term, which in baseball means the spaces between the first baseman and the second baseman and between the shortstop and the third baseman, the usual places where a ground ball will go for a hit. "Hole" is slang for the vagina as well as the anus, so this idiom could also mean to enter a person sexually.

A *large sausage* in baseball is a term for a grand slam home run, but in sexual nomenclature, it refers to an extra-large penis. A *power stroke* is a hitter with a good strong hit of the ball for extra bases, but it could also be a man having good strong action during intercourse. A *squeeze play* is a tactic used to attempt to score a runner from third on a bunt. On the other hand, a squeeze play is what female kegel muscles can do to a penis. *Struck out swinging* in baseball is when a batter is called out on strikes, though the term could also easily mean that a couple did not have any luck finding another couple at a swing party. *Throwing seeds* is when a pitcher's fastball is so good it seems as though the baseball is the size of a seed and therefore hard to hit, but sexually speaking, throwing seeds could equally mean to ejaculate sperm. *Tie him up* is getting a pitch in on the hitter's hands, making it impossible for him to swing. It could also mean the action of a dominant, actually tying up a submissive for rope play. An *unassisted play* in baseball is when a fielder single-handedly completes an out that is more often completed by multiple fielders. An unassisted play could also denote a man who makes a play for a woman and does not require a wingman to help him. *Went deep* is to run a home run, but it might also mean a deep penetrating thrust of the penis during intercourse.

Sexual Commentary

This sport, in particular, has more sexual synonyms, euphemisms, and metaphors attached to it than any other sport. A lover gaining momentum with something more sexual at every "base" has a built-in confirmation of attaining most of the stages of intimacy. The baseball field represents the female body with a step-by-step process for achieving intercourse. Surprisingly, these metaphors have been put to use in middle school sex education classes, providing a vehicle for instruction in a progressive process of sexual achievement.

Even the bat, being long and extending out with a wider head, is an obvious metaphor for the penis. *Batting 1000* means that every time a batter has stepped up to the plate, there is a hit. One might even consider the baseball term *covering one's base,* when a player actually covers a base to keep a runner from safely reaching it, could also be understood as a man protecting "his" lover from another man. Even the saying, to *knock the cover off the ball,* could be interpreted as having such sexual abandon as to throw the covers off the bed. To "play ball" takes on a whole new meaning, either playing with a scrotum or engaging in intercourse. There is a soft ball, hard ball, beanball, curveball and a ground ball, all of which constitute a description of what testicles might be like. And of course, a screwball, which is an erratic and crazy pitch, may be the craziest term of all, as it contains two words joined that mean the same thing in sexual slang, a ball *and* a screw.

All told, with the entire game having so many sexual meanings, it's no wonder it is the second most popular sport in America.

Chapter 24
Billiards

Billiards is a generic term for sports played with a cue stick and balls. There are three major subdivisions: carom billiards, pool, and snooker. Carom billiards is played on a table without pockets, and other carom games include balkline, straight rail, cushion carom, three-cushion billiards, artistic billiards, and four-ball. Pool is played on a table with pockets. Pool games include one-pocket, eight-ball, nine-ball, ten-ball, straight pool, and bank pool. Snooker and English billiards are played on a snooker table, also with pockets. This chapter will give an overview of all these games and include terms from them.

The word billiards comes from a combination of the French words for stick, *billart* or *billette,* and ball, *bille.* The first cue stick was wooden with a rubber tail called a mace (similar to a golf club), and the French word for tail is *queue.* The original game of billiards was thought to have been played outdoors on a lawn and was called ground billiards, and then the game moved indoors.[169] When acceptance of the game increased, the nobility began to play and make it popular. When King Louis XI

---

[169] Victor Stein and Paul Rubino, *The Billiard Encyclopedia: An Illustrated History of the Sport* (2nd ed.), (La Jolla, CA: Blue Book Publications, 1996).

of France came to the throne in 1461, he was the first to have a billiard table in his palace.[170] By the mid-1700s billiards was a common game found in cafés all over Paris, and had spread to England.

The balls were originally pushed by a mace stick, but by 1770 players found that they could score better if they turned the mace around and used the narrower end of the stick, now called a cue, to strike at the ball. Edmond Hoyle wrote about billiards in his book on games, which was revised many times after his death in 1769.[171] According to E. White's 1807 book, *A Practical Treatise on the Game of Billiards*, it was more common to use the narrow cue, than the tail of the mace.[172] Since the balls were getting hit harder, cushions were added to the inside edge of the table so the balls could rebound better.

The early games of carom or carambola billiards were played with three or four balls. The cue stick was used to strike a cue ball that then rebounded off a side cushion to strike an object ball. There were no pockets on the overly long table, and there were no hoops or obstacles, although the hoop eventually became the pockets in pool. Billiards became known as a sport beginning in 1893, when international competitions began.

---

[170] Clive Everton, *The History of Snooker and Billiard*, (Haywards Heath, U.K.: Partridge Press, 1986), 8–11.

[171] Edmond Hoyle and Thomas Frere, *Hoyle's Games: Illustrated Edition. Embracing All the Most Modern Modes of Play, And the Rules Practised at The Present Time, In Billiards, Whist, Draughts, Cribbage, Backgammon, And All Other Fashionable Games*, (London: Andesite Press, [original print: 1779]. Reprint, 2017.

[172] E. B. White, *A Practical Treatise on the Game of Billiard*, (London: Carter Adams [Original print, 1807]. Reprint - London: The British Library, 2007), 1-8.

Carom billiards is played with three balls, two cue balls, and one object ball, on a billiard table with no pockets. In straight rail billiards, the goal is to contact as many balls as possible with the cue ball. In balkline, the cue ball must drive each object ball past a line that runs parallel to the end of the table called the balkline, after each couple of points. In three-cushion billiards, the player's cue must bounce off three rail cushions before contacting the other two balls.

Pool has several games with different goals. There are six pockets around the green pool table, one in each corner and one in the middle of each long side of the table. Eight-ball is played with a cue ball, cue stick, and fifteen balls, of which seven are solidly-colored, seven are striped, and one, called the 8-ball, is black. The goal is to pocket either all of the solids or all of the stripes and then the 8-ball last, because then it is the eighth ball to go in a pocket. In nine-ball, at each turn the cue ball must hit the lowest-numbered object ball left on the table, and then the 9-ball. The goal in straight pool is to call any ball into a called pocket, with the last object ball not pocketed but left on the table for the opponent to re-rack with the remaining balls.

Snooker is also played on a green cloth table with six pockets, a cue, and twenty-two colored balls. The first eight balls are solid colors, with the eighth ball black, and balls nine through fifteen striped, with the last ball unnumbered and white. The goal is to strike the white cue ball and then pocket the balls in the correct numbered sequence. Each game is called a frame and several frames are a match.

English billiards, also just called "billiards" in the U.K., has two cue balls, one white, and an object ball for the first player. The second player uses a white ball with a spot or a yellow ball, a cue ball, and the red object ball.

Opponents use either the white or the yellow cue balls. The goal is to pocket as many balls in a frame. Points can be gained by striking the cue ball so it hits the other cue ball and the red ball for two points, called a cannon. A winning hazard gains two points for having their cue ball strike the opponent's cue ball into a pocket, or by striking the red object ball so that the red is pocketed for three points. A losing hazard for two points is having the other cue ball hit first, or if the red and cue ball are hit at the same time. For three points with a losing hazard, one must hit the red ball first.

Now for the equipment used in the game: the tables and cloth, the balls, cues and chalk, the rack and mechanical bridge.

The table sizes differ, but most pool tables have a 2:1 length to width ratio. Pubs usually have 7-foot (2.13 m) tables, homeowners generally choose 8-foot (2.44 m) tables, the standard pool hall table is 9 feet (2.74 m), the normal carom billiard table is 10 feet (3.05 m), and snooker and English billiard tables can be up to 12 feet (3.66 m) long. The base of all tables is slate; one piece for the smaller tables and up to three pieces for the largest tables. All tables are covered in a felt-like cloth of woven wool, or a blend of wool and nylon called *baize*. The quality of the cloth is designated slower or faster, depending upon the friction of the ball upon the material, and whether the ball runs with or against the nap of the material. Most are a green color in remembrance of the green lawns the game was originally played on, but the cloth can also be seen in blue or red.

Billiard balls differ depending upon when the balls were made and the country in which the different games are played. Balls were first made of clay and wood. Other balls have been made of plastic or steel, an early plastic called Bakelite, the first thermoplastic called celluloid, and the compressed grains of microscopic crystals called crystallite. The early and wealthy players, however, preferred to have theirs made of ivory.

There are different-sized balls for different games. In the billiard games of *kaisa* (Finnish) and Russian pyramid, the balls are 2 11/16 inches (6.83 cm) in diameter. Kaisa is played with two white cue balls, two red object balls, and one yellow ball. In Russian pyramid there is one cue ball of red and fifteen more numbered white balls. Carom Billiard balls are 2 7/16 inches (6.19 cm) in diameter. American pool balls are 2¼ inches (5.72 cm) in diameter with seven striped and seven solid, a black eight-ball, and white cue ball. British-style pool balls are 2 3/16 inches (5.56 cm) and come as unmarked yellow and blue or red balls. Snooker balls are smaller at 2 1/16 inches (5.24 cm) in diameter. English billiard balls are the same size. There are three balls with two cue balls, and a red object ball. There are also smaller 2-inch (5.08 cm) balls for children.

Cue sticks are made of wood and are 57 to 59 inches (144.78 cm to 149.86 cm) in length. Cheap ones are made of pine with plastic tips. Better-quality cues for billiards are made of maple, and ash for snooker. Cues are usually one piece, although two-piece sticks may be made to divide in half for travel. The larger end for gripping is called the butt. The shaft tapers to a point where a fiberglass or brass ferrule is attached, and a rounded leather tip is fitted at the end. Some cues are made from expensive woods and graphite. To avoid the tip from slipping when it hits the ball, chalk is applied to the tip before each play. It is not the usual calcium carbonate of straight chalk, but made from crushed silica and corundum or aluminum oxide with a green or blue dye. Chalk allows a good player to apply a side spin or curl to the ball.

Two more tools of the trade are used and they are the rack and the mechanical bridge. The rack is simply the wooden, plastic, or aluminum frame which holds the balls in numbered order, in place, at the beginning of a game. It can be triangular, as for eight-ball and straight pool, or diamond-shaped for nine-ball. When set, the rack is removed in preparation for the break shot with the cue. The bridge, also called the rake, crutch, bridge stick, or rest, is used to extend a player's reach. It is a stick with a plastic or metal groove at the end where the cue can rest and then slide on to make a shot. There are different types of bridges which all perform the same function but look slightly different: the cross, spider, giraffe, or swan.

Billiards Terms and Slang

Bank shot
Billiards: With pocket games, this is a shot where the object ball is driven to one or more cushions before it goes into a pocket.

Sexual: When a man ejaculates during oral sex into their partner's mouth and it banks down the throat.

Billiards
Billiards: In carom games, a successful play, count or score.

Sexual: A synonym for the testes.

Butt
Billiards: The handle at the larger end of the cue stick.

Sexual: A shortened word for the buttocks of a person.

Crotch
Billiards: The corner area of a carom table in straight-rail billiards, where a player can score up to three counts before getting one object ball out of the area. The four crotches are those spaces within the crotch lines between

the first diamond on the end rail to the second on the side rail.

Sexual: Refers to the groin area of a person.

Crutch

Billiards: Another name for the mechanical bridge.

Sexual: A person who uses a friend of the opposite sex for comfort, when their significant other is not there.

D, the

Billiards: On a snooker table, it is the half-circle having an 11½ inch (29.21 cm) radius with its straight side against the baulk line, which is 16 to 31 inches (40.64 cm to 78.74 cm) from the end of the table, determined by the size of the table.

Sexual: Short for "dick," referring to a man's penis.

Dead ball

Billiards: In pocket games, when a cue ball is stroked in such a manner that most or all of the speed or spin of the cue ball is transferred to the object ball.

Sexual: After a serious injury to the scrotum has occurred, the spermatic cord that carries blood to one or both of the testicles may have been twisted, called testicular torsion. This can affect the blood flow to the tissues, which will turn the testicle numb and may be referred to as "dead." This can also occur with too rapid growth during puberty.

Free ball

Billiards: After a foul, if the cue ball is snookered, the referee will call "Free Ball."

Sexual: When a man goes without wearing underwear under his pants, so that his scrotum may move freely.

Game

Billiards: The course of play that begins when the referee has finished racking the balls and ends at the conclusion of a legal shot, which pockets the last required ball.

Sexual: The pursuit of a sexual partner, which includes pickup lines, the skill of the pursuer, and the sex drive of both people.

Hicky

Billiards: Any foul that occurs in snooker golf.

Sexual: The result of someone sucking on the skin of another, usually on the neck during sexual activity, which leaves a red mark.

Hold

Billiards: To stop a cue ball from continuing its rolling course after being driven in a certain direction.

Sexual: Refers to holding on to a person, figuratively and physically.

Jaw

Billiards: The slanted cushion in pocket games, cut at an angle to form the opening of the bed of the table into the pocket.

Sexual: A euphemism for fellatio.

Jawed ball

Billiards: Generally refers to a ball that fails to drop because it bounces back and forth against the jaws of a pocket.

Sexual: To jaw is a euphemism for fellatio, and this slang term is also the taking of a testicle into the mouth.

Kiss

Billiards: The contact between balls.

Sexual: The pressing of lips with another person or anywhere else upon the body in greeting, reverence, sexual desire, or as a sign of affection or love to a pet, or any object.

Natural

Billiards: In carom games, it is a simple and easily visualized shot with a natural angle and stroke that results in a successful execution and score.

Sexual: Refers to a woman's breasts that have not been augmented with implants, unshaved public and underarm hair, and going naked.

Pills

Billiards: Small plastic or wooden balls numbered one through fifteen or sixteen in pocket games.

Sexual: A short word for birth control pills.

Plant

Billiards: A position of two or more red balls that allows a ball to be driven into a pocket with a combination shot in snooker.

Sexual: A man or woman who has no sexual ambitions, but accompanies one who does, to a public place. They are present more as a decoy. This person may also be asexual and only present to enjoy the company of others, but only in a social sense.

Position

Billiards: The placement of the cue ball on each shot, relative to the next planned shot. Also called a shape.

Sexual: The placement of human bodies while having intercourse.

Pyramid

Billiards: The positioning of the object balls in a triangular grouping, used to begin many pocket billiard games.

Sexual: A sexual position between two women and one man, where the man lies down, one woman sits on his erect penis, the other sits on his mouth, and the women face each other.

Rack

Billiards: The triangular equipment used for gathering the balls into the formation required for the game being played.

Sexual: Refers to a large pair of breasts on a woman.

Rails

Billiards: The top surface of the table not covered by cloth, from which the cushions protrude toward the playing surface.

Sexual: Intercourse that is usually intense or rough and performed without emotional attachment.

Red ball(s)

Billiards: The red-colored object ball in carom, and also the name of a three-cushion billiard game.

Sexual: "Balls" are a synonym for the testes, which may turn red from heat rash, dermatitis, or possibly a sexually transmitted infection.

Scratch

Billiards: In carom games, to score a point by accident. In pocket games, when the cue ball is going into a pocket on a stroke.

Sexual: A euphemism for intercourse.

Seeding

Billiards: Pre-determined initial pairings or advanced positioning of players in a field of tournament competition.

Sexual: Refers to the act of a male ejaculating into a male partner.

Shaft

Billiards: The thinner part of a cue where the tip is attached.

Sexual: Refers to the stem of a penis.

Stroke(s)

Billiards: The movement of the cue as a shot is executed.

Sexual: Refers to in and out of penetration during intercourse, or the stroke of the hand on a penis during manual genital stimulation.

Triangle

Billiards: In pocket games, it is the triangular device used to place the balls in position for the start of most games.

Sexual: This refers in general to a woman's genitals, to the shaved shape of pubic hair on a woman, and a sexual union between three people.

Other Billiards Terms with Sexual Possibilities

In this game, a *ball in hand* is when the cue ball is put into play anywhere on the playing surface of the table. No imagination is needed for this sexual connotation. It is a testicle being handled. A *bottom cushion* is the cushion located at the head of a snooker table. In sex play, this is a pillow placed under the lover's buttocks, used to raise them up so that the angle of penile insertion becomes easier. In billiards, a *shot* is an action that begins the instant the cue tip contacts the cue ball, and ends when all balls in play stop rolling. A shot can also be the process of attempting to "pick up" a woman in a public place, as in he "took a shot" at it, and a shot can also refer to an ejaculation.

Sexual Commentary

In looking at the pool balls being preset by the rack, the shape is a triangle that faces the center of the table. When a triangle points upright, it can symbolically represent the element of fire, and it is also the symbol for man; as opposed to an inverted triangle that represents water and is the symbol for woman. When the first player prepares for the opening break and the cue stick is laid out toward the triangle with the cue ball at its tip, one can anthropomorphize this as being a long penis with at least one testicle. This one ball is white (called the clear ball in carom), and the color white is associated with goodness and purity. The ball and the cue, representing one man, are about to break up the carefully laid triangle of colored balls. One might think of this group of balls as the testicles of many competitors. All of these other balls are either a different color or they have stripes. The solid color balls could represent men of different nationalities. During medieval times, stripes on garments were seen on prisoners, criminals, and hangmen. Therefore, the striped balls represent an undesirable element. With the opening move, that player attempts to break apart and scatter "other men," and one by one, get them off the table to eliminate them from the competition. During the following plays, all the balls will be "called," thrown," jumped," "shot," or "killed."

Now about the black eight ball. This ball may only be sent into a pocket once the other balls, either solids or stripes, have already been sunk. The color black is a mysterious color associated with secrecy, evil, fear, power, and death. Perhaps this is the one (man), who is an unknown factor in the competition. The color black has a negative connotation, and is associated with dark humor, someone being blacklisted, and the black death, which leaves the player with only one objective, to sink it into a black hole.

Just two more comments. One pertains to the term "pyramid," in the list of terms above, which again is the positioning of the object balls in a triangular grouping used to begin a game. In sexual terms, this describes a position in which a man lies down, one woman sits on his erect penis, the other sits on his mouth, and the women face each other. Not to quibble too much, but this actually forms a triangle. Add a person to either side and it forms a four-sided pyramid. My second comment concerns a billiard table's pockets at the four corners. Of course, a crotch is the groin area of a person. Is it any wonder that these corner holes are called a crotch, into which the balls are to go?

Chapter 25
Cricket

The game of cricket is another bat and ball game, played in the British Isles, Australasia, the Indian sub-continent, southern Africa, and the West Indies. It involves two teams, each with eleven players, and is played on a rounded cricket field. In the center of the field is a central strip where a pitch is delivered. At each end of this strip is a set of three wooden stumps with two balls on top of them, called a wicket, at which the ball is aimed and which the batsman must defend. The name comes from the "wicket gate" through which sheep were kept.[173] There are lines which mark the pitch at either end called the bowling crease, the popping crease, and the return crease. One team bats while the other team bowls and fields. After so many innings, the teams switch roles. The goal of the game is to score as many runs as possible while the opponent team attempts to minimize those runs. This chapter will get more into the game, its players, equipment, and terms, but first some history.

The earliest mention of cricket appears in written testimony from a medieval court case in approximately 1550, describing the land on which the game was played

---

[173] Swanton, E. W. (ed.), *Barclay's World of Cricket*, (London: Collins Willow, 1986).

314

by children.[174] The word "cricket" comes from the French word *crosse*, for crooked staff. In French, *ciquet* is a stick. In Old English, *cyce* is a crutch or staff, and in Middle Dutch it is *krick* for a crook. In 1611, Sussex ecclesiastical court records noted that two men failed to attend Easter Sunday Mass because they were playing cricket. They were fined and had to do penance, but it marked the first time that adults were playing the game.[175]

Regardless of where the name originated and how it started, the game caught on, although the Puritans of the time felt the game was profane. They complained that it preempted Sunday Mass, robbing the church of crowds, and sometimes involved betting on teams. At the time, gambling was prevalent in British society, especially blood sports with animals, horseracing, and prizefighting. It continued unabated until 1664, when the Gambling Act began limiting betting amounts (which were still quite high), yet not outlawing the practice.[176] Less than a dozen years later, interest in the game spread across England, and by the late 1600s cricket was being enjoyed not only by townspeople, but also the gentry. They became patrons of the game and consequently began to play, though there were separate changing rooms and dining rooms for each class.[177] However, the professionals that played the game were of the working class, so the nobles claimed they were amateurs and were able to join in. The professionals were paid to play and

---

[174] Ibid.

[175] Timothy J. McCann, *Sussex Cricket in the Eighteenth Century,* (Lewes, England: Sussex Record Society, 2004), xxxi.

[176] Derek Birley, *A Social History of English Cricket,* (London: Aurum Press Ltd., 1999), 7-8.

[177] John Major, *More Than a Game,* (London: HarperCollins, 2007), 268-69.

the amateurs were supposed to undertake the financial burden of the game. They could also claim expenses for reimbursement, which led to some obvious problems.

During the eighteenth century, game rules developed and the sport began to draw large crowds. At first, there was only a single wicket and the ball was rolled to the batter. Then in 1760, they began to pitch the ball to the batsman, which meant the bat design had to advance.[178] That same year, the first cricket club was formed, called the Marylebone Cricket Club, which became the overseeing organization and protector of the forty-two laws of cricket. Controversies arose over round arm and overarm bowling, in contrast to the underarm method. There also began the three-stump wicket, when part of the batter's body purposely stopped the ball from hitting the wicket, and the batter could be eliminated for doing so.

By the mid-1800s the game had spread to Australia, the Caribbean, India, New Zealand, North America, and South Africa; and by the end of the century there were eight leading clubs in the county championships. Before the beginning of the First World War in 1914, cricket experienced a "Golden Age." Cricket spread to the West Indies in 1928, New Zealand in 1930, India in 1932, and Pakistan in 1952. In 1933, Don Bradman of Australia had a test batting average of 99.94, the highest any person has ever batted, and became the greatest batsman of all time. He was finally inducted into the International Cricket Council Hall of Fame in 2009.[179]

---

[178] John Nyren, *The Cricketers of My Time,* (London: Robson Books, 1998), 153-154.

[179] Brett Hutchins, *Don Bradman: Challenging the Myth,* (Cambridge: Cambridge University Press, 2002), 21.

In 1963, England introduced Limited Overs cricket, a one-day match, which got its name from the rule that says that each team bowls a set number of overs.[180] An "overs" is when six consecutive balls are bowled by a single bowler to a batsman. Afterward, the umpire calls "over," and the teams switch. From the early 1980s to 2000, Sri Lanka, Zimbabwe and Bangladesh began to form teams.

Now for a closer description of the bat and ball used in cricket. It has been suggested that the earliest games were played with a shepherd's crook, but historians are only certain that the early cricket bat, before the eighteenth century, was more like a hockey stick. After that, the bat changed to the current design. White willow wood is used for the larger part of the flat-fronted striking side of the bat. The ridge on the reverse side of the bat is called the blade. The top edges by the handle are called the shoulders, and the bottom of the blade is called the toe. The attached handle is made of cane, spliced on to the blade, and is covered with a rubber grip. All this makes the bat lightweight, shock-resistant, and strong. New bats must go through a process called "knocking in" so that the softer fibers are compacted to better withstand the hard cracks of a full game, after which linseed oil is added to fill in the fibers.

One of the laws of cricket is that a bat cannot be any wider than 4¼ inches (10.80 cm), and no longer than 38 inches (96.52 cm). A standard for weight is not set, but most weigh between 2.7 and 3 pounds (1.23 kg to 1.36 kg). There are also child sizes designated zero to six, and a youth's size called a Harrow. There have been

---

[180] John Wisden, "One-Day Knockout Competition, 1963," In *Wisden Cricketers' Almanack, 100th Edition.* (London: Sporting Handbooks Ltd., 1963) 1074–1076.

innovations as well, such as the Slazenger bat without shoulders in the 1960s, the double-sided bat in 1970, the GN100 Scoop in 1974 which had the extra wood in the back removed, an aluminum bat in 1979, and a bat with a carbon fiber-reinforced polymer down the spine that was tried but rejected in 2005. There were other bats redesigned purely for marketing purposes, but not used professionally. One bat had a second face on the base of the back of the bat, and another had an offset handle. In 2008 a bat was created with an offset edge which increased performance, and it won awards. In 2009, the Uzi with a truncated blade and elongated handle came into use for the new Twenty20 game. There were also bats called the Mongoose, the Big Hitter, and the Joker.

The cricket ball has its own history, standards of production, and regulations. It begins with a central core of cork, layered with tightly wound string, and is covered with leather and a raised sewn seam. Top quality balls have four elongated pieces of leather stitched together. The circumference is stitched with a string of six rows of stitches and measures 9 inches (22.86 cm) around.

White balls are used for one-day limited overs cricket matches. However, they get dirty fast, taking on the brownish color of the field, so two more white balls might replace the first throughout the game. Otherwise, a pink ball was developed in 2000, and is now used for test cricket, first-class matches, and night games, as they are easier to see. Kookaburra, Dukes, and SG are the main producers. Balls get dirty throughout a game and players will often rub them against their clothes to polish a side, and if a ball loses its shape it can be replaced by the umpire. The rules forbid a ball to be scuffed with fingernails, be picked at, have a seam lifted, be rubbed on the ground, or have anything other than saliva or sweat applied. The one other thing about a cricket ball is that it is potentially lethal, which is why protective equipment is required. During practices and games played by youths, where safety, availability, and cost can enter the equation, a softer ball is used, such as a yellow leather ball or a tennis ball.

The positions of the players, how the game is played, and many of the rules will be discussed within the listing of terms, which are next.

Cricket Terms and Slang

Ball
Cricket: The object that the batsman attempts to strike.
Sexual: A synonym for one testicle, and "to ball" is a euphemism for intercourse.

Bang (it) in
Cricket: To bowl a delivery on a shorter length with additional speed and force.
Sexual: A euphemism for intercourse.

Bat (ting)
Cricket: The wooden tool which a batsman swings to strike the ball, and the process of doing so.
Sexual: An acronym for <u>B</u>ig <u>A</u>ss <u>T</u>its, and a euphemism for masturbation.

Belter
Cricket: A pitch offering advantage to the batsman.
Sexual: A synonym for a beautiful girl.

Biffer
Cricket: A term for a defending attacking batsman, opposite of a blocker.
Sexual: An unattractive woman or one without any sexual appeal, the opposite of a belter.

Blocker

Cricket: A defensive or slow-scoring batsman who blocks a bowl, rather than trying to swing and score a run.

Sexual: Short for "cock-blocker," a person who blocks another from relating sexually with someone.

Bosie

Cricket: A deceptive spinning delivery by a leg spin bowler, which spins in the opposite direction to the stock delivery.

Sexual: A Scottish word for a hug or embrace, derived from bosom.

Box

Cricket: A half-shell protective item inserted into the front pouch of a jockstrap with cup pocket, worn underneath a player's trousers to protect his genitalia.

Sexual: A synonym for female genitalia.

Bump ball

Cricket: A delivery that bounces very close to the batsman's foot after he has played a shot that appears to have come directly from the bat without ground contact.

Sexual: Both words are euphemisms for intercourse.

Bunny

Cricket: An incompetent batsman, more suited to being a bowler.

Sexual: An inexperienced male who thrusts too fast during intercourse, much like a rabbit.

Captain

Cricket: The person in command of a team.

Sexual: A euphemism for an erect penis. It is also the term used for a leader in a gay sex orgy, who takes the central role and often directs what participants should do.

Catch(er)

Cricket: When a fielder catches the ball after the batsman has batted it and before it hits the ground, which puts the batsman out.

Sexual: A "catch" is an attractive man or woman that a person desires. A "catcher" is the person who receives ejaculate in their hand, mouth, vagina, or anus.

Cherry

Cricket: Another name for the ball, and the red mark made by the ball on a bat.

Sexual: This can be a woman's erect nipples, or when a woman's hymen is torn during first penetration, this may be referred to as "popping her cherry." More likely it is a misunderstanding of the clitoris, as when it is stimulated it turns red, flushed with blood.

Cut

Cricket: What the batsman does as he swings for the shot.

Sexual: Refers to a penis that has been circumcised.

Dead ball

Cricket: The state of play between deliveries in which batsmen may not score runs or be out, when the ball becomes lodged in the batsman's clothing or equipment, when the ball is bowled and the batsman is not ready, when a bowler aborts his run up without making a delivery, and when the batsmen attempts to run after a ball that has struck the batsman's body.

Sexual: After a serious injury to the scrotum has occurred, the spermatic cord that carries blood to one or both of the testicles may have been twisted, called testicular torsion. This can affect the blood flow to the tissues, which will turn the testicle numb, making it feel as if it is "dead." Can also occur with too rapid growth during puberty.

Dead rubber

Cricket: This describes a match in a series where the result has already been decided by earlier matches, as when the match would have no effect on the series other than the number of matches won and lost.

Sexual: A condom that can no longer be used.

Dink

Cricket: This is a gentle shot.

Sexual: A synonym for penis, which comes from 1888 America, from "dingus," meaning "a thing." Also a dinkle.

Dolly

Cricket: A very easy catch.

Sexual: An attractive woman a man can "play" with.

Double

Cricket: The scoring of 1000 runs and the taking of 100 wickets in the same season.

Sexual: Short for double penetration, when a man penetrates a woman vaginally and another man does so anally. It is also when one man is engaged in sex play with two women at the same time.

Drag

Cricket: When a rear foot is dragged forward before releasing the pitch behind the bowling crease.

Sexual: "In drag" refers to someone who dresses in clothes of the opposite gender just for fun or for sexual pleasure.

Drive

Cricket: A powerful shot hit along the ground or in the air.

Sexual: A euphemism for the action of intercourse.

Duck

Cricket: A batsman's score of zero.

Sexual: Refers to a dumb and unattractive woman.

Eagle eye

Cricket: A computer-generated graphic which tracks the trajectory of a ball delivery between the bowler and a batsman if the ball were not hindered by the batsman. Same as a Hawk-Eye.

Sexual: What someone has, because they can spot an attractive person from a distance.

Edge

Cricket: A slight deviation of the ball off the edge of the bat.

Sexual: A masturbation technique where one intentionally comes to the brink of an orgasm but stops and repeats, to increase the length of time for the pleasure to build. Also, "edge play," which is risky sexual activity.

Fine

Cricket: A position on the field behind the batsman, closer to the line of the pitch.

Sexual: An attractive and sexy woman.

Fishing

Cricket: Being tempted into throwing the bat at a wider delivery outside or off-stump and missing.

Sexual: A man or woman who taunts others for attention or compliments.

Flash

Cricket: To wield the bat aggressively, often hitting good line and length deliveries, indiscriminately.

Sexual: To suddenly remove a piece of clothing to reveal a body part, performed in public as an act of exhibitionism.

Flick

Cricket: A gentle movement of the wrist to move the bat.

Sexual: An older term for film or a photograph depicting adult sexual activity.

Flipper

Cricket: When a leg bowler delivers with under spin, so it bounces lower than normal.

Sexual: A woman who performs sexual favors with more than one man in the same place within the same evening.

Glove

Cricket: Part of a batsman's kit worn to protect the hands from accidental injury.

Sexual: A synonym for condom.

Grafting

Cricket: Batting defensively under difficult conditions with a strong emphasis on not getting out.

Sexual: A Scottish term for a guy who works at flirting, often unsuccessfully.

Hat trick

Cricket: A bowler taking a wicket off each of three consecutive deliveries bowled in a single match.

Sexual: Having sex three times in one day with three different partners. Also, penetrating a female partner vaginally, anally, and orally within one session.

Hook

Cricket: A shot played so that the ball is struck when it is above the batsman's shoulder.

Sexual: One "hooks up" with a partner for sex. Also, what a hooker or a prostitute does to obtain a paying client.

In

Cricket: Refers to the batsman that comes up to bat.

Sexual: When a man has his penis already inside his partner in intercourse.

Jaffa

Cricket: An exceptionally well-bowled ball that may be unplayable.

Sexual: A male who cannot produce viable sperm. Comes from a variety of oranges with few seeds.

Lolly

Cricket: An easy hit by a batsman or easy catch by a fielder.

Sexual: Another term for fellatio. Short for lollipop.

Meat of the bat

Cricket: The thickest part of the bat from which the most energy is given to the ball.

Sexual: This refers to the thickness of a penis.

Nibble

Cricket: A small amount of movement by the ball off the seam.

Sexual: To make tiny bites, tenderly and repeatedly, usually on the neck with the intention of exciting the person.

No

Cricket: A batsman's call of not to run.

Sexual: Despite what some men might think, when a woman says "no" to an offer of intercourse, she means NO!

No Ball

Cricket: An illegal delivery.

Sexual: Exactly the same as No, above.

On strike

Cricket: The batsman currently facing the bowling attack.

Sexual: When one partner is angry with the other and withholds any sexual contact.

Out

Cricket: The state of a batsman who has been dismissed, and the word spoken by the umpire when answering an appeal for a wicket in the affirmative.

Sexual: A gay man or lesbian who decides to openly declare their sexuality.

Pair

Cricket: This can refer to a "pair of spectacles" or a "pair of ducks," that is, a zero to zero score.

Sexual: A pair of breasts or a pair of legs, usually in an exclamation of how attractive a "pair" a woman has.

Peach

Cricket: An excellent ball delivered by a fast bowler.

Sexual: A euphemism for the mons pubis or fatty tissue on the outside of the vulva, nicely shaved and shaped.

Pitch

Cricket: The rectangular surface in the center of a cricket field made of earth or clay where the bowler pitches the ball, and to bounce a ball before reaching the batsman.

Sexual: The territory, area, or street that a prostitute works along, and the words a person tells another to get them to agree to a sexual liaison.

Pull

Cricket: A cross-batted shot played to a ball bouncing around waist height by swinging the bat in a horizontal arc in front of the body, pulling it around to the leg side toward a mid-wicket or square leg.

Sexual: An Australian slang term, "on the pull," means that a man is all dressed up and out looking for a sexual partner.

Rabbit

Cricket: A poor batsman.

Sexual: Refers to a particularly popular vibrator that has a phallus, plus two rubber prongs used for clitoral stimulation.

Roger

Cricket: This term comes from the Warwickshire and New Zealand player Roger Twose, a top cricket batsman, who greatly contributed to New Zealand winning the 2000 International Cricket Council Championship.

Sexual: A late 1800s word for a penis, and an older English euphemism meaning to have intercourse.

Roller

Cricket: A cylindrical implement used to flatten the pitch before play.

Sexual: A woman who goes from one man to another.

Rough

Cricket: A worn-down section of the pitch.

Sexual: Describes a wild and hard session of intercourse.

Runner

Cricket: A player from the batting side who assists an injured batsman by running between the wickets. Not allowed in International cricket.

Sexual: A woman who goes from one man to another for sex. Same as a roller.

Scorer

Cricket: Someone who scores the progress of the game.

Sexual: One who has "scored," that is, had intercourse.

Session

Cricket: A period of play, from start to lunch, lunch to tea, and tea until end of the day.

Sexual: A period of time for masturbation or intercourse.

Short stop

Cricket: When the wicket keeper stands upfront and the fielder is right behind the wicket keeper.

Sexual: Refers to an unfinished session of fellatio or manual genital stimulation.

Splice

Cricket: The joint between the handle and the blade of a bat.

Sexual: To engage in sexual intercourse.

Stroke

Cricket: An attempt by the batsman to play at a delivery.

Sexual: The movement of the hand upon a person's body or specifically on a penis going up and down, or the act of intercourse with penis going in and out of the vaginal or anal cavity, each leading to orgasm and ejaculation.

Sweet spot

Cricket: The small area on the face of the bat that gives maximum power for minimum effort when the ball is hit with it.

Sexual: A place on the body that responds pleasurably when touched. Most often refers to the clitoris, or the "G" spot within a woman's vaginal canal.

Swing

Cricket: A bowling style used by medium to fast bowlers.

Sexual: To have an open sexual relationship with one's partner within a select group of other partners or swingers. Or can refer to a person that swings both ways, that is, bisexual.

Swish

Cricket: A rapid or careless attacking stroke by the batsman.

Sexual: An effeminate gay man.

Switch hit (ter)

Cricket: A shot played by a batsman who reverses both his stance and his grip during the bowler's run-up so that a right-handed batsman plays the shot as a left-hander, and vice versa.

Sexual: To masturbate with a sub-dominate hand, wife or girlfriend swapping, and also a bisexual person.

Tea

Cricket: The second of the two intervals between innings during a full day's play.

Sexual: Used in the drag community for gossip.

Tickle (ing)

Cricket: An edge to the wicket keeper or close fielder, or a delicate shot played to the third man.

Sexual: A way of touching another that causes involuntary twitching and laughter. Tickling can also be a paraphilia (knismophilia or titillagia), in which the receiver derives sexual arousal, pleasure, and orgasm from the action.

Tied down

Cricket: Run-making restricted by a bowling side.

Sexual: Refers to bondage in BDSM, being secured with ropes or other restraining devices.

Timber

Cricket: The wooden stumps, and the call when they are hit.

Sexual: A synonym for a large, hard erection.

Toss

Cricket: The tossing of a coin at the beginning of the game to determine who gets to decide which team bats first.

Sexual: To masturbate (toss off), and a promiscuous woman.

Track

Cricket: Another term for the pitch.

Sexual: An area in the city where prostitutes and pimps work.

Worm

Cricket: The cumulative runs scored or the progressive run rate by a team against the over number in limited-overs cricket.

Sexual: A synonym for a small penis, a "worthless worm."

Yes

Cricket: A batsman's call for a run.

Sexual: An affirmative word that a person hears from a potential lover when asked if they can have intercourse.

Other Cricket Terms with Sexual Possibilities

Cricket has the term *appeal,* which is the act of a bowler or fielder shouting at the umpire to ask if his last ball took the batsman's wicket. This term could also be used for sex appeal, which is the attractiveness of a possible sexual partner. There is an *asking rate,* which is the level at which the team batting second needs to score in order to catch the opponent's score in a limited overs game. No surprise here, as one can easily interpret this term being applied to a man who inquires of a prostitute's asking rate. To *beat the bat* is when a batsman narrowly avoids touching the ball with the edge of his bat, through good fortune rather than skill. Beating a bat can also be interpreted as masturbation.

There is the *corridor of uncertainty*, which is a narrow area on and just outside a batsman's off stump. This could also easily be the corridor of space between a car and a woman's front door of her house, after a date. Will she ask him in for sex or not? *Covers* is the next term, which is a fielding position between point and mid-off, and the equipment used to protect the pitch from rain. No debate here, it's under the covers that all the fun sexual things happen. A *daisy cutter* is when a ball rolls along the pitch or bounces more than twice. As for a sexual connotation, perhaps the reader has heard of the sexual linking of many people in a circle enjoying each other, called a daisy chain. A daisy cutter would be a person who cuts in and joins the group. *Featherbed* is a term meaning a soft, slow pitch of predictable bounce that is good for batting. Like covers, it is in a featherbed, any bed actually, where it is presumed that one does a lot more than sleep.

To *follow on* is when a team is up to bat first in the second inning, because they batted second in the first inning. To follow on in a sexual sense would be to follow a person home for sex after being picked up in a bar. In cricket, *good length* is the ideal place for a stock delivery to pitch its trajectory from the bowler to the batsman. A good length, which every woman who enjoys a penis must know, is not necessarily as long as possible, but depends on how well a penis fits within her vaginal canal. *How's that* is the necessary question the fielding team must ask when appealing to an umpire, before he calls a batsman out. "How's that?" could equally be the inquiry of a man of his partner after having sex, as all men like to know how their performance was.

A *keeper* in cricket is the shortened name for the wicket-keeper, and to the rest of us, a keeper is a lover who is so close to being perfect that they are worth holding on to. A *king pair*, also called a *golden pair,* is a dismissal for zero runs off the first ball faced in each of a batsman's two innings of a two-inning match. In sex-speak this term may apply to two well-shaped, well-hung, and attractive testicles, usually shaved. A *line* in cricket refers to the deviation of the point along the pitch where a delivery bounces from the line, from wicket-to-wicket. A well-delivered line is the one thing a male says that will get him into bed with his prospective partner. Another term is *maiden over*, which means no runs are scored off the bat and no wides or balls are bowled. Maiden over could also have a sexual meaning, that a woman is no longer a virgin. *Playing time* is the amount of time a game is played. First-class cricket matches are played over three to five days. One-day matches will last for six hours. Playing time for two lovers can be for any amount of time they choose. *Straight up-and-down* is a pejorative term for a fast or medium-paced bowler who cannot swing or seam the ball. This could also be a guy who is strictly heterosexual.

Sexual Commentary

Cricket definitely has the widest "stick." Let's take a descriptive review of a cricket bat. Starting with the handle, it is joined to the blade with a section called the shoulder. Then comes the splice, which is wood shaped into an upside-down triangle. This increases the strength of the bat to hit the ball. Running along the blade is the edge of a bat that may come in different thicknesses, which increases the mass of the bat, helps to evenly distribute the weight, and still provides a surface to hit the ball. Midway, there is a swell in the bat where it is thickest, called the sweet spot, the absolute best place to hit the ball with the most impact and force. Running lengthwise along the blade is a raised spine, and at the very end is the toe. Overall, all bats will have some degree of bow.

There are obvious references to the human body here with a shoulder, spine, and toe, but there are other aspects which also align with describing a penis, and that is the swell and the bow. All penises have a slight curve or bow, either to the left, right, or upward. And of course, when they become engorged they swell. Glory to the penis that enters the vaginal canal and finds a woman's sweet spot!

We cannot forget the cricket ball, which comes in white, pink and red. In the early days of cricket, the players always wore white, so a red ball made a nice contrast and was easier to see. Then when the shorter one-day cricket format began, as with limited-overs matches, the players began wearing more colorful clothes and the white ball was easier to spot. A pink ball has now been introduced for night games because yellow floodlights will turn a red ball brown, which is harder to see. One cannot correlate the outer color of a man's testicles (balls) with the color of a cricket ball, because of course, color depends upon the coloration of a man's skin. But inside the testicle sack, because of all the ducts, nerves, and blood vessels, the coloration can range from whitish to pink to red. One might think that there is also a weight or size equivalent, but there is not. A cricket ball is larger and heavier. The average man's testicle has a volume of 18 cubic centimeters. The average volume of a cricket ball is 180 cubic centimeters. Interestingly, that is exactly ten times the volume.

Chapter 26
Croquet

Croquet is an outdoor lawn game played by two, four, or six players. The stick is a mallet that strikes croquet balls through a course of sequenced hoops, with the goal of getting them to the final peg before the other players.

The hoops have a particular placement. Hoop one is in the southwest corner, hoop two is in the northwest corner, hoop three is in the northeast corner, hoop four is in the southeast corner, hoop five is north in the center, and the last hoop, called the rover, is in the south in the center. The balls must pass through each hoop and then reverse before hitting the central peg to finish. The central peg rises 18 inches (45.72 cm) above the ground, so everyone knows exactly where it is located at all times. There are also colored clips that match the balls, and they are placed on the hoop to indicate the next point for each ball. In the U.S. and Canada the hoops are called wickets, and instead of running the balls through the wickets, they are said to be "passed" through.

There is debate about where the game got its beginnings, as there were many similar games played that employed a stick, ball, and hoops. A game in Italy was called *pallamaglio*, which was a combination of two words, *pall* for ball and *malleus* for mallet. There was also the Italian game of *trucco*, which means a "trick or a gimmick," which eventually became lawn billiards. In France, it was *jeu de mail* or *paille-maille*, which translates to "straw mallet" because the hoops were made of bound straw, and later became ground billiards.

The first documentation of croquet was in Samuel Johnson's dictionary published in 1755, which describes the game of pall-mall as "a play in which the ball is struck with a mallet through an iron ring."[181] In 1810, Joseph Strutt in his book, *The Sports and Pastimes of the People of England,* also describes a game called the Pale-maille. By 1860, Nicky Smith's book, *The History of Croquet,* relates two origin theories. One is that the game came to England from France and then made its way to Ireland during the Norman invasion of Ireland in 1169, and the second is that the game came from Brittany and then went to Ireland.[182] Dr. Prior, a historian on the sport, claims that croquet came from a game that was played at Castle Bellingham in County Louth, Ireland, called *crookey* in 1834, and that by the following year it was called croquet.[183]

The circuitous route of the game's history is rather like the game of telephone with changing names, but regardless, it became very popular to play, especially during the 1860s. In Scotland, a book was published about the laws and regulations of the game. In England, the Earl of Essex even produced the Cassiobury croquet set, named after his home where many games were played. Ten years later, croquet ran into competition with

---

[181] Samuel Johnson, John Walker, and Robert S. Jameson, *A Dictionary of the English Language,* Vol. 1, 2nd Ed., (London: William Pickering, 1828), 519.

[182] Nicky Smith, *Queen of Games: The History of Croquet,* (London: Trafalgar Square, 1991).

[183] Clive Martin and Simon Williams, *A History of Croquet in Ireland,* Croquet Association of Ireland, 2004.
http://www.croquetireland.com/node/4

the then-popular game of lawn tennis, but survived into modern times. Tournaments are still held at the All England Lawn Tennis and Croquet Club in Wimbledon, and the headquarters for the game is located in Cheltenham, England.

There are many variations of the game still played in different countries with their own courts, rules, shots, and scoring. Gateball is played in Japan, southeast Asian countries, and North and South America. There is also an advanced level of the game called Association Croquet, played internationally. In this game, each player has two balls of either red and yellow or blue and black, to run through six hoops. A player chooses which of his balls to strike at each turn, getting both of his balls through all hoops and back again, to strike the central peg. Each hoop for each ball is one point and a final hit of the peg is one more, for a total of twenty-six points to win. Extra shots can be given when a ball hits an opponent's, called a *roquet*. In American six-wicket croquet, a ball can have "deadness" if it does not get through a hoop. A Deadness Board is used to keep track.

In golf croquet, the players must take turns taking a stroke in order of their color: blue, red, black, and yellow, and the object is to be the first one to go through each hoop. All first hoops are added up for the winner. It is a simpler game, growing the quickest of them all, with its Golf Croquet World Championships.

The U.K. particularly favors garden croquet on a 32-by-40-foot (9.75 by 12.19 m) lawn. The rules are similar to Association Croquet with a few differences. There is a boundary starting point for all balls, 3 feet (0.91 m) from hoop number one. There is no penalty for a ball that goes off-course, it just comes back in within the same 3 feet. And a croquet ball does not have to move when a striker's ball is struck. There are 170 clubs in England and Wales belonging to the Croquet Association.

There is also a nine-wicket variety with six balls, nine wickets, and two stakes which is played in a double-diamond pattern. The rules differ again with additional terms, and this game is most popular in Canada and the U.S. There is one more game, called ricochet, a simple game that can be played with up to six people. When a ball has been hit or roqueted, the player who hit it earns two free shots, thus the name of the game. North America has the United States Croquet Association, with about two hundred clubs participating.

Mallets used to be made entirely of wood. A standard mallet weighed 3 pounds (1.36 kg), had a length of 36 inches (91.44 cm), and the round wooden head was between 9 and 11 inches (22.86 cm to 27.94 cm) long. Now there are very few restrictions on a mallet's composition, length, weight, or size. The days of all-wooden mallets are long gone, at least for professionals. Now, the mallet head may be squared and made of stainless steel or carbon fiber with either a hard plastic or metal component on either end. Or it might be made of solid plastic, or a composite, or have a brass or tungsten face. The shaft can still be made of ash or hickory wood, but can also be made of fiberglass or carbon fiber tubing with beveled edges on the face. There are some players who even use a 12-inch-long (30.48 cm) mallet head.

Croquet balls used to be made of wood, but now they are made of cork or nylon in very hard polymer plastic. They come in different sizes, weights and colors, depending upon whether the play is for home recreation or professional tournament play. The smaller ball weighs about 9 ounces (255.15 g) and measures 3 5/16 inches (8.41 cm) in diameter. And the official full-size ball measures 3 5/8 inches (9.21 cm) and can weigh between

12 to 16 ounces (340.19 g to 453.59 g). They come in four different sets of colors: the primary colors of blue, red and yellow with black; those primary colors in stripes over white; or they are muted in secondary colors of white, pink, light brown and light green; in tertiary colors of either lilac, turquoise, orange and purple; or in porridge, peach, slate and aubergine. Each ball has a texture of two directions of perpendicular milling, which looks like a diamond pattern.

The World Croquet Federation holds a world championship every couple of years in a different country. The countries most involved are Australia, Canada, Egypt, England, New Zealand, South Africa, and the U.S.

Croquet Terms and Slang

Ball in hand

Croquet: A ball that the striker can pick up to change its position when it leaves the court. Then it must be placed next to a roqueted ball. Also, when the striker's ball is entitled to a lift.

Sexual: When a man cups a testicle, often in masturbation.

Block

Croquet: A ball on which the striker is dead and intrudes into the path where a striker ball would go to score a wicket.

Sexual: Interference by a "cock-blocker," or a person who blocks another from connecting sexually with someone.

Block play

Croquet: A tournament playoff when players must play one game against other players in their block.

Sexual: Exactly the same meaning as "block," above.

Condone

Croquet: The failure of a player to claim a fault within the limit of claims.

Sexual: To accept and allow sexual behavior to continue that is considered morally wrong or offensive.

Dead(ness)

Croquet: What a ball has after it roquets another ball.

Sexual: After a serious injury to the scrotum has occurred, the spermatic cord that carries blood to one or both of the testicles may have been twisted, called testicular torsion. This can affect the blood flow to the tissues, which will turn the testicle numb, and may be thought of as "dead." This can also occur with too rapid growth during puberty.

Double tap

Croquet: A fault in which the mallet makes more than one audible sound when it strikes the ball.

Sexual: A sexual style of dancing that is done standing up but bumping with a dry hump to the music. It also refers to intercourse with the same woman twice in the same evening.

Hoop

Croquet: The U-shaped gate pushed partially into the ground that the ball travels through. Also called a wicket.

Sexual: A synonym for the anal ring.

Hot ball(s)

Croquet: The opponent's next ball to play. Also called a danger ball.

Sexual: Occurs when the scrotum becomes overheated.

Pass

Croquet: To give up a turn.

Sexual: An amorous or sexual advance to someone.

Peel

Croquet: To send a ball, other than the striker's ball, through its target hoop.

Sexual: To either sensually or quickly take off one's clothes in anticipation for sexual activity.

Peg

Croquet: The center stake in a game.

Sexual: A synonym for the penis. A strap-on dildo a woman uses to penetrate another during intercourse. It is also an acronym for Post Ejaculatory Guilt Syndrome, which may occur after a sexual encounter, whereby the person experiences feelings of self-reproach or guilt.

Pioneer ball

Croquet: In a three or four-ball break, a ball that is positioned at the wicket, following the one a player is attempting to score.

Sexual: The first experience of intercourse with a virgin, referring to "ball" as an act of intercourse.

Rover

Croquet: A ball that has scored all twelve wickets but has not yet hit the stake or central peg.

Sexual: One that cruises bars and parks for sexual encounters.

Stroke

Croquet: It begins when the striker's mallet contacts the ball and ends when the ball comes to a rest.

Sexual: A hand movement that brushes another's body, and the action of placing the index finger and thumb around the penis along the shaft and moving the skin up and down to produce a pleasurable sensation leading to orgasm and ejaculation. Also, a man's penetrations delivered full-length during intercourse.

Tice

Croquet: A ball sent to a location that will entice an opponent to shoot at it but miss.

Sexual: A combination word for tight and nice, which is used by men to describe a woman.

Other Croquet Terms with Sexual Possibilities

In croquet, a *round robin* is the same as a block play, where players are assigned to other players for a playoff, but a round robin in a sexual context might also describe a sexual process with multiple couples who trade off partners in a swinging context. A *shot clock* in croquet is used during a game to measure the striker's allowed 45 seconds to play each shot. Sexually speaking, this term shares the same as in basketball, a clock shot (reversed) is an ejaculation on the face, as a clock has a face. Another term is *split shot,* which is when a croquet shot sends the striker ball and the croqueted ball in different directions. In sexual parlance, a split shot is when a man begins to ejaculate in one place and then moves to another place to complete the process.

Sexual Commentary

Some names for parts of the croquet mallet also have sexual connotations. The hitting end of the mallet that is set perpendicularly on to the base of the mallet is called the head, and the long part of the mallet held in the hands is called the shaft, both also used to describe a penis. There is also the shank which is inserted into the hole in the head, which is a slang term for a prostitute or a woman without virtue.

In playing the game, usually one turn constitutes one stroke of the mallet. If a player hits one of their balls through a hoop and scores a point, they get another turn, called a continuation stroke. That sounds as if one has gained sexual entry into a partner, and then they get to have another go at it. And, if a player touches any ball other than the striker's ball with the mallet, that is a foul. So keep your hands and balls to yourself.

Chapter 27
Golf

In the sport of golf, the playing field is called a "course," the stick is a slender metal "club," and the small hard ball must fly across vast green lawns into a series of small holes, each one called a "cup," with as few swinging strokes as possible.

Like so many ancient games, golf has several possible origins. Some say golf started with the first century BCE Roman game called *paganica*, with a ball stuffed with feathers. Others say it was a fourteenth century Chinese game called *chuiwan*, meaning to strike a small ball. There was the Dutch game of *kolven* or *kolf*, the Dutch sport of *beugelen* and *klosbaan*, and the Belgian game of *chole*. There was also the English Middle Ages game of *cambuca*, which translates as a hooked rod or stick. Also, the game of *chambot* was played in France, and the game of *chaugan* was played in Persia. However, Scotland claims to the be the origin of the modern game now played.

The first written record of the Scottish sport was in 1457, when King James II banned the game because it competed with his favorite game of archery.[184] In 1502, his grandson lifted the ban when *he* began to enjoy the game. The Old Course at Saint Andrews dates to 1574,

---

[184] The Golfer's Guide to Golf, "The Complete History of Golf." http://www.golf-information.info/history-of-golf.html

344

though historians say that Mary Queen of Scots played there earlier, in 1567. The Musselburgh Links date to 1672 and it is this site that is listed in the *Guinness Book of World Records* as the oldest golf course still operating.[185] The oldest surviving rules of golf come from the book, *The Honourable Company of Edinburgh Golfers*, published in 1744.[186] In 1764, the standard of playing twenty-two holes was reduced to eighteen holes, and 1860 marks the year of the world's first and oldest major tournament called The Open Championship.[187]

The popularity of the game spread around the word, so that by 2005 it had also become popular in Australia, Canada, England, Ireland, New Zealand, Sweden, the United States, and Wales. Although the number of people who played the sport in the U.S. began to decline in the year 2000, the game spread to the rest of the world. Nine more countries took up the sport: Japan, Germany, France, South Africa, South Korea, Spain, Argentina, Italy, and India. In 2015 there were just over 34,000 golf courses worldwide.[188] The one person who took golf beyond the earth was Alan Shepard on Apollo 14, when he smuggled a club and two balls onboard. He hit a ball

[185] David Brice, "Recognition for the World's Oldest Links, at Last." http://web.archive.org/web/20110604120255/www.pgatour.com/2009/tourlife/travel/03/23/course_of_week/index.html

[186] Neil Laird, "1744 Honourable Company of Edinburgh Golfers," Scottish Golf History. http://www.scottishgolfhistory.org/oldest-golf-clubs-societies/1744-honourable-company-of-edinburgh-golfers/

[187] David Brice, "The Open Championship – More Scottish than British." https://web.archive.org/web/20121002214520/www.pgatour.com/2007/travel/07/16/trans_071607/index.html

[188] Neil Laird, "How Many Golf Holes are There in the World?" http://www.scottishgolfhistory.org/news/how-many-golf-holes-are-there-in-the-world/

200 yards, surprisingly only an average distance for a golfer on earth.[189]

Now on to describe the course. A full golf course has eighteen holes, but nine-hole courses are also common, depending upon the available area. Each course has a teeing ground where one begins the game, and the fairway is the stretch between the teeing ground and the putting green. Anything out-of-bounds, or where the grass is cut higher and is coarser, is called the rough. Between each putting green there is a predetermined number of strokes that a golfer is expected to complete in order to reach each hole, which is called a par. There can be holes which are par-3, par-4, or par-5. The path between holes can be straight, but some are bent, called a dogleg. Along the way between holes, there may be hazards, such as slopes, areas of sand, bodies of water, depressions, trees, ravines, or rocks, which the golfer must negotiate. There is also a course called an executive or short course of nine holes, which can be played once through, or twice through for a full round of eighteen holes. Or a short game can be played on an eighteen-hole course, playing the front nine or the back nine. There are private, commercial, municipal, and associated golf courses.

The putting green is the meticulously short-trimmed grass surrounding the hole. To accurately get the ball to go into the hole, the player carefully reads the physical area of the green, then "putts" the ball with a light stroke. Each hole is fitted with a flag on a metal pole, called a flagstick or pin, so one can see where to hit the ball from a distance. The green is grown from sod, but later has the

[189] Mark Aumann, "Remembering Alan Shepard's Lunar Golf Shots, 47 Years Later." https://www.pga.com/news/golf-buzz/feb-6-1971-alan-shepard-plays-golf-moon

soil washed from it, is rolled and laid, and then topped with fine sand. This kind of sandy soil, typically found along coastlines, makes for the best golf links. Different grasses are used on a course, which can influence the shot and the roll. The various grasses used on a course may be Bent grass, Bermuda grass, Kentucky bluegrass, and Zoysaigrass. Sometimes a small portion of the grass is clipped with the hit of the ball, called a divot.

Next is the equipment used, and first up is the ball with its history, design, and regulations. In the latter 1300s, the first balls were believed to have been made of carved beech and box tree hardwood. Beginning in 1486 in the Netherlands, balls were made with leather stuffed with cow's hair.[190] Later, the leather ball was stuffed with chicken or goose feathers and painted white, called a *featherie*.[191] Although this type of ball was used into the nineteenth century, it had its problems when it got wet, and when hit hard too many times it would split. In 1848, a new ball was made from the rubbery sap of the gutta-percha tree, and thus got the name *guttie* ball.[192] It was cheap to produce, was not affected by moisture, and kept its shape. However, it was not impervious to nicks or dents when struck by a club. Players were surprised when these nicks seemed to improve the ball's flight, so makers then began to produce balls with a texture, and these marks became known as *brambles*, because they look like bramble fruit.[193]

Almost fifty years later, the ball changed again, when it was discovered that a rubber thread wound into a ball

---

[190] Neil Laird, "Golf Ball."

[191] Ibid.

[192] Ibid.

[193] Ibid.

had a greater bounce. The new ball was filled with either a liquid sap or had a solid round core, surrounded by a layer of the wound rubber thread, and then covered by another sap called *balata*. This ball was called the rubber Haskell golf ball.[194] A few years later, it was found that by dimpling the ball with overall indentations, it gained flight, spin, and better trajectory. By the mid-1960s, the outer layer of balata was replaced by a synthetic resin called Surlyn. Balls then came to be classified by the number of layers they had, either two, three, or four-piece balls. By 1967, Spalding began replacing the caustic liquids that were once used inside with a solid core that is still used today.

A golf ball is small, only 1.68 inches (4.27 cm) in diameter, and weighs no more than 1.62 ounces (45.93 g). Regulations state that the ball must be completely spherical and the dimples on its surface symmetrical. Until 1990, the English had a slightly smaller ball called the British ball, which flew further. Balls can also be produced with harder high compression or softer low compression. Typically, a softer ball is preferred, but a higher compression ball will allow for further distance. Basically, a ball is made for either recreational or advanced play. A recreational ball will be made with two layers, while an advanced ball will be made with three. The recreational ball is for a slower swing speed and is less expensive, while an advanced ball offers greater spin, is for a higher speed of swing, and costs more. Players need to differentiate their balls from those of other players. Some balls come with a pre-marked letter, number, or symbol; but if not, each player will mark their balls with a particular color or with their initials.

---

[194] Ibid.

If you thought that the description of the ball was extensive, wait until the clubs are described! A single club is not sufficient to play the game of golf. Although every club is made up of a grip, a shaft, and a head, different clubs are needed for different reasons. The game requires up to fourteen different golf clubs, which are numbered, with the higher the number the shorter the shaft and the higher the ball will fly for a shorter distance. It is the loft which is the most important aspect of hitting a ball, while the swing is secondary.

Types of clubs include the wood, iron, wedge, hybrid, putter, and chipper. A wood is the most powerful, with a long shaft and a large head, used for the tee shot and for driving the ball long distances down the fairway. Originally, the heads were made of persimmon wood, and some were laminates of different woods. Beginning in 1979, the "woo" club began to be made of steel. Since then, they have also been made with composite, carbon fiber, scandium, and titanium. The largest wood is called a driver, made of hollowed out titanium, reaching up to 45.5 inches (115.57 cm) long, and with a head that can be up to 28 cubic inches (71.12 cm) in volume. There may be three or four woods in a set. Even though they are not made of wood any more, they are still called "wood" clubs.

Next is the iron club, which has a shorter shaft and a solid all-metal head with a flat angled face. They were originally made from forged iron, but modern irons are made out of steel alloys. They are used along a course in many situations, like getting out of a sand bunker, tall grass, over trees or lakes, or around doglegs. There may be up to nine irons in a set, all numbered according to the intended distance the ball must travel, which also corresponds to their shaft length. Numbers nine and eight are short irons, numbers seven to five are medium irons, and numbers four to two are long irons. A number one is almost never used.

Another club is the wedge, which is really a different kind of iron, but in a class by itself. Wedges are generally used for short distances when high altitude and high accuracy are needed, such as a lay-up shot down the green, an approach shot onto the green, or for chipping to get out of a rough or hazard. There are five types of wedges with different angles ranging from 45° to 64°: the pitching wedge, gap wedge, sand wedge, lob wedge, and the ultra-lob wedge.

There are also hybrid, putter, and chipper clubs. The hybrids combine the usefulness of a wood and an iron club and are often used in place of them. They offer a wood's higher launch and distance and an iron's easier swing. The head is smaller than a wood and has a slightly convex shape. A putter is useful on the putting green to get the ball into the hole. Its head has a minimum loft of 5° and may have grooves on the face to help the ball roll along. A chipper is used to lift a ball out of a rough. If it has a loft up to 10° it is a type of putter. Above 10° and it is a type of iron.

A common set of clubs will include the following: a 1-wood driver, a fairway wood, seven irons of numbers 3-9, a sand wedge, putter, and two more of either a hybrid, gap wedge, lob wedge, or a chipper, making fourteen different clubs.

The rules and regulations of the game are far too numerous to relate, but some may be explained in the terms which follow.

Golf Terms and Slang

The 19th Hole

Golf: The clubhouse bar, where one goes after playing eighteen holes.

Sexual: Meeting up with a lover after a game.

Ace

Golf: When a player hits the ball directly from the tee into the hole with one stroke. Also known as "a hole in one."

Sexual: A shortened word for an asexual person.

Ball

Golf: The small white sphere used in golf, which is struck by a club, and meant to land in a cup in a hole in the green.

Sexual: A synonym for one testicle, and a euphemism for intercourse.

BIGGA

Golf: The United Kingdom's professional association for golf management.

Sexual: A term used by men for describing exceptionally large women.

Birdie

Golf: A hole played in one stroke under par.

Sexual: A 1915 British word for a maiden or young woman, a euphemism for penis, and a hand gesture with the derogatory meaning of "screw you," with the upturned middle finger symbolizing the penis.

Bite

Golf: A particular spin on a ball which causes it to stop immediately when it hits the green.

Sexual: The French word for a "cock," meaning a penis.

Blade

Golf: A type of iron with weight evenly distributed across the back of the head, a type of putter with a wide striking face, and a shot struck with the bottom of an iron high on the ball.

Sexual: The strolling place, track, or pitch where prostitutes and pimps hustle.

Blast

Golf: A shot that sends the ball and sand explosively out of a bunker.

Sexual: An explosive ejaculation.

Blind

Golf: A shot that does not allow the golfer to see where the ball will land.

Sexual: Refers to someone in love who does not see the faults of their lover.

Block

Golf: A shot played severely to the right.

Sexual: Interference by a "cock-blocker," a person who deters another from connecting sexually with someone.

Bounce

Golf: The measurement of the angle from the front edge of the base of the club to the point that rests on the ground when addressing the ball. In a wedge club, it is when the back edge of the base of the club is lower than the front edge.

Sexual: A euphemism for intercourse.

Club

Golf: An instrument used by a player to hit a golf ball, an organized group of golfers, and the entirety of a golf facility.

Sexual: A synonym for a penis.

Cut

Golf: An elimination of players from a tournament, and a shot that is usually higher in trajectory but curves off in a different direction.

Sexual: A euphemism for a circumcised penis.

Dead (ball)

Golf: TV-broadcaster slang for a shot in which there is no favorable outcome possible.

Sexual: After a serious injury to the scrotum has occurred, the spermatic cord that carries blood to one or both of the testicles may have been twisted, called testicular torsion. This can affect the blood flow to the tissues, which will turn the testicle numb, making it feel as if it is "dead." This can also occur with too rapid growth during puberty.

Drive

Golf: The first shot off each hole, made from the tee box, usually with a driver club.

Sexual: A euphemism for intercourse.

Duff

Golf: Denotes a horrible shot.

Sexual: An abbreviation for Designated Ugly Fat Friend, referring to the one unattractive woman among several attractive women.

Eagle

Golf: A hole played in two strokes under par.

Sexual: The spread-eagle sexual posture of lying with the legs and arms stretched out.

Foursome(s)

Golf: A group of two pairs of people in a match play, where the two partners hit alternate shots on one ball, or any group of four players on the course.

Sexual: A group of four people, usually two men and two women, who engage in intercourse together.

Grand slam

Golf: Winning all of golf's major championships in one calendar year.

Sexual: Refers to intercourse while maintaining penetration in a continuous set of positions; a man attaining sexual reward by having vaginal, anal, and fellatio with one woman; and having had intercourse with three different women in one night.

Groove

Golf: The crevices on the face of a club that are designated to impart spin on a ball, and a well-practiced swing that is easily repeatable by a player.

Sexual: A synonym for the crease between the buttocks on men and women.

Good-good

Golf: When both players in a match agree to concede each other's putts.

Sexual: The best kind of sexual organs, male or female, that will not fail to please.

Handsy

Golf: A player with too much wrist movement in their golf swing or putting stroke, causing inconsistent shots or puts.

Sexual: A person, male or female, who engages in inappropriate touching of another on any part of the body.

Hole

Golf: A 4.25 inch (10.80 cm) wide circular hole with a cup in the ground on a green, where the ball is supposed to fall into.

Sexual: A synonym for the vagina or anus, or a general derogatory euphemism for a promiscuous woman.

Hole in one

Golf: Hitting the ball from the tee into the hole in one stroke.

Sexual: Intercourse on a first date.

Hook

Golf: The curved flight of a ball with an unintentional spin that is a miss or out of control.

Sexual: A "hook up" for a partner in sex. It is also a shortened word for what a hooker or prostitute does.

Jab(s)

Golf: A putting stroke that is short, quick, and often erratic.

Sexual: An Irish slang term for pointed breasts.

Knock-down

Golf: A type of shot designed to have a low trajectory, employed to combat strong winds.

Sexual: Intercourse just for the sex, without feelings.

Lag

Golf: A long putt designed to get the ball close to the hole, or during a downswing how far the club-head will delay behind the hands prior to the release.

Sexual: A "sex-lag" is when a couple has so much sex their bodies become disoriented with time. A "jetlag" is when someone misses another after being with them sexually. And a "fuck-lag" is when a couple takes a few moments to pause during intercourse.

Lay up

Golf: A stroke played with a short-range club that is used in order to position the ball in a certain spot. This may be done to avoid a hazard on the course.

Sexual: A casual "meet-up" and or an easy "pick-up" of a person, solely for sex.

Misread

Golf: To incorrectly discern the correct line of a putt.

Sexual: A misunderstanding of the signal one receives in a bar or club as a sexual invitation, but it is not.

Pin(s)

Golf: Slang for a flag-stick, or marker, usually a metal pole with a flag at the top to indicate the position of the hole on a green.

Sexual: This may refer to a small penis or to intercourse, meaning that the vagina is a pincushion to be stuck with a penis. It can also refer to a woman's long skinny legs.

Pitch

Golf: A short shot played with a higher lofted club and made using a less than full swing toward the hole at the green.

Sexual: The territory or area that a street prostitute works along, and the words a person tells another to get them to agree to a sexual liaison.

Pro

Golf: A professional golfer who plays or teaches golf for financial reward.

Sexual: A short word for a prostitute.

Pull

Golf: A shot that unintentionally travels on a trajectory on the same side of the ball from which the player swings.

Sexual: The ability to draw a potential sexual partner by seduction, touching, or kissing. An Australian slang term, "on the pull" means that a man is all dressed up and out looking for a sexual partner.

Putt(s)

Golf: A shot played on the green with a putter.

Sexual: This comes from "putting from the rough," which is a metaphor for gay sex.

Release

Golf: A powerful downswing when the wrists open, creating a lag with a late delivery.

Sexual: The critical moment at the point of climax when an orgasm is achieved and an ejaculation is produced.

Rough

Golf: The tall, coarse grass that borders the fairway.

Sexual: Describes a wild and hard session of intercourse.

Rutter

Golf: A small headed niblick (an iron with a heavy, lofted head) used for hitting the ball from a cart track.

Sexual: A man who is especially sexually active.

Shank

Golf: An erratic shot in which the golf ball is struck by the hollow part of the club head where the shaft is attached.

Sexual: A prostitute or a woman without virtue.

Shrimp(ing)

Golf: A severe hooked shot, named because it resembles the shape of a shrimp.

Sexual: To lick or suck on someone's toes.

Skin

Golf: A skin game pits players in a type of match play in which each hole has a set value of money or points.

Sexual: Describes someone in the nude, and "getting skin," meaning intercourse.

Skull

Golf: To contact the ball with the leading edge of an iron, resulting in a low shot that goes further than expected, usually a mishit.

Sexual: A euphemism for fellatio.

Slice

Golf: An unintentional shot of the ball on the same side from which the player swings but curves from a sideways spin.

Sexual: A comment about a sexy woman, as if wanting a slice of sweet pie, which also resembles the triangle of a crotch.

Spray

Golf: To hit the ball in a seemingly random and inconsistent direction, compared to the intended target.

Sexual: A man who ejaculates with force.

Stroke

Golf: A swing of a golf club by the player who is trying to strike the ball, and each stroke is counted as part of keeping score.

Sexual: A hand movement that brushes another's body, and the action of placing the index finger and thumb around the penis along the shaft and moving the skin up and down to produce a pleasurable sensation leading to orgasm and ejaculation. Also, a man's penetrations delivered full-length during intercourse.

Sweet spot

Golf: The location on the club face where the optimal ball-striking results are achieved.

Sexual: A place on the body that responds pleasurably when touched, usually upon the clitoris, or the "G" spot within a woman's vaginal canal.

Swing

Golf: The movement a golf player makes with his or her body and club to hit the ball.

Sexual: To have an open sexual relationship with one's partner, and with a select group of other partners or swingers.

Tip(s), the

Golf: The championship tees on a golf course.

Sexual: The end of a man's penis, or erect nipples.

Toe

Golf: The far end of the club-head, opposite the grip.

Sexual: A short word for camel toe, which refers to the outline of a woman's labia majora seen through her pants.

Topped

Golf: An errant shot where the club-head strikes on top of the ball, causing the ball to roll or bounce rather than fly.

Sexual: In BDSM, being dominated.

Up and down

Golf: When a player holes the ball in two strokes or pars, starting from off the green.

Sexual: This indicates how a person is looking at and "checking out" another's physical attractiveness.

Waggle

Golf: A pre-shot routine where a player adjusts his body, the club, or practice swings at the ball.

Sexual: The movement of raising the eyebrows with a gesture of sexuality, the shaking of one's hind end, or a group of men showing their penises.

Wedge

Golf: A type of golf club, which is a subset of an iron, designated for short range strokes.

Sexual: A slang synonym for female genitalia.

Wood

Golf: A type of club where the head is bulbous with extra weight for hitting far down the green.

Sexual: A synonym for a hard and erect penis, to get a "wood" or "a woody."

Zinger

Golf: A ball hit high and hard.

Sexual: A particularly large and engorged penis.

Other Golf Terms with Sexual Possibilities

An *angle of approach* in golf is the angle at which the club head strikes, affecting the trajectory of the ball. An angle of approach with a sexual connotation, much like the angle of entry in bowling, refers to the angle of penile insertion for direct entry. A *bare lie* in the sport is when the ball sits directly on hard ground without any grass to buoy the ball up. A bare lie could only be lying about in the nude. The *best ball* is a form of team play using two, three, or four people on a team. The team score on each hole is the lowest score obtained by one of the team members. And since "to ball" is also another term for intercourse, the best ball would be the best sex. A *bump and run* in golf is a low-trajectory shot that is intended to get the ball rolling along the fairway and up onto the green. And since bump is a euphemism for intercourse, a bump and run would be someone who has a quick sexual connection with someone and then, just as quickly, departs. A *fairway* in golf is the area of the course between the tee and the green that is well-maintained allowing a good lie for the ball. A fairway sometimes can have the meaning much like "alley" or the short stretch between the anus and the sexual organs, but it could also be the close-cut pubic hair that forms a fairly attractive entry to the vaginal opening.

Grounding the club is to place the club-face behind the ball on the ground at address, although not allowed in bunkers or marked hazards. Since a club is a synonym for the penis, and grounding someone is meant as a punishment, grounding the club, might be grounding one's partner to stay home and not allowing him to go out with the boys or to a strip club. An *interlocking grip* is a grip style where the pinkie finger of the right hand is hooked around the index finger of the left when holding a golf club. An interlocking grip could also be a couple in yab-yum, that is, a man and woman in union with each sitting and facing each other with their legs wrapped around the other. A *pro shop* is a shop at a golf club, run by the club professionals, where golf equipment can be purchased. A pro shop could also be a brothel where many prostitutes are available. A *stroke play* is a style of scoring in which the player with the fewest strokes wins. Stroke play can also refer to the playing and stroking of a penis or the playing and stroking of the female body.

Sexual Commentary

The basic premises of golf are clear: 1. Play the ball as it lies, 2. Play the course as you find it, and 3. If unable to do either, do what is fair. This makes complete sense, both for the game and for a sexual player. A man can have his scrotum played with while he is lying down, most usually on a couch or bed. If he is not lying down on a couch or bed, perhaps he is sitting or standing. Above all, be fair. Don't just play around. Allow time for him to climax.

Who plays golf and their ages is interesting to note. Here are two sets of statistics that show what a difference was made in only four years, just in the U.S. A 2014 report by the American Golf Corporation stated that 24% of golf players were fifty years of age and older, with the average age being 54. The number of players was 29 million, 77.5% men and 22.5% women.[195] In a 2018 study conducted by the Statistics Portal, only 8.64% were 50 and older. Also, the number of players had dropped to 24 million.[196]

Sexually speaking, within the age range of fifty years and older, one finds that the majority of men begin to have erection difficulties. Is it no wonder that these older men decide to play a sport where their "stick" is made with an extremely hard shaft made of a hollow rod of titanium or steel? The club called a wood also has the largest head of all the clubs. And they can take comfort in the fact that they can now "play" with a tremendous swing of that club.

The average time it takes for four men to play eighteen holes of golf is four hours. In 2009, AARP did a random sex, romance and relationships survey of 1,670 Americans forty-five and older. It found that men in their fifties had intercourse an average of once a week, spending an average time of 5.4 minutes—and that is the average time for males of all ages. It is no wonder that a man over fifty decides to swing his golf club rather than

---

[195] Tyler Pringle, "The Demographics of Golf – Inside the Mind of a Golfer," American Golf Corporation.
https://www.americangolf.com/blog/mulligans/the-demographics-of-golf-inside-the-mind-of-a-golfer/

[196] The Statistics Portal, "Share of People Who Played Golf in the Unites States in 2018, by Age."
https://www.statista.com/statistics/227420/number-of-golfers-usa/

362

his penis as often as he does. The results end up being far
greater a reward.

Chapter 28
Hurling & Camogie

In hurling, the stick is a *hurley* (called a *caman* in Irish), the ball is a *sliotar*, the outdoor field is called a hurling pitch, and the fifteen players are called hurlers. The goal is to hit the ball into the opponent's pitch area and either get the ball over the crossbar, when a white flag signals one point, or under the crossbar, past the goalkeeper into a net, for a green flag that designates three points. Camogie is almost identical to hurling, but it is only played by women, and the few differences will be discussed below.

Hurling is played with three forwards, three half forwards, two midfielders, three half backs, and three full backs. Up to five players can be substituted. The sliotar can be hit in the air, struck by a hurley on the ground, kicked, slapped, caught and carried for four steps, bounced once to keep the ball in play, or for the best trick of all, the ball is balanced on the end of the stick! Eight pairs of eyes watch all plays to make sure calls are made correctly. There is the referee on the field, a linesman on each sideline, a sideline official or standby, and two umpires at each end who watch a seventy-minute game with a ten-minute halftime. As one of the fastest field sports on earth, it also has its risks because no protective padding is required except a helmet with a faceguard.

The sport has been around for about 2,000 years, finding its origins through Gaelic and Irish players, back to the Celts.[197] In Seamus King's book, *A History of Hurling*, he references the game being played as early as 1200 BCE, in Tara, County Meath, Ireland, describing it as a village game played for days by men of the area.[198] Hurling shares its history with the game of *cammag* played on the Isle of Man, *bando* in England and Wales, *shinty* in Scotland, and *camogie* in Ireland. The Golden Age of Hurling is thought to have been during the eighteenth century when the gentry amused their tenants with local teams on their estates.

In 1879, the first formal set of rules was formed at Dublin's Trinity College by the Irish Hurling Union. The Gaelic Athletic Association, founded in 1884, still administers the games and terminology. The first All-Ireland hurling final was played in 1891. There were also equipment changes midcentury which became official. The old Claddagh boot spikes were no longer used, the hurley stick became flatter, and a ball was introduced. Over twenty of Ireland's thirty-two counties have teams. In 1904, hurling was introduced into the Summer Olympics, but never became an official Olympic sport. However, about a dozen different cups are awarded for all the different championship games, named after star players.

Since 2000, hurling is played throughout southern Ireland, centered in County Kilkenny, and has spread throughout Europe from Britain, to South Korea, South Africa, and across the sea to North America, Argentina, Australia, and New Zealand. Next to Ireland, the Milwaukee Hurling Club in the U.S. has the largest

---

[197] Kidzworld, "Traditional Celtic Sports."
https://www.kidzworld.com/article/5426-traditional-celtic-sports/

[198] Seamus J. King, *A History of Hurling*, (Dublin: Gill & Macmillan Ltd., 2005), 15.

hurling club membership in the world. In 2002 the St. Louis Gaelic Athletic Club was founded, and now there are teams in eighteen cities, and a thirty-member camogie league for women. In 2009 an informal game of hurling between Berkeley and Stanford colleges was played. In 2011, the first championships between the national colleges were played.

Also in 2011, Camogie was being played by over 100,000 women. Although most of the rules are the same, there are a few differences. The goalkeepers wear the same colors as the outfielders, hand passes are allowed, the game lasts for two 30-minute halves with a 10-minute halftime, one can drop their stick to hand pass, and the sliotar is smaller at size 4 as opposed to a men's hurling sliotar which is a size 5. If a defending player hits the sliotar wide, a near 50-yard (45 m) puck is awarded to the opposition, as opposed to about a 70-yard (65 m) puck in hurling. After a goal, a goalkeeper will puck from the 14.22-yard (13 m) line. The metal band on the camogie stick must be covered with tape, side-to-side changes are forbidden, and two points are awarded for a score from a sideline cut. Wearing shorts is not allowed, so players must wear either a skirt or skorts (a combo of a skirt over shorts). There are 537 camogie clubs in the world, most of them in Ireland.

This chapter won't delve into the different plays of either game, but some will be presented in the terms and slang section. Now on to describing the playing field and equipment.

Both camogie and hurling are played on a large rectangular grassy pitch, 87.49 to 98.43 yards (80 m to 98.43 m) wide by 142.17 to 158.57 yards (130 m to 145 m) long. Large H-shaped goalposts are at each end, standing 20 to 23 feet (6.09 m to 7.01 m) high and 21 feet (6.40 m) apart, connected above the ground by an 8.2-foot (2.50 m) crossbar. A net is connected between the crossbar and lower posts. From side to side, down the pitch, white lines are drawn at 14 yards (12.80 m), 21 yards (19.20 m), and 65 yards (59.44 m).

The first piece of needed equipment is the helmet with faceguards protecting the mouth and nose. It became compulsory for hurlers of all ages to wear a helmet by 2010.

The hurley stick, or as the Irish call it, the *camán,* is made of the upper root of an ash tree. It can measure between 18 and 40 inches (45.72 cm to 101.60 cm) long, depending upon the size of the player. With a hurley held upright next to a person and the hurley toe on the ground, the handle should come to the player's hip. At the other end of the handle, the wood widens out to a vertically-flat foot where the metal band is and the sliotar is hit.

In the 1970s the hurley was made of plastic. By 2012, plastic was phased out and a synthetic material was used. In hurley, there are steel or copper bands that lie across and bind the wood. In camogie, no metal bands are allowed to be exposed, for safer play. Still, a hurler will go through several hurleys in a season from rough play. "The clash of the ash" is the collision of two hurleys. There are different names for the parts of the hurley. The very end, on the other side of the metal band, is the *toe,* which is used to roll lift or jab lift the ball for possession. The flat base of the hurley is called the *bas,* and on the stick side of the metal band is the *heel.* The handle end also has a lip so that the hurley does not slide away from the handgrip.

The sliotar is the hard ball used in the game, and the name is from the Scots Gaelic meaning "slot." It is made of cork and covered in two leather pieces with a heightened rib stitch. It resembles a baseball, but is used in hurley, camogie, and the game of rounders. It is 2.7 to 2.8 inches (6.86 cm to 7.11 cm) in diameter and weighs from 3.9 to 4.2 ounces (110.56 g to 119.07 g). The ball was originally made of wood, rope, animal hair, leather, or hollow bronze. In 1886, Ned Treston fashioned a horsehair and leather ball, but it got lumpy and became heavy with the moisture, and the dark leather was difficult to see. In 1896, Johnny McAuliffe began using cork inside the balls and white leather on the outside, making the ball sturdier, lighter, water resistant, and easier to see. For a brief time in the early 2000s, the cork was replaced with rubber, but the bounce ended up being too unpredictable, so manufacturers returned to using cork.

Hurling Terms and Slang

Alley

Hurling: Aside from a hurling field, hurling can be played indoors in what is called a hurling alley, which is about 5½ yards (5.03 m) in height. It should be enclosed with floodlights and have an overhanging barrier or net for catching the sliotar.

Sexual: The shortened term for "shaft alley," which is the area from the vaginal opening to the anus. It is originally a nautical term for the passage from the engine room to the stern.

Backdoor

Hurling: A knockout championship in which defeated teams are not immediately eliminated from the competition and remain to win. Such teams re-enter the championship through the back door.

Sexual: Refers to the buttocks, the anus, and anal intercourse.

Bas (Boss)

Hurling: The flattened and curved end of a hurley stick, which provides the striking surface.

Sexual: An expression for a top-notch, sexy man or woman.

Block

Hurling: When a player prevents an opponent's strike by trapping the ball between his and the opponent's swinging hurley.

Sexual: A deterrence by a "cock-blocker," a person who blocks another from "hooking up" sexually with someone.

Book

Hurling: A referee's notebook where he marks a tick against a player who has committed a certain type of foul. When two ticks are noted that player is given a warning with a yellow card.

Sexual: An analogy used by men for women. The cover of the book is how attractive she is and the plot is her personality. A quick read is a one-time sexual encounter and a lasting relationship is a novel. Having read the whole book means he had intercourse. If disappointing, she goes "back on the shelf."

Club

Hurling: The basic organizational unit of the Gaelic Athletic Association throughout Ireland; i.e. the Hurling Club.

Sexual: A synonym for a large penis.

Double, (a)

Hurling: In Gaelic games, this means that a county wins the All-Ireland Senior Football Championship and the All-Ireland Hurling Championship in the same year.

Sexual: Short for double penetration, when a man penetrates a woman vaginally and another man does so anally. It is also when one man is engaged in sex play with two women at the same time.

Fetch(ing)

Hurling: To catch the ball above one's head.

Sexual: When someone is fetching they are attractive, alluring, charming, eye-catching, intriguing, and captivating.

Green flag

Hurling: When a team scores a goal of the sliotar under the crossbar, the judge waives a green flag for three points.

Sexual: A person who wears a green handkerchief in their back pocket is relaying sexual code via a "flag" to mean there is money involved as in hustling or prostitution.

Hook(ing)

Hurling: A defensive tactic where a player approaches from a rear angle and uses his stick to hook or stop the attempted swing of another player.

Sexual: Refers to the act of "hooking up" or meeting another person for a sexual encounter. It is also the action of a hooker or a prostitute at work.

Junior

Hurling: A grade of competition for players not quite good enough to play at the intermediate or senior levels.

Sexual: A euphemism for a penis.

Park

Hurling: Hurling is often played on a sports ground park.

Sexual: A euphemism for sex in a car.

Pitch

Hurling: The field that hurley is played on.

Sexual: The territory, area, or street that a prostitute works along, and the words a person tells another to get them to agree to a sexual liaison.

Solo(ing)

Hurling: To run with the sliotar balanced or bouncing on the end of the hurley, known as a solo run.

Sexual: Known in the porn industry as a videotape sequence of only one woman who masturbates or uses sex toys.

Strike (ing)

Hurley: The action of hitting the sliotar ball with a hurley.

Sexual: From "sex-strike," in which one or multiple persons refrain from sex with their partners to achieve certain goals.

Tackle (ing)

Hurley: Using the hurley to interfere with another player's stick, and initiating shoulder-to-shoulder contact with another player in pursuit of the ball.

Sexual: Refers to a man's genitals, his "fishing tackle," also known as his "wedding or man tackle," for that special night.

White flag

Hurling: When a team scores a point by hitting the sliotar over the crossbar, the goal judge will waive a white flag.

Sexual: In the gay man's hanky code, when a man wears a white handkerchief in his back pocket, he is relaying a coded sexual message with a variety of meanings depending upon whether the kerchief is in the left or right back pocket.

Other Hurling & Camogie Terms with Sexual Possibilities

A *dual player* is someone who plays both football and hurling at a high level. A sexual meaning for a dual player would be a person who can be a sexual giver and taker, or a switch who can be a submissive one time and a dominant another time. A *hand-pass* in hurling is when a ball is slapped with the palm of the hand, rather than throwing it. It can't be used to score goals, but it will garner points. A possible sexual meaning for a hand-pass might be an actual pickup pass, but instead of being spoken is done with a hand.

There is also *lift and strike,* which is the method used to take frees, 65s, and penalty strikes. The ball is placed on the ground and a player uses their hurley to lift the ball into the air, where it is then struck. A lift and strike could also mean that a man lifts a woman's skirt and has intercourse with her. With a *sideline ball,* a puck is awarded to the opposite team when the ball passes over the sideline. A sideline ball could also be a lover kept on the side, outside a relationship.

Sexual Commentary

When scoring the game, if a ball sails high between the opposition's goal posts, an umpire raises a white flag, and one point is awarded. If the ball goes below the crossbar, the umpire raises a green flag indicating that the goal is worth three points. Men sometimes refer to the successful completion of sexual intercourse as a "score." In urban-speak, a crossbar in sex refers to the knees or legs raised during coitus. If a man ejaculates outside of the body and instead directs his ejaculation between the knees, that is one thing, but if he ejaculates within the vaginal canal, that is more within the description of a "score," because it has more value. The color white means innocent, goodness, safe, pure, virginal, and clean. The color green means fertility, renewal of life, and growth. It becomes easy to see the meaning of these colors and scores when it comes to a sexual interpretation.

The hurley stick has a wooden handle top and middle, and between them is the grip. Where the handle meets the "bas," it forms the "foot," although only the toe and heel are official names. For a hurley stick played by men, there is a metal band around the toe to help reinforce the wood, but this is taped over for camogie when women play. This sounds like the use of a covering or condom when there is sex with another.

The hurley stick shape is unique and unlike any other stick in sports. Remember the three shapes of a dart's barrel? The torpedo shape is the thinnest at the base and widest at the point. So too, is the hurley stick, which again, is what some penises look like, being thinner at the base and wider at the tip. But the bas or foot of the stick, rather than being rounded, is wide and flat with a slight curve toward the toe. This area is the playing surface where the sliotar is hit and carried. It is the only sport where the stick can carry its own ball. Oh, you mean like how a penis has testicles that are carried wherever the penis goes? Yes.

Chapter 29
Lacrosse

The contact team sport of lacrosse is played with a lacrosse ball and a lacrosse stick on a lacrosse field. Its players use the stick to carry, catch, pass, and shoot the ball into a goal in the opponent's field for points. There are four different lacrosse games and they have different equipment requirements and rules. There is box lacrosse (men's indoor), field lacrosse (men's outdoor), intercrosse (played by both genders with no body contact and other differences), and women's lacrosse (no body contact, with little protective gear, but protective eye-gear). Men's games require a helmet, gloves, shoulder and elbow pads.

Lacrosse has its beginnings in North America, quite possibly as early as 1100 CE, by the Iroquois people in the area of New York and Pennsylvania.[199] Stories from Jesuit missionaries talk of games in Canada involving hundreds of men on a huge field, lasting for several days. This was not so much a sport as symbolic warfare being played out in a ceremonial ritual for their creator. In 1637, a French missionary saw the game being played with a wide-ended stick, and described the word for "stick" in his

---

[199] Howard Liss, *Lacrosse*, (New York: Funk & Wagnalls, 1970), 13.

native language as *"la crosse,"* and the name stuck.[200] By
the 1830s the game was being played in Montreal, and in
1856 the first Lacrosse Club was founded. Four years
later, the game was codified, a rubber ball was
introduced, and a new design for the stick was made. The
number of players was set at twelve per team and the
length of play was shortened to four 15-minute periods.
Women's games were introduced in Scotland in 1890,
and by the early 1900s, lacrosse was being played in
Australia, Canada, England, New Zealand, and the
United States.

In 1904 and 1908, field lacrosse was in the Summer
Olympics as a medal sport. After that, it was only present
for demonstration, as the sport has yet to meet the
qualification of being played in at least seventy-five
countries. In 1987, the only team ever made up solely of
Iroquois nationals which has been sanctioned for
international competition in any sport was admitted to
the international field lacrosse competition.[201] In 1995, the
European Lacrosse Federation was established with its
championships. In 2004, the Asia Pacific Lacrosse Union
was founded for the teams of Australia, Hong Kong,
Japan and South Korea. In 2008, the governing bodies for
men and women merged to become the Federation of
International Lacrosse, which hosts five world
championship tournaments, each held every four years.
In 1990 the federation had only four countries, but by

[200] Peter Bailey Lund, "Lacrosse: A History of the Game."
https://web.archive.org/web/19991008114420/ www.e-
lacrosse.com/laxhist4.htm

[201] Tabitha Marshall and Jim Calder, "Lacrosse: From Creator's Game
to Modern Sport," The Canadian Encyclopedia.
https://www.thecanadianencyclopedia.ca/en/article/lacrosse-
from-creators-game-to-modern-sport

2014 there were thirty-eight countries. A survey conducted in 2016 found that there were over 825,000 participants in the sport at collegiate and professional levels.[202]

One of the unique aspects of the game is the "faceoff," which occurs at the beginning of each fifteen-minute quarter and when a goal is achieved. Parallel to the midline, two players place their stick heads on the ground on either side of the ball. When a whistle blows, both sticks toss up the ball and each team volleys to take possession. There are various strategies to the game, with personal and technical fouls that can bring penalties, and the team may be one man up or down.

All of the intricate rules and different plays of the game will not be discussed, but some of them will be described when the different terms are listed. This chapter will next look at the field played on, the equipment used, protection worn, and the sticks and balls used in the game.

All fields are about the same, but the rules change with each type of lacrosse game. A men's lacrosse field is 60 yards wide by 110 yards long (54.96 m by 100.58 m). But in women's lacrosse the field is slightly larger, 70 yards wide by 120 yards long (64 m by 109.73 m). The field is divided into three areas: the defensive zone at one end, the wing zone in the middle, and the attack zone at the far end. On one sideline of the wing area is the limit line and on the other side are the benches, the coach's area, and the timer. Each team of ten has one goalie, three defensemen, three midfielders, and three attackmen. Only a maximum of four sticks are allowed at one time

[202] Brian Logue, "National Lacrosse Participation Tops 825,000 Players." https://www.uslacrosse.org/blog/national-lacrosse-participation-tops-825000-players

for the defensemen and one midfielder. And only the goalie has a wider head on his stick to defend his 6-by-6-foot (1.83 m) goal area, called a "crease."

Box lacrosse gets its name from the enclosed shape of the indoor soccer field it is held in. There are several differences in this game. For one, box lacrosse is a quicker game and because the ball is moving faster, there is more risk of injury, so the goalie wears a lot more protective padding, especially since the goals are smaller, 2 feet (60.96 cm) deep and only 4 feet (121.92 cm) wide. The players wear rib pads, shoulder and elbow pads, and a hockey helmet with a box lacrosse facial cage. There is also a shot clock, which is a timer designed to increase the game's pace and scoring, which requires the attacking team to take a shot within thirty seconds of gaining the ball. This game is the National Lacrosse League and the Canadian Lacrosse Association's highest level of play.

There are notable differences between the men's and women's games, created when the first women's team was established in 1926. A faceoff is not how a women's game begins. They begin with a draw, similar to a faceoff but the sticks and ball are horizontal at the waist. There are twelve players on a women's lacrosse team, there is no pocket or loose net on the stick, there is no physical contact, and only a mouth and eye guard are required. There are boundaries in this game with an 8.75 to 12-foot (2.67 m to 3.66 m) fan (an arched marking on the field) and the draw circle in the center of the field. No more than three seconds are allowed for defending players to stand in the fan. A foul can result in the opposing team getting a free shot. There's also "checking" (body contact) in men's games, which means rough play.

Intercrosse is played by any adult, so it is non-physical. The intercrosse stick is made of soft plastic, and the ball is larger and hollow. This game is played on a court that is 21.87 yards wide and 43.75 yards long (20 m by 40 m). It is still a competitive sport in Canada, the Czech Republic, France, Germany, Hungary, Italy, Poland, Slovakia, and Switzerland. There are five players on each team and the goal is to get the ball into the 4-foot-wide (1.22 m) goal net. The end goal of a seasoned player is to be able to participate in the Fédération International d'Inter-Cross (FIIC) World Championship.

The earliest lacrosse balls were made of solid wood covered with stitched deerskin with the fur facing inward. The early Iroquois sticks were made of hickory wood, sometimes with attached hawk feathers or wolf fur. A stick pocket was made from leather strips crisscrossing a wooden loop, or from hardened cow or deer intestine. In 1937, Robert Pool created the double-walled lacrosse stick, making it much easier to handle.[203] By 1970, the first synthetic plastic head was made, making restringing easier, and by 1980 lighter mesh laces were used. Now, the shaft is made of hollow metal and the shaft is capped with a plug called a *butt*, made of rubber.

At the other end of the shaft, a wooden head is attached and bent into a triangle shape. It is drilled all around the triangle, so that a woven pocket can be formed about 6 inches (15.24 cm) across. Nylon string is now used, woven loosely to form the net with a top string, two sidewalls, and a bottom string. At the throat of the stick is a drawstring to adjust the tightness. With the ball caught in the net, it can be cradled along, passed to a teammate, or swung for a shot to the goal. In men's

---

[203] Lacrosse in America, "Robert Pool's Contribution: Double Walled Lacrosse Sticks – 1937."
https://americanlacrosse1865.wordpress.com/2017/03/28/robert-pools-contribution-double-walled-lacrosse-sticks-1937/

lacrosse, a head can be up to 10 inches (25.4 cm) wide, and a goalie's stick head can be from 10 to 15 inches (25.4 cm to 38.1 cm) wide. The circumference of the shaft cannot be more than 3½ inches (8.89 cm). The stick length can be 40 to 42 inches (101.6 cm to 106.68 cm) long for offensive players, 40 to 72 inches (101.60 cm to 182.88 cm) long for goalies, and 52 to 72 inches (132.08 cm to 182.88 cm) long for defensemen.

Lacrosse Terms and Slang

Ball or Ball down

Lacrosse: Players shout "ball" when the ball is on the ground. Also, when a player goes after the ball instead of a man.

Sexual: Ball is a synonym for one testicle, and a euphemism for intercourse.

Box, the

Lacrosse: The rectangular shaped area around the crease and goal. Defenders seldom press players outside of the box. The distance involved makes it all but impossible to score from outside of the box. The rules state that the offense can only possess the ball for so long without entering the box. At the end of a game the team that is ahead must keep the ball inside of the box.

Sexual: A synonym for vagina.

Butt

Lacrosse: The end of a lacrosse stick opposite the head. All shaft ends need to be covered with a butt-cap.

Sexual: A shortened word for the buttocks of a person.

Clamping

Lacrosse: On the face-off, a player pushes the back of his stick down on the ball in the attempt to gain control of it.

Sexual: In bondage and S&M, clamping of the nipples, vaginal lips, and other body parts is common.

Crease

Lacrosse: The 18-foot (5.49 m) diameter circle surrounding each team's goal.

Sexual: The crevice separating the buttocks.

Head

Lacrosse: The plastic part of the stick connecting the handle.

Sexual: The tip of the penis, and the act of giving or receiving oral sex, fellatio or cunnilingus.

Man-to-man

Lacrosse: A defensive setup in which each defending player guards a specific offensive opponent.

Sexual: A homosexual pairing.

Pocket

Lacrosse: The head of the stick in which the ball is held and carried. The pocket is strung with leather and or mesh netting. In order to be legal, the top of a ball cannot be seen when looking at the pocket from the side, while the pocket holds the ball. This indicates that the netting has been properly adjusted so that the tension does not raise the ball in the net.

Sexual: A synonym for the vagina.

Poke Check

Lacrosse: This is when a defender jabs his stick at the exposed stick end or hands of an opposing ball carrier in an effort to jar the ball loose. These checks are very effective in that the checking player stays in balance and keeps a cushion of space between himself and the ball carrier.

Sexual: Refers to anal fingering, in masturbation or in sexual play by another person.

Release

Lacrosse: Players shout "release" when they succeed in scooping a ground ball. This indicates to teammates that they can no longer contact an opponent to drive them away from the ball.

Sexual: The energetic discharge of sexual tension with orgasm.

Riding

Lacrosse: When an attacking team loses possession of the ball it must quickly revert to playing defense in order to prevent the ball from being cleared back out.

Sexual: Refers to a woman sitting astride a man in coitus and moving up and down as if riding a horse.

Scooping

Lacrosse: The manner in which a player picks up loose ground balls. He bends toward the ground, slides the pocket of his stick underneath the ball and lofts it into the netting of the stick.

Sexual: When a male puts his hands under a woman's shirt and bra to grab hold of her breasts.

Shaft

Lacrosse: The hollow aluminum or composite pole connected to the head of the lacrosse stick.

Sexual: Refers to the stem of a penis.

Slide

Lacrosse: When an offensive player with the ball has gotten past his defender, a defending teammate will shift his position to pick up that advancing player.

Sexual: A woman used for intercourse with no obligation.

V Cut

Lacrosse: A maneuver used by an offensive player to get open for a pass. The offensive player feigns going in one direction, causing his defender to react and move. The offensive player then cuts sharply away, completing the V shape.

Sexual: Refers to the V-shape of the human groin area.

Other Lacrosse Terms with Sexual Possibilities

A *body check* is when a player defensively uses the body to hit an opposing ball carrier, only done above the waist and from the front or side, or while contesting an opponent for a player or a loose ball. A body check is recommended before having intercourse with someone new, to make sure no open sores or problems are present. Along with the butt of a lacrosse stick, there is a *butt-cap* at the end of the shaft. A butt-cap in sexual terminology would be a butt-plug, which is inserted into the rectum for sexual pleasure. *Cradling* is when a lacrosse player turns his or her wrists and arms to cradle the ball in the stick pocket, done to maintain control of the ball when moving along the field. There is also the use of cradling in a sexual fetish called infantilism, which is when an adult chooses to role-play as an infant. *Face dodging* is when a player with the ball cradles the stick across his face in an attempt to dodge a stick-poking defender. In sex-speak, this sounds like what a woman does when she does not want ejaculate in her eye.

A *man down* describes the team which has lost a player to the penalty box and must play with fewer men on the field. A man down in an orgy is when a man orgasms and needs to pull back and recuperate, leaving the group with one less penis for play. In lacrosse, a *quick stick* is when the ball reaches an offensive player's stick on a feed pass. He catches it and then shoots it toward the goal in one swift motion. A quick stick could also refer to someone coming to orgasm too quickly with a premature ejaculation. *Raking* is a face-off move by a lacrosse player, who, in trying to gain possession of a ground ball, places the head of his lacrosse stick on top of the ball, and sweeps it back. Raking is also a BDSM action, done by raking a brush, spur, or any other semi-sharp object over the skin for stimulation, usually done with the person blind-folded so they don't know what the tool is, for a heightened sensory experience. A *stick check* is done by a defending player in an effort to dislodge the ball from the pocket of an opposing ball carrier in a controlled manner. Stick checking, also as in ice hockey, would be the process of closely looking over the penis before having intercourse with someone new, to make sure no open sores are present, and all appears normal.

Sexual Commentary

Let's address the lacrosse stick. The handle is either short or long, and the shaft is capped at the end of the handle with a butt end. Where the shaft joins the head is called the neck. Where a ball is held is called the pocket, and deep within that pocket at the throat is where a ball comes to rest, called a ball stop. The pocket is a mesh net made up of runner strings that run lengthwise with a few shooting strings that run widthwise. The pocket is held in shape by the sidewalls. When the player is ready to shoot the ball, it is rolled to the widest end called the scoop and the ball is propelled forward with the help of the shooting strings. In women's lacrosse the pocket is made up of strips of leather or synthetic thongs.

One can see where this will go, as the terms are expressed with names for parts of the human body. A shaft is the shank of a penis, the butt is the buttocks. The head is joined to the body by a neck. If a testicle is taken into the mouth it will go no further than the throat. In urban slang, a pocket, also called a hot or sex pocket, is the vagina with flexible sidewalls. After intercourse, a penis can be ejected by the vagina's side muscles. And a thong is a woman's G-string panties. The analogies are obvious.

Chapter 30
Polo

In polo, the ball is a polo ball and the stick is a mallet. The sport is played on a large grassy field with riders mounted on polo ponies, all with the aim of hitting a small hard ball across the field into the opposing team's side to score a goal. Outdoor field polo is played with four players, whereas indoor arena polo is played with three players and the ball is slightly larger and air inflated. The players are numbered, one to three or four, and each has a position and certain responsibilities. They play for one to two hours divided into time periods called *chukkas* or *chukkers*. Other variations include beach polo, cowboy polo, horseball, pato, polocrosse, and other games of polo not played on horseback, such as ones played in autos, on cycles, elephants, motorcycles, canoes, and Segways.

It's possible that polo traces its beginnings to the nomads of Iran and Turkey in Central Asia, and during the Middle Ages was used for training cavalry.[204] The sport spread during the Parthian Empire (247 BCE to 224 CE) to China, Iran, India, Mongolia, and Pakistan. Mongolian rulers supported the sport through the eleventh century, when it was known as the "sport of

---

[204] Horace A. Laffaye, *The Evolution of Polo*, (Jefferson, NC: McFarland, 2009), 5-6.

kings."[205] A Persian emperor, Shapur II, learned the game as a child in 316 CE. In 408 to 450 CE, the eastern Roman emperor, Theodosius II, built the *tzykanisterion*, a stadium inside the Great palace of Constantinople, for playing the game of *tzykanion*, the Byzantine word for polo.[206] The Sultan Saladin played the game and encouraged others to play it, even though it had its dangers.[207] A Persian miniature from 1546 depicts a group of courtiers riding horses holding mallets on a brown field. The word "polo" may have come from the Balti language of Tibet, with the word "pulu" meaning ball.[208]

The game, however, continued its migration to Manipur, India, where the sport was established as the first polo club in 1833. The winged-pony god of polo was represented at the Lai Haraoba festival, which worshipped the sylvan deities of the Meitei people of northeastern India. Manipur also has the oldest polo playing area at the Imphal Polo Ground, described in a royal chronicle in 33 CE. In 1850, Major General Joseph Ford Sherer became the father of modern polo. In 1862 the Calcutta Polo Club was established and still exists.

From India, the game traveled to England where more polo clubs were established, rules were codified, and the Hurlingham Polo Association set its parameters for

---

[205] Darren Heitner, "The Economics of Polo, The Sport of Kings," Forbes Online.
https://www.forbes.com/sites/darrenheitner/2015/05/17/the-economics-of-polo-the-sport-of-kings/

[206] Christopher Kelly, *Theodosius II: Rethinking the Roman Empire in Late Antiquity*, (Cambridge: Cambridge University Press, 2013), 4.

[207] Mark Cartwright, "Saladin," Ancient History Encyclopedia. https://www.ancient.eu/Saladin/

[208] Robert Crego, *Sports and Games of the 18th and 19th Centuries*, (Westport, CT: Greenwood Press, 2003).

British players in 1874. This produced a slower and more methodical game with fewer passes, fewer methods, and less skill necessary to play and ride. A league finally formed in 2016 in Jaipur, India with six teams, called the Champions Polo League. The game went on to Argentina, where they have five teams with three major tournaments known as the Triple Corona: the Hurlingham Polo Open, Tortugas Polo Open, and the Palermo Polo Open.

The United States began organizing the game in 1876, forming the Westchester Polo Club, and later, the United States Polo Association. As the new century began, polo began to slowly change to a faster game, with the fast break, long passes downfield to riders at full gallop, and a four-period match. The game spread to a total of seventy-seven countries. Polo was an Olympic game from 1900 to 1939, but it was only recognized as a sport with an international governing body in 1998. The Federation of International Polo offers the World Polo Championships every three years.

This chapter won't get into the rules and strategies of the game, but a description of the field and equipment is necessary before getting on to its terminology. The outdoor polo field is 160 yards by 300 yards long (146.30 m by 274.32 m), the size of five football fields. It is played in seven-minute chukkas (segments) with four-minute intervals and a ten-minute halftime. An indoor polo arena is 12.5 by 25 yards (11.43 m by 22.86 m) long. There is also a 4-foot-high (1.22 m) wall around the space, and it is played on dirt. The goal posts are centrally located at each end of the field, 8 yards (7.32 m) apart.

The basic equipment the polo rider wears is white pants, a numbered shirt stating the player's position and in the team's color, which is also seen on the helmet with a chin strap, and riding boots. Other items not required but which might be worn are a face mask, gloves, wristband, kneepads, spurs, and a horse whip.

The most fascinating piece of equipment is the full-grown horse, which is still called a polo pony. They are selected for their temperament, speed, responsiveness, agility, and maneuverability, and can account for up to seventy-five percent of a player's skill and net worth. The horse's training begins at three years of age, and a horse may play the game for fifteen years. Each player will use two to six ponies during a game, depending upon the level of competition, changing between or during chukkas.

The saddle is English-style, with a flat seat and no knee support, so that the rider will lean forward and close the knees. There are many variations in this kind of saddle, but two are that the stirrup leather is wider and thicker and the irons are heavier to support standing. During a game, the horse's legs will often be wrapped with team colors from the fetlock up to below the knee, for protection. The horse's mane is often shaved off down to the neck, and the tail is braided.

The next piece of equipment is the polo ball, which has been made from several different materials since its inception. The first ones were made of carved wood but they were also heavy. Players in India fashioned them out of bamboo, and this lighter material was used throughout the twentieth century. They were also made with a willow root center, and then a cork center covered with leather or hard rubber. By the 1970s, for the outdoor game, they were made of high-impact plastic, 3.0 to 3.5 inches (7.62 cm to 8.89 cm) in diameter, and 3.5 to 4.5 ounces (99.22 g to 127.57 g) in weight. The indoor arena ball is inflated leather, at 4.5 inches (11.43 cm) in diameter.

The polo mallet, or polo stick as the British call it, has a shaft, a handle at one end, and a cigar-shaped mallet head at the other. The shaft is usually made of cane for flexibility, though some are of a composite material. The handle is a rubber grip with a webbed thong sling for the thumb to hold on to. The head is made of a hardwood called *tipa*. The head is 9.25 inches (23.50 cm) long and weighs 5.6 to 8.5 ounces (158.76 g to 240.97 g). The length of the entire stick depends upon the stretch of the arm and the height of the horse, averaging from 50 to 53 inches (127cm to 134.62 cm).

Polo Terms and Slang

Back shot
Polo: A backhand swing, changing the flow of play by sending the ball in the opposite direction.
Sexual: From rear-entry intercourse, a penis is withdrawn and the ejaculate lands on the person's back.

Ball
Polo: The small white plastic sphere that a mallet hits and seeks to make a goal with.
Sexual: Ball is a synonym for one testicle, and a euphemism for intercourse.

Bump
Polo: When a player directs his pony into the side of an opponent's pony.
Sexual: A euphemism for intercourse.

Equipment
Polo: Tools needed for the game. Hard helmets are compulsory, but knee-pads, whips, and spurs are optional.
Sexual: A euphemism for male sexual genitals.

Field

Polo: The playing area, usually 160 by 300 yards (146.30 m by 274.32 m), is outlined by sideboards.

Sexual: From "playing the field," meaning to date or have sex with multiple people.

Handicap

Polo: A team's handicap is based on ability with the total of its player's goal ratings. The team with the lower handicap is awarded the difference in goals at the start of the match.

Sexual: Refers to a lover giving manual genital stimulation instead of fellatio.

Hook(ing)

Polo: Catching an opponent's mallet in swing below the level of the horse's back, and to leave or turn the ball for a teammate.

Sexual: Refers to the act of "hooking up" or meeting another person for a sexual encounter. It is also the action of a hooker or a prostitute at work, "hooking" a client for business.

Made pony (ponies)

Polo: A polo pony that is well-trained for polo and has been playing for some time.

Sexual: A fetish called "pony play" is when a person has been outfitted with the equipment of the trade, a bridle, bit, reins, halter, saddle, collar, hoof boots, gloves, and a pony's tail butt-plug.

Pass

Polo: To hit the ball forward or laterally to a teammate.

Sexual: An amorous or sexual advance to someone.

Stick

Polo: The polo mallet.

Sexual: A synonym for the penis.

Stick and ball(s)
Polo: Personal practice time.
Sexual: Refers to the penis and the testes.

Swing
Polo: Hitting at the ball with the mallet using one of four basic shots: the forehand, backhand, neck, or tail shot.
Sexual: To have an open sexual relationship with one's partner, and with a select group of other partners or swingers.

Throw in
Polo: When the umpire starts or resumes the match, he rolls the ball down the center of a lineup of players and horses.
Sexual: From "throw in the towel," meaning what a man does (figuratively) after his long pursuit of a particular woman, when she does not want to be intimate with him and turns him down.

Wrap(s)
Polo: Protective bandages the polo ponies wear on their legs.
Sexual: A synonym for a condom.

Other Polo Terms with Sexual Possibilities

In polo, *appealing* is a claim by players for a foul, expressed by the raising of mallets above the head. This term could also be used for a person being sexually appealing, which is the attractiveness of a possible sexual partner. A *goal* is scored any time the ball crosses the line between the goal posts, regardless of who knocks it through. In sexual nomenclature, a goal is met whenever a sexual conquest has been achieved. *Neck shot* is hitting the ball under the horse's neck. A neck shot could also be when a person is giving fellatio, the man pulls out to splash the face, but misses and hits the neck. A *knock-in* is awarded when a team hits the ball across the opponent's backline during an attack, and the defending team resumes with a free hit from the backline where the ball went over. In urban sexual nomenclature, a knock-in is when a guy tries to convince a prostitute that he would be a better pimp for her.

There are four player *positions* in polo, numbered one through four, each with different responsibilities. The Kama Sutra outlines sixty-four sexual positions. A *sudden death* in polo is overtime play, when the score is tied at the end of the last regular chukker, and the first team to score wins. A sudden death could also refer to the little death, or the experience of orgasm. *Tack* is all the equipment used on a pony, but *tacked* means empty, as in a man has ejaculated so many times in one session that he cannot come again. A *tail shot* in polo is hitting the ball behind and under the horse's rump, but in sexual slang, a tail shot, like a backshot, might also be when a man is having intercourse with rear entry and ejaculates upon the tailbone.

Sexual Commentary

This is the only sport that is played upon a horse. Not so much sexual, but horses are universally symbolic of freedom without restraint, and represent the action of movement. In Native American tribes, the horse represented power, as the more horses a tribe had, the more powerful the tribe was, and better able to win battles. In ancient Rome, horses were linked with Mars, the god of war. In Celtic mythology they were the harbingers of good fortune. When seen in dreams, they can represent strength, endurance, stamina, and male sexual energy. In literature, the horse symbolizes victory.

Now let's look at the polo mallet, followed by a sexual interpretation. The mallet is usually made from cane, but now players are switching to composite materials with fiberglass. A shaft should be stiff at the handle and more flexible near the tip. Attached to the end are the heads which strike the ball. Different heads come in different weights, from 5.30 to 7.76 ounces (150 g to 220 g). Most heads are similar in that they are about 9 inches long (228 mm), with one end squared and the other smaller, with a rounded end. There are arena polo heads, mango wood polo heads, and Argentine tipa polo mallet heads. Arena heads are made with lighter woods such as cane, are stiffer, and have a larger diameter head. The mango is made of Indian mango wood, and it is slightly longer at 9 1/8 inches (230 mm) long. Tipa is made from *Tipuana blanco* wood, and they are the heaviest of the three.

Such a description deserves interpretation. Suffice to say, mallets need to have a shaft that is long and strong. It comes to a tapered end to allow for more flex action, offers a wide sweet spot to hit the ball, and produces movement with maximum impact for speed with less effort and enhanced power. The relevance to a penis is obvious. This sounds like a commercial for women who are able to choose the penis they want.

Chapter 31
Quidditch (Muggle Quidditch)

The fictional game of Quidditch was created by J. K. Rowling in 1997 for the *Harry Potter* series. By 2005, with the popularity of her books, Quidditch turned into a real game played on American college campuses and in England with real tournaments. Now it is played on six continents, in twenty-six countries, with hundreds of teams. The U.S. hosts the World Cup Quidditch tournament, and there are the European Games, the Asian Quidditch Cup, Canadian Nationals, and the Global Games which are held every two years in different countries. The International Quidditch Association oversees all national governing bodies and all team competitions by developing officiating standards and maintaining official rules.[209]

Quidditch is a mixed-gender, full-body-contact stick and ball sport with up to twenty-one players on a team, but only seven on a field at one time: three chasers, one keeper, two beaters, and one seeker. It is unusual in that the players move about the pitch with brooms (or sticks representing a broom) between their legs, and a bat. The game is played on a hockey rink-sized pitch of a long oval, 36 by 60 yards (32.92 m by 54.86 m) with line

---

[209] International Quidditch Association, "About-Activities." http://iqaquidditch.org/about.html.

markings. There is a goal line at each end of the pitch. Two more yards inward (1.83 m) is the starting line, and 6 yards (5.49 m) from the goal line is the keeper zone line. There is also the center of the field where the balls are set to begin.

At both ends of the pitch are mounted three hoops, 2.45 yards (2.24 m) apart, at different heights; one at 1 yard (0.91 m) the second at 1.5 yards (1.37 m), and the third at 2 yards (1.83 m) high. It is one of these hoops that a team's chasers or keepers hope to get their quaffle ball through for ten points. Beaters use their bludgers to take out opposing players, and when an opposition player is hit, they must dismount their broom, drop any ball, and return to and touch their hoops before being allowed back into the game. There is also the snitch, which is guarded by an official. All the plays and rules of the game will not be given in this chapter, but one can consult the International Quidditch Association Handbook, found online.

Quidditch is the only sport to use three different balls, the quaffle, bludger, and snitch. The quaffle is a slightly-deflated volleyball, the bludger is a slightly-deflated dodgeball, and the snitch is a tennis ball, held in a long yellow pouch attached to the back of a snitch runner's shorts, like a tail. Only seekers can approach the snitch runner, but it must be done without forceful contact.

There are two sticks in this game. One is a broom held between the player's legs, and one is a bat used only by the beaters. The broomstick can be a household broom, a handcrafted piece, or even a PVC pipe, but it must remain between a player's legs at all times, except when hit by a bludger. It is best if it is lightweight and short. Lacrosse goggles and mouthguards are also required for official play, and differently-colored headbands are worn for different team positions.

Quidditch Terms and Slang

Beater(s)

Quidditch: The two beaters on each team wearing black headbands are the only players on the pitch who have bats. Their job is to keep the bludgers away from their team and at the same time try and aim the bludgers toward the opposite team.

Sexual: A man who "beats his meat," a *beater*, is one who masturbates. In BDSM, it may also refer to a person who beats or spanks a willing participant.

Chaser

Quidditch: These are players in the game who go after the opposing chasers to impede the quaffle from advancing down the pitch in the wrong direction.

Sexual: A person who is sexually attracted to an overweight person and pursues them for sexual play and gratification. Also known as a "chubby chaser."

Foul

Quidditch: A violation of the rules.

Sexual: When someone is physically dirty, nasty, raunchy, or foul-mouthed to the point of being unpleasant.

Game

Quidditch: The course of play that starts when the referee has finished racking the balls and ends at the conclusion of a legal shot, which pockets the last required ball.

Sexual: The pursuit of a sexual partner which includes pickup lines, the skill of the pursuer, and the sex drive of both people.

Game time

Quidditch: The official time of any given game, measured from the first call of "brooms up," until the end of the final period of the game, aside from the stops called by a referee and between periods.

Sexual: The time it takes for a person to pursue a sexual partner, which includes pickup lines, the skill of the pursuer, and the sex drive of both people.

Grab

Quidditch: A form of wrap consisting of holding an opponent or any part of an opponent with a closed hand.

Sexual: Refers to a successful approach toward taking hold of a person, with the intention of a sexual goal.

Hoop(s)

Quidditch: The upright and self-supporting structure through which the quaffle must pass to score a goal, and a player must touch after a knockout effect.

Sexual: Refers to the anal ring on men and women.

Keeper

Quidditch: This is the quaffle player on each team, who wears a green headband and prevents opponents from scoring with their quaffle.

Sexual: Refers to someone who makes a perfect companion.

Overtime

Quidditch: An extra period in a game that occurs when a snitch is caught in regular time, which causes a game to be tied. Overtime lasts five minutes or until the snitch is caught again. There can also be a second overtime.

Sexual: Refers to having sex at the end of a workday, and to the continuing of intercourse even after ejaculation has occurred.

Period

Quidditch: A segment of a game that may occur up to three times during a regulation game.

Sexual: Refers to a woman's time of menstruation.

Pitch Boundary

Quidditch: The playing field on a hockeyrink-sized area that is rectangular with rounded corners, 36 by 60 yards (33 m by 54.86 m), with three hoops of varying heights at either end.

Sexual: The claimed territory, area, or street that each prostitute walks and works along, and the words a person tells another to get them to agree to a sexual liaison.

Push

Quidditch: A form of physical contact which consists of initiating force upon an opponent with an extended arm, be it extended during or before initiation of contact.

Sexual: An 1800s British slang euphemism for intercourse, from "do-a-push."

Tackle

Quidditch: Physical contact between players consisting of *wrapping* (see *wrap* below) a player and bringing that player to the ground.

Sexual: A U.K. word for a man's genitals, his "fishing tackle," also known as a man's "wedding or man tackle," for that special night.

Wrap

Quidditch: A wrap consists of encircling an opponent's torso or any part of an opponent with one or both arms.

Sexual: Can refer to kissing and touching, and to a condom.

Other Quidditch Terms with Sexual Possibilities

Once enough points have been made by getting enough quaffle balls through the hoops, the team must find the one impartial official dressed in yellow and take the *snitch*, which is a tennis ball, found in a long sock hanging from the shorts of that official. Successfully completed, that team makes thirty points and the game ends. But a snitch can also be someone who tattles to a friend that his girl has slept with another man. *Possession* is the quidditch team that has complete control of the ball. Possession can also be when a dominant partner takes complete control over their submissive. Especially if the submissive wears a collar, they are possessed by their "owner." On each team there is a *seeker*, who wears a gold or yellow headband, and they attempt to catch the snitch. Although there is no direct sexual meaning, a seeker could be identified as a person who is truly seeking a steady sexual partner.

Sexual Commentary

What a great idea it was to turn this into a sport, and apparently thousands have thought so too. From the call for "brooms up!" to get the players to make sure those sticks are secured between their legs, to tagging their team hoops after being carded, as if they had to go home to mom in order to get permission to go out again, to grabbing a golden ball, to "brooms down," this contact sport has it all. It is truly an egalitarian sport, allowing mixed genders on a team, having three different sizes of balls which could be interpreted as representing manhood in three major proportions, to the hoops which when viewed standing together with three different heights, appear as if they are stick figures representing a family. The tallest is the father, the middle-sized is the mother, and the shortest one is a child. They may also represent the vaginal or anal rings of three men or women of different heights.

Chapter 32
Rounders

Rounders is a non-contact sport for children played in England, Ireland, and Scotland. But don't let that throw you, that's seven million children playing this stick-and-ball game. Two teams of nine trade-off being batters and fielders. The field is in the form of a diamond with four bases, around which players run counterclockwise. The ball is a hard baseball and the bat is shorter than a baseball bat. Each point is called a rounder. There are two innings with nine outs per team played in each match.

The game, which most likely originated with the common people in the British Isles, was discouraged by the church, but its popularity continued. Early games such as stool ball, with milkmaids using their stools as bases, contributed to rounders development, which in turn contributed to the development of baseball. In 1745, a small book was published called *A Little Pretty Pocket-Book,* which first referenced the game in a poem as being played since Tudor times.[210] William Clarke's 1828 book, *The Boy's Own Book,* was the first to describe the play of the game.[211] By 1884, the Gaelic Athletic Association in

---

[210] West Midlands Sports Development, "Rounders." https://www.wmsd.co.uk/component/k2/item/320-rounders

[211] David Block, *Baseball Before We Knew It: A Search for the Roots of the Game,* (Lincoln, NE: Bison Books, 2005), 86-87.

Ireland decided to nationally formalize the rules for rounders. England and Scotland then formed their own associations in 1889, and in 1943, the game was formally regulated by Rounders of England. Now there are over forty rounders leagues in the U.K., and international games are played annually.

Rounders has many similarities with baseball, but there are some striking differences. The shorter rounders bat is swung with one hand, and each batter only gets one swing at a good pitch. There are no misses, no walks, and no strike-outs. Wooden posts encased in plastic are used for the bases, but they are called posts. The ball is bowled with an underarm pendulum motion. The ball must be delivered to the batsman above the knee and below the head over the batting square. Even if the batsman misses the ball, he must run to the next base. If he or she hits the ball and it is caught, or if the ball is thrown and touches the base before the runner gets there, they are also out.

A batsman (or female batter) stands at the batting square in front of the backstop, which is part of the backward area. To the right is the position for a substitute runner and the umpire. Beyond the batting square is the forward area. The first post fielder stands at first base or post, the second post fielder stands at the second post, and the third and fourth fielders stand at their respective posts. There is a bowler's umpire behind the second post, so there are two umpires per game. There are also three deep fielders, and the bowler (pitcher) stands in the center at the bowling square.

Now for descriptions of the field, ball and bat. The playing field is an open pentagon 39.5 feet (12 m) long on three sides and 28 feet (8.53 m) on the other two sides. The outdoors rounders ball is made with a cork core with soft white leather around it with red stitching, or is red with black stitching. It weighs between 2.5 and 3.0 ounces (70.87 g to 85.05 g) and measures 7.5 inches (19.05 cm) in circumference. An inside ball, or one for beginners, is a synthetic hollow air ball. The stick bat is rounded and either wooden, plastic, or metal, with a non-slip rubber grip. The bat is not more than 18 inches (45.72 cm) in length, 6¾ inches (17.15 cm) around at the thickest part, and does not weigh more than 13 ounces (368.54 g). There are some bats that are flattened, which are for training juniors.

Rounders Terms and Slang

Ball
Rounders: The ball that is used, which is either white with red stitching or red with black stitching.
Sexual: A synonym for one testicle, and a euphemism for intercourse.

Bat (ing)
Rounders: That which hits the rounders ball and the action of doing so.
Sexual: An acronym for Big Ass Tits, to flutter the eyelashes, and "batting" is a euphemism for masturbation.

Club
Rounders: A stick for rounders players.
Sexual: A synonym for a large penis.

Court
Rounders: The area on which the game of rounders is played, the pitch area.
Sexual: The act of dating a person with the intent to marry, meaning that sexual intercourse will most likely take place in preparation for getting to know one another.

404

Duration

Rounders: The time it takes for all the batters to have been struck out over two separate innings.

Sexual: Refers to the length of time it takes for a person to reach orgasm.

Equipment

Rounders: The tools needed to play rounders are a bat, a rounders ball, and four posts as bases, for a full set.

Sexual: A euphemism for male sexual genitals.

Glove(s)

Rounders: Rounders catching gloves are usually made from leather with a padded palm and sturdy Velcro wrist fastening.

Sexual: A synonym for a condom.

Kit

Rounders: The numbered vests that rounders' players wear with different colors for each team.

Sexual: An acronym for Keep in Touch, said after a sexual encounter. A young woman who seeks the company of an older man, which derives from either the kit of a young fox, or a kitten.

Out(s)

Rounders: When a batter is not fully in the batting box, when making a run on the inside of the post, when a fielder or ball reaches the post before the runner, and when they are caught out. Also, any time the batter deliberately blocks a fielder, overtakes another batter, or moves from a post before the ball has been thrown.

Sexual: A person who is open with their new sexual identity.

Rounder

Rounders: A successful score awarded to the batter when they bat the ball and reach the fourth post before another ball is bowled.

Sexual: An adulterer, seducer, debaucher, ravisher, or womanizer; a dissolute man who is morally unrestrained.

Stick

Rounders: The truncheon-like wooden bat with a flat end that rounders players use.

Sexual: A synonym for a penis, and the act of sticking the penis into something.

Other Rounders Terms with Sexual Possibilities

A *batting area* in rounders is the 39.37-foot (12 m) zone which houses the batting square. In urban utterance, a bat is a synonym for a penis, batting is a euphemism for masturbation, and therefore a batting area is a bed or place where one might masturbate. A *field* in rounders is where all the players are involved in the game. A sexual field is an arena of social life wherein individuals seek intimate partners and vie for sexual status, and refers to a currency of erotic energy. *Jokes* are a selection of children's rounders jokes which are meant for amusement only. Example: Why did Cinderella get thrown out of the rounders team? Because she kept running away from the ball. If it is a joke, there are millions of sexual *jokes*. What's the difference between a G-spot and a golf ball? A guy will actually search for a golf ball.

A *no-ball* in rounders can be when the bowler's under-arm action is not continuous, when the bowler does not keep his feet inside the bowling square, when the bowler directs the ball on to the wrong side of the batter, or when the bowled ball reaches higher than the batter's head or lower than the knee. A no-ball can also have the simple meaning of no-nookie, no "balling," no intercourse. An *obstruction* can be a fielder blocking a batter's hit or run, or a batter deviating from the track. An obstruction to intercourse could also be a tampon. *Posts* in rounders are the four vertical poles of 4 feet, supported on bases at the corners of the running track, but not fixed into the ground. Since a pole is another synonym for a penis, certainly a post for a stout penis might be inferred. Also, there is the term *post-sexual*, which means that a person has reached a time in their life when they no longer feel like being sexual. The *start of play* in rounders begins with the two captains tossing a coin to see who will take the first inning. It could also mean the time when two people begin to sexually play together. Rounders *worksheets* are task and activity sheets with diagrams and teaching points, designed to promote learning. This could also mean the bed sheets that a prostitute uses for her customers.

Sexual Commentary

It is so sweet that the bat in rounders is smaller for children, as opposed to the larger bat used in baseball. But unlike baseball, rounders rules state that the batter must run with their bat. That seems to make sense. Would the game be teaching them that no matter where they go in life, their phallus (a man's penis and a woman's clitoris) may be the tool that will help them advance in the world?

Chapter 33
Shinty

In the Scottish and Irish contact team sport of shinty, the ball is a shinty ball, the long, curved stick is a caman, and the wide grassy field is a pitch. The goal is to have the caman get the shinty ball into the goal, called a "hail," which is over the goal line and under the crossbar. There are twelve players on a men's team and ten players on a women's team, plus each team has a goalkeeper, and a match is played in two halves of forty-five minutes.

Shinty is part of a group of early stick and ball games from several places. It has similarities to Irish hurling, cammag from the Isle of Man, and cluich-bhal, hailes, cammock, knotty, or shinnins from Scotland. It was a winter game, and competitions were traditionally held on New Year's Day. The game was formalized in Glasgow and London, with one of the first games played in 1887. Shinty has been governed by the Camanachd Association since 1893.[212] In 1981, the game was restructured and reorganized from a volunteer game to players getting paid, and clubs were formed in nine major cities, with a team associated with every major university in Scotland.[213] Women formed their own shinty teams in the

---

[212] Roger Hutchinson, "Camanachd: The Story of Shinty." https://www.shinty.com/mens/about-us/history

[213] Ibid.

mid-1900s, and they have the Valerie Fraser Trophy cup and the Challenge Cup.

The highest competition in the premier national leagues is for the Camanachd Cup and the MacAulay Cup, between North and South Scotland. There are also the Bullough Cup, the Glasgow Celtic Society Cup, and the Lovat Cup. Shinty is also played by the British Army with the Scots Shinty Club. Shinty came to North America in the early nineteenth century, but did not really grow until the twenty-first century. By then, 2000 teams had formed in several states, and their first international game was in 2009, under the direction of the US Camanachd Association.

In the game, a player is allowed to use the slanted side of his caman to block and to tackle, but not to crash down upon an opponent's caman, which is called "hacking." Fouls are penalized by a free-hit, which is indirect unless the foul is committed in the penalty area, commonly referred to as "The D." This results in a penalty hit from 20 yards (18.29 m). Other examples of dangerous play which are penalized include playing the ball while a player is grounded, or recklessly swinging the caman in the air in a way that might endanger another player. Players may tackle using the body as long as it is shoulder-to-shoulder.

Now to discuss the field and the equipment used. This chapter won't get into all the rules and strategies of the game, but some aspects will be addressed within the following descriptions as well as in the terms.

Either artificial turf or a grassy pitch will run from 70 to 80 yards (64.01 m to 73.15 m) wide and 140 to 170 yards (128.02 m to 155.45 m) long. At both ends of the pitch is a goal area, and 10 yards out (9.14 m) is a 10-yard-wide (9.14 m) half-circle that curves toward the goal box. Twenty yards (18.29 m) in from the goal box on both sides is a penalty spot. There is also a corner hit area in each corner of the pitch.

The ball is spherical with a cork center and an outer shell made of leather. The circumference is between 7.5 and 8 inches (19.05 cm to 20.32 cm) and the weight between 2.5 and 3.0 ounces (70.87 g to 85.05 g). The ball is white with raised black and white stitching. A player may stop the ball with his caman, his chest, two feet together, or one foot on the ground. It is a foul and dangerous to play with the head. No one can touch the ball with their hands except the goalkeeper. The goalkeeper is not allowed to catch it, but they can touch it with an open palm. A player is allowed to play the ball in the air or balance the ball on the edge of a caman, called a "keepie-uppie." A ball played by a team over the opposing bye line results in a goal hit from the edge of the "D" while a ball played by a team over their own line, results in a corner. A ball hit over the sideline results in a "shy." A shinty shy involves the taker tossing the ball above his or her head and hitting the ball with the shaft of the caman directly overhead.

Before the 1980s the caman stick was made of one piece of ash or hickory. Now they are produced with several layers of laminated wood. A stick is 3.5 feet (1.07 m) long with two slanted faces and the head which is wedge-shaped. There is no blade like the Irish caman, but from the Gaelic word found in both games, *cam* means "bent or corked."

Shinty Terms and Slang

Ball

Shinty: The small leather-covered sphere made of cork which is hit by the caman stick.

Sexual: A synonym for one testicle, and a euphemism for intercourse.

Center spot

Shinty: The spot in the center of the pitch from where the game is begun.

Sexual: Refers to either a woman's clitoris or her G-spot.

Crossbar

Shinty: A pole connecting the front two goalposts at each end of the field, which measures 12 feet (3.66 m) long and is 10 feet (3.05 m) above the ground.

Sexual: A horizontal bar is used in BDSM, to which a person is attached for sex play.

Duration

Shinty: The length of the game, ninety-minutes, plus halftime and any extra time permitted.

Sexual: Refers to the length of time it takes for a person to reach orgasm. On average, for a woman it is approximately twenty minutes, and for a man five minutes or less.

Field

Shinty: The rectangular playing area that is 80 by 110 yards (73.15 m by 100.58 m).

Sexual: From "playing the field," meaning to date or have sex with multiple people.

Players

Shinty: A men's team has twelve players, a women's team has ten, each with a maximum of two substitutes.

Sexual: People who date more than one person at a time, or who are open to many different acts of sexual pleasure.

Shy

Shinty: When a ball is hit over the sideline, the taker tosses the ball up and must strike the ball directly above their head with the shaft of the caman.

Sexual: A bashful, fearful, and introverted person who is afraid of approaching the opposite or same sex for sexual play.

The D

Shinty: When a foul is committed in the penalty area. This results in a penalty hit from 20 yards (18.29 m).

Sexual: The "D" is an abbreviation for "dick," meaning the penis.

Whistle(s)

Shinty: A referee will blow whistles whenever there is a foul.

Sexual: A "wolf whistle" is given by whistling one rising note and one falling note when someone sexy walks by; usually done by men for women.

Other Shinty Terms with Sexual Possibilities

An *attacker* in shinty is a player whose role is to score as many points as possible. Outside of sports, an attacker in the sexual arena is one who is a sexual assaulter. A keepie-uppie is a player who can move down the field while either balancing or bouncing the ball on a caman. This also sounds like a fun slang term to use in describing how a man stays excited so that his penis does not go flaccid before or during sexual play. A *penalty spot* in this sport is the spot from where a penalty hit is taken. And for any couple in a relationship, if one does something wrong, that person may be told to sleep on the couch instead of in bed with their partner. That couch is definitely a penalty spot. *Protecting the ball* in shinty is a way of shielding the ball as long as the person is playing the ball and not the opponent. Protecting the ball or both

412

testicles is the work of a jockstrap that may have a hard cup, or a man may simply cup them with his hands to protect them.

Sexual Commentary

The shinty stick or caman is a long stick, slanted on both sides, with a 90° curved turn at the end. There are four types: a forward, midfield, defender, and goalie. Each has a slightly different bevel and shape that will influence the arc of the ball. The stick with the least angle is the forward, while a defender and goalie have the greatest angle, which are helpful to lift the ball. There will also be a slightly different curve to the stick depending upon the maker, and the toe might even be cut on a different angle. The toe is in the shape of a triangle, with some smaller or larger and with a narrower or wider shape.

A penis will never have this kind of a bend at its end, nor will the head ever be in the shape of a triangle, but a penis as a whole can have a great variety of angles. Factors that can change this angle are the tension of the suspensory ligament, the level of arousal, the age of the person, and the size, thickness, and shape of the penis. Steven Lamm, M.D. wrote a book called *The Hardness Factor*[214] which addresses the angle of the dangle for an average man throughout his life. An eighteen-year-old will have the greatest angle, 135 to 145 degrees from the ground. A twenty-five-year-old male will have a range of 120 to 135 degrees. A thirty-five-year-old man will have a range of 100 to 120 degrees. A forty-five-year-old man will have an average angle from 90 to 110 degrees. A

[214] Steven Lamm, *The Hardness Factor*, (New York: HarperCollins Publishers, Inc., 2005) p. 90.

fifty-five-year-old man's penis will have a range from 80 to 100 degrees. And a man sixty-five years old will have an erection angle of 80 to 90 degrees.

This talk of penis angles doesn't have much to do with the angle of a caman stick, but the angle at which a man ejaculates does, as the greater the angle the more the ejaculate will arc. In the end, a stick is a stick and whatever angle is used, if it gets the owners ball(s) to the goal, it will have achieved the same thing.

Part Five
Rackets and Paddles

There are twenty-eight sports games that use a racket or a paddle to hit a ball or birdie. The fifth section of this book will focus on five of these games: badminton, table tennis (ping-pong), racquetball, squash, and tennis.

Granted, a racket is not *just* a stick, it is a highly augmented stick with a wooden frame holding tightly woven strings that create a bounce when a ball or shuttlecock (birdie) rebound from it. The rackets used in badminton, racquetball, squash, and tennis are each a little different in their size and shape, but basically work in the same way. Table tennis, also known as ping-pong, is the only game that does not use a racket. Instead it uses a paddle, which still acts as a mechanism to bounce a ball. The balls are all a little bit different, too. The racquetball is a hollow rubber ball, usually blue. A squash ball is black with either one blue, one red, one yellow, or two yellow dots on it. A tennis ball is covered in a fibrous felt material, usually of fluorescent yellow. A table tennis ball is made from celluloid and is either white or orange, and a shuttlecock is a ball with a feathered cone attached. In badminton, table tennis, and tennis, there is a net, but not in racquetball or squash, although there is a designated area in which the ball must be played.

However, they all have one thing in common that makes them similar to every other stick and ball game: many of their terms have sexual meaning.

Chapter 34
Badminton

Badminton can be a casual game played for fun or a highly-competitive sport played between nations. In this sport, the stick is a racket, the ball is a shuttlecock, the field is a court, a play is a rally, a foul is a hinder, and a game is a match. The goal is to hit the shuttlecock over a net and onto an opponent's side without the opponent being able to return it. A match is the best of three games of twenty-one points each. Badminton can be played with two individuals one against one, called singles, or four individuals two against two, called doubles. A player on each side of the net may strike the shuttlecock only once before it must pass back over the net, and the rally ends when the opponent fails to return the cock or it lands outside the court area.

The sport of playing with a racket and a shuttlecock has been an entertainment since the middle of the 1800s, especially in Europe and Asia.[215] Earlier games that most likely influenced badminton were battledore, shuttlecock, and *jeu de volant* (the flying game). Battledore comes from

---

[215] Wikipedia, "Hanetsuki,"
https://en.wikipedia.org/wiki/Hanetsuki

an earlier term for a racket.[216] The history of one British home in particular is associated with the beginning of the game, namely Badminton House, in Gloucestershire, England. In 1863, the eighth Duke of Beaufort devised a game which his children could play indoors in the winter. It is said that feathers were added to a small lightweight ball to soften the blows against interior paintings.[217] The game, and others like it, became popular when the British went to India, and there its appeal exploded and it was widely played by 1873. By 1878 the sport had spread to the United States, in 1882 to South Africa, and by 1890 to Canada. The Badminton Association in Southsea, England, was founded in 1893 to organize matches and tournaments for their nine teams.

By the 1920s there were already 300 badminton clubs. In 1934, the Badminton Association changed its name to the Badminton Association of England, with England, Ireland, Scotland, Wales, Denmark, Holland, Canada, New Zealand, and France as international participants. By 1945, after the Second World War, the number of badminton clubs rose to 9,000, and the International Badminton Federation became the Badminton World Federation with over 176 different nations participating. In early 1979, the federation revised and adopted new rules, and held the first open badminton tournament where players received money for playing. With the adoption of the new rules, the game was finally introduced into the 1992 Olympics. After soccer,

---

[216] Henry Jones, "Badminton," T.S. Baynes, (Ed.). *Encyclopedia Britannica*, Vol. 3 (9th ed.), (New York: Charles Scribner's Sons, 1878), 228.

[217] Hugh Chisholm (ed.), "Badminton (game)," *Encyclopedia Britannica*, Vol. 3 (11th ed.). (Cambridge: Cambridge University Press, 1911), 189.

badminton has become the second most popular participatory world sport. Britain alone has four million players.

The rules, strategies and terms of the game will not all be discussed in this chapter, although some will be touched upon in the descriptions of the court, equipment and the terms.

A badminton court is rectangular, 44 feet (13.41 m) long, but the width is determined by whether it is a game of singles at 17 feet (5.18 m) wide, or doubles at 20 feet (6.10 m) wide, with lines that mark both. This changes the legal bounds of the court during a rally, and the position from which the server stands to serve.

The early English racket went through changes. At first, the racket was shorter and made of wood, which made it heavier. In India, they produced the longer and lighter *slakot* "bat" with more of a tear-drop shape, and that design has remained popular in India to this day. The earlier battledore racket had strings made of twisted parchment, which changed to catgut, then to nylon.

In 1908, a new racket came on the market. The designers carved a fish's tail at the end of the handle and called it the fishtail handle—the new standard. The flared end of the fins added support to the edge of the wrist, on top of the already long comfortable handle. Later the handles were made from aluminium. Some aluminium rackets can still be found, but not wooden ones. The modern racket is made from different composites of carbon and fiber, or graphite-reinforced plastic, to solid steel, and now carbon nanotubes and fullerenes are added for durability. Rackets weigh between 2.5 and 3.4 ounces (70.87 g to 96.39 g), not including the grip or strings. A variety of grips are available to players, such as polyurethane synthetic or toweling grips that are either replacement grips that make the handle thicker, or over-grips that are thinner. The strings are thin and high-performing, which means they can retain a tension of between 18 and 36 pounds (8.17 kg to 16.33 kg) of force.

The shuttlecock, also known as a birdie or shuttle, is designed not for speed, but for drag. For informal matches, the shuttlecock is made of a small ball of either cork, synthetic foam or nylon, with a plastic cone or skirt around it. In professional matches, the ball is a leather-covered piece of rounded cork and the cone is made of sixteen small overlapping white feathers. In the late 1800s, most of the world's shuttlecocks were made in France and the design was known as the "barrel."

The only other items in badminton are the net and shoes. The net stretches across the center of the court with a height of 5 feet (1.52 m) at the center. It is made of black polyethylene and polyamide knotless square mesh with a braided textile cord that runs across the top as a tensing line. Badminton shoes have rubber soles made out of non-marking materials and are lightweight, which allows the player a lower center of gravity with strong lateral support. The largest museum in the world for the sport is the National Badminton Museum in Buckinghamshire, England, which houses a collection of archives, artifacts, memorabilia, and all things on badminton.

Badminton Terms and Slang

Baseline

Badminton: The back-boundary line at each end of the court that runs parallel to the net.

Sexual: The bare minimum standard of attractiveness that a man or woman might consider for an intercourse partner.

Bird (Birdie)

Badminton: Another name for the shuttlecock.

Sexual: A 1915 British word for a maiden or young woman, a euphemism for a penis, and a hand gesture with the derogatory meaning of "screw you," with the upturned middle finger symbolizing the penis.

Court

Badminton: The area of play as defined by the outer boundary lines.

Sexual: The act of dating a person with the intent to marry, meaning that sexual intercourse will most likely take place as part of getting to know one another.

Drive

Badminton: A fast and low shot that makes a horizontal flight over the net.

Sexual: A powerful penile thrust in intercourse.

Flick(s)

Badminton: A quick wrist and forearm rotation that surprises an opponent by changing an apparently soft shot into a faster passing one. It is used primarily on the serve and at the net.

Sexual: An older term for pornographic movies on film.

Kill

Badminton: A fast, downward shot that cannot be returned, often called a put-away.

Sexual: The number of different people one has had sex with, usually compiled on a list.

Service

Badminton: A player puts the shuttlecock into play for points by serving it to the opponent by hitting it over the net into a special part of the court near their opponent.

Sexual: A euphemism for intercourse. Often referred to the "services" a prostitute offers.

Smash

Badminton: When a shuttle is floated high into the air and a player has time to unleash a powerful overhand shot straight to the floor of the opposing court.

Sexual: A euphemism for intercourse.

Other Badminton Terms with Sexual Possibilities

In badminton, the *long service line* is the back-boundary line where the serve may not go past, and the *short service line* is a line several feet from the net which a serve must reach to be legal. One could easily interpret both terms as a long line (like on a Saturday night) or a short line (like on a Monday night) of men at their favorite brothel, waiting for a woman to service them. There is also the term *wood shot*, which is a shot that results when the base of the shuttle is hit by the frame of the racket. However, because a synonym for a penis is a wood or woody, this could easily be interpreted as an erect penis that reaches a point of ejaculation.

Sexual Commentary

Something the sport and sexual terms in the body of this chapter did not reveal in their definitions was the use of the badminton net and the shuttlecock, which play into their own sexual symbolism. The first constructed nets set the rule. They must be exactly 5 feet high (1.52 m) and hang all the way to the ground. When the game was in its beginnings in the mid-1850s, skirt lengths were to the ground.

A badminton net is an open-meshed material woven together at regular intervals, which can act as a division, but allows one to see through it to the other side. A net can also be an entrapping device for an animal or human, something that covers or encloses, a barricade, or can even catch a person if they fall. In badminton, birdies often get caught in the net, and that is why it is important for them to sail over and clear the net. A net can be a passageway or network, and a conduit for communication. And lo and behold, the Internet was invented, which offers open and regular communication connections, including cybersex. Also, something most people don't know is that behind eBay, which sells everything from ant farms to zebra towels, there is a huge back section that offers explicit adult items for sale. One just needs to register to see and buy from it.

Then there is the shuttlecock. A "birdie" is another name for a shuttlecock, and a birdie was a term of endearment for a young woman. A shuttlecock was made of a rounded end of cork, covered in leather, and surrounded by a crown of feathers. If I were to give you a description of the early shuttlecocks, you might be surprised to learn that its description would be similar to a woman's design of dress at the time. The skirt was bell-shaped, supported by a cage skirt underneath. The dress neckline was open to the shoulder, and finished with a tucked net trim or eyelet edging in ruffle, ribbon, lace, sash, or sheer netting.

As an extension of a man's arm, a racket gives breadth and length, and when two men rally back and forth, they are asserting their power through each stroke to get the birdie over the net in a particular place within the bounds of the court. And lest we forget, a "cock," from the term shuttlecock, is a synonym for the penis.

Still, this particular "bird" has to be the most frilly and feminine ball of any sport. No wonder it has been very popular for women to play ever since 1804.[218]

---

[218] Beulah Folmsbee: *A Little History of the Horn-book*. London: The Horn Book Inc., 1942. "Battledore was a precursor to Badminton, and one of the few competitive sports that were considered appropriate

for the middle and upper classes of women to play during the early 19th century."

Chapter 35
Table Tennis (Ping-Pong)

In table tennis, also known as ping-pong, the play area is a table, the ball is a table tennis (or ping-pong) ball, the stick is a hand paddle (sometimes called a bat or a racket), a game is a set, a play is a rally which makes a match, a hit is a stroke that can be flat or have spin, and a winning shot is called a kill.

There are two players in a singles game and four players in a doubles game, which can be played by men, women, or mixed. They bounce a small ball back and forth on a table over a small net. The ball must bounce once before hitting a return, and a point is scored when an opponent fails to return the ball. After every two points, the service alternates between opponents. Players switch sides of the table after each game. The winner is the one who reaches eleven points first and a match is the best out of an odd number of games, of which either five or seven games are played in competition.

Table tennis may have been brought to England from India between 1860 and 1870, when military officers returned to imitate the game by lining up books in the center of a table to serve as a net, using a book as a paddle, and a golf ball to rally with.[219] In 1901, two

---

[219] Wikipedia, "Table Tennis."
https://en.wikipedia.org/wiki/Table_tennis

important discoveries were made. A man named James W. Gibb discovered celluloid balls, which were the perfect ball for the game, being very light with an excellent bounce.[220] And E.C. Goode, who invented the modern paddle by attaching a rubber sheet onto each side of a wooden paddle, improved the handling of the ball.[221] In the same year, J. Jaques & Son Limited trademarked the game, calling it "ping-pong." The popularity of the game took off, with articles and books touting the game, and the first world championship was held in 1902. By the early 1920s, Jaques & Son sold the trademark to the American gaming company Parker Brothers. Since they then possessed the only rights to the ping-pong name, all the other producers of the game were forced to call the same game "table tennis."[222]

The Table Tennis Association was founded in 1921, the International Table Tennis Federation in 1926, and the U.S. Table Tennis Association in 1933. During the 1950s, a layer of sponge was added underneath the rubber sheet on the paddle, giving the play on the ball greater speed, bounce, and spin. Other changes in the game have occurred over the years. The change of serve was reduced from every five points to every two points. The ball must be tossed up in the air before it is hit to give the opponent time to see that a serve is being made. And, the point system has changed from twenty-one points to eleven points.

The game was finally introduced into the Olympics in 1988. Competitions are held around the world, including the European Championships, the Europe Top-16, the

---

[220] Ibid.

[221] Ibid.

[222] Ibid.

Asian Championships, and the Asian Games. The Chinese are the top world players and have been for many years, but other Asian and European countries compete, such as Austria, Belarus, Belgium, France, Germany, Hong Kong, Japan, South Korea, Portugal, Singapore, Sweden, and Taiwan.

Not all of the rules, strategies, scoring, and manner of play are covered in this chapter, but a description of the table, paddle and ball follow. And where each term is given below, these aspects will be addressed and explained.

The size of the table is 5 by 9 feet (1.52 m by 2.74 m), and 2½ feet (0.76 m) above the ground on table stands. The net rises 6 inches (15.24 cm) above the flat, wooden table. The table is painted in a dark color, usually green, blue, or grey, with a matte finish and a white line down the long center for distinguishing a game of singles from doubles. The table must produce a uniform bounce over its entire surface, tested by dropping a ball next to a standing ruler from 12 inches (30.48 cm) to produce a 9-inch-high (22.86 cm) bounce.

Now for the "stick" information. The International Federation calls it a racket, in the U.K. they call it a bat, and in the U. S. it is a paddle. The handle may be flat, straight, rounded, or rounded and flared. The wooden blade is made of many layers of laminated wood, usually balsa, cypress, limba, or Japanese *hinoki* wood. Wood must comprise eighty-five percent of the blade. Some blades add a thin layer of aluminum fiber, carbon fiber, cork, glass fiber, or Kevlar. An average blade is 5.9 inches (15 cm) wide, 6.7 inches (17 cm) long, and weighs between 2.6 to 3.35 ounces (74 g to 95 g).

Each side of the paddle can have its own special surface in red or black, depending upon whether the shot is intended to spin or not. The rubber used on both sides may have different thicknesses and textures, called pimples or pips. Short pips are good for blocking, long pips are helpful for defense, and an inverted pip is smooth for good ball control. Even the glue used to affix the rubber to the blade is important, as it can affect the speed of the ball. A water-based, non-volatile glue is preferred.

There are three ways to hold a paddle: the penhold, between the thumb and index finger, preferred by Asian players; the western, as if shaking hands with the handle; and the Seemiller, named after Danny Seemiller, who used it in the 1985 World Championships. In the Seemiller hold, one places their thumb and index finger on either side of the bottom of the paddle head and the rest of the fingers hold the handle. There are offensive and defensive strokes a player can use. Offensive strokes are a flip, hit, a counter-hit, loop, and smash. Defensive strokes are a block, chop, lob, and push. There are also different types of spin that can be placed on the ball, such as a backspin, corkspin, sidespin, or topspin.

The table-tennis ball is made of celluloid plastic and is white for play on a green or blue table, or orange for play on a grey table. The ball has a matte finish. There is a star rating for quality, from one to three stars. The balls were originally 1.5 inches (3.81 cm) wide, but in 2000, the International Federation required the ball to be slightly larger, 1.57 inches (4 cm) wide. With the additional bounce from the rubber on the paddle, the earlier ball moved exceedingly fast, especially for a televised audience, making it too difficult to keep an eye on. The larger size increased the ball's air resistance, and helped to slow the ball down enough to follow the game. As of 2014, a new poly material ball is required in International games.

Since most readers in the U.S. are more familiar with the name ping-pong, that name will be referred to in the terms below.

Table Tennis (Ping-Pong) Terms and Slang

Bat
Ping-pong: The British term for the racket or paddle.
Sexual: An acronym for <u>B</u>ig <u>A</u>ss <u>T</u>its, and is a British euphemism for being bisexual, to "bat for both sides."

Blade
Ping-pong: The wooden part of the paddle.
Sexual: British slang for penis, or a gay man. It is also the strolling place or track where prostitutes and pimps hustle. A *Gillette blade* (with two blades) is a bisexual person.

Block
Ping-pong: A quick, off the bounce return of an aggressive drive done by just holding the racket in the ball's path.
Sexual: To impede one from connecting sexually with another, a "cock-block."

Chop
Ping-pong: A heavy underspin shot, usually executed away from the table and below the tabletop, which forces the ball to drop downward when it hits an opponent's paddle.
Sexual: The art of getting a woman's phone number to date her. "Chopped" is a euphemistic slang word for a circumcised penis.

Chopper
Ping-pong: A style of play where chopping the ball is the primary shot.
Sexual: A euphemism for the penis.

Dead (ball)

Ping-pong: A ball without any spin.

Sexual: After a serious injury to the scrotum has occurred, the spermatic cord that carries blood to one or both of the testicles may have been twisted, called testicular torsion. This can affect the blood flow to the tissues, which will turn the testicle numb, making it feel as if it is "dead." This can also occur with too rapid growth during puberty.

Drive

Ping-pong: The basic topspin shot executed close to the table. Also called a counter, counter drive, or smash.

Sexual: To have sexual intercourse, and the action of the penis in penetration. Also, to have "sex drive."

Flat

Ping-pong: A ball that has no spin but has good pace.

Sexual: Refers to a woman with very small breasts or buttocks.

Flick

Ping-pong: A topspin shot generated over the table close to the net, usually with the power generated only from the upper arm or the wrist, used to start an offense on a short ball.

Sexual: An older term for pornographic movies on film.

Game

Ping-pong: A set with each game played to eleven points unless a deuce occurs.

Sexual: The pursuit of a sexual partner, including pickup lines, the skill of the pursuer, and the sex drive of both people.

Junk

Ping-pong: Anti-spin and long-pip rubber on a paddle, which does not produce any spin.

Sexual: A euphemism for the male genital organs.

Lob

Ping-pong: Usually used when a player is in the backcourt in a defensive situation. The player hits the ball as high as they can, usually with a combination of topspin and sidespin.

Sexual: A semi-erect penis, and to have sexual intercourse.

Open

Ping-pong: Refers to the hold of the paddle with the hitting surface aimed forward and the top edge leaning toward the player.

Sexual: Someone who is easy to connect with for intercourse, and a person willing to try new sexual things. Also, an open relationship, where partners are willing to be sexual with a person outside of the paired relationship.

Paddle

Ping-pong: What Americans refer to as the racket or bat used in the game to hit the ball.

Sexual: Both the implement and the act of paddling, a spanking between consenting adults with sexual dynamics in mind.

Pips

Ping-pong: The small conical bits of rubber that cover a sheet of a table tennis paddle.

Sexual: May refer to very small female breasts, just the seed-like size of the nipple, or an excellent or very attractive person.

Point

Ping-pong: A unit of scoring in table tennis.

Sexual: A euphemism for the glans (head) of the penis.

Push

Ping-pong: An underspin shot executed over the table, and usually close to the net. This is a passive shot that is used when it is impossible to attack a ball.

Sexual: An 1800s British slang euphemism for intercourse, from "do-a-push."

Rating

Ping-pong: A number that is assigned to players after their first tournament. The better the player the higher the rating.

Sexual: A number that is assigned by men specifically to women, in evaluating and ranking their face, breasts, and buttocks.

Smash

Ping-pong: A ball that is hit with enough speed so that the opponent cannot make a return shot, a "putaway" shot.

Sexual: A euphemism for a good session of intercourse.

Stroke

Ping-pong: Any shot used in the game, including the serve.

Sexual: The gentle slide of a hand across the body, or the action of the index finger and thumb around the penis along the shaft moving the skin up and down to produce a pleasurable sensation leading to orgasm and ejaculation. To stroke in masturbation. A man's penetrations delivered full length in and out during intercourse.

Twiddle

Ping-pong: The twirl or turning of the paddle, meant to confuse the opponent as to which side of the paddle will be used.

Sexual: A British term for intercourse. Also, the rubbing stimulation given to a woman's clitoral area. A combination of the words, "tweak" and "diddle."

Other Table Tennis (Ping-Pong) Terms with Sexual Possibilities

A *counter-drive* is a drive (a topspin shot) made against a drive. Some players specialize in counter-driving. A counter-drive could also be the opposite of sex drive, that is, having no desire to have sex with anyone. The meaning of *deep* in ping-pong is a ball that lands deep or at the far edge of the table. A serve that will not bounce twice on the opponent's side, if given the chance, is also considered deep, but it might also mean a deep penetrating thrust of the penis during intercourse.

Sexual Commentary

Once one sees a sex performance called "ping-pong," one is not likely to forget it. Under the auspices of doing research, of course, while traveling in Thailand, this author went to the famous red-light district called Patpong, where strip clubs abound and their female performers can do amazing things with their bodies. An entire page could be filled with what women can do with their vaginal muscles, such as blow darts, drop razor blades, hold weights, blow out candles, open bottles, write with a pen, drink liquids, whistle, spin tops, and shoot out lots of things from this orifice. Ping-pong is one of the classic and iconic shows, in which women use their vaginal and pelvic muscles to shoot ping-pong balls across a stage with more force than you can imagine.

Warning: observing this act may make any other woman feel abjectly inadequate with the ordinary things their vagina can do.

Chapter 36
Racquetball

In this sport the ball is called a racquetball and the stick is a racquetball racquet. The playing area is in a fully-enclosed racquetball court, but there is no net, and every court's surface is a legal playing area. The game can be played as singles, doubles, or with three people. A three-player game is called several things: California, Cut-throat, In-and-out, Ironman, King of the Court, or Sevens, each with a variation in the rules.

A player stands in a service box to serve the ball. It must bounce on the floor before hitting the front wall, otherwise it is a foul. Once it bounces behind the short line or the receiving line, the ball is in play. A server is given two tries to put the ball into play correctly. Afterward, the players alternate hitting the ball against the front wall, after which it can rebound off any other surface. The server scores a point if he or she wins the rally. If the opponent wins, no point is scored but they become the server. In an American match, the first two games are to fifteen points and the third game is to eleven points. In Canada, the matches are also best of three with a two-point margin.

Historically speaking, racquetball is a relatively new sport, having been invented in 1950 by Joseph Sobek when he saw the potential of a stringed racquet for his paddleball game, giving him more control and the ball more velocity. He called his new game "paddle rackets," and wrote the rules based on squash, handball and paddleball.[223] The following year he founded the National Paddle Rackets Association. However, the name did not hold. It was a professional tennis player named Bob Mcinerney who coined the name racquetball.[224] In 1969, the International Racquetball Association was founded. Sobek, along with Robert W. Kendler, president of the U.S. Handball Association, wrote about and promoted the sport, and because the game could be played on any handball court, its popularity climbed to 3.1 million by 1974, when the association held the first professional tournament.

In 1976, Ian D. W. Wright created a version of the game in the United Kingdom using a smaller ball, squash courts, and scoring like squash, up to eleven points.[225] The game's popularity increased, and so did the demand for dedicated racquetball clubs and courts. But in the latter part of the decade, the focus on racquetball at these clubs shifted to other physical fitness services. In 1981, the International Racquetball Federation held the first World Racquetball Championships and has held them ever since, biennially in August. The countries that participate are Argentina, Australia, Bermuda, France, Germany, Ireland, Malaysia, Netherlands, New Zealand,

[223] David Walker, *Skills, Drills & Strategies for Racquetball,* (Scottsdale, AZ: Holcomb Hathaway, Inc., 1999), 112.

[224] Bud Muehleisen, "How Racquetball Got Its Name," Racquetball Museum.
https://racquetballmuseum.com/wpcontent/uploads/2017/10/howrballgotitsname.pdf

[225] England Squash and Racquetball, "Racketball."
https://web.archive.org/web/20150210232150/
www.englandsquashandracketball.com/play-squash-and-racketball/rules-of-play/racketball

North America, South Africa, and Sweden. In 1988, the British Squash Rackets and Racquetball associations merged into England Squash & Racquetball, with a U.K. Tournament Series.

In 1995, the American organization was renamed the United States Racquetball Association, only to change the name again in 2003 to U.S.A. Racquetball. In 2016, a change was made to the name of the game played in Britain, as it was played slightly differently. The World Squash Federation now calls that international British game Squash 57, which refers to the diameter in millimeters of the smaller-sized ball. Racquetball isn't included in the Olympic Games, but is included in the Pan American, World, Central American, and Caribbean games.

Not all of the sport's moves, strategies, rules, and terms will be discussed, except when the terms of the game require an explanation. However, the court and the equipment will now be fully reviewed.

The racquetball court is 40 feet (12.19 m) long, 20 feet (6.10 m) wide, and 20 feet high. Running across the middle of the court, dividing it in half, is the short line. Toward the front wall, 5 feet (1.52 m) from the short line is the service line, and toward the back wall, 5 feet from the short line is the receiving line. Between the short line and service line is the service zone, screen line, and doubles box on both sides. All lines are a solid red color and 1½ inches (3.81 cm) wide.

The racquet is made up of a handle, throat, and head. The handle is comprised of the shaft with the butt end where there is a butt cap, and the grip of the handle. The throat is where the shaft splits and forms an open Y to connect with the racquet head. The racquet head includes the beam or thickness of the wood, the strings, grommets, and bumper guard. There is a grommet to protect each string. The strings are woven across the head, which can range from 95 to 110 square inches (241.30 sq. cm to 279.40 sq. cm) of a bouncing surface, and comes in a variety of materials and thicknesses, with a bigger head having more power. The bumper guard is made of durable plastic to protect the edge of the racquet. The maximum length of a racquet is 22 inches (55.88 cm), including the frame, bumper guard, and any part of the handle. The frame includes an 18-inch (45.72 cm) cord that attaches to the player's wrist, and the strings of the racquet must be made of graphite, gut, metal, monofilament, nylon, or plastic.

The balls are hollow and pressurized, made of soft rubber, and measure 2.25 inches (5.72 cm) in diameter. They come in an assortment of colors and each has a meaning. The black ball is a durable slow ball for longer rallies, often played by seniors. A blue ball is the most common indoor ball with a medium speed and durability. Green balls are fast for indoor play. Purple balls are the fastest for indoor use, but they are some of the least durable. There are slightly heavier red balls, the fastest for outdoor use, which are very durable. Pink balls are fast, good for indoors, and a portion of the proceeds from their sale goes to fight breast cancer research. Players also wear a glove to better hold the racquet, and protection for the eyes. A short-sleeved shirt and shorts are worn with special racquetball court shoes for better lateral movement.

Racquetball Terms and Slang

Ace

Racquetball: A serve that isn't returned, which results in a point for the server.

Sexual: A shortened word for an asexual person.

Alley

Racquetball: The area along the court's side walls, a "down the line" shot is targeted along this lane.

Sexual: A shortened term for "shaft alley," referring to the area from the vaginal opening to the anus. Originally a nautical term for the passage from the engine room to the stern.

Around the world (also called around-the-wall shot)

Racquetball: This is a three-wall defensive shot that travels around the court in a high trajectory.

Sexual: Refers to a man who attains sexual reward from having vaginal, anal, and oral sex with one woman in one night.

Blue ball(s)

Racquetball: A ball of this color is the most commonly used ball for beginners. There are also green for tournament play, purple for International Pros, black for senior tournaments, and red balls for the fastest players.

Sexual: This condition of the testicles can be painful, caused by prolonged sexual arousal that does not end in ejaculation.

Court

Racquetball: Either a fully enclosed indoor or outdoor area, 20 by 40 feet (6.10 m by 12.19 m), with red lines defining the service and serve reception areas.

Sexual: The act of dating a person with the intent to marry, meaning that sexual intercourse will most likely take place as part of getting to know one another.

Dead ball

Racquetball: The ball at the end of a rally that is no longer being played, until it is served again.

Sexual: After a serious injury to the scrotum has occurred, the spermatic cord that carries blood to one or both of the testicles may have been twisted, called testicular torsion. This can affect the blood flow to the tissues, which will turn the testicle numb, making it feel as if it is "dead." This can also occur with too-rapid growth during puberty.

Dink

Racquetball: An effective offensive shot designed to end the point.

Sexual: A synonym for the penis, which comes from 1888 America, from "dingus," meaning the "thing." Also, a dinkle.

Doubles

Racquetball: Four players divided into two teams of two.

Sexual: Short for double penetration, that is, a woman being penetrated by a man vaginally and another man anally. It is also when one man is engaged in sex play with two women at the same time.

Drive

Racquetball: An aggressively hit, fast moving ball.

Sexual: A powerful penile thrust in intercourse.

In-and-out

Racquetball: A racquetball game played with three players, also called "Cut-throat," "Ironman," "Sevens," and "California."

Sexual: A British euphemism for intercourse.

Lob Serve

Racquetball: A defensive serve. A plain lob serve is a ball hit with a long, high arch into either back corner. A junk lob takes a shallower arch and lands close to the side wall.

Sexual: A semi-erect penis, and to have sexual intercourse.

Plum

Racquetball: A good setup for an offensive shot, often occurring at knee level or lower.

Sexual: A synonym for a man's testicle.

Rating

Racquetball: An evaluation of player's ability levels based on their success versus local opponents.

Sexual: A number that is assigned by men specifically to women, in evaluating and ranking their face, breasts, and buttocks.

Receiver

Racquetball: The player waiting for the server to hit the ball.

Sexual: A submissive who is being sexually dominated by a "server" either orally, vaginally, or anally.

Server

Racquetball: The player hitting the serve and the only player who can score for that round.

Sexual: The person who "serves" for fun or for payment, when understood as a euphemism for intercourse.

Setup

Racquetball: A shot placing the ball in a great position for an aggressive offensive shot that might be a kill shot or a plum shot.

Sexual: A man that has a woman ready and available for sexual indulgence.

Wallbanger

Racquetball: Slang for a squash or racquetball player.

Sexual: Sexual intercourse that occurs vertically, against a wall.

Other Racquetball Terms with Sexual Possibilities

When a serve in racquetball accidently hits the corner of the front wall, it is called a *crotch serve*. The term could also apply to a woman sitting on the edge of a dining table who reveals to her lover her open legs and her crotch, being served up hot and ready. A *donut* is a shutout game in which one player loses without scoring for a final score of 15-0. The zero resembles a donut. A donut is a euphemism for the rounded entrance of the vagina with a "hole" in the middle. In racquetball the *service box* is formed by the short solid red line running the court's width parallel to the front and back walls, and the service line which runs parallel to the short line. Although it is not a very nice or accurate synonym, a "box" is a slang word for the vagina, therefore, a service box could be interpreted as that which a prostitute uses to service her customers. And a *service line*, referring to the back-boundary line, is where the serve may not go past. Although unfound in any sexual slang listing, a service line could refer to a line of men at their favorite bordello waiting for the woman they want.

When a racquetball server enters the safety zone before the ball strikes the court behind the short line, it is a *safety zone violation*. This could also pertain to a male lover who kept going after the condom broke. That would definitely be a safety zone violation. The *splat shot* in racquetball is an elongated pinch that strikes the side wall toward the back part of the court, making a distinctive splatting sound. But the term can also be an ejaculation upon the lower part of a woman's back where she has a tattoo, for a tat splat shot. A *straight-in shot* is meant to hit the front wall as low as possible so that it's difficult for the opponent to return a shot. A straight-in shot could also be a direct ejaculation into an open mouth.

Sexual Commentary

The racquet, the ball, the court, and its walls are made for commenting on. First, the racquet is similar in shape to the head of a lacrosse stick, with an elongated and rounded triangle in a frame, but the strings are quite taut. The racquet in racquetball has a short handle with little to no neck, so the grip directly attaches to the head, which tends to give the player more power to swing. The ball is a hollow rubber ball. They come in several colors, but a pink ball is the official ball of professional women's racquetball. The official colors for U.S. tournaments are blue and green, though blue has been more traditional. The court is an elongated box, and although the walls and ceiling must be of the same color, most tend to be white.

So, we have a short, wide stick that likes to knock its balls against a pure white wall within an elongated box. Women like to whack those pink balls hard, and men like to bang their blue balls about, until each can score. Yeah, that sounds about right. So players, you just go right ahead and continue banging those balls around if it makes you happy.

Chapter 37
Squash

The game of squash is played by two people, one against one, called singles, or with four people, two against two, called doubles, in an enclosed court with four walls. The hollow rubber ball is called a squash ball because of its squashable quality. Players alternate serving and hitting the ball between score lines on the walls. A match is best of either three or five games of eleven points each.

To begin the game, a player spins the racket to see who it points to. That person stands in a service box at the rear of the court and strikes the ball. The ball must land above the service line and below the outline on the front wall, and bounce back to the opposite back quarter court. They take turns serving and rallying the ball, until one person makes fifteen points, though only eleven points are required in the English form of the game.

It was in the late sixteenth century that ball and racket games became popular, including tennis, badminton, and a game called rackets. Squash didn't begin until 1830, at Harrow School in London. The areas available to play were the inner city, outdoors between buildings, waterways, and slopes, so the spaces were confined and somewhat hazardous. Consequently, a shorter racket was used.[226] That all changed later.

The first squash court was built in 1884 for St. Paul's School in New Hampshire. Twenty years later, the first national association of squash was formed in Philadelphia, now known as U.S. Squash. In 1907, the first standards for the game were set. The game was so popular that in 1912 the Titanic had a squash court for their First-Class passengers. In 1923, the rules and regulations were finally set down.

A squash court has four walls with lines dividing the court. There is a front line and a back line, a half court line, and a left and right-hand side line providing three boxes: the large front half, and the back right and left quarters. But the court lines only matter when serves are made. A court is about 32 feet long and 21 feet wide (9.75 m by 6.40), and 18.5 feet (5.64 m) high. On these high walls are marked parallel lines. There is an out line that runs along the top of the wall and descends on the sides to the back wall. Shots that land above or touch the line are out. About 1½ feet (0.46 m) from the base is another line, and striking below it means the ball is also out.

The rackets at first were made out of laminated ash wood, but in the 1980s their construction shifted to composite materials and metals for strength, including graphite, aluminum, boron, Kevlar, and titanium. The strings were once made of gut but became synthetic. The racket was to weigh between 3 to 5 ounces (85.05 g to 141.75 g), but could weigh up to 9 ounces (255.15 g).

The ball is always made of two pieces of natural rubber, glued together. They are hollow and have a matte

[226] James Zug, "The History of Squash in 8 Chapters," U.S. Squash Archive. https://web.archive.org/web/20110717181310/ www.ussquash.com/functions/content.aspx?id=1252

finish, measuring about 1½ inches (3.81 cm) in diameter and weighing less than an ounce (28.35 g). Different compositions of rubber are used which produce variation in bounce, and the warmer the temperature, the better the bounce. A ball's bounce is noted on the ball with a colored dot. There are blue dots for a beginner, with a very high bounce for easier play; red for a medium player, with a high bounce; yellow for an advanced player, which bounces more slowly; and a double yellow dot for the experienced player, with a very slow bounce that is difficult to hit. The balls are also known as pro, progress, competition, and pro grade. A ball with an orange dot is made for high altitudes.

In 2009 there were almost 50,000 squash courts in the world, with twenty million players. The International Olympic Committee recognizes the game but it has yet to be accepted into the games.

Squash Terms and Slang

Attack

Squash: An aggressive play, to take the ball on the volley, to give the opponent less time, and to generally force the opponent to feel rushed or threatened by a player's presence on the court.

Sexual: It can mean a sexual attack, or in Japan it simply means to approach someone (without harm) of the opposite gender.

Box

Squash: A square area in each quarter court bounded by part of the short line, part of the side wall, and by two other lines, from where the server serves from.

Sexual: A slang synonym for the vagina.

Down

Squash: The expression is used to indicate that an otherwise good return has struck the lowest horizontal marking on the front wall or has failed to reach the front wall.

Sexual: Refers to "going down," meaning to perform oral sex, fellatio or cunnilingus. Also, to "get down and dirty" means to have intercourse.

Game

Squash: This is part of a match, commencing with a service and concluding when one player has scored or been awarded nine or ten points.

Sexual: The pursuit of a sexual partner, including pickup lines, the skill of the pursuer, and the sex drive of both people.

Hand

Squash: The period from the time a player becomes server until they become the receiver.

Sexual: Refers to a "hand job," manual genital stimulation during masturbation.

Knackered

Squash: When in complete exhaustion.
Sexual: When sexually spent.

Out

Squash: When a ball in play strikes above the outline or below the base line and deflects back into the court.

Sexual: When someone "comes out" as in "out of the closet," meaning that they are openly expressing their homosexuality.

Stroke

Squash: A stroke is awarded to a player as a penalty against the opponent for interference.

Sexual: The gentle slide of a hand across the body, or the action of the index finger and thumb around the penis along the shaft moving the skin up and down to produce a pleasurable sensation leading to orgasm and ejaculation. To stroke in masturbation. A man's penetrations delivered full length in and out during intercourse.

Stop

Squash: A call made by the referee to stop the play.

Sexual: An abbreviation for <u>S</u>have <u>T</u>hat <u>O</u>vergrown <u>P</u>ussy.

Time

Squash: A call made by the referee to indicate that a period of time prescribed in the rules has elapsed.

Sexual: From "making time," to engage in sexual activity.

Turning

Squash: This occurs when the striker has physically followed the ball around and turned, or the ball was passed around the striker, and the striker strikes the ball to the right of the body after the ball has passed to the left or right.

Sexual: A euphemism for intercourse.

Other Squash Terms with Sexual Possibilities

An *appeal* is a player's request to the referee to consider an on or off court situation, varying a marker's decision, or to allow a let. The correct form of an appeal by a player is "appeal, please." This term could also be used for a person having sexual appeal, which is the attractiveness of a possible sexual partner. *Excessive swing or dangerous play,* is when the swing is performed with a straight arm, instead of bent, which can merit a conduct warning or a conduct penalty. If an injury results from a dangerous play, the referee will award the match to the injured player, and the player who caused the injury will forfeit that point but retain all points won. Excessive swing(ing) or dangerous play might also be said about a person in a swingers' group who fails to use protective measures by not wearing a condom. *A not up* in squash is when the server attempts but fails to hit the ball correctly. In sex-speak, not up could mean that a male partner could not get an erection, for any number of reasons.

A *service box* is a square area in each quarter court bounded by part of the short line, part of the side wall, and by two other lines which the server serves from. As in racquetball, since a slang word for vagina is a box, a service box could be interpreted as that which a prostitute has and uses to service her customers. A *service line* is the line upon the front wall, the top edge of which is above the floor and extends the full width of the court. In sexual nomenclature, a service line could also refer to a line of men at their favorite bordello. A *slow game* is how some people play squash with lobs, high serves, and few hard drives. The game might be played deliberately slowly to upset the opponent's rhythm, or to catch one's breath. A slow game could also be the slow pursuit of a sexual partner, which includes pickup lines, the skill of the pursuer, and the sex drives of both people.

Sexual Commentary

At the start of a game, it is interesting to note that the spin of the racquet is what determines which side of the court the spin winner chooses for the first serve. The logo at the end of the grip will land either up or down. This smacks of the situation when two men who are friends in a bar both take an interest in the same woman, so they flip a coin to see who gets to approach her first. And just like in squash, where a player only gets one serve, if the first guy strikes out with the girl, he cannot keep trying. The loser must let his friend now have a try.

If a squash player loses the rally, then the opponent gets the point and the serve. To carry this analogy further, if the squash opponent looks like he might interfere with a player's direct swing, he must say "let please," to warn the other player not to interfere. If the opponent does interfere, then it should be a "stroke," or the first player's point. If the interference is from more than a meter away, and the player closest could have gotten the ball, it is a let. If the interference is less than a meter from the ball, it is a stroke. How close did each get to catching the attention of the woman? Did they have to "let" the other guy get her or did he win her attention and get to have a stroking (sexual) good time with her?

Chapter 38
Tennis

In the game of tennis, the stick is a tennis racket, the ball is a tennis ball, the playing area is an outdoor tennis court with a net, and the players are a server and a receiver. A serve starts the game when the server hits the ball with his or her racket, it goes over a net, and the opponent returns the ball with his or her racket over the net. When the ball is in play it is a rally, a set is a number of games, and a match is a sequence of sets. Scoring is unique, with zero points called "love," one point called "15," two points called "30," and three points called "40." If the score is 40 to 40, that is called a "deuce." If a player gets one more point, the score of the game is his or her "advantage."

Tennis can be played one against one for singles or two against two for doubles, and the markings on the court indicate the bounds for each. There are three officials: the line judge, net judge, and the head judge or chair umpire. An electronic review system called the "Hawk-Eye" is now used, which can more closely identify any foul.

Only the Grand Slam tournament offers a grand prize for Junior tennis team competitions. Most Juniors must progress by competing in the Challenger, Future, Satellite, and International tournaments for the Junior Fed Cup and the Davis Cup. There are also the men's Masters 1000, 250, and 500 Series, the Challenger Tour,

Futures tournaments, and the women's Premier and International events.

A playbook of tennis history dates to the late 1100s in northern France, with players using their hands instead of a racket.[227] It was said that Louis X liked to play a similar game with a small ball and the palm of his hand called *jeu de paume*. He also designed the first indoor tennis court, but unfortunately, he died after playing a game in Paris, having drunk too much wine to cool himself down.[228]

Up until the 1500s, the game had been played with the palm, but then using a racket became popular and it earned a new name. A server would get the receiver's attention that a serve was coming by calling out *tenez* in French (meaning to "hold, receive, take").[229] The game spread to England, and the English heard the French word *tenez* as "tennis."[230] When it arrived in England it was only played indoors, and the ball was bounced off a wall. Of all things, it ended up being the invention of the lawn mower in 1830 that allowed the game to go outdoors on short-cut grassy courts.

In 1872, the world's first tennis club was formed and the sport was referred to as "lawn tennis." A year later, British officer Major Walter Clopton Wingfield devised a version of the game, calling it by the Greek name *sphairistikè,* meaning "ball-playing." He did much to promote and popularize the game by producing and

---

[227] Heiner Gillmeister, *Tennis: A Cultural History,* (New York: New York University Press, 1998). 117.

[228] Ibid, 17-21.

[229] Online Etymology Dictionary, "Tennez." https://www.etymonline.com/search?q=tenez

[230] Robert Crego, *Sports and Games of the 18th and 19th Centuries,* (Westport, CT: Greenwood Press, 2003), 115.

shipping out thousands of sets of the game with the rules.[231] In 1874, a young Mary Ewing Outerbridge saw sphairistikè being played in Bermuda, so she brought the game to America. By 1877 tennis was introduced at the Wimbledon Championships in London, and three years later, the U.S. National Lawn Tennis Association was created to set up competitions and to standardize the rules, just in time for the first Men's Singles Championship. The first Women's Championship was held in 1887.

By 1891, France had their first French Championships, but only French club members could compete. In 1900, lawn tennis was being played in Canada, the Davis Cup was first held for men's national teams, and the sport was introduced as singles and mixed doubles at the Olympic Games. In 1905, the Australia Open held its first championships. Then, the four International championships held by Australia, Britain, France, and the U.S. became known as the Majors. When a player participates in all four, it is referred to as a Grand Slam. The International Tennis Federation formed in 1924 to oversee international tennis and added a tiebreaking system for tied games. From 1928 to 1988, tennis was not included at the Olympic, due to a long-standing dispute between the Olympic Committee and the International Federation. Demonstrations of the game were offered in 1968 and 1984, and tennis was finally reinstated as a medal sport in 1988.

Since the majority of terms deal with the court, the racket, and the ball, those descriptions will be offered

---

[231] Gary Morley, "125 Years of Wimbledon: From Birth of Lawn Tennis to Modern Marvels."
http://edition.cnn.com/2011/SPORT/tennis/06/14/tennis.wimble don.125th.anniversary.museum/index.html

next. Not all aspects of the game, with its long list of rules, will be discussed unless they pertain to the terms presented below.

The tennis court is narrower for singles, at 27 feet by 78 feet (8.23 m by 23.77 m). For doubles, the court is 36 feet (10.97 m) wide. A net is stretched across the middle of the court widthwise at 3 feet (0.91 m) high in the center, and 3 feet 6 inches (1.07 m) at the posts. At each end is a baseline and a center mark. Thirty-six feet (11 m) in from the baseline is the service line, on both sides. Linking the two service lines is the center service line, running 42 feet (12.80 m). Courts can be made of acrylic-topped asphalt, artificial turf, carpet, clay, concrete, or grass, and are usually a shade of green or blue, but can also be found in grey, purple, and red.

A tennis racket is very similar to a racquetball racquet, and consists of a handle, throat, and head. The handle is comprised of the shaft, the butt with butt cap at the end, and the grip of the handle. The throat is where the shaft splits and forms an open Y to connect with the racquet head. The racquet head includes the beam or thickness of the wood, the strings, grommets, and bumper guard. There is a grommet to protect each string. The strings are woven across the head, 12.5 inches by 29 inches (31.75 cm by 73.66 cm), for a good bouncing surface. Most laminated wood rackets gave a racket the best strength until metals were used, then carbon graphite composites, ceramics, and titanium were introduced. The bumper guard is made of durable plastic to protect the edge of the racquet.

Early balls were strips of white cloth stuffed with feathers. Now they are vulcanized rubber, covered in yellow felt. The ball must be 2.58 to 2.7 inches (6.54 cm to 17.78 cm) in diameter and weigh between 1.98 and 2.10 ounces (56.13 g to 59.53 g). There are eight basic shots that a player can make: the serve, forehand, backhand, volley, half-volley, overhead smash, drop shot, and a lob.

Tennis Terms & Slang

Ace
Tennis: A serve landing on or near one of the corners at the back of the service boxes that the receiver is not able to return.

Sexual: A shortened word for an asexual person.

Action
Tennis: Another word for spin on a ball.

Sexual: What a person hopes for in a possible partner for intercourse.

Alley
Tennis: The area of the court between the singles and doubles sidelines, known as the tram lines.

Sexual: A shortened term for "shaft alley" referring to the area from the vaginal opening to the anus. Originally a nautical term for the passage from the engine room to the stern.

ATP
Tennis: The men's Association of Tennis Professionals.

Sexual: In the porn, ATP stands for "ass to pussy" for anal to vaginal entry.

Baseline
Tennis: The chalk line at the farthest ends of the court indicating the boundary of the area of play.

Sexual: The bare minimum standard of attractiveness that a man or woman might consider in a partner for intercourse.

458

Block

Tennis: A defensive shot with little backswing when returning a serve.

Sexual: Short for "cock-block," one who impedes another from connecting sexually with someone.

Breadstick

Tennis: A way of expressing a set of 6 to 1, of either winning or losing.

Sexual: A synonym for the penis.

Break

Tennis: To win a game as the receiving team, thereby breaking serve, meaning to have in a set, one break less than the opponent. A double break is two breaks more than the opponent.

Sexual: When a couple decides to spend some time separated from their sexual activities; and a term used by a prostitute for collecting money from a customer to "break" her luck with the first money of the night, and to depart with a client to conduct business.

Buggy whip

Tennis: Describes a forehand hit with a follow through which does not go across the body and finish on the opposite side, but goes from low to high and finishes on the same side (similar to the driver of a horse-drawn carriage whipping a horse).

Sexual: A type of thong whip with a tough rigid core and flexible cracker at its end, used in BDSM scenes for consensual flogging of a person, or for self-flagellation.

Chop

Tennis: A shot with extreme underspin.

Sexual: The art of getting a woman to agree to a date and getting her number.

Court

Tennis: The area designated for playing a game of tennis.

Sexual: The act of dating a person with the intent to marry, meaning that sexual intercourse will most likely take place as part of getting to know one another.

Cross-over

Tennis: This occurs when a player crosses the net into the opponent's court, accidently or on purpose.

Sexual: A crossover sexual offense is one in which victims are from multiple age, gender, and relationship categories.

Cyclops

Tennis: A device used on center court to detect if a serve lands long past the service line. It emits an audible noise when the serve is long.

Sexual: A euphemism for the penis, as it has one eye.

Dink

Tennis: Refers to hitting a shot with no pace.

Sexual: Or a dinkle. A synonym for penis, which comes from 1888 America, from "dingus," meaning a "thing."

Doubles

Tennis: A game played by four players, two on each side of the court.

Sexual: Short for double penetration, that is, a woman being penetrated by a man vaginally and another man anally. It is also when one man is engaged in sex play with two women at the same time.

Flat

Tennis: A flat serve with relatively little spin.

Sexual: Refers to a woman with very small breasts or buttocks.

GOAT

Tennis: An acronym for the <u>G</u>reatest <u>o</u>f <u>a</u>ll <u>T</u>ime, which can refer to a player, the team, or the game.

Sexual: The same acronym, but specifically refers to an excellent lover.

Grand slam

Tennis: Winning the four most prestigious tournaments within the same year: the Australian Open, the French Open, Wimbledon, and the U.S. Open.

Sexual: Refers to intercourse while maintaining penetration in a continuous set of positions; when a man attains sexual reward with vaginal, anal, and oral sex from one woman; and having had intercourse with three different women in one night.

Hail Mary

Tennis: An extremely high lob, for defensive purposes.

Sexual: When a person in a bar or club at the end of the night "hooks up" with who remains.

Hawk-eye

Tennis: A high speed computer system used to track the path of the ball and used with the challenge system for overall line calls.

Sexual: Refers to what someone possesses, because they can spot an attractive person from a distance.

Head

Tennis: The portion of the racket that contains the strings.

Sexual: The end of the penis, and the act of giving or receiving oral sex, fellatio or cunnilingus.

Hold

Tennis: Winning the game when serving.

Sexual: Refers to holding on to a person, figuratively and physically.

Jamming
Tennis: To serve or return straight to the opponent's body.

Sexual: A euphemism for engaging in sexual intercourse.

Lob
Tennis: A stroke where the ball is hit high above the net.

Sexual: A semi-erect penis, and to have sexual intercourse.

Love
Tennis: A zero score.

Sexual: Erotic love or eros that is primal, powerful, and arouses romantic and sexual feelings.

Love game
Tennis: A shutout game, won without the opponent scoring.

Sexual: A person who teases and plays hard to get, or attempts any other purposeful play to test their lover.

Out
Tennis: Any ball that lands outside the play area.

Sexual: When someone "comes out," as in "out of the closet," they are openly expressing their homosexuality.

Receiver
Tennis: The person who is being served to.

Sexual: A submissive who is being sexually dominated by a "server," either orally, vaginally, or anally.

462

Round Robin

Tennis: A tournament format in which players are organized into groups of three or four players and they compete against all other members of the group, who are ranked by games won.

Sexual: A swinger's game in which couples meet and play with others, one after another, for sexual pleasure.

Seed

Tennis: Players with the highest ranking who have the best chance of winning a tournament.

Sexual: Refers to semen.

Shank

Tennis: A mis-hit whereby the ball contacts the racket frame during the swing, resulting in a shot that is misdirected.

Sexual: A prostitute or a woman without virtue.

Singles

Tennis: A tennis game played one person against one other.

Sexual: When a person is not currently in a sexual relationship with anyone.

Slice

Tennis: Rallying a tennis ball with underspin or serving with a sidespin.

Sexual: A sexual reference for an attractive and sexy woman, as in relishing the taste of a sweet slice of pie.

Smash

Tennis: An overhead shot that bounces off the opponent's court at an angle difficult to return.

Sexual: A euphemism for good intercourse, also known as a "smashing buttflap" and "smashing pissers."

Spank

Tennis: To hit a groundstroke flat with a lot of pace.

Sexual: The action of whacking a partner on the buttocks, back, or thighs, with a hand or various tools.

Strings

Tennis: The material woven through the face of the racquet, and the area where contact with the ball is supposed to be made.

Sexual: When a person controls the situation in a physical relationship, having "strings attached." "No strings" is to have a physical relationship, but without responsibility.

Stroke

Tennis: A striking of the ball.

Sexual: The gentle slide of a hand across the body, or the action of the index finger and thumb around the penis along the shaft moving the skin up and down to produce a pleasurable sensation leading to orgasm and ejaculation. To stroke in masturbation. And a man's penetrations delivered full length in and out during intercourse.

Sweet spot

Tennis: The central area of the strings on the racket head which is the desired location for contacting the ball.

Sexual: A place on the body that pleasurably responds to a touch or caress. Also refers to the "G" spot and the clitoris.

Touch

Tennis: This occurs when a player touches any part of the net when the ball is still in play, resulting in losing the point.

Sexual: A synonym for sexual intercourse.

Tweener

Tennis: A trick shot which involves hitting the ball between the legs from front to rear while retrieving an offensive lob.

Sexual: A lesbian or bisexual person who has equal qualities of male and female.

Other Tennis Terms with Sexual Possibilities

A *ball person* is tasked with retrieving tennis balls from the court that have gone out of play and supplying the balls to the players. For a sexual meaning, this could be a person who favors playing with another's scrotum. A declaration that a play was outside of the play area is a *call* made by a line judge. A call can also mean a prostitute "on call," waiting for a client to phone. Or it can mean a "booty call," which is when a summons has been made to a friend for a sexual liaison. In tennis, a *dead rubber* refers to a Davis cup match which is played after the victor of the tie has already been decided. The term seems perfectly obvious to also mean "a used condom." A shot that lands near the baseline, as opposed to near the net, is said to be *deep* on the court. Deep can also have a sexual connotation, that is, a deep penetrating thrust of the penis during intercourse.

An *entry system* is the ranking system that determines whether a player has a sufficiently high ranking to gain direct acceptance into the main draw of a given tournament. An entry system could also be the means of sexual entry into the body as with fellatio, vaginal, or anal penetration. An *exhibition* is a tournament in which players compete for the purpose of entertaining the crowd but not ranking points. A sexual term very close to this is exhibitionism, and an exhibitionist is one who enjoys showing off their naked body and their sexual prowess when in sexual congress with someone. A *ground stroke* is a forehand or backhand shot that is executed after the ball bounces once on a court. A ground stroke could also be intercourse while lying on the ground. And a dirt baller has a similar sexual meaning. In tennis, a *dirt baller* is a colloquial term for a clay court specialist.

In tennis, a *moon ball* is a medium-high offensive lob hit with topspin. A moon ball could also be having intercourse under the light of the moon, since "to ball" is to copulate. *New balls* is a set of new tennis balls that replace old ones during the game. New balls could also be the addition of a new man joining a group of sexual players. *Singles sticks* are a pair of poles placed under the net near the singles sideline for the purpose of raising it for single play. Singles sticks could also be phallic toys that a single person might use for sexual pleasure with masturbation. An *unseeded player* is one who is not a "seed" (a high-ranking player) in the tournament. An unseeded player could also be a man in an orgy who has already ejaculated.

Sexual Commentary

The one very unique thing about tennis is the scoring terminology, with the use of "love" for a zero score. The word itself isn't sexual per se, but the reasons for it might just be. There are different possibilities for its use. The word is thought to come from a misunderstanding of the French word, *l'oeuf,* "the egg," meaning "nothing." Americans sometimes use the term "goose egg" to refer to a score of zero, meaning a failure or a defeat. The Dutch translate "lof" to mean praise or honor, so maybe just playing the game is an honor. It was once a game only for the nobility. The Oxford Dictionary states that the term may have come from the phrase "to play for love." Could that mean that one may not have a stake in the game? Does one play tennis because they love their partner or just because they love the game? Or does that mean that the loser misses out on "getting some"? Eggs are a synonym for the testes because they are very similar in size. Regardless, if one loves tennis and loves eggs, eat, play, and be merry!

Appendices

Appendix 1
Ratio of Sexual Terms to Sports Terms

Two lists follow. The first list has each of the thirty-five sports listed alphabetically and gives the percentage of sexual words compared to their total list of official terms. The number of each sports' official terms were calculated using their respective international terminology lists.

Archery: 15 out of 176 = 8.52%
Badminton: 8 out of 30 = 26.66%
Bandy: 12 out of 49 = 24.49%
Baseball: 146 out of 1,164 = 12.54%
Basketball: 35 out of 175 = 20.00%
Billiards: 27 out of 172 = 15.70%
Bocce ball: 9 out of 46 = 19.56%
Bowling: 21 out of 84 = 25.00%
Cricket: 68 out of 611 = 11.13%
Croquet: 15 out of 113 = 13.27%
Curling: 50 out of 224 = 22.32%
Darts: 22 out of 163 = 13.50%
Dodgeball: 14 out of 44 = 31.81%
Fishing: 42 out of 368 = 12.50%
Football: 53 out of 370 = 14.32%
Golf: 55 out of 291 = 16.00%
Handball: 29 out of 128 = 22.66%
Hurling: 17 out of 25 = 68.00%
Ice Hockey: 47 out of 227 = 20.70%

Kickball: 7 out of 14 = 50.00%
Lacrosse: 15 out of 47 = 31.91%
Ping-Pong: 21 out of 51 = 41.18%
Pole Vault: 8 out of 18 + 44.44%
Polo: 14 out of 41 = 34.15%
Quarterstaff: 9 out of 29 = 31.03%
Quidditch: 14 out of 64 = 21.88%
Racquetball: 17 out of 105 = 16.19%
Rounders: 11 out of 51 = 21.57%
Rugby: 45 out of 195 = 23.08%
Shinty: 9 out of 37 = 24.32%
Shuffleboard: 21 out of 87 = 24.14%
Soccer: 11 out of 41 = 26.83%
Squash: 11 out of 75 = 14.67%
Tennis: 40 out of 195 = 20.51%
Volleyball: 43 out of 97 = 44.33%

The same sports above are now listed in order below, from the lowest percentage of sexual words to the highest.

Archery: 15 out of 176 = 8.52%
Cricket: 68 out of 611 = 11.13%
Fishing: 42 out of 368 = 12.50%
Baseball: 146 out of 1,164 = 12.54%
Croquet: 15 out of 113 = 13.27%
Darts: 22 out of 163 = 13.50%
Football: 53 out of 370 = 14.32%
Squash: 11 out of 75 = 14.67%
Billiards: 27 out of 172 = 15.70%
Golf: 55 out of 291 = 16.00%
Racquetball: 17 out of 105 = 16.19%
Bocce ball: 9 out of 46 = 19.56%
Basketball: 35 out of 175 = 20.00%
Tennis: 40 out of 195 = 20.51%
Ice Hockey: 47 out of 227 = 20.70%

Rounders: 11 out of 51 = 21.57%
Handball: 29 out of 128 = 22.66%
Quidditch: 14 out of 64 = 21.88%
Curling: 50 out of 224 = 22.32%
Rugby: 45 out of 195 = 23.08%
Shuffleboard: 21 out of 87 = 24.14%
Shinty: 9 out of 37 = 24.32%
Bandy: 12 out of 49 = 24.49%
Bowling: 21 out of 84 = 25.00%
Badminton: 8 out of 30 = 26.66%
Soccer: 11 out of 41 = 26.83%
Quarterstaff: 9 out of 29 = 31.03%
Dodgeball: 14 out of 44 = 31.81%
Lacrosse: 15 out of 47 = 31.91%
Polo: 14 out of 41 = 34.15%
Ping-Pong: 21 out of 51 = 41.18%
Volleyball: 43 out of 97 = 44.33%
Pole Vault: 8 out of 18 = 44.44%
Kickball: 7 out of 14 = 50.00%
Hurling: 17 out of 25 = 68.00%

Summary

Here is how these sports measure up. Although baseball has the greatest number of official terms, at 1,164, its percentage of sexual terms is pretty low, the fourth-lowest. Only archery falls below 10% of sexual terms compared to its total number of official terms. Eleven sports fall between 11% and 19.99%: cricket, fishing, baseball, croquet, darts, football, squash, billiards, golf, racquetball and bocce ball. Fourteen sports range between 20% and 29.99%: tennis, basketball, ice hockey, rounders, quidditch, handball, curling, rugby, shuffleboard, shinty, bandy, bowling, badminton, and soccer. Four sports are within the range of 30% to 39.99%:

dodgeball, quarterstaff, lacrosse, and polo. Three sports are between 40% and 49.99%: table tennis (ping-pong), volleyball, and pole vault. Fifty percent of kickball's terms are sexual, and hurling wins with 68% of its total official terms being sexual. Of the thirty-five sports listed within this book, the *average* percentage of sexual terms came to 26.58%, just over one-quarter of the total number of sports terms!

With all that has been presented, the reader is sure to agree, sexuality finds a comfortable home within sports. There is also the possibility that in the future, more sexual terms might find their way into sports terminology, and more sports terms might find their way into sexual nomincalture. Whether you are an athlete, a sports fan, or one who enjoys sexual word play, there is something for everyone to enjoy. Now there is no reason to even mention what might be going on beneath that sport's blanket.

Appendix 2
Sexual Slang Word Lists

The following lists of words and phrases are from the English language found in the United States, the United Kingdom, and Australia. There are only eight headings of genitalia and activities among the many sexual topics that could be listed, but they serve as more than enough to show the variation and diversity which the human mind has adopted in order to describe sexuality from the past to the present. These lists only compile a fraction of the made-up words out there. A complete list is not possible, as it would be a book all on its own.

Looking at the amount of substitute words, it is obvious that they were created simply because a person did not know or did not want to use the proper name for a body part or sexual activity. Terms that were unintelligible, words with references that could not be found, and truly gross descriptions were eliminated, but all the rest were kept. The reader will see named cities, countries, famous people, and movie references. All abbreviations have their meanings written out in parentheses. If curious, one can find a majority of these terms with definitions online at http://www.sex-lexis.com. At the end of the bibliography, the reader will find a list of online sites that can be visited to find thousands more descriptive sexual terms.

474

Male Genitalia

The Penis:

#/A/B - 100% all-beef thermometer, Aaron's rod, ABD (all but dissertation), abominable pants worm, Abraham, accordion, accoutrements, ace poker, acron, action Jackson, Adam's dagger, Adam's whip, adamantine organon, Adolph, agate, Alabama black snake, albino cave dweller, Aleck, all-beef sausage, almond, almond rock candy, ambassador, amblyopic organ, anaconda, anal impaler, angle of the dangle, animated ivory, anteater, antenna, a piece of meat, apparatus, appendickle, appropriate member, arbor bitae, Ares, arm, arrow, arse-opener, arse-wedge, artillerie de Cupidon, ass-wedge, atomic turtle, Athenaeum, auger, auxiliaries, awaken the bacon, axe, baby-arm, baby fetcher, baby-maker, bag of tricks, bald-headed sailor, bald-headed yogurt slinger, baloney pony, banana, basilisk, bat, bayonet, BBC (big black cock), BBD (big black dick), beak, beard splitter, beaver basher, beaver cleaver, bedfellow, bed snake, beef thermometer, beef whistle, bellend, bell on a pole, bellpiece, belly-ruffian, best leg of three, big Dick and the twins, big Italian salami, billy-my-nag, bird(ie), bludgeon, bicho, bishop, bita, bite (Fr.), bobby, bobby dangler, Bob Dole, bob-my-nag, boga, bookworm, bollocks, bologna pony, Boomstick, bone(er), boom stick, boomerang, boonga, braciole, branch, brat-getter, bratwurst, bread in the basket, breadstick, brocos, broner, bud, bulge, bum-tickler, burrito, bush-whacker, butcher

C - cabeza de gato, cack, caduceus, cane, candle, chap, captain Standish, captain Winky, carrot, cave hunter, cazzo, Chairman Mao, champion, charmer, child-getter, chin-chin, chien, chink-stopper, choad, choada, chode, chota, concern, chopper, chub, chubbie, chubby, chup, chut, cigar, clam hammer, clarinet, club, cob, cobra, cock, cock rocket, cocktapus, comholder, cod, cony-catcher, copper-stick, corndog, cornholer, corporal, corporal of the guard, cracksman, crank(er), cranny axe, cranny hunter, cream stick, crumb, cuckoo, cucumber, cum gun, custard launcher, custard launcher, customs officer, cut, cutlass, cyclops

D/E - D (dick), dagger, danger noodle, dangler, dard, deep-V diver, dhanda, dick, dickie, dicklet, diddle, diddy, ding-a-ling, ding dong, dingbat, ding dong Mcdork, dingle, dingus, dingy, dink, dinkle, dipstick, dirk, disco stick, divine rod, dodger, dog bone, dog head, dolly, doinker, domepiece, dong, donger, Dong Johnson, dongle, donkey kong, doodle, dopper, Dora the explorer, domick, dork, down, dragon, drill, Dr. Johnson, drum stick, D train, ducey, dude piston, Easy Rider, eggroll, electric eel, elephant, elevator, e-peen, enemy, energizer bunny, equipment, erection, Excalibur, eye-opener

F/G - family jewels, family organ, fang, father confessor, ferret, fiddle, fire hose, flapdoodle, flesh flute, flesh tower, floppy drive, flute, footlong, foreman, fornicating engine, fornicating member, fornicating tool, foto, frankfurter, Frank n' beans, froto, fuckpole, fuck puppet, fuck rod, fuck stick, fuck truck, fudge sickle, fun stick, garcha, gearshift, general and two colonels, generlissimo weenis, gherkin, genitalia, get it up, giant redwood, giggle stick, gigi, Godzilla, goober, goofy goober, gospel-pipe, groin heat-seeking moisture missile, groin ferret, gun, gut wrench

H/I - hairy canary, hairy hotdog, halfmast, hambone, hammer, hammer-headed meat stick, hard drive, hard-on, hardware, Harry Johnson, head, helmet, helmet head, Herman von longschlongenstein, hockey cocky, hog, hollow point, homeboy, hooded, Hoover Tower, horn, horse cock, hose, hot beef injection, hotdog(er), hot dog popsicle, hot member, hotrod, hooter, how's your father, humperdink, hung

I/J/K - ice cream cone, inanimate carbon rod, intromittent organ, it, jackhammer, Jack-in-the-box, Jacob, jade stalk, jamoke, jigger, Jimmy, John, jock, John Thomas, Johnson, joystick, junior, junk, Jurassic Pork, Justin-in beaver, katana, kielbasa, kickstand, king kong, king Sebastian, knick-knack, knight, knob, knobgoblin, krull the warrior king

L - lad, lamb kebab, lance of love, langer, langolee, lap rocket, leaky hose, leather-dresser, leather-stretcher, length, life preserver, Lil' Billy, Lil' Buddy, Lil' Friend, Lil' Steve, lingam, Lincoln log, lipstick, little Alex, little Bob, little chubby, little Davy, little Elvis, little fella, little soldier, live rabbit, lizard, lobster, lodger, lollipop, long dong silver, long John silver, loom, Lord Hardwick, love dart, longfellow, love muscle, love rod, love shaft, love staff, love steak, love stick, love truncheon, love whistle, lu, Luigi, lullaby, lunch box

M - machine, magic mushroom tip, magic stick, magic wand, main vein, male member, manhood, male organ, mallet, man meat, meat popsicle, man muscle, manroot, man's best friend, man's affair, man umbrella, mast, master John Goodfellow, male member, manhood, maypole, master of ceremonies, master sword, mayo shooting hotdog gun, meat, meat and two veg, meat constrictor, meat injection, meat popsicle, meat puppet, meat rod, meat scepter, meat skewer, meatstick, meat thermometer, member, membrum virile, merrymaker, meter long king kong dong, mickey, Mickey Finn, microphone, middle leg, middle stump, milkman, Moby Dick, moisture and heat seeking venomous throbbing python of love, mole, morning wood, mule, mulkku, Mr. Happy, Mr. Knish, Mr. Winky, mushroom head, mutton, mutton dagger, my Asian buddy, my little pony, my oldest friend, my other head

N/O - nabo, nail, nature's scythe, Nebuchadnezzar, needle, needle dick, netherrod, nerve, nightstick, nimrod, nippy, nob, noodle, nuclear missile, nymphaea, okra, old boy, old chap, old fellow, old man, ol' one-eye, one-eyed monster, one-eyed rattlesnake, one-eyed snake, one-eyed trouser-snake, one-eyed trout, one-eyed wonder weasel, one-eyed Willie, one-eyed worm, one-eyed wonder worm, one-eyed yogurt slinger, organ, organ grinder

P - P (pecker), package, packer, patootie, patz, pecker, Pedro, pee-pee, peen, peeper, pee-wee, pencil, pencil dick, pene, Percy, Peter, peg, pego, petter-nikias, Ph.D, phallus, philly cheesesteak, pica, pickle, piece, pico, Pied Piper, Piers Morgan, pig skin bus, pijo, pillicock, pin, pino, pinga, pink cigar, pink oboe, pink torpedo, pink tractor beam, pike, pingas, Pinocchio, pintle, pinto, pipe, pipecleaner, pipi, piroca, pisser, piss weasel, piston, pito, pizzle, pleasure pump, plonker, plug, plumtree shaker, pocket rocket, poloroid, poinswatter, pole, pop a chub, popeye, poronga, pork sword, power drill, prick, Prince Everhard of the Netherlands, Princess Sophia, private eye, private part, privy parts, propagator, ptak a vejce, privates, pud, Puff the one-eyed dragon, pulling prick, purple-headed soldier(man), purple-headed warrior, purple-headed yogurt flinger, purple-helmeted warrior of love, putz, P-word, pyramid, python

Q/R - quadibun, quimstake, quiver bone, rabo, Ramburglar, ramrod, rape tool, redcap, remote control, reproductive organs, rod, rod of pleasure, reed, Richard and the twins, Roger, rooster, root, roundhead, Rumpleforeskin, runnion, Russell the love muscle, Russell the one-eyed muscle, rutter

S - salami, sausage, schlong, schlong dongadoodle, schlort, schmeckel, schmuck, shmuk, schnitzel, schwanz, schwantz, schwartz, sconge, screw, screwdriver, Sebastianci sword, sea biscuit, sea monster, secondary sex characteristic, sexcaliber, sex pistol, sex organ, sex tool, shaft, shlittle, shlong, short arm, shmeki, shotgun, shrinkage, silent flute, single-barreled pump action yogurt server, single serving soup dispenser, Skaufi, skin flute, skyscraper, slut slayer, snake, snausage, sniper rifle, sododalist, soldier, Snickers bar, soupbone, spaetzli, spam dagger, spam javelin, spam trumpet, spawn hammer, sperm cannon, spindle, spitstick, steamin' semen roadway, St. Peter, steamin semen truck, skin shift, staff, stretcher, stick, stinky pickle, straw, summer sausage, super-secret agent hosepipe, surfboard, stiffle, stiffy, sweetener, sweet spot, swelling, swimmeret, swipe, sword

T - taladro de carne, tallywacker, tallywhacker, tadger, tagger, tail, tallywacker, tan banana, tarse, tassle, tater, tentpeg, tent pole, testes, the assault rifle, the bald man, the battleship, the blue-veined aristocrat, the bone ranger, the colonel, the D, the dictator, the goods, the grenade, the ground squirrel, the hardware, the key, the land mine, the lawnmower, the lieutenant, the lightsaber, the Lincoln memorial, the machete, the machine, the major, the member, the mongoose, the monkey, the mustang, the pendulum, the pleasure pump, the pocket monster, the pocket rocket, the salamander, the seaman, the sequoia, the shotgun, the silver bullet, the spear, the sticky grenade, the tank, the Titanic, the trombone, the trouser snake, the Washington monument, the water gun, the worm, thing, thingy, third leg, thumper, thunderbird, thundersword, throbber, tickle-faggot, Timothy tool, tinker, tiny tim, tockley, todger, tonk, tonka, tonsil tickler, tool, toothpick, tramp killer, tripod, trouser meat, trouser monkey, truncheon, trouser snake, tubesteak, tuna torpedo, turca, twig, twinkie, twix

U/V/W/X/Y/Z - uberaffengeil, Uncle Dick, Uncle Reamus, undercover brother, unit, urinary path, vagina miner, vein, veiny love tree, verge, verga, virile member, Vlad the impaler, wand, wang(er), wang doodle, wanger, wanker, wankie, water hose, weapon, weapon of ass destruction, wedding tackle, wedding wrecker, wee, wee-wee, weenie, weeny, whang, whanger, whiskey dick, wick, Wilson, womb broom, womb raider, whoopee stick, who-who dilly, widgie, widdler, wiener, Weiner Schnitzel, willie, willy, willy-winky, wing dang doodle, wingwang, winkie, winkey, winkle, wood, woody womb pecker, yard, yingyang, yogurt gun, yogurt hose, yogurt slinger, yogurt slinger, Zayyin, Zeus, zip, yoo-hoo, zubra, zucchini

The Testes and Scrotum:

Numbers: 3-t scrot, <3m, ←8

A – acorns, adjusticle, afronads, afronuts, aggots, aintya, ala alsas, Alabama crag dangle, Aladdin's magic carpet, Alaskan parachute, aleksi, alien brain, air brushin', angry poodle, angry Shannon, alien facemask, anicles, a nurse purse, anusbag, anal annihilator, anal

480

noobage, anniation, Antarctican nosering, applesack, aqua scrotum, Arabian goggles, Arabian sandgoggles, Arabian teabag, Asian pear, assneck, assticles, Austrian rubdown, Austrian sack race, avraj

B - baby bag, baby crib, baby hedgehog, baby in a bean bag, baboon ass, baby's brains, backsack, back-sack, backside ball bag, bac2pray, bad sack, bag buffer, bagdrag, bageria, baggage handler, baggins, baggyballbag-syndrome, bag licker, baginton, bagrot, bagsack, bag tap, bag weld, bald breasted pigeon, bales, balf, ball bag, ballbag snuggy, balch, ball balloon, ball balm, ballbanñero, ball beg, ballbust, ball cat, ball cheese, ball crack, ball crumbs, ball curtsy, ballfap, ballfart, ball-fucking, ball fro, ballgasm, ballhuggers, balljob, ball lift, ballpumper, balls, ballsack, ballsac eclipse, ball salad, ballsauce, balls of Jericho, ball sac, ballsack blues, ballsackery, ball sack ninja, ballsagna, balls ass, ballsaxons, balsamic vinegar, balls chin, balls deep, ballseam, balls on your face, ball spike, ball suckling, ball-sweat, ball tickler, ball tingle, ball wedgie, Balzac, ballzinall, bamboo, banana nut muffin, barber shopped, barce, bat balls, batflaps, batwings, batch satchel, bat signal, Bavarian snorkler, bawbag, baw bagbaw, bawbaggery, bawhum, bawsack, beadle's fist, beanbagger, bean bags, bean sack, beard sex, bearded clown, beef tarp, Beethoven blow job, beiver spout, bengay, Benjamin clamp, bennie logan, berry gasket, berry lick, betlog, biffkin, bite my bag, birection, bitchsack, bixmorph, bizallz, blow a bubble, boardwalk fries, bobbing for scrotum sauce, bodek, boesker, bogley, boite, bollock face, bollocks, bollucks, bologne pouch, bombs over dad's bag, bonch, bond your boys, boner phone, boogley, borp, bosack, Bosnian goggles, bossin frumunda, Boston tea farty, bouche, bouncing scrotum of doom, bozak, bradham, brain bag, brain balls, brain matter greflin, brain sac, brain monster, Brazilian hickey, bretum, bridger, brock pizza, brown bag lunch, brown bagging, bufuna, brown baling, brubble, bruntlett, bubblegum, buffalosack, buland ballix, bulk and skull, bully gag, bumballed, bumper balls, bungle sack, bunnock, burnley wallet, butt sack

C - California water omelet, California stickies, camelscrow, captain tatty bo jangles, cat brain, catch this work, Catskill blackbeard, caverned, CBT, chafe, cello scrotum, chain the tires, chamwaff, chapped sack, chaster, cheeg, chickenskin, chicken skin dust mask, cheese crease, cheese wagon, cherry muffin, cherry cream, chest scrotes, chew toy, Chinese wonton dip, chocoball mukain, chocolate freezy, choad, choda, choda hair, chodal, chode, chode butter, chodum, chowder bag, Cincinnati bowtie, cleft bag, class, Cleveland scrape, Cleveland steambagger, Cincinnati bowtie, clism, clobe, clown, cheesy scrotum, chindit, chocolate dipped cherries, chowder bags, cider, cockophobia, cock pouch, cock tugger, concbag, cooksac, cods, codsack, coin purse, cootum, Cornish game hen, cornpouch, cowbell, crab step, crack sap, cradle the balls, creef, crelum, crevice juice, crinkly demons, croistable, crotchpod, crypt orchid, cryptorchid, cuddlefinger

D - dack, daddybag, dairy frog, dandy slap, danglers, Danish sack, dartos, day after balls, dearth, de-balled, dees nuts, desert potato, devil's ladder, dibble dong, dickbag, dick chops, dick crumb, dick cyst, dick spine, dicktrum, dictum, dillbag, dilly balls, dinglebag, dingle-berry, dingle set, dinklage, dinner roll, dirtbagging, dirty muffin, dirty squirrel, d my s, dog in a bathtub, doggy bagging, dogs in the tub, dongal, donkey cheese, donkey hammer, doorknob, down under, droopy, drop a nut, dropping a Paul Kelly, dry hammock, dry sack, duck butter, duckwater, dufflebag, dugdales, dungeon butter, dunking, durf, dusters, Dutch blind fold, Dutch puddle

E - Eabag, early morning tea, eat sack, e-bagged, ecastrate, elbow scrotum, elephantitis, emo job, empty my bag, epon, equipment, escroto, estavan, eteabagging, expectacle, extreme teabagging

F – fagball, fage, fairway, famundachese, fanbangho, farch, favnum, fawaffle, fester, fever junk, fiddler, firewall, fish nuts, fish hook, flaming bagpipe, flanski, flat tire, fleur de lèche, flesh bagpipe, fishily Schneider, flesh scarf, flip and drag, flobe, flop clap, flot, flumunda cheese, flying squirrel, flying scrotums, flying teabag, footjob, forbidden speedbag, forward fart, fosbas, fraiser, franich, freckelnut, French hobble, French Mary's balls, frog goggle, frogwallet, fromunda cheese, from under cheese, frotum, frumundacheese, fruit roll-up, fudge balls, fugnuts, fuhmunda cheese, funky sac, funtle, fun sack, fupples, furmunda, fusac, fushigi, fuzzy chandelier

G - Gayper, German lawnmower, giggle berries, ginive, gisp, gleeba, glitterbag, glimzak, glowing balls, goatgag, goat scrote, gobbler's knob, gock, godemiche, godi, godsmacked, god's stitches, goggles, golden kangaroo-pouch, gonad, gnarph, gooch, gooche cramp, gooch rover, goochirama, goodysac, gootchie, Gordon Brown, gorilla nuts, gotte, gouch, grabbing a slice, grape peeler, gribbin, griggles, grim reaper, grotum, ground beef, grow a sack, grumble, grundle, grundle fudge, grundleitis, grundula, g.u.e.s.s, guiche piercing, gugular, gunny snipes, guppo, guttering, gutter nuts

H - Haanooten, hafadas, hairy beanbag, hairy brain, hairy lollipop, hairy parachute, half-walnut, hammocking, handful of dough, hanging brains, hangy down bitshappy sack, hardcakes, hazelnut, hemisphere, Herman, hernia, hine bag, hip stick, hittin' it old school, hoagie slap, hoch, hodensac, Hofmann, hort, hot as balls, hot map, hot Paul, hug my wallies, hum job, honey badger, Houston towel

I/J/K - Ian pa, icky, icky ball, iggl, I'm befuddled by your waffling scrot, insurrection, Italian boiler, itch, itchy sac, itchy scrot, Japanese welsch, jargun, jerky sack, jewelry bag, Jewish *piñata*, Jimmy Carter, jiz-nuts, jizzbag, jobby jabber, jock itch, Joel Loweing, John Ritter, Jonas brothers, joobag, joot, juncture, jungle nuts, junk-jiggler, jixizit, Karl Malden, kegel, ketchupballs, kicked in the nuts, kicker, kick flop, King John, king pair, kittyballs, kjer, knackercracker, knar dukes, koala ball, kojak balls, konk, kontol, krang bang, krinkleknuckle, kroge, krum, krotch buddy, krufu, kumiho, kunder, kuxling, kyph

L – lap my bag, lap-ricots, latching, lawfin, leather balls, leather face, legs bag, levy, lick my pouch, liquid kids, little dick with a fat sack, little nemo-ing, lobster balls, lolly bag, loin-purse, lolskerotimy, long nut, lost buddy, love mound, love sac, lowhangers, lubbing, luft, luigi, Luke, lumberjack sack, lusticle, lynskey

M – majestic scrotum, male pattern balls, male queef, manatomy, man basket, mancrease, man junk, mankey nuts, manmal tow, man musk, mannequin, man pouch, man udder, marble bag, mark sack, marsupial, matbag drag, mcdrag, mean bean, machinemeat bridge, Meg Lunching, meat cabbage, meet my sisters, Meltzer melt, menthstruate, Merriam, Mexican lampshade, Mexican

484

pizza, midget brain, milking the cock, Minneapolis bullfrog, miropenis, Mississippi plunger, mmmbop your shenanigans, money-clipped, Mongolian meat mask, Mongolian mask, Mongolian shephard's piemonkey brain, monkey-scrotum face, moonbag, mooples, motor scroting, ms, muggis, mumple frumps, mushroom, mustynuts, muttox, my balls itch son

N – naculars, nadhere (nadhesion), nad pack, nad sack, nad satchel, nadsq, Nagasaki teabag, nanodick, napkin, Nathan, nerch, New England grape picker, nie, nifins bridge, nifkin, nimsack, ninja yanked, nitbag, nithishka ranasinghe, Nixon, noila clap, nudicles, nugbag, nugget pouch, nullus, numbnuts, nutbag, nut bat, nutbeard, nut bubble, nut butter, nut-cheeks, nut cleavage, nut cramp, nutcysts, nut dreads, nut flap, nutfuck, nut gargler, nutgas, nutless dick sac, nut licker, nut necking, nut musk, nut powder, nut sack, nutsatchel, nutsicle, nutslapper, nut to sack ration, nuts, nutsbumbridge, nut suck, nuts to the face

O – olb, oh my sac, ole Canadian flapjack, olos, onion bridge, oriental butterfly, oral fighter, Osama bin Laden, osf, ostrich sac, ovech-skin

P – package, paddidas, pain Olympics, Panamanian pumpernickel, panda bacon, Panhandle flapjack, parking lot, patio, patty sack, peachnutz, peanut butter balls, peanuckle pool balls, peaugh, peenits, pekerectomy, pelican beard, pemdas, pendulum position, pengus, penile perpetrator, penis cape, penteriferous doogler, percher, perenium, phantom nut syndrome, pickleberry butternut, pickler tickler, pig skin pouch, pinch and pull, pinch and roll, ping ponging, pink butter, pink pancakes, pink scooter, Pittsburgh plow, pizza dough, pläp, plisskin, pony nibble, pope soap on a rope, pope slap, poopscraint, poopynuts, poor-john, pork missle, porn sack, Portuguese man of war, Portuguese Wesley, porp, potato sack, powerformer, pre-baggin grease, pre-ejaculation pumps, pressed fruit salad, prickly pair, prison eye-patch, protum, pterodactyl, pulling leather, pumpernuts, punching the sack, pung, pwans

Q/R – quanza, quilbone, qum, q-bag, raisin sack, rantallion, rancid sack, rat brains, rathbone, rathe, rat satchel, reach, red bagging, red sack, red velvet treatment, reitel, Rifkin, rigby, ripped Damian, roast beef and cheddar cunt, rock tumbler, roster, rotum, rubber tortilla, rubbing my suburban, ruby red bag, rumple stiltskin, runkle, Russian boil, rusty nickels

S – sac fungi, sack, sack attack, sack brand, sackdazzling, sackface, sack inch, sacking, sack licker, sack lint, sack lunch, sack meat, sack 'n' balls, sackne, sacknut, sackola, sack rolling, sack-slurping, sack spackle, sacksnack, sack swipe, sack tack, sack warmer, sack whack, sackwraps, salami, sac magique, sac race, sacreligion, sacsquatch, sac-stitch, sac strangler, sac-tap, saddle bag, saggy ball syndrome, saggy sisters, sag sack, Salisbury, saltsack, salty tea cup, Sam Hornish Jr., San Bernardino sailboat, sanctum, sandbags, Sandilands, sansack, satchel, sat in gum, saumunda nuts, sausage and meatballs, saz, scaftom, scaif, scallop dragger, scally, scantchbar, scarp, scass, scqueef, scuba gear, scholz, schkeef, sckwards, scordor, scotch egg, scotrun, Scottish headmask, scrabs, scraddle, scrag bag, scrainus, scraitch, scranal, scranus, scrapage, scrapuation, scrass, scratamotobota, scratchy satchel, scraumica, screat, scredgie, screenis, screetum, screevage, schwub, screnis, scricky scagum, scrig meat, scrimples, scro, scroatch, scroatee, scroaterboat, scroat lobes, scrobadiving, scroberries, scrobow, scroche sallypat, scrodazzle, scrodom testicular crucifixion, scrodomy, scrodumb, scro-fro, scroggles, scrogurt, scrohawk, scroinal, scrojob, scrollocks, scrondle, scronis, scronus, scroodilydoo, scro pei, scrota, scrotal, scrotal assembly, scrotal doo rag, scrotal seam, scrotard, scrotch, scrot(s), scrote, scrote bite, scrotebutter, scrote face, scrot gag, scrote goat, scroteless, scrote punt, scroteration, scroterboat, scrotex, scrotiferous, scrotily, scroatmeal, scrotomima, scrotoplasm, scrototomy, scrotorboat, scrotox, scro-yo, scrotongous, scroid, scroaching, scrotacular, scrotalicious, scrotang, scrotrim, scrotii, scrottin, scroteome, scrotum lick, scrotal, scrotanic disaster, scrot sack, scrot slap, scrozipped, scrotash, scrotate, scrotdent, scrotesqu, scrotesqueula, scrotastic, scrot float, scrotic, scroti-coat, scroticular, scrotizzle, scroatjinx, scrotograph, scrotole, scrotology, scrotometer, scrotometry, scrotopussy, scrotumbleweed, scrotum boner, scrotum bopper, scrotum champ, scrotum chin, scrotum clap, scrotum coat, scrotum delight, scrotum docker, scrotum face, scrotumhagen, scrotum head, scrotum neck, scrotum knight, scrotum licker, scrotum lobe, scrotum pirate, scrotum roper, scrotum sandwich, scrotum scrambler, scrotumscribe, scrotum slammer, scrotum sniffer, scrotum snogger, scrotum spheres, scrotum stick, scrotum totem, scrotum toter, scrotumnal, scrotum stamp, scrotum troll, scrotum-wanking, scrotund, scrotus, scrozy, scruffnut, scruffocate, scrullet, scrumble, scrundle, scruple, scrust, scruttock, scruttocks, scrutux, seabag, seed satchel, semen shuttle, Serbian scratch, shaggnatts, shambag, sharpie scrot, shatnips, shavacado, shitesticles, shock and awe, shoogle ma plooms, shower cap, showing brain, shrimp nuggets, silver strainer, Singapore buttslug, siznac, secret sack, seed bag, seed sack, skaf, skin beard, skin Mohawk, skin pinching, skin roller, skrot, skrut, skruttle, slater, slater ballz, sleepy Christmas, slerg, sloblock, smack the sack, SMB(suck my balls), smcp, smell-bridge, sneck, snorkeling, snuffleupagus, spabba, spankter, speed-bag, speedbagging, sperm churner, sperm purse, spiky balls, splooge nozzle, spooge nozzle, spudbag, squirff, squirrel brains, squirrel on a trampoline, squirrel pocket, sqwedgie, s.s.s. (sorry so sloppy) stair clap, stank, steamed dumpling, steaming teabag, stench tickler, sticky balls, stingray, stinky bridge, stuff job, stuff the cannon, stumbling monkey, stumbling monkey, stump grinder, suck my balls, summer balls, summer length sack, summer sag, summertime sac, swamp nuts, swampy balls, swastickles, sweaty gumball, sweaty sleep mask, Swedish earmuffs, Swedish meatballs, syndrome

T – tacos at midnight, taffy bag, taffy sac, t'aint, taintoo, taffy sack, talc up, tambourine, tatte, t-bake, t-bag, t-bell, teabag and sandwich, teabagger, tea baguette, teabags, teabagging, tea-bazzling, tea berry, teacup, tea drop, teasing, testes satchel, teetle, testicide, testicles, testicle satchel, testicle ticklin', testify, tetlies, Tiajuana trampoline, tiert, tinder-bridge, tiggleywitted, titsack, 'tisn't, tittygooch, thackwhap, Thai orchid, the abc, the butterfly, the career ender, the chad, the degrees, the devils inch, the gizmo, the nut duster, the old switch-er-oo, the quarter mile, the royal American, the sack, the Shapiro, the sleeping bag, the southern toboggan, third testicle, the tongue, thousand elves, thrash metal, thunder clap, thunderclapscroobs, tillman tickle, tiss, toat scrota, toich, tongalangas, tornado, tortoise shell, total scrotal, tote the scrot, to the sack, traumerx, tree scrotum, tricky dicky, trolling motor, truck balls, trucker nuts, tts connectors, turkey goggler, turkey trapped, Turkish tissue, turkle, turtle-back sack, tweenis, twins playpen

U/V – ultimate cheese curl, under balls, underdog, under luggage, undernuts, upside down trumpet, urungus, veiny blanket, vagitis, vampire tea bagsacknave, vasocongestion, velcrosac, venis, vibrating orchid, Viking ship

W – waggling, wallies, wallyfincher, walnut juice, wang, wasabi, wasserbag, water closet, wedding vegetables, wee sack, weldage, wetbags, wet ones, wenis, werewolf scrotum, wet tortilla, whackbag, whacky sack, wombat combat, wufwagy, wizened, wizzak

X/Y/Z – xionix, yagballs, yam bag, yampouch, yamsack, yeti, y'idiot, zybe, zorbing

Female Genitalia

The Vagina:

A/B – ABC, Abraham's bosom, abyss, ace-of-spades, agreeable ruts of life, air bags, air pipe, alley, almanac, alpha and omega, altar of hymen, altar of pleasure, anal alternative, another thing, Anthony Blunt, Antipodes, aperture of bliss, Apostle's grove, apparatus, apron, arm sleeves, artichoke, arsenal, aunt Annie, aunt Maria, baby vending machine, bald eagle, ball backboard, bearded clam, beef curtains, black hole, beaver, bloomin' big Bertha, bloody Mary, bloomin' onion, bone collector, bottle holder, box, box-on-the-jack, buried treasure

C - can, camel toe, carp carnival, cauliflower, chang-chang, chatterbox, cherry, cherry pie, chlamydia canal, chonch, church box, clam flavored pothole, clit crate, cock cubby hole, cockpit, cock holster, cum catcher, cock sheath, cock sock, crank case, cum sponge, coochie, cooter, cooze, cozy, crotch sink, cum dumpster, cum muffler, cunny, cunt, cuntilocks and the three hairs, cuntzilla

D/E - daddy's dead end, devil's ditch, dick microwave, dick skinner, dinner, douche caboose, duck billed fatapuss, eager dildo mating canal (edmc), ecd, ecf, erection correction trench, extremely durable penis orifice

F - fag mace, fancy, fat fold, female genitalia, fetus factory, finger warmer, fertilization plantation, fish farm, flapper, flitter, flower bud, fork, front butt, front door, fuck hole, fuck funnel, fuck knuckle, fuck trophy receptacle, fun bag, fur burger, furby, fur pipe, furry flounder, fuzzy credit card, fuzzy grape, fuzzy taco

G/H - glory hole, grassy knoll, gonorrhea gainer, great red ravine, hair pie, hairy dime slot, hallway, hatchet wound, Hawaiian hairball, hole, hot pocket, humpadelic hymen, horny harry's hobby hole, ho chi minh trail, holiest of holies, horny halo, honey pot

I./J/K/L - inni, infection connection, jiz creek, joy trail, key hole, kiki, knuckles, land down under, landing strip, lasagna lips, lesbian lunch box, limpy's hump palace, long wanger hanger, love muffin, lovin' oven

M - main vein drain, mama joe, masturbation contingency plan, meat tunnel gash (bleeding), meatball sub tub, meat drapes, meat wallet, miss flappy, misty crevice, moist monkey mauler, money maker, moose knuckle, mound, mr. happy's flappy garage, muff, muscle

N/O - Nappy dugout, next to the butt nut hut, nut cam, one eyed one horned flying purple penis eater, one eyed monster's cave, oval office, one eyed al's beef corral, one eye's wonder hole, organ formally known as pussy

P - panty perch, panty puppet, park & ride, peach, pee-wee grinder, pelvis sperm jacuzzi, penis coffin, penis fly trap, penis garage, penis piñata, penis slide, penis parking lot, penis warmer, pin cushion, pink penis caddie, pink penis pooker, penis receptacle, pike purse, pimp's paycheckpink void, pink room, pinoché, plump pink penis cushion, pudunda, punani, puntang, pussy, porch, port of entry, prick road, pride land, pretty little penis purse, purple headed party shack, purple headed pit stop, pussy pot pie

Q/R - queef quarry, quim, quiver, rabbit hole, red snapper, rite of passage, roast beef, royal slut envelope (rse), rubber rimmed romper room

S - sausage delivery orifice, semen locker, sex, shaft alley, shrimp bed, sideways smile, skanky hood, skirt scampi, slime well, slip & slide, slit, small aquatic animal, snake pit, snake ranch, snatch, snoop nappy snatch, snuffleufapuss, soft shelled tuna taco, sperm bank, split tail, spunk bucket, stabin' cabin, stinky pink, sweaty love box

T - tampon tamer, tar pit, testicle tub, yellow Texas tunnel, the mouth, the other white meat, the q, tinkle bird, toothless grin, trouser trout, tuna melt, tuna town, tunnel of love, twat

U/V/W/Y - uterine hatch, vagina, vajayjay, velvet-lined pee-pee, velvet underground, warm apple pie, watertight door, weiner wagon, weiner getter wetter, whisker biscuit, womanhood, yeast factory, yeast pinochtitlán

Female Breasts:

A/B/C – amply endowed, apple dumplings, apple dumpling shop, apples, appurtenances, assets, atom bombs, babaloos, balcony, bazongas, bee stings, bongos, boobs, bosom, bouncers, bra stuffers, breasticles, bristols, bumpers, bust, butter bags, cantaloupes, chest, chesticles, chitty chitty bang bangs, cleavage, cock muffs/warmers, coconuts, cupcakes

D/E/F/G/H/I/J/K - dirty pillows, dual airbags, flesh bombs, flotation devices, fun bags, gazongas, the girls, globes, grapefruits, flapjacks, flesh bombs, hand warmers, hangers, headlights, head rests, high beams, hills, honkers, hood ornaments, hooters, hot dog buns, howitzers, humps, itty bitty titties, jolly jigglers, jugs, jumbos, kaboobers, kazongas, knobs, knockers

L/M/N - lactoids, the ladies, lemons, loaves, love bubbles, muffins, lungs, mammaries, mammary glands, mammies, mangoes, man pacifiers, mangos, meatballs, meat loaves/puppets, melons, milk bags, mild duds, milk jugs, milk makers, milkers, milkshakes, mosquito bites, mounds, money makers, muffins

N/O/P/Q/R - niblets, nose warmers, nubbies, nubs, oranges, orbs, ottomans, pancakes, paper weights, peaches, pears, personalities, pillows, pumpkins, puppies, rack, rib bumpers, rib cushions, roundies

S/T/U/W/Z - sandbags, sauce shelf, scones, shimmies, snuggle pups, speed bags, spheres, spuds, stacks, stuffing, sugar lumps, sun deck, sweater meat, sweet rolls, ta tas, teats, tee tees, tetons, Thelma & Louise, tidbits, tits, titties, tooters, torpedoes, Tweedledee and Tweedledum, twin peaks, twins, udders, umlauts, upper decks, warheads, watermelons, whoppers, window washers, wobblers, and zeppelins

Sexual Acts

Cunnilingus:

Numbers: $7.82 special, $50, 68, 69, 69 cream pie, 69 Hold

A - aer lingus, air lingus, Albuquerque jackhammer, alphabet, alphabet soup, April 14, alligator, alternating flame, Amish twizzler, anal cunnilingus, antifish, ass potato pancake, at C level, aurilingus, Aussie or Australian kiss, autocunnilingus, axillingus

B - banana slit, barking at the, badger, baseball analogy, bean crusher, beanjob, bean omelet, beefeater, beard pie, beard ride, beardsquidj, beaver cake, beaver mask, beaver tennis, beef job, beefslap, befborstel, belly button test, bichic, biscuiterian, biscuitian, bitch scarf, black swan, blood clot sandwich, blood muffin, blumpette, blumpkina, blumpy choad, bnk, bobo Brazil, bog snorkeling, booty tooth, boozied, Boston bouffant, Boston clam chowder, Boston cream, both sides of Christmas, bounty, boss nass, boxgrazer, boxjob, box lunch, box lunch at the Y, boxmunchin' by proxy, bowcat, bowel growl, Brazilian, breakfast in bed, breakfast of champions, breakfast, turnover, broiler, Bronx taco, brown chin syndrome, brunching, buck house, bunchmox, buntal, burble, bushhogging, butch pudding, bum tickler, buttberry

C - Caligula, Canada's history, canalingus, canine bushing, cannibalingus, canyon yodeling, captains pie, captain tampon, carlingus, carpal tongual, carpal tonsil, carpet cleaner, carpet jockey, carpet licker, carpet mopping, carpet muncher (munchies), cave yodeler, CFB, Cicil's moustache, casuallingus, chainsaw, chaw clit, Charleston chew, cherilumpkin decker, cherries jubilee, cherry pie, chewin' cunt, chewing the chotch, cheeseburger, chili over the kitchen sink, chin duster, Chinese blumpkin, Chinese bricklayer, chipotlingus, chodist, chow fucking down, chox, chunkylingus, cinnamon face, cinna snatch, clamdabble, clam diving, clam-grappler, clam job, clamkin, clam scrubber, clamster diving, clamtastic, clean the kitchen, cleaning the carpet, clibbling, clickey, cligging, clit caddy, clit dweller, cliterature, clitlash, clit liquor, clit mop, clitorungus, clittering, clit whisperer, clownalingus, coiltalingus, coker poked, coksucker by proxy, cold Nixon, Colombian condor, colonel angus, conealingus, congratullatio, consultant, contralingus, cooch face, coochsmooch, cookie and cream, coon-doom, cootchsmooch, cooter smoocher, cooter smooth(er), copper crown, crab, cracksnacker, croc bite, crotch broom, cuddliness, cummage, cuni, cunilinguist, cunna, cunnilangus, cunnilick, cunnilingually, cunnilingue, cunniligus, cunnilingus interruptus, cunnilingus rice, cunnilincoln, cunnilinctus, cunnilinctusest, cunniling, cunnilingass, cunnilingo, cunnilingual drift, connilingual symphony, cunnilingue, cunnilingus exception, cunnilingus forehead pillow, cunniloiterer, cunnilumpkin, cunnilumpkin decker, cunnilinquint, cunnilynguist, cunning linguist, cunninglingus, cunnilinguaphilia, cunnilinguate, cunningulus, cunniringus, cunniwingus, cuntalickus, cunt-brooming, cunt CPR, cuntimated, cuntkin, cuntlapper, cunt-mouth, cunton-mouth, cunt raptor, cuntsuck, cunt wanger, curly kneel, curtain call, cuntkin, cupcake and cunnilingus day, cupidge, cyoon, daisy chain

D – daisy chain, daisy dookie, darryn, decker special, deep in the muffin, deep sea diving, deep tongue spelunking, degnan, devil's mustache, devil's omelet, dickalungus, dine (or dining) at the Y, dirty Carla, dirty Dracula, dirty hairbear, ditch licker, diving for grouper, diving for oysters, dogbowling, dometologist, down at the Y, downtowner, downtown sushi restaurant, draculingus, drap crusader, drink from the furry cup, drink honey from the holy land, drinking red sea, dusty mustache, Dutch taco

E - eau de femme, egg in face, Elkhart air show, earlingus, ear muffs, earning red wings, eat, eat a furburger, eat & play combo, eat a peach, eat at the Y, eatboxing, eat fur pie, eat hair pie, eat it, eat mouth, eat pussy, eating pussy, eat the watermelon, eating out, eatinout, eat rice, eat some clams, eat the box, eat the fish, eggnog pie, el zabricabra, ETP

F - facebang, face-crotch, face hugger, face massage, face party, facesit, face sitting, facial bird bath, FBC, faire minette, fanny kiss, feastin, femblumkin, fanny fun, flangulate, flavor crevasse, fleagle, feastin, feast on the yeast, fellatio (to cunnilingus) ratio, fielding, fennilitus, fetish bracelets (gold), filacio, first course, fish eater, fisherman's best friend, fish queen, flap nap, flickering one, flishkin, Florida feedbag, flunching, flying helmet, foaming the milk, friendilingus, fuckin's, full koala, fumilingus, fungilingus, funnilingus, fur burger, fur lapper, furry tea cup

G - gamahauche, gamahuche, Gene Simmons, George W. bitch, get head, get your cooch smooched, gimme da head, gineevitis, gingalingus, girlie cum, give face, giving face, give head, glaze goatee, going down south, going down to the warf, gonorrhea turnover, goodmornilingus, goof tooth, go out to lunch, gorilla lawn mower, grand slam breakfast, grass grazer, gravy geyser, growl, growling, growling at the badger, gummilingus, gummy bears, gunt curtain, gynophobe

H/I - hairy duke, handyman, happy cobra, happy raccoon, have a box lunch, headbutt the buffalo, headette, heady murph, heartburn pussy, hiawani, Hitler's handshake, hojay, hole-foods, honeybum, honey-hoover, honey mown, Hoover maneuver, hot air balloon, hot cap, hot Rhonda, hummilingus, hungry howie, hungry lion, hymenlick manoeuvre, iain, imt, izar-band qui dhili

J/K - jabbaing, Jamaican taco, jelly bracelets, Jew's harp, jofpit, joker's smile, Johney rocket teeth, juice sucker, Juneau watershed, kama sutra, kapowie, karch, Kayden kross, kennebunkport surprise, Kenosha typewriter, king fucker, king of feasts, kiss the bean, kissing Abraham Lincoln, kitty tongue massage, kitty tossing, knocklebutting, koif, kunch, kwamejob, kylynne, kiwi cootchie

L - labbajuice, labia loofa, labial lunch, lady altar, lady dragon, lady glaze, lady job, laguna sunrise, lalposuction, lappin lab, lesbionic tongue, lickabout, lickathon, lickfucker, lick her lock, licketty split, licking the bloodloins, lickin the wound, lick job, lick me off, licksomaniac, lick the lox, licus, lighthouse, lingalingus, lingbie, lip biting animal, lip cross, lips & lobster day, lip service, liquor in the front (poker in the rear), lobster diving, London fog, loompa'licker, love floss, love jam, love puttin', low job, lunching at the Y, lunch meat toupee

M - mack the cat, made her dessert, magnolia minge, mcmuff diving, meal on heels, making a phone call, making noise, meals on wheels, meatballing, meat beard, Merlyn style, metal mouth, minge bogey, minge binge, mirandized, Missouri lawnmower, moist wipe, momlick, munging, Mongolian beefeater, mooseburger, moose munch, mopshee, Moses, moundsville, moustache dip my dream sickle, moustache ride, moustache rodeo, mouth, mouthhug, mouth to the south, mouth to vagina, Mr. Belding, mrluvstoeatpussy, muck her barn, mudda likka, muff dive, muffication, muffin buffin, muffinman, muffin munchies, muffin munching, muffivore, muff job, muffkin, muffmuncher, muff munching, muffocation, muff piggy, muff slave, muff tucka, muffy, multigasm, munch a box lunch, munch box, munch carpet, munch on, munch on her waffle, munchstache, munch task, mundtalingus, mungfishing, musburger, mustard snack, my place on your face

N/O - nattiligusoral, nattilingus, Nebraska nasty, Nevada hot pocket, ninjalingus, nookie duster, northern delight, noseinringlingus, oblickatory, okey dokey, here, we go, omega mongoose, one-man band, oral, oral-eo, oralexciter, oral permission, oral sex, oral top, oral unicorn, oral vaginosis, orváge, osq, oyster soup

P - paintballing, parseltongue, parsley, peaches and cream, peach gobbler, pearl lipstick, pearlwaxing, pecking, p.e.e.p., pek, pels, perilingus, Persian heat tent, Peruvian salchitranca, photo frolick, pie-in-the-sky, pink caviar, pink honey, pink Kleenex, pink turtle, Pillsbury dough boy, place on my face, playing the hairmonica, plenty to eat at home, plowman's lunch, poon chow, poon job, poonlash, poonspeeding, porcelingus, porkling, pornastics, post gym pre-shower, post lick, portalingus, power lick, predalingus, psls, pudding cat, pudding sucker, pulling a Westmancoat, pumpkin muffin, pun-job, pussassium, pussicles, pussyassy, pussy fart, pussy feed bag, pussyflaps, pussy fox, pussy handle, pussy licker, pussy sandwich, pussy shaman, pussy snorkel, put the beard on

Q/R - queef, queening, queening chair, querp, quimling, racos, rainbow kissing, rainbow warrior, Ralph Lauren, rap on the mic, raspberry cave, raspberry swirl, ready brek, red delicious, red wine cork surprise, red wing bandit, red wings, re-queef, reverse 69, reverse cunnilumpkin, reverse hug, Rhode Island clam stand, ric flair, rick moranis, rip van tinkle, roadalingus, road head, road pie, roast beef curtain, roly poly, Romanian handshake, rorschach kiss, rug muncher, Russian fruit tart, Russian stash, rusty clam digging, rusty Humphrey, rusty trombone

S - saddleface, Saint Louis steam boat, salty walter, San Diego shit sandwich, sassin' the donald, say hello in Italian, scuba dive, scuba diving, sclerenchyma, scratch and sniff, scruffin' the muffin, scutterbotch, seafood lover, seafood platter eater, second hand vagina, semi-poon, sex bracelets, sex diamond, shark special, sharp tooth, Shawcross, sheep sandwich, shimmy slurp, shminge, shrimp boat to tuna town, shwanee, siga pi, silver tongue, sister suck, skorpion, skudouche, skyrimjob, skunk diving, skunky lunch, slabberwash, sligo kiss, slither, slobbery tongue, sloppy dan, sloppy falafel, slurpie, slurping oyster, slurp that stew, smell my face, smell the hole, smunnilingus, snack lobstering, snatch boat, sneeky Castro, smoked salmon, smoking the birth cigar, snapper licker, snatch snacker, sneezin' in the heater, sniggling, snod, snowball fun dip, snowball impregnator, soapie, sondag, south town face plant, spam-sloth, speedwolf, spicy tom, spit dred, square away, square meal, squash, stache ride, stank baiting, stand her up like a tulip, stanking, stank lip, stanky pudding, Staten Island surprise, steak Diane, Stephan Jenkins, strawberry kiss, stray frog, stoneclam, subconjunctival, hemorrhage, suck my clit, sucky sucky, sugar pussy, sun-dried tomatoes, sunrise grunt, surf the crimson tide, swamp logging, SWD dirty, snowball, sweet & sour, swigging muesli, swimming for mussels, swipe test

T - taco burn, tacosnoball, talaba, taste, teabagger, teapotting, tease, terlingua, Texas tongue torch, the angry Edmunds, the blue velvet, the motorboat, the party pleaser, the sampler, the selleck, the Steve, the Wilson, third base, thorndike confused cat, tickle the teapot, tip the velvet, thigh tickler, thunderclapping, titilingus, toledo takedown, tongue fu, tongue in chic, tongueilingus, tongue jack, tonguekwando, tongue of hazard, tongue plow, tongue punchbag, tongue ride, tongue sandwich, tongue sweater, tongue trap, tongue twister, tongules, too drunk to fucktion, tootsie roll mustache, tummilingus, tuna fish taco, tuna oatmeal sandwich, turf tongue, twat broom, twatnap, twat rangoon, twat snot, twat spider, twattoo, twirling the cherry, twing-twang

U/V - uncle earl, uncle mung's chunky shrimp buffet, undercarriage marauder, underground boombox, underwater swimming, unfumpkin, vadge goggles, vagappetite, vagaterian, vagitarian, vagiterian, vagitarianism, vag batter, vagilean, vagiking, vaginal vagire, vagina bolognese, vaginalitosis, vagina sucking, vagire, vagita, vaglika, vampirilingus, vanillingus, veggie sex, vehicular nomicideue, venkateshwara, victory tong, Vietnamese hot box, VJ, vobble

W/Y/Z - warm bloody Mary, war stripes, watsy chowdown, wax, west coast chopper, wet knocker, whale eye, whisker mechanic, wild berries, Wilsoning, wingilingus, wriggling, yodeling in the canyon, yodel in the gulley, yodel in the valley, yogalingus, yoster toaster, yummy down, zesty taco, zinc pink, zune

Fellatio:

Numbers: 0<=3, 3rd base, 5-second sam, 6, 7 digits, 8, 10-cent job, 10-points for hufflepuff, 20th base, 49, 69, 84, 747

A – A+, Abraham Lincoln, acorn-picker, addressing the court, Amish blowjob, airhead, Alabama breathalyzer, Alabama picroast, Alaskan firedragon, Alaskan snowdragon, all mouth, American tombone, angry dragon, angry gremlin, aquabob, auquabop, a ride to the airport, Alaskan snow blower, altoid hummer, Arabian goggles, Arizona blowdryer, Arizona diamond dick, Arkansas slider, artichoke, Artiste, astrojob, A to M (ass to mouth), aul, Austin job, Austin strangler, autodome, auto-fellatio, austad, ava devine, avsugning, ayuga

Ba/Be/Bi - bacca, backfire, B & G (blow & gag), bad blowjob barb, bagpiping, bag toss, bajatt, bajowski, ballcuzi, ball handling, ball spit, bamjam, banana blow job, bandido favorite, banjo, barflo, barry jon, basket lunch, batgirl, battle creek blowjob, bauks, Bavarian cream sickle, BBBJ (bareback blowjob), BBBJCIMSW (bareback blowjob, cum in mouth and swallow), BBBJCIMWS (bareback blowjob, cum in mouth with swallow), BBBJNQNS (bareback blowjob, no quit, no spit), BBJTC (bareback blowjob to completion), BBBJTCNQNS (bareback blowjob to completion, no quit, no spit), BBBJTCWF (bareback blowjob to completion with facial), BBBTNQNS (bareback blowjob to completion, no quitting no spitting), B & BJ (bed & blowjob), bean cap, beanerjob, beanski, bearclaw, beasted on, beaujean, beaver trimming the wood, becky , beej, beejer, beerlowme, bejo, BK bj (blowjob in a burgerking), Belgian curtsy, belljob, belowjob, best hug ever, B for B (blow for blowjob), Bj and P (blowjob and pussy), BFF (blowjob, fuck & facial), bico, bieb job, big j, B job, Bi-j, Bill Clinton, Billy, Billy bee, bivens, bitchjob, bingo dabber, bingy, birthday blowjob, birthday candling, birthday present, bitejobbj(s) blow job, bjam, bjawesome, bj central, bjf (blowjob face), Bjtt (blowjob, tea & toast), blumpy

Bl - blacon, black ops blumpkin, blackout blowjob, blandjob, blandy, blanwich, blasen, blaze job, blaze and glaze, blee, bleedge, bleejebe, blewter, blidget, blimpkin, blind but made to see, blinjout, blipy, bloagie, blobo, blod, blogie, bloitering, blojob, blokin, blomkin, blomper, blompkin, blondjob, blonde with pigtails, blone, bloogle, bloompkin, blooper, bloopy, blop tart, blorange, blossieblow(ing), blow a big pole, blowbasaur, blowbee jobee, blowbob, blowbox, blowcap, blow cheeks, blow-chopper, blowcraft, blowdge, blow dry(er), blowdunk, blowfish, blow for snow, blowhow, blowie, blowing the love whistle, blowjab, blowjack, blowjay, blowjobbery, blowjob ninja, blowken, blowkin, blowkob, blowha, blowjob sandwich, blowmance, blow me, blow, blow blow, blowjizzle, blowjo, blowjob(s), blowjob administration, blowjob artist, blowjob bar, blowjob betty, blowjob choke, blowjob city, blowjob club sandwich, blowjob denial, blowjob eyes, blowjob face, blowjob fever, blowjob handlebars, blowjob kiss, blowjobless, blowjobligation, blowjob master, blowjob nose, blowjob surprise, blowjob susan, blowjob syndrome, blowjob week, blowjob with handles, blow massage, blowpon, blowrider, blowsob, blowsty, blowtask, blowtella, blow the bottle, blowtion, blowtonium, blow trabajo, blowy, blozner, blozza, blozzer, blubjub, bluegrass blast, bluejob, bluetooth blowjob, blumken, blumpatola, blumpkin(s), blumper, blumper decker, blumpersal, blumpie, blumpken, blumpkin backsplash, blumpkinator, blumpkin decker, blumkin-con-munch, blumpkwich, blumpy, blumptendo, bluntkin, bluppet, blurger, blurgle, blurjobbmj (blowjob from someone with temporal mandibular joint disorder)

Bo/Bu - bob, bobe, bobbin on the knob, bobbing for apples, bobble, Bobby Jones, bob head, bob my knob, bob on a knob, bob on the d, bob scootles, bobskeet, bobs marley, bob some knob, bocchino, bocky, boeyen, bomb dome, bomb neck, bonejob, boner breakfast, boneless bites, bone-lipping, bonesmooch, bonophone, bop(s), bop off, bopsicle, boquete, border dog, boris johnson, boston cream tease, bowjob, bowl job, boxerjob, bracejob, brain(s), brain damage, brain job, brain work, brainzino, branjob, brankin, bravo julliet, brazilian blowjob, breakfast sausage, breathing dragon, breejetwa, brentwood hello, bridgehead, broche, brojob, bronx blowjob, brosh, brown bunny, brown pappy, bro-yob, bbjm (big titted blowjob machine), brushing teeth, buccal onanism, buckley fuckley, buff, buff buff, bumjob, bumkin, bumpin gums, bumy, burny, bust me a shine, butterjob, buttery alarm

C - cabeza, Canadian service, can suck chrome off a tail pipe, can suck chrome off a trailer hitch, cap, captain's eye, car jacked, car park karaoke, catch the neck, cbluntkin, Charles Barkley, charming the snake, cheeky chewy, cherry tootsie pop, chewbacca blowjob, chewybacca, Chicago-style blumpkin, Chicago surprise, chicken head, chik-fil-atio, chilly middis, chin buster, Chinese blowjob, Chinese firetruck, chocolate milk, chocolate-vanilla snow cone maker, chock, choc-o-hawk, choke on an almond, chomp job, Christian bone, chubbuck, chumbly, chunk a hunk, chunky chomper, chupamela, chrome one's dome, circus jiffy, classy blowjob, clean(ing) your rifle, CLH (chair lift head), climbing the corporate ladder, Clinton, Clinton job, c-mac, coastal postal, cob job, clockblowalypse, clockblock shower, cockbreath, cockdog, cock-gobbling, cockinthemouth, cock lips, cockmeat mcgriddle, cock on the rocks, cock rocking, cock sandwich, cocksuckee, cocksucker, cock wheeze, coddie, codjob, cold jeffrey, cold smoker, come down, comp sci help, connor-kelly, cop a beej, copping a doodle, cop some dome, corpse bride, cottonwood, count blumpkula, country blumpkin, courting the gay vote, cout, covered bj, cox, cranium, crooked mettle, crossblow, crown, cuban sandwich, cum, cum catcher, cumcicle, cum guzzling dumpster slut, cumtumer, cum yodel, cup of fuck

D - dandelion, dangers, danza slap, das it mane, day player, deeger, deep throat, deep throat trauma, dentist appointment, derb, derve, devil's blowjob, dickalingus, dick burp, dick fluffer, dick-n-biscuits, dick nibber, dick pockets, dick snorkeling, dicksterity, dick twizzler, dine at the dome, dingle dangle, dirty bagpipes, dirty bj, dirty Chewbacca, dirty gherkin, dirty jovi, dirty madden, dirty sandbox, discount double-check, dishwash, ditch bitch, dodger, doggy blowjob, dome, domeburger, domecast, dome shot(s), domeskie, dome than rome, do my head, dong chomper, donut smile, doodle bop, doodoo lips, double blowie, double blowjob, double decker blumpkwich, double dome, double hoover, dragging your teeth, draw the curtains, drinking a slurpee, drink someone under the table, drool monster, drop down, drop knowledge, dropping on it, drops neck, duck face, DTBBBJ (deep throat, bareback, blowjob) DT (deep throat) gooch, dungbar, dunkachino, D-up, durb, durbz, duty dome

E - eahhh, earning your keep, ear sex, eat my piece, eating latex, eating the cheese, edghead, Eiffel tower, eggnoggin, English toothbrush, e. peters, erskine, erob, essin' the dee, Eskimo hobo blumkin, ewit ewit, exorcism head

F - face-frosting, facelift, facepump, fadoink, faggot blumpkin, failatio, faisal, falle, family foreplay, fatty beej, fatty blowjob, feed, fellacial, fellarski, fellasian, fellated, fellatio sanz, fellatious reasoning, feltkin, fera, ferratio, fifty cent, fire and ice, firehead, fizzjobflat tire, flayed penis, fleshlight, floopy, flop gobs, floppy jalopy, flumkin, fluting, fog horn, forehead, fore play, foursome, foven, French abortion, French blowjob, French pickle, French release, friend job, fries, frosty mitten job, frothing walrus, fruit cup from chick-fil-a, frumpel, fuck me ears, fudge job, fudgesicle, fukoshimo, fun dip, furious b

G - gam gam, game blover, gas chamber, gas money, gator mouth, G-blob, George bush blowjob, German Geronimo, getting crown, getting a facial, getting a Lewinsky, getting a throat culture, getting Nintendo, getting some brain, getting to the cream filling, get head, getting head in the whip, get in your pants, get one's knees dirty, get on your knees, getting' a Guttenberg, getting skull, getting some, ghosty, giff, give(ing) brain(s), give(ing) cone, give(ing) face, give(ing) head, give(ing) oral, give(ing) skull, give(ing) Scully, give(ing) top, giving Big Jim and the twins a bath, giving cap, glazed donut, glimzak, glowjob, glug, glumkin, glup, gobbi, gobbies, gobble, gobble and cheese, gobble knob, gobble one's knob, gobblers point, gobbling pork, gobby, gobby bogs, gobstabber, gob tug, go downtown, golden guzzle, golden rod, gonk, going down, going south, good dome, goodheadsucker, good service, gotten head, graped up, grapefruit technique, gratehead, greasy torres, greyhound shuffle, grumplet, guacamole hotdog, guac guac guac, Guatemalan blumpkin, gug, gumblumpkin, gulp gummer, gummie, gumming the green bean, gumming the root, gummy, gummy gam, gum-rooting, gumster, gurp, guzzle guzzle

H - hada, haeger, hairy lollipop, hairy poppins, half bone, hamburguesa, hardhat, hardjob, hate job, hat trick, HBO go and blow, head, head bang, head bopper, head buff, head fuck, head job, headphones, headwind, heady mo, headywop, heblow headrush, heddy moe, helmet hummer, hersty, heywood jablome, Hilary Duff grateful, hillbilly mouth hug, hingham lockjaw, hobo blumkin, Holland's gift, Hollywood head, hoodie wash, hookitup, hoover, hoover cocksucker, honkin' Bobo, hobjob, honk on bobo, how much da head do for, huffing bone, humding, humjob, hum drum boogie, hummer, hummer blowjob, hummer gummer, Hungarian cocktail

I/J/K - ice job, ice leopard, icicles, ideepthroat.com, I learned the clarinet at school, ILLEEJ (bj from an underaged illegal individual), I lub joo, imitatio, Indian head massage, ineedmorecowbellatio, infallatio, insta-bj, interrogating the prisoner, intern, it aint gonna suck itself, Italian blowjob, Italian job, jawbreaker, jaw pussy, jaw surgery, jbeat, Jeff smoker, jingle bob, jinski, John Cena, jolly rodger, juicy hobknocker, Julia bird, junkin, kabloosh, keg head, kempolicious, kiffy, kneeling at the altar, knob(ber), knob job, knowledge, king my whopper, kolecki flicker, kowee, Krispy Kreme job, kwamejob, Kyle Fischer, lakey, lallygaggin, lam lam, lamp, lap kiss

L - larking, laying some lip, lemonade stand, lemon tart, letterboxing, Lewinski, libby suck, licking the lollipop, lick me up, like a dog eating hot chips, ling ming'd, linzz, lipsdick, litscher, lober, lollypop love, lolly, longjaw, lowbob, loopy trambone, LRL (lollipop – blowjob-, rub down, lollipop) lucky dick, lumpkin

M - maggag, making mouth music, making the blind see, mamar, mamilucos, mamone, mango cake, March 14, massage with a happy ending, master chief, masturbation, mayer mc'cheese, MBJ (massage and bj), mcsuckit, mcgovern, meat on the grill, mecca blowjob, meeting with Mr. one-eye, messy Martinez, Mexican blowjob, Mexican blumpkin, Mexican dentist, Miami handshake, Michael Brannen, mile-high turban, millet-ed, Missouri forklift, mistleblow, modern warjob, mogle, Mohegan steamer, Mongolian meatpie, Mongolian slurpee, monocle Lewinsky, moojob, moosewood, monkey wrench, monsoon, morehead, mount rush smore, mouthbrezy, mouth-fuck(ing), mouth-hammered, mouth-holstering the nightstick, mouth hug, mouthhump, mouthie, mouth milking, mouth to junk resuscitation, mouthwash, Mr. freezey, Mr. Hardy, Mrs. Jones special, muddy monster, muppet necking

N/O - natural conversation, NBAB (nothing beats a blowjob), neck, necklace, neins fellatio, nerd job, Netflix and fill, new old fashion, niggerdome, no denture adventure, noodle chewer, nopper, Nordic blowjob, nose job, nose sex, nosh(ing), NQNS (no quit, no spit), notley, now and later, nunfer, ocean surprise, oofsk, one's turn in the barrel, opening wide for Dr. Chunky, oral history, oral sex, oral sodomy, orphan the balls

P - pagar boquete, paleese, Pasadena mudslide, paveblow, PBJBJ (peanut butter and jelly blowjob), Pecker ripper, pecker wrecker, peeling the banana, peenie polish, penguin, penilingus, penis mouth, peppermint faddy, peppermint patty, perpetual blowjob machine, pete, phillddogg, philosophical discussion, piablow, pickle martini, pig roasted, pigtails, pijpen, Pillsbury blow boy, pink smoothie, pipa, pipe, piping, piston cup, piston job, pitching a tent, play(ing) Pan's pipes, play(ing) the pink oboe, play(ing) the skin flute, plompy, plumpkin, pokéjob, pokey bum blowjob, pole-smoking, Polishing the trailer hitch, Polish lawnmower, pompano, poonjob, poop dick carwash, pop rocked, popsicle, porkjob, porno eyes, portablumpkin, Portland trout, pot-head, pricknicking, Princeton cheesecake, prison bj, pro job, protein milkshake, puffin ham, pulling a Melissa, pumpkin blumpkin, punching, purple mushroom, purple slurpee, put some lipstick on it

Q/R - quagging, queerios, quid pro quo-job, rabies, racing stripes, radford, radiohead, railer, rail head, rainblow job, rainbow job, rainbow nut crunch, rakejob, ramp, rasha, receiving Holy Communion, red cum dragon, redneck facial, regurgitated cum wad, respecting your superiors, reverse brother blumpkin, reverse reach around, rickjob, road dome, road head, roadjob, road throatie, rock the mic 'till you bleed, roethlisberger, roufokavletta, rowboat, rubber ducky, ruebon, rumpleblumpkins, rune special, rusty barfield, rusty top, rusty train, rusty trombone

S - sacond, sack jester, sada pop, salty peanut, sampling the sausage, sandjob, sandy balls, sandy social, Sasquatch waterfall, sausage, schoon trubert, scooby-snacking, Scottish garlic bread, scrape job, screamin' on the mic, Seattle blowjob, Sebastian, secretarial duties, second hand semen, self blumpkin, self-fellatio, self-suck, sepong, set head, shakuhachi, shamjob, shark fin, shine, shnoggin, short stop, short story, shoryuken, shotgun headjob, shower blowjob, showjob, shumpkin, sick brains, silent alarm, s'ing d's, singing into the pink karaoke machine, singing to the choir, sket, skiing pterodactyl, skittledicking, skull, skul-buggery, skull fuck(ing), skull job, skyjob, slackjob, slemmy, slippery Josh, sloaner boner, slobjob, slob my knob, slob on bob, slob on my nob (like the corn on the cob), slob one's knob, slob on the knob, slob the knob, slobbin' the knob, slogo, slop-chop, slopdog, sloppy Benjamin, sloppy blowjob, sloppy j, sloppy joe, sloppy Susie, sloppy yawn, slow blow, slow deep, slowie, slowjob, slunk, slurpjob, slurp-n-gulp, slurp off, slurpie, slurp-the-salami, slurping turtle, slurp the gherkin, slut's eye, sly blowy, slythican, smile like a donut, smiling at Mr. Winky, SMK (swallow my kids), smoam, smokeblast, smokin' da cockpipe, smocko, smojob, smoke one's Johnson, smoking blowjob, smoking the pink pipe, smokin' mulch, smoke(ing) pole, smoky blowjob, smurfjob, snake throat, snarfle, snarling, sneezle, snickerdoodle, snowball, snow cone, snowjob, snurfing, soffocotto, soggy bone, souder, sour apple altoid, sour Pablo, soska, Southern France, space dome, Spanish bandana, speak to the judge, speaking into the bonophone, speaking low genitals, special bond, spence, spider-man style, spit-shining the baseball bat, spit trail, splaque, splout, splunchkin, spongejob, spraying the tonsils, sprechen sie dick, squabblenecks, squal, squalo, squeesh, squirrely beej, standing blow-vation, stas, steak and blowjob day, steam boat delight, stemwinder, stereo, still hard, stucking, strauss khan, strawberry swirl, street blowjobs, succ, succotash, succulent, suck & go, suck a monkey off, suckbuggy, suck(ing), suck dick, suckjob, suck me tender, suck my dick, sucked off, suck(ing) off, sucked up, suck one's dick, suck rape, sucksholaxtion, suck-starting the harley, suck the chrome off a ball hitch, sucky-ducky, sucky fucky, sucky sucky char char, sucky sucky for a bucky, sugejobb, suicide blumpkin, surprise blumpkin, swallow, swallowing the baloney pony, Swedish blowjob, Swedish trumpet, sweet dome, swimmer's ear, swizzling, sword-swallowing, S your D (suck your dick)

T - tadpole frappe, take care of, taking one's temp with a meat thermometer, Taliban mustache, talking into the mic (mike or microphone), talking to the root, tankjob, tapioca destroyer, taylar, team top, teeds, teej, teethin, teethy, telling it to the judge, tejob, Tennessee sobber, Tennessee swimming pool, tetro, Texas roundhouse, Texas weed wacker, TGI Fridays, textalacio, text n head, thank job, theater head, the back alley lolly, the Bill Clinton treatment, the double creamer, the Italian ice job, the fizzy jizzy drink, the James Deen, the menthol, the Nixon, the rocket launcher, the walking head, the way you're on my dick must really hurt your knees, the wonder kiss, the woody woodpecker, the zombie mask, third base, threebie, three b's (backrub, blowjob, breakfast), three-j, throatmeal, throwin' dueces, thurty, tier 15, Tim teblow, tip-licking, tipping, Tina Turner, tizzies, toecurl, toiched, Toledo depth charge, tomjon, tonsil hug, tonsil teaser, toothy blow, top, Toronto b-jay, torque blow, tornado, tornado blowjob, tortling, tototte, touchbase, toupee, townhouse Betty, tubesteak, tug and chug, Turkish earthquake, turkey stern, turtle snorkel, trailor jaw, trainwreck, trapezoidkin, treasure chest, trolly waffle, trophy head, trouser friendly kiss, trouser kiss, trumpetface, tsibouki, tsibuki, twerk and blow, twirl, two headed woodpecker, Tyler Shanklin

U/V - uncle Jesse, uncle sloppy sam, unconventional toothbrush, undead head, underground railroad, unemployed, unique blowjob, un pete, upper decking, upper Dutch blumkin, vacuum blowjob, VCP (vocal cord penetration), vertically curved Canadian mango, video game road head, volcano job, Voltron

W - waffling the yogurt cannon, waps, warhead, wawis, waxing the carrot, Welsh breakfast, westside glaze, West Virginia mud pie, wet axe, wet dome, wet steak, whale head, whaps, wheel of fortune, whirlpool, windy city shitter, while you're down there, whistlehead, whistling-Canadian, white dophin, white dragon breath, whorechata, willy, Willow Smith, windpipe, windshield wiper, wingnut overhang, wireless, wizjob, Wo-j, wolbem, wolf cookie, wolfing, wonderjob, woodchuck, work it, world cup, worshiping at the altar, wowkin, woweez, wringing it dry, wrong beverage, WTW (wet the worm), wurthjob

X/Y/Z - XJ (giving a blow job while crying), x-ploge, yawning the worm, yersuked, yubb, yum yum, zbin, zees, zipper dinner, Z jay, zoggle job, zoog, zombkin, Zuckerberg

Intercourse:

A – a bit of: beef, brown, butt, crumpet, cuddle, flat, fork, front door work, hair, hard for a bit of soft, "how's yer father?," meat, nifty, nobble, nookey, raspberry, ring, rough, rumpy-bumpy, skin, snug for a bit of stiff, the old in and out, the other, a-bucking, a capella, accommodation, act of: darkness, generation, kind, love, pleasure, shame, sport, Adam-and-Eve it, adamize, a dash up the channel, adult naptime, afternoon delight, afternooner, afternoon gig, aggressive cuddling, agreeing on stuff, a knee trembler, a little one-on-one, a little o the one with tother, all the way, alley job, amorous congress, anal borer, anal job, anal lovemaking, anal rampooning, androsodomy, Apache, a piece of: flesh, fluff, goods, patch, skirt, snatch, stuff, tail a poke through the whiskers, arsometry, arse worming, ashes hauled, a spot of Cupids archery, a spot of hard (or heavy) breathing, a squeee and a squirt, ass-fuck, assault with a friendly weapon, asshole plugging, assume the position, a straight shot, at it, attacking the pink fortress

B - baking the potato, balling, bam-bam in the ham, banana in a fruit salad, bandicooting, banging, barney mugging, basket-making, batter-dipping the corn dog, beard-splitting, beating guts, bedroom rodeo, being intimate, belly-bumping, bending her over a barrel and showing her the fifty states, bisecting the triangle, bit of bouncy-bouncy, bit of fat, bit of fun, bit of it, bit of pork, bit of rumpty-tumpty, blitzkrieg mit dem fleischgewehr, blowing the grounsils, bludgeoning the flaps, bodging, boffing, boinking, bonestorming, boning, boom-boom, boppin' squiddles, bouncy-bouncy, bow-chick-a-wow-wow, bringing an al dente noodle to the spaghetti house, bruising the beef curtains, buckwilding, bulging the back of the old onion bag, bump(ing), bumping uglies, buttering the biscuit, burping the worm in the mole hole, burying the weasel, bushwacking, buying frisbees, buzzing the brillo

C - carnal knowledge, cattle-prodding the oyster ditch with the lap rocket, caulking the tub, cave-diving, charvering, checking the oil, chesterfield rugby, christening the yak, churning butter, cleaning the cobwebs with the womb broom, clicketing, clunge plunge, commixtion, completing the jigsaw puzzle, corking the onion, crashing the custard truck, creaming the twinkie, crunching guts, crushing buns, cully-shangying

D - dancing in the sheets, dancing the goat's jig, daubing the brush dickening, digging up the sand crab, dinky-tickling, dipping the crane in the oil well, dipping the stinger in the honey, dipping the wick, disappointing the wife, docking, doddling, doing it, doing squat thrusts in the cucumber patch, doing the devil's dance, doing the dirty deed, doing the dipsy doodle doing the do, doing the hibbety-dibbety, doing the horizontal, greased-weasel tango, doing the mystery dance, doing the nasty, doing the wild thing, doinking, doodle-bopping, doodling, drabbling, driving miss daisy, dunking the dingus

512

E/F - enraging the cave, entangling the lower beards, entering the castle, exploring punarnia, extreme flirting, feeding the kitty, fenorking, ferking, fettling, fickey-fick, fidgeting the midget in bridget, filling her out like an application, filling the cream donut, filling the gas tank, fishing for kippers, fixing the clap flap, fletching, flimp-flopping, forbidden polka, four-legged foxtrot, frickle-frackle, frigging, fucking, funny business, furgling

G - getting a bellyful of marrow, getting busy, getting down, getting it on, getting laid, get some ass, getting some, getting up in them guts, getting one's banana peeled, getting one's bean waxed, getting one's bone honed, getting one's canoe shellacked, getting one's kettle mended, getting one's twinkie stinky, getting some stank on the hang down, giving her the beans, giving the dog a bone, going all the way, going balls-deep, going crab fishing in the dead sea, going heels-to-Jesus, going in the nappy dugout, going to the grocery store, gland-to-gland combat, glazing the donut, greasing the loaf pan, grummeting, gutsticking

H/I - hanging 20 toes, hanging at the y, hanky panky, harpooning the salty longshoreman, having relations, having hot pudding for supper, hiding the bishop, hiding the Nazi, hitting a home run, hitting the skins, hitting the upvote button, hot beef injection, humpy-squirty, horizontal refreshments, hot yoga, humping, huntching, interior decorating, introducing charley, intromission

J/K/L - jamming the clam, jerking it where she's twerking it, jerking off with someone to talk to, jiffy-stiffing, jiggery-pokery, jingle-jangling, jinking, jiving, joint session of congress, jumping bones, jumping the turnstile, knobbing, knocking boots, knowing someone in the biblical sense, launching the meat missile, laying pipe, loading the clown into the cannon, locking legs and swapping gravy, lust-and-thrust

M - makin' bacon, making a magical sandwich, making it, making love, making one's way downtown, making the beast with two backs, making whoopee, marital congress, mashing the fat, mattress-dancing, matrimonial polka, midnight jockey ride, mingling limbs, mishing, moistening the pope, mollocking, monkey business, monster mashing, mort douce, mortar and pestle, moving furniture, myrtling

N/O – naffing, nailing, negotiating the forested chasm, nobblingnoddy, nubbing, nugging, nurtling, nut in the gut, nygling, occupying, opening the gates of Mordor, organ grinding, oscillating the unmentionables

P - paddling up coochie creek, palliardizing, pants-off dance-off, parallel parking, parking the beef bus in tuna town, parting the pink sea, passing the gravy, patching the hatchet wound, paying the rent, peeling the tree bark, pelvic pinochle, phutzing, pickling the prime meridian, pile-driving, puzzling, planting the parsnip, playing a game of Mr. wobbly hides his helmet, playing dungeons and dragons, playing hide the cannoli, playing peek-a-boo with your vein cane in the flesh pipe, playing tetris, playing with the box the kid came in, plonking, plooking, plowing through the bean field, plugging, pogo in the shrub, poking squid, pole-varnishing, polishing the porpoise, pondering the unicorn, porking, posting a letter, pounding the paternal piston, pounding the punani pavement, puddle-snuggling, pranging, praying with the knees upwards, pressing dangly parts, pressing the baby button, pressure-washing the quiver bone in the bitch wrinkle, prick-scouring, prigging, pronging, pully-hawly, pumping fur, punch-fucking the rosebud, punching the cow, putting condensed milk on the waffle,putting ranch dressing in hidden valley, putting the bread in the oven, putting the email in the spam folder, putting the wand in the chamber of secrets

Q/R – queef, quelching, quimsticking, releasing the kraken, riding st. George, riding the bolonga pony, riding the bony expressrip-'n'-dip, roasting the broomstick, rocking 'n' rolling, rogeringrolling in the hay, rooting, roughing up the suspect, rubbing the fun bits, rubbing wet spots, rumbusticating, rummaging in the root cellar, rumpling, rumpy-pumpy, rutting

S - schnoodlypooping, scoring, scragging, screwing, scrogging, scrimping, searching for pocket change, seeing a man about a dog,sending out for sushi, sexual congress, sexy time, shaboinking,shafting, shagging, shaking sheets, shampooing the wookie,sharpening the pencil, sheathing the meat dagger, shocking the monkey,, shooting the meat rocket into the sausage wallet,, shrimpin' the barbie, shtupping, shucking the oyster, sinking the pink, skeet-shooting, skinning the cat, sklooging, slamming the clam, slap and tickle, slapping sloppies, slaying the vadragon, sliming the banana, slippin' and slidin', slophockey, smacking the salmon, smashing buttflaps, smashing pissers, smeggingsnabbling, snubbing, snu-snu, souring the kraut, spearing the bearded clam spelunking the slime cave, splitting the hamster, splooge bathing, splurgin' the nurge, spray-painting the cervix, squat-jumping in the cucumber patch, squishin' the gibbly bits, sticking it in the slop box, sticking the llama's head up the lift shaft, stirring guts, stirring the up-skirt yogurt, struggle snuggling,stuffin' the muffin, stuffing the taco, swanky swirling, sweeping the chimney, switcheling

T - taking grandma to Applebee's, taking ol' one-eye to the optometrist, taking the bald-headed gnome for a stroll in the misty forest, taking the magic bus to Manchester, taming the strange, tapping ass, testing the humidity, testing the suspension, the act, thumping thighs, thrashing the gash, threading the needle, thrumming, tickling her tummy from the inside, tiffing, tonking, torpedoing the eel, tripping down the mine shaft, tromboning, tube-snake boogie, tubular wedging, tumbling, tunnel patrol, twirling the dum dum, two-ball in the middle pocket, two-person push-ups, tying the true lover's knot

U/V/WZ - using a telescope to explore the black hole, venerean mirth, venery, violating the prime directive, vulcanizing the whoopee stick, waka-waka, waxing ass, wetting the willy, whitewashing the picket fence, whittling the love branch, wiggling the toothpick, yentzing, yiffing, zig-zagging

Masturbation:

A – abusing the wicked stick, accordion solo, accosting the Oscar Meyer, acting out the grapes of wrath, activating cruise control, a date with: Palmela Handerson, Senorita Mano, and Manuela. addressing Mr. Palmer, adjusting the antenna, adjusting your set, aiding and abetting a known felon, a little southern romance, ambidexterity, answer the bone-a-phone, applying for a fishing license, applying lip gloss, applying the hand brake, arguing with Henry Longfellow, arm aerobics, arm breaker, armswing, arm-wrestle with your one-eyed vessel, Arthur, articulate the archdeacon, assault on a friendly weapon, attacking the one-eyed purple-headed warrior, auditioning the hand-puppet, a visit from mother fist

B - backing your fist, backstroke roulette, badgering the witness, bang yourself, barking up the wrong tree, bash the candle, basting the ham, battling the purple-headed yogurt slinger, being rough with the sex stick, beat, beat off, beating the bishop, beating my meat, be your own best friend, beat the beaver, beat the bishop, beat the bologna, beat the dummy, beat the meat, beat the pud, beat the stick, beat up your date, beef tips stroking off, bleed the weed, blow your own horn, bludgeon the beefsteak, bop the bologna (or baloney), bop the bonzo, box the Jesuit, box with Richard, brushing up on your typing skills, bugger your hand, building upper-body strength, burp the baby, burp the worm, butter the corn, buff the banana

C - calling in the secret service, caning the vandal, caulking the cracks in the bathroom tile, charm the snake, check for testicular cancer, cheese off, choke Kojak, choke the chicken, choke the sheriff and wait for the posse to come, calling down for more mayo, crank the shank, crimp the wire, crown the king, crushing pop cans in the dark, cuddle the kielbasa, cuff the carrot, clamp the pipe, clean your rifle, cleaning out your account, clear the snorkel, climb the tree, closet frisbee, combing the hair on your bald pig sally, combing your hair, communing with nature, consulting with your silent partner, corral your tadpole, couch hockey for one, crank the love pump, choking the chicken, clap your clit, clean the bean, clicking the mouse

D - dating Hannie Palmer, diddle my skittle, diddling, Donald Trump firing his apprentice, double clicking the mouse, daisy-chaining, dancing in the dragon's fiery breath, dancing with the one-eyed sailor, date Miss Michigan, date Mrs. Palmer and her five daughters, date Rosie Palm and her five sisters, debugging the hard drive, defrosting the fridge, digital penile oscillation, discovering your own potential, distributing free literature, do handiwork, do it your way, do the janitor thing, do the white knuckler, doing your homework, drain the monster, dry humping the ottoman

E/F - eating grapes with the one-armed man, electing the president, engage in safe sex, exercise one's right, exercising your right to privacy, evicting the testicular squatters, fastening the chin strap on the helmet of love, feed the ducks, feeding bologna to the smurfs, feeling your way around, fiction friction, fire off some knuckle-children, five finger shuttle, fiddle the flesh flute, firing the pound gunfishing with dynamite, fist your mister, five knuckle shuffle, flick your bic flickin' the kitten, flicking the bean, fling your phallus, flip the bishop, flipping your omelet, flog the bishop, flog the dolphin, flog the dong, flog the log, flog the mule, flogging the egg man, fly fishing, fondle your flagpole, free willy, frost the pastries, frosting your maple bar, frying up the corndog, fucking yourself

G – gallop the old lizard, gardening with the golden trowel, genital stimulation via phallengetic motion, get a date with slick mittens, get the German soldier marching, get to know yourself, get your pole varnished, getting trigger happy, give it a tug, give your low five, giving the half-blind dog a run for his money, go a couple of rounds with ol' josh, go blind, go on a date with Fisty Palmer, go

518

on a date with Handrea and Palmela, go the blow, going fishing with the man in the boat, going Hans Solo on Darth Vader's head, going to the palm prom, goose the gherkin, grease the pipe, greasin' the gash, greasing the three-legged cow

H - hand to gland combat, hard labor, have one off the wrist, having a knee trembler, helping put Mr. Kleenex's kids through college, hit the slit, hitchhike to the sky, holding your sausage, hostage hand job, hitchhike to heaven, hitchhike underneath the big top, hitting too close to home, hoisting your own petard, hold the bishop, hold the sausage hostage, holding your own, hone the cone, honk your horn, hosing down the driveway, hotfooting it to the nearest exit, hug the hog, hump your hose

I/J/K/L - Indiana Jones finding a sweet dig, investing in pork bellies, invoking the Oscar Meyer love spell, Jack hammer, jacking off, jazz yourself, jerk Jamby, jerk the gherkin, jerking off, jerkin the gerkin, jibber jab, jilling off, left to your own devices, let the beaver swim, letting the cat out of the bag, liquidating the inventory, locking the bathroom door, look for ticks, looking for clues with Fred and Daphne, lope the mule, love the muppet, love's labor's lost, lubricating the love monkey, lubing the tube

M - make a foreskin cone, make instant pudding, make the bald man puke, making a cash withdrawal, making chowder with sailor Ned, making it up as you go along, making it snow, making magic with leftovers, making my girl happy, making soup, making stomach pancakes, making the bald man cry, making the bread rise, making the world safe for democracy, mangle the midget, manipulate the mango, manual labor, manual override, master bacon, meet Rosie Hancock, meat with mother thumb and her four daughters, milking the cow, milk the lizard, milk the moose, milk the self, mount a corporal and four, much goo about nothing

N/O - nerk your throbber, null the void, oil the glove, Onan's Olympics, one-gun salute, one-man band, one-night-stand with yourself, opening the flood gates, one handed baseball

P - pack your palm, paddle the pickle, paint the ceiling, paint the pickle, painting the flag pole, painting the picket fence, painting the ceiling, palm the calm, paying at the turnpike, peel the banana, perform diagnostics on your man tool, pet the lizard, pet the poodle, petting the kitty, pip the pumpkin, playing air guitar naked, playing pocket pool, playing tug of war with the cyclops, play a little five-on-one, play a one-stringed guitar, play five against one, play in a one-man show, play peek-a-boo, play pocket pinball, play pocket pool, play tag with the pink torpedo, play the skin flute, play tug-o-war with cyclops, play Uno, playing it safe, playing the one-stringed melody, playing the single-string air guitar, plugging in the toaster, plunk your twanger, pole dancing, polishing the pearl, Polish Percy in your palm, polish the family jewels, polish the helmet, polish the rocket, polish the rock-hard staff of St. Peter, polish the sword, pound off, pound the bald-headed moose, pound the pud, pound your flounder, pounding the fence post, prepare the carrot, prime the pump, pull rank, pull the bologna pony, pull the carrot, pull the goalie, pull the pole, pull the pope, pull the pud, pull your own leg, pull your taffy, pulling your own weight, pulling yourself up by your own bootstrap, pumping the keg, pump the python, pump the stump, punch the clown, punch the munchkin, punish Percy in your palm, putting your best foot forward, putting your foot down, putting your thumb in the porridge

R - raining on your parade, ram the ham, relishing your hot dog, revving the engine, roll your own, rolling it off the lot, Romeo and himself, rope the pony, rope the pope, rub one out, rub the pink eraser, rubbing buddha's tummy, run off a batch by hand, roughing up the suspect, rub the nub, rubbing one out, rubbing Rob Reiner, ruin your eyesight

S - sacrifice sperm to the god of lonely nights, safest sex, sailing the, mayonnaise seas, saluting the general, sampling the secret sauce, sand wood, scratch and sniff, scraping off the scabs, scratch n' sniff, scour the tower of power, scraping the bottom of the barrel, scratch the itch, screwing your courage to the sticking place, secret handshake, self-abuse, self-induced penile regurgitation, sex with someone you really love, shake and steak, shake hands with Abe Lincoln, shake hands with the midge, shake hands with the unemployed, shake hands with your John Thomas, shake hands with your wife's best friend, shake hands with Yul Brynner, shake the sauce, shake the sausage, shake the snake, shaking hands with Dr. Winky, shellac the shillelagh, shemp the hog, shift gears, shine the helmet, shine your pole, shoot for the moon, shoot putty at the moon, shoot the airplane, shooting yourself in the foot, shuck your corn, shuffle your ipod, sizing things up

Sl - slam the clam, slam the ham, slam the salami, slam the salmon, slam the spam, slapping the salami, slap high fives with Yul Brynner, slap it, slap pappy, slap the carrot, slap the clown, slap the donkey, slap the purple-headed yogurt pistol, slap the salami, slapping Johnny on the back, slicking willie, sling the jelly, smack the salami, smiting the pink knight, snap the monkey, snap the rubber, snap the whip, solo flight, solo marathon, solo sex, spank Elvis, spank the bishop, spank the frank, spank the monkey, spank the salami, spank the wank, spanking the monkey, spanking the rooster, spending your Christmas bonus, spinnin' a record, squeeze the cheese, squeeze the juice, squeeze the toothpaste in the middle of the tube , squeeze your cheese-dog, squeezing the happy lumberjack, squishing the squidgy, stewing in your own juices, stinky pinky, stir the batter, stir the yogurt, stranger, stranger on the rocks, strangers in the night, strain the main vein, straining your cabbage, stretching the truth, strip-mining with the spaghetti man, stroke the carrot, stroke the mole, stroke the one-eyed burping gecko, stroke the satin-headed serpent, stroke your poker, stroke your twinkie, stroking it, stroking the one-eyed snake, strumming the one-string harp

T - take matters into your own hands, take part in population control, take the fifth, take the monster for a one-armed ride, taking care of my business, taking a few practice shots, taking a load off, talk quietly to yourself, tame the shrew, tapping the wookie on the head, taunt the one-eyed weasel, teaching the cyclops the lambada, tease the weenie, tenderize the tube steak, tending to your own affairs, test your batteries, that crazy hand jive, thinking of your mom, thrash your thing, thump the pump, thump your thong, tickle the ivory, tickle the pickle, tickle the taco, tickle your pickle, tickle-wiggle-jiggle-pickle, tipping off the inspector, toss the snag, toss the turkey, toss yogurt, tug the slug, turning Japanese, twang the wire, tweak your Twinkie, twist your crank, two-finger tango

U/V - unleashing the alabaster yak, unloading the gun, unpacking the moving van, varnishing the banister, varnish the flagpole, visiting with Papa Smurf, visit from the five-fingered aunty, visiting Rosy Palms and her five sisters

W - wake the dead, walking the dog, walk the dog, walk the plank, walking a mile in Mr. Wiggly's shoes, wallowing in self-pity, wank with the one-eyed wonder weasel, wash the meat, wax the Buick, wax the carrot, wax the dolphin, waxin' n' milkin', western grip, whack it, whack the weasel, whack willy, whip the dummy, whip the one-eyed trouser snake, whip the one-eyed worm, whip the rat, whip the stiff, whip the wire, whip up some sour cream, whip your dripper, whitewashing with Huck and Tom, whittle the stick, wiggling your walrus, windsurf on Mount Baldy, wonk your conker, work things out, working at your own speed, working late at the office, working up a foamy lather, working without Annette, wrestle the dragon, wrestle the eel, wrestling the one-eyed monster, wrestling with the bald champ, wring out your rope, wrist aerobics

Y - yank the crank, yank the yo-yo, yank your plank

Bibliography

The following books, journal articles, and websites were consulted while writing of this book.

Books

Benn, Charles. *China's Golden Age: Everyday Life in the Tang Dynasty*. Oxford: Oxford University Press. 2002.

Birley, Derek. *A Social History of English Cricket*. London: Aurum Press Ltd., 1999.

Block, David. *Baseball Before We Knew It: A Search for the Roots of the Game*. Lincoln, NE: Bison Books, 2005.

Buss, David M. "Evolutionary Theories of Dominance and Status." In *Evolutionary Psychology: The New Science of the Mind*, 4th Ed., 351-353. Austin: University of Texas, 2012.

Chisholm, Hugh, (ed.) "Badminton (game)." In *Encyclopedia Britannica*, Vol. 3 (11th ed.). Cambridge: Cambridge University Press, 1911.

Crego, Robert. *Sports and Games of the 18th and 19th Centuries*. Westport, CT: Greenwood Press, 2003.

Dunbar, Robin, and Louise Barrett (Eds.). *Oxford Handbook of Evolutionary Psychology*. New York: Oxford University Press, 2009.

Epstein, Randi Hutter. *Aroused: The History of Hormones and How They Control Just About Everything*. New York: W. W. Norton & Company, 2018.

Everton, Clive. *The History of Snooker and Billiard*. Haywards Heath, U.K.: Partridge Press, 1986.

Folmsbee, Beulah. *A Little History of the Horn-book*. London: The Horn Book Inc., 1942.
Gardiner, E. Norman. "Athletics in the Ancient World." New York: Courier Dover Publications. 2002.

Gillmeister, Heiner. *Tennis: A Cultural History*. New York: New York University Press, 1998.

Glória, M.B.A. *Encyclopedia of Food Sciences and Nutrition*, 2nd Edition. Amsterdam: Elsevier Science Ltd., 2003.

Grabowski, Michael, (Ed.). *Neuroscience and Media: New Understandings and Representations*. New York: Routledge. 2015.

Haliburton, Thomas Chandler. *The Attaché: or Sam Slick in England, 2nd Series*. London: Richard Bentley, 1844.

Hoyle, Edmond, and Thomas Frere. *Hoyle's Games: Illustrated Edition. Embracing All the Most Modern Modes of Play, And the Rules Practised at The Present Time, In Billiards, Whist, Draughts, Cribbage, Backgammon, And All*

Other Fashionable Games. London: Andesite Press, (original print: 1779). Reprint, 2017.

Huizinga, Johan. *Homo Ludens, Proeve Ener Bepaling Van Het Spelelement Der Cultuur*. Original 1938. Dutch ed. by Groningen, Wolters-Noordhoff. Translated into German. Translated from the 1944 German edition into English. Translator unknown. London: Routledge & Kegan Paul Ltd., 1949.

Hutchins, Brett. *Don Bradman: Challenging the Myth*. Cambridge: Cambridge University Press, 2002.

Johnson, Jan, and Ruse Versteeg. *Illustrated History of the Pole Vault*.
Atascadero, CA: Sky Jumpers, 2008.

Jones, Henry. "Badminton," T.S. Baynes, (Ed.). *Encyclopedia Britannica,* Vol. 3 (9th ed.) New York: Charles Scribner's Sons, 1878.

Joyce, Patrick Weston. *English as We Speak it in Ireland*. Dublin: Longmans, Green, & Co. 1910.

Kanter, Rosabeth Moss. *Confidence: How Winning Streaks and Losing Streaks Begin and End*. New York: Crown Business, 2006.

Kelly, Christopher. *Theodosius II: Rethinking the Roman Empire in Late Antiquity*. Cambridge: Cambridge University Press, 2013.

King, Seamus J. *A History of Hurling*. Dublin, Ireland: Gill & Macmillan Ltd., 2005.

Klinge, C.M. "Steroid Hormone Receptors and Signal Transduction Processes." In *Principles of Endocrinology and Hormone Action*. A. Belfiore and D. LeRoith (ed.). Cham, Switzerland: Springer International Publishing, 2008.

Laffaye, Horace A. *The Evolution of Polo*. Jefferson, NC: McFarland, 2009.

Lamm, Steven. *The Hardness Factor*. New York: HarperCollins Publishers, Inc., 2005.

Linney, E. J. *A History of the Game of Bowls*. Edinburgh: Edinburgh Press. 1933.

Liponski, Wojciech. *World Sports Encyclopedia*. Minneapolis: MBI-UNESCO Publishing Company LLC, 2003.

Liss, Howard. *Lacrosse*. New York: Funk & Wagnalls, 1970.

Major, John. *More Than a Game*. London: HarperCollins, 2007.

McCann, Timothy J. *Sussex Cricket in the Eighteenth Century*. Lewes, England: Sussex Record Society, 2004.

Nyren, John. *The Cricketers of My Time*. London: Robson Books, 1998.

Powers, Albert Theodore. *The Business of Baseball*. Jefferson, NC: McFarland Books. 2003.

Riess, Steven A. (Ed.) "Rise of Organized Bowling." From *Sports in America from Colonial Times to the Twenty-First Century.* New York: Routledge. 2015.

Robertson, Ian. *The Winner Effect: The Neuroscience of Success and Failure.* New York: Thomas Dunne Books, 2012.

Rowley, C. *The Shared Origins of Football, Rugby, and Soccer.* Lanham, MD: Rowman & Littlefield Publishers. 2015.

Ruiz-Cortés, Zulma Tatiana. *Gonadal Sex Steroids: Production, Action and Interactions in Mammals.* Chapter 1, pp. 3-39. London: IntechOpen. 2012.

Selke, Frank. *Behind The Cheering.* Toronto, Canada: McClelland and Stewart Ltd., 1962.

Smith, Nicky. *Queen of Games: The History of Croquet.* London: Trafalgar Square, 1991.

Stein, Victor, and Paul Rubino. *The Billiard Encyclopedia: An Illustrated History of the Sport* (2nd ed.). La Jolla, CA: Blue Book Publications, 1996.

Swanton, E. W. (ed.). *Barclay's World of Cricket.* London: Collins Willow, 1986.

Walker, David. *Skills, Drills & Strategies for Racquetball.* Scottsdale, AZ: Holcomb Hathaway, Inc., 1999.

Ward, William Arthur. *Fountains of Faith: The Words of William Arthur Ward.* Anderson, S. Carolina: Droke House, 1970.

528

Weinberg, M. S. "The Nudist Camp: Way of Life and Social Structure." *Human Organization*. Vol. 26, No. 3 (1967):91-99.

White, E. B. *A Practical Treatise on the Game of Billiards*. London: Carter Adams (Original print, 1807). Reprint - London: The British Library, 2007.
Williams, Gardon. *A Dictionary of Sexual Language and Imagery in Shakespearean and Stuart Literature*. London: Athlone Press. 1994.

Willughby, Francis. *Book of Games*. Nottingham, England: Ashgate Publishing Co., 2003.

Wisden, John. "One-Day Knockout Competition, 1963." In *Wisden Cricketers' Almanack, 100th Edition*. London: Sporting Handbooks Ltd., 1963.

Journal Articles

Arce, J. C., and M. J. De Souza. "Exercise and Male Infertility." *Sports Medicine,* Vol. 15 (1993):146–169.

Bernhardt, Paul, J. M. Dabbs, J. A. Fiedern, and C. D. Lutter. "Testosterone Changes During Vicarious Experiences of Winning and Losing Among Fans At Sporting Events." *Physical Behavior,* Vol. 65, No. 1 (1998):59-62.

Blaicher, W., D. Gruber, C. Bieglmayer, A. M. Blaicher, W. Knogler, and J.C. Huber. "The Role of Oxytocin in Relation to Female Sexual Arousal." *Gynecologic and Obstetric Investigation*. Vol. 47, No. 2 (1999):125–126.

Broneer, See O. "The Isthmain Victory Crown." *American Journal of Archaeology,* Vol. 66 (1962): 259-263.

Buss, David M. "Evolutionary Theories of Dominance and Status." *Evolutionary Psychology: The New Science of the Mind*, No. 4 (2012): 351-353.

Cappelletti, M., and K. Wallen. "Increasing Women's Sexual Desire: The Comparative Effectiveness of Estrogens and Androgens." *Hormone Behavior*. Vol. 78 (2016):178–93.

Carmichael, M.S., R. Humbert, J. Dixen, G. Palmisano, W. Greenleaf, and J. M. Davidson. "Plasma Oxytocin Increases in the Human Sexual Response." *The Journal of Clinical Endocrinology and Metabolism*. Vol. 64 (1987):27–31.

Corbyn, Zoë. "Archaeologists Land World's Oldest Fish Hook." *Nature: International Weekly Journal of Science.* doi:10.1038/nature.2011.9461.

Cumming, Sean P., Frank L. Smoll, Ronald E. Smith, and Joel R. Grossbard. "Is Winning Everything? The Relative Contributions of Motivational Climate and Won-Lost Percentages in Youth Sports." *Journal of Applied Sport Psychology,* Vol. 19, No. 3 (2007):322-336.

Elias, A.N., and A. F. Wilson. "Exercise and Gonadal Function." *Human Reproduction*, Vol. 8 (1993):1747–1761.

Gauquelin, G., G. Geelen, F. Louis, A.M. Allevard, C. Meunier, G. Cuisinaud, S. Benjanet, N.G. Seidah, M. Chretien, and J. J. Legros. "Presence of vasopressin, oxytocin and neurophysin in the retina of mammals,

530

effect of light and darkness, comparison with the neuropeptide content of the neurohypophysis and pineal gland." *Peptides*. Vol. 4, No. 4 (1983):509–515.

Hackney, A. C. "The Male Reproductive System and Endurance Exercise." *Medicine and Science in Sports and Exercise*, Vol. 28. (1996):180–189.

Irwig, M. S. "Testosterone Therapy for Transgender Men." *The Lancet: Diabetes & Endocrinology*, Vol. 5, No. 4 (2017):301–311.

Lever, Janet, David A. Frederick, and Letitia Anne Peplau. "Does Size Matter? Men's and Women's Views on Penis Size Across the Lifespan." *Psychology of Men & Masculinity*, Vol. 7, No. 3. (2006):129-143.

Lombardo, Michael. "On the Evolution of Sport." *Evolutionary Psychology Journal*, Vol. 10, No. 1 (2012): 18.

Lynch, Jerry. "The Way of the Champion." *Podium Sports Journal*, Vol. 1, No. 1 (2007):5.

MacLennan, Hugh Dan. "Shinty's Place and Space in the World." *The Sports Historian* No. 18 (1998):23.

Rastrelli, G, G. Corona, and M. Maggi. "Testosterone and Sexual Function in Men." *Maturitas: The European Menopause Journal*. Vol. 112: (2018):46–52.

Weinberg, M. S. "The Nudist Camp: Way of Life and Social Structure." *Human Organization*. Vol. 26, No. 3. (1967): pp. 91-99.

Wibowo, E., and R. J. Wassersug. "The Effect of Estrogen on the Sexual Interest of Castrated Males: Implications to Prostate Cancer Patients on Androgen-deprivation Therapy." *Critical Reviews in Oncology/Hematology*, Vol. 87, No. 3 (2013):224–38.

Wrangham, Richard. "Evolution of Coalitionary Killing." *American Journal of Physical Anthropology.* Vol. 110, no 29. (1999): pp. 1-30.

Yang, Hai-Peng, Liwei Wang, Liqun Han, and Septhani C. Wang.
"Nonsocial Functions of Hypothalamic Oxytocin." *International Scholarly Research Notices* Vol. 2013 (2013): Article ID 179272. doi: 10.1155/2013/179272.

Websites

Advocates for Youth. "Personal Responsibility & Work Opportunity Reconciliation Act of 1996." Title V, 510(b) (2) (A-H) of the Social Security Act. Accessed April 2, 2018.
http://www.advocatesforyouth.org/publications/publications-a-z/597-abstinence-only-until-marriage-programs-ineffective-unethical-and-poor-public-health.

Aumann, Mark. "Remembering Alan Shepard's Lunar Golf Shots, 47 Years Later." PGA. Accessed August 22, 2018. https://www.pga.com/news/golf-buzz/feb-6-1971-alan-shepard-plays-golf-moon.

BBC Sport. "Sergey Bubka's Pole Valt Record Broken by Renaud Lavillenie." BBC Sports. Accessed March 30, 2018. https://www.bbc.com/sport/athletics/26208821.

Becker, Wilhelm Adolf. "The Game of Ball." In *Gallus: or, Roman Scenes of the Time of Augustus.* Rev. Frederick Metcalfe, (trans). London: Longmann, Green, and Co. 1603: p. 402. Accessed March 28, 2018. Archive.org. https://archive.org/details/Gallus/page/n9.

BocceVolo. "Rules – Chapter 2: The Game - Points to be Made and the Duration of the Match." BocceVolo.com. Accessed May 8, 2018.
  http://www.boccevolo.com/about/ch2.html.

Branch, John. "Curlers Are Finicky When It Comes to Their Olympic Ice." NYtimes.com. Accessed March 6, 2018.
https://www.nytimes.com/2009/08/17/sports/17curling.html.

Brice, David. "Recognition for the World's Oldest Links, at Last." PGA Tour. Accessed May 28, 2018.
  http://web.archive.org/web/20110604120255/www.pgatour.com/2009/tourlife/travel/03/23/course_of_week/index.html.

Brice, David. "The Open Championship – More Scottish than British." PGA Tour. Accessed April 29, 2018.
  https://web.archive.org/web/20121002214520/http://www.pgatour.com/2007/travel/07/16/trans_071607/index.html.

Briggs, P. "Ethiopia." Health and Fitness History. Accessed February 20, 2018.
  https://healthandfitnesshistory.com/ancient-sports/ethiopian-genna-field-hockey/.

Cartwright, Mark. "Saladin." Ancient History Encyclopedia.
Accessed September 30, 2018.
https://www.ancient.eu/Saladin/.

Celizic, Mike. "Smooth Operators: They Make Olympic Ice Nice." Today.com. Accessed March 12, 2018.
https://www.today.com/news/smooth-operators-they-make-olympic-ice-nice-wbna35537168.

Chandler, John H. "Robin Hood: Development of a Popular Hero."
The Robin Hood Project, University of Rochester.
Accessed March 31, 2018.
http://d.lib.rochester.edu/robin-hood/text/chandler-robin-hood-development-of-a-popular-hero.

Chaplin, Patrick. "The History of the Dart." Patrick Chaplin.
Accessed March 17, 2018.
http://www.patrickchaplin.com/Darts.htm.

China Tungsten Online (Xiamen) Manufacturers & Sales Corp. "Tungsten Barrell Shape." Chinadart.com. Accessed March 14, 2018.
http://www.chinadart.com/tungsten_dart_barrel_shape.htm.

Collins Dictionary. "Boccia." Collinsdictionary.com.
Accessed May 7, 2018.
https://www.collinsdictionary.com/dictionary/english/boccie.

Lacrosse in America. "Robert Pool's Contribution: Double Walled lacrosse Sticks – 1937." Accessed June 5, 2018.
https://americanlacrosse1865.wordpress.com/2017/03/28/robert-pools-contribution-double-walled-lacrosse-sticks-1937/.

Curling Canada. "History of Curling." Curling.ca. Accessed March 12, 2018.
https://www.curling.ca/about-the-sport-of-curling/the-history-of-curling/.

Eden. "What is the Phospholipid Bilayer and What Determines Its Fluidity?" Cambridge Coaching. Accessed March 22, 2018.
http://blog.cambridgecoaching.com/what-is-the-phospholipid-bilayer-and-what-determines-its-fluidity.

England Squash and Racquetball. "Racketball." Accessed June 28, 2018.
https://web.archive.org/web/20150210232150/http://www.englandsquashandracketball.com/play-squash-and-racketball/rules-of-play/racketball.

Federation of International Bandy. "Members." Worldbandy.com.
Accessed May 12, 2018.
http://www.worldbandy.com/members.html.

FIFA World Cup Russia. "More than half the world watched record-breaking 2018 World Cup" FIFA.com, accessed May 29, 2018,
https://www.fifa.com/worldcup/news/more-than-half-the-world-watched-record-breaking-2018-world-cup

Fédération Internationale de Volleyball. "FIVB History." Web.archive.org. Accessed October 17, 2018. https://web.archive.org/web/20070919033125/http://www.fivb.ch/EN/FIVB/History.htm.

Folmsbee, Beulah. *A Little History of the Horn-book*. London: The Horn Book Inc., (1942). Accessed September 2, 2018. https://commons.wikimedia.org/wiki/File:Battledore_-_Youthful_Sports.png.

Gates, Zachary. "The Story of Marn Grook." Sydney Swans.
Accessed February 21, 2018.
http://www.sydneyswans.com.au/news/2018-05-28/the-story-of-marn-grook.

Johnson, Samuel, John Walker, and Robert S. Jameson. *A Dictionary of the English Language*. Vol. 1, 2nd Ed. London: William Pickering, 1828. Books.google.com. Accessed May 28, 2018.
https://books.google.com/books?id=z3kKAAAAIAAJ&pg=RA2PA519&dq=pelmel#v=onepage&q&f=false.

Google Books. "Kick Baseball." Chapter, in *The Playground: The World at Play*. Vol. XI, No. 1. New York: Cornell University. 1917:240. Google.com. Accessed March 18, 2018.
https://books.google.com/books?id=x70vAAAAYAAJ&printsec=frontcover&source=gbs_ge_summary_r&cad=0#v=onepage&q&f=false.

Harper, Douglas. "Fooball." Etymology online. Accessed May 29, 2018.

https://www.etymonline.com/word/football#etymonline_v_11761.

Heitner, Darren. "The Economics of Polo, The Sport of Kings." Forbes Online. Accessed February 15, 2018.
https://www.forbes.com/sites/darrenheitner/2015/05/17/the-economics-of-polo-the-sport-of-kings/#4bd51438ea14.

Help with Bowling. "The History and Origins of Bowling."
Accessed on April 2, 2018.
http://helpwithbowling.com/history-origins-of-bowling.php.

Hill, Bryan. "Ulama, The Mesoamerican Ball Game: Deadly Sport of the Ancient Americas." Ancient Origins. Accessed March 29, 2018.
https://www.ancient-origins.net/news-history/ulama-mesoamerican ball-game-deadly-sport-ancient-americas-003156.

Hutchinson, Roger. "Camanachd: The Story of Shinty."
Accessed June 20, 2018.
https://www.shinty.com/mens/about-us/history.

International Quidditch Association. "About-Activities." Iquidditch.org. Accessed June 15, 2018.
http://iqaquidditch.org/about.html.

Kidzworld. "Traditional Celtic Sports." Kidzworld.com.
Accessed June 2, 2018

https://www.kidzworld.com/article/5426-traditional-celtic-sports/.

Kubala, Jillian. "Essential Amino Acids: Definition, Benefits and Food Sources." Healthline Newsletter. Accessed March 2, 2018. https://www.healthline.com/nutrition/essential-amino-acids.

Laird, Neil. "1744 Honourable Company of Edinburgh Golfers." Scottishgolfhistory.org. Accessed May 28, 2018.
http://www.scottishgolfhistory.org/oldest-golf-clubs-societies/1744-honourable-company-of-edinburgh-golfers/.

Laird, Neil. "Golf Ball from Hairy to Haskell." Scottish Golf History. Accessed April 29, 2018.
http://www.scottishgolfhistory.org/origin-of-golf-terms/golf-ball-feathery-gutty-haskell/.

Laird, Neil. "How Many Golf Holes are There in the World?" Scottish Golf History. Accessed April 29, 2018.
http://www.scottishgolfhistory.org/news/how-many-golf-holes-are-there-in-the-world/.

Latham, Richard C. "Polo Sport." Encyclopedia Britannica Online. Accessed February 15, 2018.
https://www.britannica.com/sports/polo.

Logue, Brian. "National Lacrosse Participation Tops 825,000 Players."
US Lacrosse. Accessed June 4, 2018.
https://www.uslacrosse.org/blog/national-lacrosse-participation-tops-825000-players.

Lund, Peter Bailey. "Lacrosse: A History of the Game." E-lacrosse.com. Accessed June 3, 2018.
https://web.archive.org/web/19991008114420/http://www.e-lacrosse.com/laxhist4.htm.

Mark, Joshua J. "Games, Sports & Recreation in Ancient Egypt." Ancient History Encyclopedia. Last modified April 11, 2017.
Accessed February 5, 2018.
https://www.ancient.eu/article/1036/.

McCarthy, Thomas A. "Quarter-Staff: A Practical Manual." Reprinted from the Journal of Manly Arts. London: W. Swan Sonnenshein & Co., 1883. Accessed on March 31, 2018.
https://ejmas.com/jmanly/articles/2001/jmanlyart_mccarthy_0901.htm

Medieval Chronicles. "Medieval Quarterstaff Weapon."
Accessed March 31, 2018.
http://www.medievalchronicles.com/medievalweapons/quarterstaffweapon/.

Maguire, Joseph Anthony, William N Thompson, David Charles Rowe, and Allen Guttmann. *Encyclopedia Britannica, Inc.* "Sports." Chicago: Encyclopedia Britannica, 2018. Accessed February 16, 2018.
https://www.britannica.com/sports/sports.

Marshall, Tabitha, and Jim Calder. "Lacrosse: From Creator's Game to Modern Sport." The Canadian Encyclopedia. Accessed May 12, 2018.
https://www.thecanadianencyclopedia.ca/en/article/lacrosse-from creators-game-to-modern-sport.

Martin, Clive, and Simon Williams. "A History of Croquet in Ireland." Croquet Association of Ireland. Accessed May 28, 2018.
http://www.croquetireland.com/node/4.

Masters, James. "The History of Darts and Other Useful Information."
The Online Guide to Traditional Games. Accessed March 13, 2018.
http://www.tradgames.org.uk/games/Darts.htm.

McCall, Pete. "Exercise and Hormones: Eight Hormones Involved in Exercise." American Council on Exercise. Accessed March 23, 2018.
https://www.acefitness.org/education-and-resources/professional/expert-articles/5593/exercise-and-hormones-8-hormones-involved-in-exercise.

McClure Tables. "Shuffleboard Game Rules." Mccluretables.com.
Accessed April 1, 2018.
https://www.mccluretables.com/t-Shuffleboard_Game_Rules.aspx.

Medieval Chronicles. "Medieval Quarterstaff Weapon."
Accessed March 31, 2018.
http://www.medievalchronicles.com/medieval-weapons/quarterstaff-weapon/.

Major League Baseball News. "World Series Trophy Profile."
Accessed April 24, 2018.

https://www.mlb.com/news/world-series-trophy-profile/c-155729034.

Marshall, Tabitha, and Jim Calder. "Lacrosse: From Creator's Game to Modern Sport." The Canadian Encyclopedia. Accessed May 12, 2018.
https://www.thecanadianencyclopedia.ca/en/article/lacrosse-from-creators-game-to-modern-sport.

Morley, Gary. "125 Years of Wimbledon: From Birth of Lawn Tennis to Modern Marvels." CNN.com. Accessed July 8, 2018.
http://edition.cnn.com/2011/SPORT/tennis/06/14/tennis.wimbledon.125th.anniversary.museum/index.html.

Muehleisen, Bud. "How Racquetball Got Its Name." Racquetball Museum. Accessed June 28, 2018.
https://racquetballmuseum.com/wpcontent/uploads/2017/10/howrballgotitsname.pdf.

Muska, Scott. "What Happens To Your Body and Your Brain When You Watch Football." Better Wellness. Accessed March 24, 2018.
https://www.nbcnews.com/better/health/what-happens-your-body-brain-when-you-watch-football-ncna814401.

Naismith Basketball Foundation. "About Dr. James Naismith."
Naismithbasketballfoundation.com. Accessed April 1, 2018. https://naismithbasketballfoundation.com/about-dr-james-naismith/.

New England Historical Society. "In 1895, William Morgan Invents Mintonette." Accessed Oct. 17, 2018.
http://www.newenglandhistoricalsociety.com/leroy-shear-therespected-vermont-banker-who-wasnt/.

Norris, Shawn T. "The Sport of the Roman Army." Rome Across Europe. Accessed April 3, 2018.
http://www.romeacrosseurope.com/?p=1118#sthash.E9a2XlwU.dpbs.

National Public Radio. "Sex Education in America." The Kaiser/Kennedy School Poll. Accessed May 19, 2018.
https://www.npr.org/templates/story/story.php?storyId=1622610.

National Center for Biotechnology Information. "Histidine," "Isoleucine," "Leucine," "Lysine," "Methionine," "Phenylalanine," "Threonine," "Trytophan," "Valine." PubChem Compound database.
Accessed March 2, 2018.
https://pubchem.ncbi.nlm.nih.gov/.

O'Houlihan, Patches. "Dodgeball – A True Underdog Story." Wikipedia. Accessed March 3, 2018.
https://en.wikipedia.org/wiki/DodgeBall:_A_True_Underdog_Story.

Olympic Games. "Welcome to the Ancient Olympic Games." Olympic.org. Accessed February 15, 2018.
https://www.olympic.org/ancient-olympic-games/long-jump-javelin-discus.

Online Etymology Dictionary. "Tennez." Etymonline.com.
Accessed August 2, 2018.

https://www.etymonline.com/search?q=tenez.

Phillips, Brian. "Why Do We Call It Soccer?"
Slate.com.
Accessed March 4, 2018.
https://slate.com/news-and-politics/2010/06/most-countries-think-of-the-world-cup-as-a-football-tournament-why-do-we-call-the-game-soccer.html.

Pluckhahn, J. Bruce. "Bowling Game." Encyclopedia
Britannica.
Accessed April 2, 2018.
https://www.britannica.com/sports/bowling.

Pringle, Tyler. "The Demographics of Golf – Inside the
Mind of a Golfer." American Golf Corporation. Accessed
June 9, 2018.
https://www.americangolf.com/blog/mulligans/the-demographics-of-golf-inside-the-mind-of-a-golfer/.

Quora. "How Did Jerry West Become the NBA Logo?"
Quora.com. Accessed May 7, 2018.
https://www.quora.com/How-did-Jerry-West-become-the-NBA-logo.

Rebounderz. "Where Did Dodgeball Start? A Brief
History Lesson." Rounderz.com. Accessed May 20, 2018.
https://www.rebounderz.com/lansdale/where-did-dodgeball-start-a-brief-history-lesson/.

Reilly, Jill. "It's a Hard Job but Someone's Got To Do
It: Scientists Visit Sex Club for Research Into Testosterone
Levels." DailyMail.com.
Accessed March 23, 2018.

https://www.dailymail.co.uk/news/article-2239621/Researchers-test-mens-testosterone-levels-rise-arousal--visiting-sex-club.html.

Ritchie, Marlene. "How Are Our Children Learning about Sex? The Responsibility of Parents and Schools to Teach Kids about Human Development and How to Form Caring Relationships." Child Research Net. Accessed April 2, 2018.
http://www.childresearch.net/papers/rights/2016_02.html.

Rules of Sport. "What is the Difference Between Rugby League and Rugby Union?" Rulesofsport.com. Accessed March 20, 2018.
http://www.rulesofsport.com/faq/what-is-the-difference-between-rugby-league-and-rugby-union.html.

Scarsbough, V. L. and D. R. Wilcox, "The Mesoamerican Ballgame." Health and Fitness History. Accessed February 5, 2018.
https://healthandfitnesshistory.com/ancient-sports/mesoamerican-ball-game/.
Schmidt, J. R. "Steve Nagy's 300 Game on Championship Bowling." Set Them Up Knock Them Down. Bowl-A-Roll Lanes.
Accessed April 3, 2018.
http://bowl-a-roll.blogspot.com/2011/11/perfect-tv-drama-steve-nagy-is.html.

Smith, Ian. "This is the earliest surviving Ice Hockey film footage, taken in 1898." The Vintage News. Accessed March 26, 2018.
https://www.thevintagenews.com/2016/03/15/earliest-surviving-ice-hockey-film-footage-taken-1898/.

544

Smothers, Hannah. "Where are Schools Teaching Kids How to Use a Condom?" Splinter News. Accessed February 19, 2018.
https://splinternews.com/where-are-schools-teaching-kids-how-touse-a-condom-1793850389.

Spector, Felicity. "Belly up: Why men don't like their bodies," 4 News, (Jan. 6, 2012).
https://www.channel4.com/news/belly-up-why-men-dont-like-their-bodies

The Statistics Portal. "Share of People Who Played Golf in the Unites States in 2018, by Age." Accessed November 7, 2018.
https://www.statista.com/statistics/227420/number-of-golfers-usa/.

Sulat, Nate. "Why Isn't Baseball More Popular in the U.K.?" BBC News Magazine (online). July 26, 2013. BBC.com. Accessed May 29, 2018.
https://www.bbc.com/news/magazine-23425907.

The Golfer's Guide to Golf. "The Complete History of Golf." Golf Information. Accessed May 28, 2018.
http://www.golf-information.info/history-of-golf.html.

Thomas, Terrence B., Frank E. Eating, and Robert Lee Petri. "Fishing."
Encyclopaedia Britannica. Accessed March 21, 2018.
https://www.britannica.com/topic/fishing-recreation#ref70275.

Urban, Tim. "Why Sports Fans are Sports Fans." Wait But Why.
Accessed March 23, 2018.
https://waitbutwhy.com/archive.

USA National Shuffleboard Association. "USA – NSA Shuffleboard." NSA.us. Accessed April 1, 2018.
http://www.national-shuffleboard-association.us/.
Volleyball - General Information. "History of Volleyball." Volleyball.org. Accessed October 17, 2018.
http://volleyball.org/history.html.

West Midlands Sports Development. "Rounders." Accessed June 18, 2018.
https://www.wmsd.co.uk/component/k2/item/320 -rounders.

Whitehouse, Jordan. "The Carr-Harris Cup: Hockey's Oldest Rivalry." Visitkingston.ca. Accessed March 24, 2018. https://www.visitkingston.ca/the-carr-harris-cup-hockeys-oldest-rivalry/.

White Hutchinson Leisure & Learning Group. "What's Happening to Bowling?" Whitehutchinson.com. Accessed April 3, 2018.
https://www.whitehutchinson.com/leisure/articles/whats-happening-to-bowling.shtml.

Wikipedia. "Alexander Cartwright." Wikipedia.org. Accessed April 22, 2018.
https://en.wikipedia.org/wiki/Alexander_Cartwright.

Wikipedia. "Curling." Wickipedia.org. Accessed April 8, 2018. https://en.wikipedia.org/wiki/Curling.

Wikipedia. "Episkyros." Wikipedia.com. 2007. Accessed February 15, 2018.
http://en.wikipedia.org/wiki/Episkyros.

Wikipedia. "Hanetsuki." Wikipedia.org. Accessed June 24, 2018.
https://en.wikipedia.org/wiki/Hanetsuki.

Wikipedia. "Harpastum." Wikipedia.org. Accessed February 15, 2018.
https://en.wikipedia.org/wiki/Harpastum.

Wikipedia. "International Ice Hockey Federation." Wikipedia.com. Accessed March 27, 2018.
https://en.wikipedia.org/wiki/International_Ice_Hockey_Federation.

Wikipedia. "Target Archery." Wikipedia.com. Accessed April 7, 2018.
https://en.wikipedia.org/wiki/Target_archery.
Wikipedia. "Table Tennis." Wikipedia.com. Accessed June 22, 2018.
https://en.wikipedia.org/wiki/Table_tennis.

Wikipedia. "Walter Camp." Wikipedia.com. Accessed March 9, 2018.
https://en.wikipedia.org/wiki/Walter_Camp.

WikiVisually. "Victoria Skating Rink." Wikivisually.com.
Accessed March 28, 2018.
https://wikivisually.com/wiki/Victoria_Skating_Rink.

Wood, Robert. "About Cnapan Medieval Football." Topendsports.com. Accessed February 20, 2018.
https://www.topendsports.com/sport/extinct/cnapan.htm.

Wood, Robert. "La Soule Medieval Football." TopendSports.com.
Accessed February 20, 2018.
https://www.topendsports.com/sport/extinct/la-soule.htm.

World Curling Federation. "Mixed Doubles Curling Confirmed for PyeongChang 2018 Olympics." World Curling.org.
Accessed March 6, 2018.
http://www.worldcurling.org/mixed-doubles-curling-confirmed-for-pyeongchang-2018.

World Curling Federation. "The Rules of Curling (Oct 2018)." World Curling Federation. Accessed March 12, 2018.
http://www.worldcurling.org/rules-and-regulations.

World Handball. "History: Origins and Development." Hand-Ball.org. Accessed May 18, 2018.
http://www.hand-ball.org/historia/.

Zug, James. "The History of Squash in 8 Chapters." U.S. Squash Archive.
Accessed June 24, 2018.
https://web.archive.org/web/20110717181310/http://www.ussquash.com/functions/content.aspx?id=1252.

548

Slang Resources

Australian English Sexual Terms:
https://en.wiktionary.org/wiki/Appendix:Australian_E
nglish_sexual_terms

Australian Slang:
http://www.koalanet.com.au/australian-slang.html

British Slang Dictionary & Translator:
https://www.translatebritish.com/dictionary/c

Dalzell, Tom, and Terry Victor. *The New Partridge Dictionary of Slang and Unconventional English*. New York: Routledge, 2015.

Dalzell, Tom (Ed.). *The Routledge Dictionary of Modern American Slang and Unconventional*. (2nd ed.). New York: Routledge, 2018.

Dictionary of Obscure Sexual Terms:
http://unix.rulez.org/~calver/fun/sex.html

LGBT slang:
https://en.wikipedia.org/wiki/LGBT_slang

PseudoDictionary.com:
http://www.pseudodictionary.com/

Sex-Lexis.com. The Language of Love, Lust, Sex:
http://www.sex-lexis.com/

The Dictionary of Slang:
http://www.peevish.co.uk/slang/d.htm

The London Salad: British Slang Sex Words: 1300s –
1800s:
http://www.thelondonsalad.com/old-british-slang-
sex-words/

The Online Slang Dictionary:
http://onlineslangdictionary.com/

Urban Dictionary: https://www.urbandictionary.com

Urban Thesaurus: http://urbanthesaurus.org

Wiktionary, the Free Dictionary:
https://en.wiktionary.org

Other Books by the Author

Poetry

From the Mundane to the Magical:
A Lifetime of Poetic Moments

Poetic Emanations of Light, Life, Love & Liberty

Cookbook

The Thelemic Cookbook:
Cooking with Correspondences

Mystery and Crime

The Reynard Trilogy
Book 1 - The Collioure Concealment
Book 2 - Murder of the Mystras Nun
Book 3 – The Cypriot Secret

Forthcoming Books

Spy Novel

Hiding in Paradise

Short Stories

Merry & Scary Fairytales

Occult Mystery

The Blyth Woods Curse

About the Author

Lita-Luise Chappell has written poetry, short stories, mysteries, plays, lyrics, rituals, cookbooks, investigative articles, social commentary, reviews, and travelogues for the last 50 years. With her background in psychology, half a dozen careers, many world travels, and a magical perspective, her broad experiences and opinions are reflected in everything she writes. Her works have been published in books, magazines, journals, and online. She lives with her husband Vere Chappell, who is also a writer, in Laguna Hills, California. Visit her online at litachappell.com, and find all of her available works on amazon.com.